THE BIBLE

Modern Critical Views

Edward Albee
Maya Angelou
Asian-American
    Writers
Margaret Atwood
Jane Austen
James Baldwin
Samuel Beckett
Saul Bellow
The Bible
William Blake
Jorge Luis Borges
Ray Bradbury
The Brontës
Gwendolyn Brooks
Robert Browning
Italo Calvino
Albert Camus
Lewis Carroll
Willa Cather
Cervantes
Geoffrey Chaucer
Anton Chekhov
Kate Chopin
Agatha Christie
Samuel Taylor
    Coleridge
Joseph Conrad
Contemporary Poets
Stephen Crane
Dante
Daniel Defoe
Charles Dickens
Emily Dickinson
John Donne and the
    17th-Century
    Poets
Fyodor Dostoevsky
W. E. B. DuBois
George Eliot
T. S. Eliot
Ralph Ellison
Ralph Waldo
    Emerson
William Faulkner
F. Scott Fitzgerald

Sigmund Freud
Robert Frost
George Gordon,
    Lord Byron
Graham Greene
Thomas Hardy
Nathaniel
    Hawthorne
Ernest Hemingway
Hispanic-American
    Writers
Homer
Langston Hughes
Zora Neale Hurston
Henrik Ibsen
John Irving
Henry James
James Joyce
Franz Kafka
John Keats
Jamaica Kincaid
Stephen King
Rudyard Kipling
D. H. Lawrence
Ursula K. Le Guin
Sinclair Lewis
Bernard Malamud
Christopher Marlowe
Gabriel García
    Márquez
Carson McCullers
Herman Melville
Arthur Miller
John Milton
Toni Morrison
Native-American
    Writers
Joyce Carol Oates
Flannery O'Connor
Eugene O'Neill
George Orwell
Sylvia Plath
Edgar Allan Poe
Katherine Anne
    Porter
J. D. Salinger

Jean-Paul Sartre
William Shakespeare:
    Histories and
    Poems
William Shakespeare's
    Romances
William Shakespeare:
    The Comedies
William Shakespeare:
    The Tragedies
George Bernard
    Shaw
Mary Wollstonecraft
    Shelley
Percy Bysshe Shelley
Alexander
    Solzhenitsyn
Sophocles
John Steinbeck
Tom Stoppard
Jonathan Swift
Amy Tan
Alfred, Lord
    Tennyson
Henry David
    Thoreau
J. R. R. Tolkien
Leo Tolstoy
Mark Twain
John Updike
Kurt Vonnegut
Alice Walker
Robert Penn Warren
Eudora Welty
Edith Wharton
Walt Whitman
Oscar Wilde
Tennessee Williams
Thomas Wolfe
Tom Wolfe
Virginia Woolf
William Wordsworth
Richard Wright
William Butler Yeats

Modern Critical Views

THE BIBLE

Edited and with an introduction by

Harold Bloom

Sterling Professor of the Humanities
Yale University

CHELSEA HOUSE PUBLISHERS

Printed and bound in the United States of America

10 9 8 7 6 5 4 3

∞ The paper used in this publication meets the minimum requirements
of the American National Standard for Permanence of Paper for Printed
Library Materials, Z39.48 – 1984.

Library of Congress Cataloging-in-Publication Data
The Bible.
    (Modern critical views)
    Bibliography: p.
    Includes index.
    1. Bible as literature. 2. Bible – Criticism,
interpretation, etc. I. Bloom, Harold. II. Title.
III. Series.
BS535.B47 1987   220.6'6   86-12967
ISBN 0-87754-720-3

Contents

THE NEW TESTAMENT

Editor's Note

This book brings together a representative selection of the most illuminating *literary* criticism that has been devoted to the Bible. I am grateful to Hillary Kelleher for her aid in researching this volume.

My introduction centers upon the uncanniness or sublimity of the Yahwist or J writer, the prime or original author of Genesis, Exodus, Numbers. Kenneth Burke's exuberant "logological" exegesis of aspects of the first three chapters of Genesis is followed by Robert Alter's subtle tracing of the origins of the novel to certain elements in the Bible's sacred history.

Erich Auerbach's celebrated contrast between differences in the representation of reality in the Bible and in Homer is succeeded here by Meir Sternberg's structural analysis of the wooing of Rebekah and by two very different, indeed antithetical, readings of the story of wrestling Jacob, the first by Roland Barthes, and the second my own. The art of the Deuteronomist is the subject of Robert Polzin's account of what might be called a revisionary Moses.

Martin Buber, a spiritual dialectician but also a superb literary exegete, gives memorable readings of Job and of Psalm 73. Ecclesiastes, great stylist and dialectical skeptic, is expounded by Robert Gordis, who sees the Preacher's originality both as rhetoric and as vision. Robert Alter returns with an unmatched reading of the Song of Songs, that garden of metaphor preserved in the canon through the passion for it of the great Rabbi Akiba.

The focus moves to the prophets, commencing with Yehoshua Gitay's remarkable exegesis of Isaiah, and with Geoffrey Hartman's exposition of the poetics of Jeremiah. Leo Strauss, profound reader between the lines, contrasts Socrates and the prophets in a way very different from Auerbach's study of Greek and Hebrew representation. A last glance at prophecy is provided by Douglas Robinson's advanced consideration of the failed prophet, Jonah.

Typology, or the ways of linking the Hebrew Bible to the New Testament, dominates the five essays here on the Christian or belated Testament, starting with Frank Kermode's lively investigation of the rather troublesome "Boy in the Shirt" of the Gospel of Mark. Northrop Frye, massively setting forth his *Great Code's* phases of revelation, gives us typology in the grand style. An attack upon typology, and indeed upon the Gospel of John and all the New Testament, is mounted in my rather polemical essay on "the Original and the Belated Testaments." Herbert Marks, partly defending Pauline typology against varieties of revisionary criticism (my own included), shrewdly implies that St. Paul himself was very much a revisionary critic.

The final excerpt in this book is from D. H. Lawrence's preternaturally eloquent and apocalyptic critique of the Revelation of St. John the Divine. Lawrence, great visionary and apocalyptic poet, makes a response to Revelation that is at once a fresh creation and poetic criticism of the highest order.

Introduction

To my best knowledge, it was the Harvard historian of religion George Foot Moore who first called the religion of the rabbis of the second century of the Common Era "normative Judaism." Let me simplify by centering on one of those rabbis, surely the grandest: normative Judaism is the religion of Akiba. That vigorous scholar, patriot, and martyr may be regarded as the standard by which any other Jewish religious figure must be judged. If your faith and praxis share enough with Akiba's, then you too are a representative of normative Judaism. If not, then probably not. There is a charming legend in which Moses attends Akiba's seminar, and goes away baffled by the sage's interpretation — of Moses! But the deepest implication of the legend, as I read it, is that Akiba's strong misreading of Moses was in no way weakened by the Mosaic bafflement.

The Great Original of the literary and oral traditions that merged into normative Judaism was the writer scholarly convention rather wonderfully chose to call "J." Since Kafka is the most legitimate descendant of one aspect of the antithetical J (Tolstoy and the early, pre-Coleridgean Wordsworth are the most authentic descendants of J's other side), I find it useful to adopt the formula "from J to K," in order to describe the uncanny or antithetical elements in J's narratives. The J who could have written *Hadji Murad* or *The Tale of Margaret* was the inevitable fountainhead of what eventually became normative Judaism. But this first, strongest, and still somehow most Jewish of all our writers also could have written "The Hunter Gracchus" or even "Josephine the Singer and the Mouse Folk." Indeed he wrote uncannier stories than Kafka lived to write. How those stories ever could have been acceptable or even comprehensible to the P authors or the Deuteronomist, to the Academy of Ezra or the Pharisees, let alone to Akiba and his colleagues, is a mystery that I have been trying to clarify by developing a critical concept of what I call "facticity," a kind of brute

1

contingency by which an author's strength blinds and incarcerates a tradition of belated readership. But here I primarily want to describe the uncanniness of J's work, so as to break out of facticity, insofar as I am able to do so.

By "the uncanny" I mean Freud's concept, since that appears to be the authentic modern version of what once was called the Sublime. Freud defines "the uncanny" as being "in reality nothing new or foreign, but something familiar and old-established in the mind that has been estranged only by the process of repression." Since I myself, as a critic, am obsessed with the Sublime or Freud's "uncanny," I realize that my reading of any Sublime work or fragment is always dependent upon an estrangement, in which the repressed returns upon me to end that estrangement, but only momentarily. The uncanniness of the Yahwist exceeds that of all other writers, because in him both the estrangement and the return achieve maximum force.

Of course J himself is considered to be a fiction, variously referred to by scholars as a school, a tradition, a document, and a hypothesis. Well, Homer is perhaps a fiction too, and these days the slaves of critical fashion do not weary of proclaiming the death of the author, or at least the reduction of every author to the status of a Nietzschean fiction. But J is pragmatically the author-of-authors, in that his authority and originality constitute a difference that has made a difference. The teller of the tales of Jacob and of Joseph, of Moses and the Exodus, is a writer more inescapable than Shakespeare and more pervasive in our consciousness than Freud. J's only cultural rival would be an unlikely compound of Homer and Plato. Plato's contest with Homer seems to me to mark one of the largest differences between the ancient Greeks and the Hebrews. The agon for the mind of Athens found no equivalent in Jerusalem, and so the Yahwist still remains the mind of Jerusalem, everywhere that Jerusalem happens to be.

I do not believe that J was a fiction, and indeed J troubles me because his uncanniness calls into question my own conviction that every writer is belated, and so is always an inter-poet. J's freedom from belatedness rivals Shakespeare's, which is to say that J's originality is as intense as Shakespeare's. But J wrote twenty-five hundred years before Shakespeare, and that time-span bewilders comparison. I am going to sketch J's possible circumstances and purposes, in order to hazard a description of J's tone or of the uncanniness of his stance as a writer. Not much in my sketch will flout received scholarship, but necessarily I will have to go beyond the present state of biblical scholarship, since it cannot even decide precisely which texts are J's, or even revised by others from J. My attempt at transcending scholarship is simply a literary critic's final reliance upon her or his own sense of a text, or what I have called the necessity of misreading. No critic, whatever her or his moldiness *or* skepticism, can evade a Nietzschean will to power over a text, because interpretation is at last nothing else. The text, even if it was written that morning, and shown by its poet to the critic at high noon, is already lost in time, as lost as the Yahwist. Time says, "It was," and authentic criticism, as Nietzsche implied, is necessarily pervaded by a will for revenge against time's "it was." No interpreter can suspend the will to relational knowledge for more than an isolated moment, and since all narrative and all poetry are also interpretation, all writing manifests such a will.

Solomon the King, nowhere of course overtly mentioned by J, is the dominant contemporary force in the context of J's writing. I would go further, and as a pious Stevensian would say that Solomon is J's motive for metaphor. The reign of Solomon ended in the year 922 before the Common Era, and J quite possibly wrote either in Solomon's last years, or — more likely, I think — shortly thereafter. One can venture that Solomon was to J what Elizabeth was to Shakespeare, an idea of order, as crucial in J's Jerusalem as it was in Shakespeare's London. The Imperial Theme is J's countersong, though J's main burden is a heroic and agonistic past represented by David the King, while his implied judgment upon the imperial present is at best skeptical, since he implies also an agonistic future. J's vision of agon centers his uncanny stance, accounting for his nearly unique mode of irony.

How much of J's actual text we have lost to the replacement tactics of redactors we cannot know, but biblical scholarship has not persuaded me that either the so-called Elohistic or the Priestly redactors provide fully coherent visions of their own, except perhaps for the Priestly first chapter of Genesis, which is so startling a contrast to J's account of how we all got started. But let me sketch the main contours of J's narrative, as we appear to have it. Yahweh begins his Creation in the first harsh Judean spring, before the first rain comes down. Water wells up from the earth, and Yahweh molds Adam out of the red clay, breathing into the earthling's nostrils a breath of the divine life. Then come the stories we think we know: Eve, the serpent, Cain and Abel, Seth, Noah and the Flood, the tower of Babel, and something utterly new with Abraham. From Abraham on, the main sequence again belongs to J: the Covenant, Ishmael, Yahweh at Mamre and on the road to Sodom, Lot, Isaac and the Akedah, Rebecca, Esau and Jacob, the tales of Jacob, Tamar, the story of Joseph and his brothers, and then the Mosaic account. Moses, so far as I can tell, meant much less to J than he did to the normative redactors, and so the J strand in Exodus and Numbers is even more laconic than J tended to be earlier.

In J's Exodus we find the oppression of the Jews, the birth of Moses, his escape to Midian, the burning bush and the instruction, the weird murderous

attack by Yahweh upon Moses, the audiences with Pharaoh, the plagues, and
the departure, flight, and crossing. Matters become sparser with Israel in the
wilderness, at the Sinai covenant, and then with the dissensions and the battles
in Numbers. J flares up finally on a grand scale in the serio-comic Balaam and
Balak episode, but that is not the end of J's work, even as we have it. The
Deuteronomist memorably incorporates J in his chapters 31 and 34 dealing
with the death of Moses. I give here in sequence the opening and the closing
of what we hear J's Yahweh speaking aloud, first to Adam and last to Moses:
"Of every tree in the garden you are free to eat; but as for the tree of knowledge
of good and bad, you must not eat of it; for as soon as you eat of it, you
shall die." "This is the land of which I swore to Abraham, Isaac, and Jacob,
'I will give it to your offspring.' I have let you see it with your own eyes,
but you shall not cross there." Rhetorically, the two speeches share the same
cruel pattern of power: "Here it is; it is yours and yet it is not yours." Akin
to J's counterpointing of Yahweh's first and last speeches is his counterparting
of Yahweh's first and last actions: "Yahweh formed man from the dust of the
earth," and "Yahweh buried him, Moses, in the valley in the land of Moab,
near Beth-peor; and no one knows his burial place to this day." From Adam
to Moses is from earth to earth; Yahweh molds us and he buries us, and both
actions are done with his own hands. As it was with Adam and Moses, so
it was with David and with Solomon, and with those who come and will come
after Solomon. J is the harshest and most monitory of writers, and his Yahweh
is an uncanny god, who takes away much of what he gives, and who is beyond
any standard of measurement. And yet what I have said about J so far is not
even part of the truth; isolated, all by itself, it is not true at all, for J is a writer
who exalts man, and who has most peculiar relations with God. Gorky once
said of Tolstoy that Tolstoy's relation to God reminded him of the Russian
proverb "Two bears in one den." J's relation to his uncanny Yahweh frequently
reminds me of my favorite Yiddish apothegm: "Sleep faster, we need the pillows."
J barely can keep up with Yahweh, though J's Jacob almost can, while J's Moses
cannot keep up at all. Since what is most problematic about J's writing is
Yahweh, I suggest we take a closer look at J's Yahweh than the entire normative
and modern scholarly tradition has been willing or able to take. Homer and
Dante, Shakespeare and Milton, hardly lacked audacity in representing what
may be beyond representation, but J was both bolder and shrewder than any
other writer at inventing speeches and actions for God Himself. Only J convinces
us that he knows precisely how and when Yahweh speaks; Isaiah compares
poorly to J in this, while the Milton of *Paradise Lost*, book 3, hardly rates
even as an involuntary parodist of J.

   I am moved to ask a question which the normative tradition—Judaic,

Christian, and even secular — cannot ask: What is J's stance toward Yahweh? I can begin an answer by listing all that it is not: creating Yahweh, J's primary emotions do not include awe, fear, wonder, much surprise, or even love. J *sounds* rather matter-of-fact, but that is part of J's unique mode of irony. By turns, J's stance toward Yahweh is appreciative, wryly apprehensive, intensely interested, and above all attentive and alert. Toward Yahweh, J is perhaps a touch wary; J is always *prepared to be surprised*. What J knows is that Yahweh is Sublime or "uncanny," incommensurate yet rather agonistic, curious and lively, humorous yet irascible, and all too capable of suddenly violent action. But J's Yahweh is rather *heimlich* also; he sensibly avoids walking about in the Near Eastern heat, preferring the cool of the evening, and he likes to sit under the terebinths at Mamre, devouring roast calf and curds. J would have laughed at his normative descendants — Christian, Jewish, secular, scholarly — who go on calling his representations of Yahweh "anthropomorphic," when they should be calling his representations of Jacob "theomorphic."

"The anthropomorphic" always has been a misleading concept, and probably was the largest single element affecting the long history of the redaction of J that evolved into normative Judaism. Most modern scholars, Jewish and Gentile alike, cannot seem to accept the fact that there was no Jewish theology before Philo. "Jewish theology," despite its long history from Philo to Franz Rosenzweig, is therefore an oxymoron, particularly when applied to Biblical texts, and most particularly when applied to J. J's Yahweh is an uncanny personality, and not at all a concept. Yahweh sometimes *seems* to behave like us, but because Yahweh and his sculpted creature, Adam, are incommensurate, this remains a mere seeming. Sometimes, and always within limits, we behave like Yahweh, and not necessarily because we will to do so. There is a true sense in which John Calvin was as strong a reader of J as he more clearly was of Job, a sense displayed in the paradox of the Protestant Yahweh who entraps his believers by an impossible double injunction, which might be phrased: "Be like me, but don't you dare to be too like me!" In J, the paradox emerges only gradually, and does not reach its climax until the theophany on Sinai. Until Sinai, J's Yahweh addresses himself only to a handful, to his elite: Adam, Noah, Abraham, Jacob, Joseph, and, by profound implication, David. But at Sinai, we encounter the crisis of J's writing, as we will see.

What is theomorphic about Adam, Noah, Abraham, Jacob, Joseph? I think the question should be rephrased: What is Davidic about them? About Joseph, everything, and indeed J's Joseph I read as a fictive representation of David, rather in the way Virgil's Divine Child represents Augustus, except that J is working on a grand scale with Joseph, bringing to perfection what may have been an old mode of romance.

I have called Solomon J's motive for metaphor, but that calling resounds with Nietzsche's motive for all trope: the desire to be different, the desire to be elsewhere. For J, the difference, the elsewhere, is David. J's agonistic elitism, the struggle for the blessing, is represented by Abraham, above all by Jacob, and by Tamar also. But the bearer of the blessing is David, and I have ventured the surmise that J's Joseph is a portrait of David. Though this surmise is, I think, original, the centering of J's humanism upon the implied figure of David is not, of course, original with me. It is a fundamental postulate of the school of Gerhard von Rad, worked out in detail by theologians like Hans Walter Wolff and Walter Brueggemann. Still, a phrase like Wolff's "the Kerygma of the Yahwist" makes me rather uneasy, since J is no more a theologian than he is a priest or prophet. Freud, like St. Paul, has a message, but J, like Shakespeare, does not. J *is* literature and not "confession," which of course is not true of his redactors. They were on the road to Akiba, but J, always in excess of the normative, was no quester.

I find no traces of cult in J, and I am puzzled that so many read as kerygmatic Yahweh's words to Abram in Gen. 12:3: "So, then, all the families of the earth can gain a blessing in you." The blessing, in J, simply does not mean what it came to mean in his redactors and in the subsequent normative tradition. To gain a blessing, particularly through the blessing that becomes Abraham's, is in J to join oneself to that elitest agon which culminated in the figure of the agonistic hero, David. To be blessed means ultimately that one's name will not be scattered, and the remembered name will retain life into a time without boundaries. The blessing then is temporal, and not spatial, as it was in Homer and in the Greeks after him, who like his heroes struggled for the foremost place. And a temporal blessing, like the kingdom in Shakespeare, finds its problematic aspect in the vicissitudes of descendants.

Jacob is J's central man, whose fruition, deferred in the beloved Joseph, because given to Judah, has come just before J's time in the triumph of David. I think that Brueggemann is imaginatively accurate in his hypothesis that David represented, for J, a new kind of man, almost a new Adam, the man whom Yahweh (in 2 Sam. 7) had decided to trust. Doubtless we cannot exclude from our considerations the Messianic tradition that the normative, Jewish and Christian, were to draw out from those two great contemporary writers, J and the author of 2 Samuel. But J does not have any such Messianic consciousness about David. Quite the reverse: for him, we can surmise, David had been and was the elite *image*; not a harbinger of a greater vision to come, but a fully human being who already had exhausted the full range and vitality of man's possibilities. If, as Brueggemann speculates, J's tropes of exile (Gen. 3:24, 4:12, 11:8) represent the true images of the Solomonic present, then

I would find J's prime Davidic trope in Jacob's return to Canaan, marked by the all-night, all-in wrestling match that concentrates Jacob's name forever as Israel. The Davidic glory then is felt most strongly in Jacob's theomorphic triumph, rendered so much the more poignant by his permanent crippling: "The sun rose upon him as he passed Penuel, limping on his hip."

If Jacob is Israel as the father, then David, through the trope of Joseph, is Jacob's or Israel's truest son. What then is Davidic about J's Jacob? I like the late E. A. Speiser's surmise that J personally knew his great contemporary, the writer who gave us, in 2 Samuel, the history of David and his immediate successors. J's Joseph reads to me like a lovingly ironic parody of the David of the court historian. What matters most about David, as that model narrative presents him, is not only his charismatic intensity, but the marvelous gratuity of Yahweh's *hesed*, his Election-love for this most heroic of his favorites. To no one in J's text does Yahweh speak so undialectically as he does through Nathan to David in 2 Samuel 7:12–16:

> When your days are done and you lie with your fathers, I will raise up your offspring after you, one of your own issue, and I will establish his kingship. He shall build a house for My name, and I will establish his royal throne forever. I will be a father to him, and he shall be a son to Me. When he does wrong, I will chastise him with the rod of men and the affliction of mortals; but I will never withdraw My favor from him as I withdrew it from Saul, whom I removed to make room for you. Your house and your kingship shall ever be secure before you; your throne shall be established forever.

The blessing in J, as I have written elsewhere, is always agonistic, and Jacob is J's supreme agonist. But J makes a single exception for Joseph, and clearly with the reader's eye centered upon David. From the womb on to the ford of the Jabbok, Jacob is an agonist, and until that night encounter at Penuel by no means a heroic one. His agon, as I've said, is for the temporal blessing that will prevail into a time without boundaries; and so it never resembles the Homeric or the Athenian contest for the foremost place, a kind of topological or spatial blessing. In J, the struggle is for the uncanny gift of life, for the breath of Yahweh that transforms *adamah* into Adam. True, David struggles, and suffers, but J's Joseph serenely voyages through all vicissitudes, as though J were intimating that David's agon had been of a new kind, one in which the obligation was wholly and voluntarily on Yahweh's side in the Covenant. Jacob the father wrestles lifelong, and is permanently crippled by the climactic match with a nameless one among the Elohim whom I interpret as the baffled angel of death, who learns that Israel lives, and always will survive. Joseph the son charms reality, even as David seems to have charmed Yahweh.

But Jacob, I surmise, was J's signature, and while the portrait of the Davidic Joseph manifests J's wistfulness, the representation of Jacob may well be J's self-portrait as the great writer of Israel. My earlier question would then become: What is Davidic about J himself, not as a person perhaps, but certainly as an author? My first observation here would have to be this apparent paradox: J is anything but a religious writer, unlike all his revisionists and interpreters, and David is anything but a religious personality, despite having become the paradigm for all Messianic speculation, both Jewish and Christian. Again I am in the wake of von Rad and his school, but with this crucial Bloomian swerve: J and David are not religious, just as Freud, for all his avowedly antireligious polemic, is finally nothing but religious. Freud's overdetermination of meaning, his emphasis upon primal repression or a flight from representation – before, indeed, there was anything to represent – establishes Freud as normatively Jewish despite himself. Turn it and turn it, for everything is in it, the sage ben Bag Bag said of Torah, and Freud says the same of the psyche. If there is sense in everything, then everything that is going to happen has happened already, and so reality is already in the past and there never can be anything new. Freud's stance toward psychic history is the normative rabbinical stance toward Jewish history, and if Akiba is the paradigm for what it is to be religious, then the professedly scientistic Freud is as religious as Akiba, if we are speaking of the Jewish religion. But J, like the court historian's David of 2 Samuel, is quite Jewish without being at all religious, in the belated normative sense. For the uncanny J, and for the path-breaking David, everything that matters most is perpetually new.

But this is true of J's Jacob also, as it is of Abraham, even Isaac, and certainly Tamar – all live at the edge of life rushing onwards, never in a static present but always in the dynamism of J's Yahweh, whose incessant temporality generates anxious expectations in nearly every fresh sentence of certain passages. This is again the Kafkan aspect of J, though it is offset by J's strong sense of human freedom, a sense surpassing its Homeric parallels. What becomes theodicy in J's revisionists down to Milton is for J not at all a perplexity. Since J has no concept of Yahweh but rather a sense of Yahweh's peculiar personality, the interventions of Yahweh in primal family history do not impinge upon his elite's individual freedom. So we have the memorable and grimly funny argument between Yahweh and Abraham as they walk together down the road to Sodom. Abraham wears Yahweh down until Yahweh quite properly begins to get exasperated. The shrewd courage and humanity of Abraham convince me that in the Akedah the redactors simply eliminated J's text almost completely. As I read the Hebrew, there is an extraordinary gap between the Elohistic language and the sublime invention of the story. J's Abraham would have argued far more tenaciously with Yahweh for his son's life than he did in defense of the inhabitants of the sinful cities of the plain, and here the revisionists may have defrauded us of J's uncanny greatness at its height.

But how much they *have* left us which the normative tradition has been incapable of assimilating! I think the best way of seeing this is to juxtapose with J the Pharasaic Book of Jubilees, oddly called also "the Little Genesis," though it is prolix and redundant in every tiresome way. Written about one hundred years before the Common Era, Jubilees is a normative travesty of Genesis, far more severely, say, than Chronicles is a normative reduction of 2 Samuel. But though he writes so boringly, what is wonderfully illuminating about the author of Jubilees is that he totally eradicates J's text. Had he set out deliberately to remove everything idiosyncratic about J's share in Torah, he could have done no more thorough a job. Gone altogether is J's creation story of Yahweh molding the red clay into Adam and then breathing life into his own image. Gone as well is Yahweh at Mamre, where only angels now appear to Abraham and Sarah, and there is no dispute on the road to Sodom. And the Satanic prince of angels, Mastema, instigates Yahweh's trial of Abraham in the Akedah. Jacob and Esau do not wrestle in the womb, and Abraham prefers Jacob, though even the author of Jubilees does not go so far as to deny Isaac's greater love for Esau. Gone, alas totally gone, is J's sublime invention of the night wrestling at Penuel. Joseph lacks all charm and mischief, necessarily, and the agony of Jacob, and the subsequent grandeur of the reunion, are vanished away. Most revealingly, the uncanniest moment in J, Yahweh's attempt to murder Moses en route to Egypt, becomes Mastema's act. And wholly absent is J's most enigmatic vision, the Sinai theophany, which is replaced by the safe removal of J's too-lively Yahweh back to a sedate dwelling in the high heavens.

J's originality was too radical to be absorbed, and yet abides even now as the originality of a Yahweh who will not dwindle down into the normative Godhead of the Jews, Christians, and Muslims. Because J cared more for personality than for morality, and cared not at all for cult, his legacy is a disturbing sense that, as Blake phrased it, forms of worship have been chosen from poetic tales. J was no theologian and yet not a maker of saga or epic, and again not a historian, and not even a storyteller as such. We have no description of J that will fit, just as we have no idea of God that will contain his irrepressible Yahweh. I want to test these observations by a careful account of J's Sinai theophany, where his Yahweh is more problematic than scholarship has been willing to perceive.

Despite the truncation, indeed the possible mutilation of J's account of the Sinai theophany, more than enough remains to mark it as the crisis or crossing-point of his work. For the first time, his Yahweh is overwhelmingly self-contradictory, rather than dialectical, ironic, or even crafty. The moment of crisis turns upon Yahweh's confrontation with the Israelite host. Is he to allow himself to be seen by them? How direct is his self-representation to be? Mamre and the road to Sodom suddenly seem estranged, or as though they never were. It is not that here Yahweh is presented less anthropomorphically, but that J's Moses (let alone those he leads) is far less theomorphic or Davidic than J's Abraham and J's Jacob, and certainly less theomorphic or Davidic than J's Joseph. Confronting his agonistic and theomorphic elite, from Abraham to the implied presence of David, Yahweh is both canny and uncanny. But Moses is neither theomorphic nor agonistic. J's Sinai theophany marks the moment of the blessing's transition from the elite to the entire Israelite host, and in that transition a true anxiety of representation breaks forth in J's work for the first time.

I follow Martin Noth's lead, in the main, as to those passages in Exodus 19 and 24 that are clearly J's, though my ear accepts as likely certain moments he considers only probable or at least quite possible. Here are Exod. 19:9–15, 18, 20–25, literally rendered:

> Yahweh said to Moses: "I will come to you in a thick cloud, that the people may hear that I speak with you and that they may trust you forever afterwards." Moses then reported the people's words to Yahweh, and Yahweh said to Moses: "Go to the people and warn them to be continent today and tomorrow. Let them wash their clothes. Let them be prepared for the third day, for on the third day Yahweh will descend upon Mount Sinai, in the sight of all the people. You shall set limits for the people all around, saying: 'Beware of climbing the mountain or touching the border of it. Whoever touches the mountain shall be put to death; no hand shall touch him, but either he shall be stoned or shot; whether beast or man, he shall not live.' When there is a loud blast of the ram's horn, then they may ascend the mountain."
>
> Moses came down from the mountain unto the people and warned them to remain pure, and they washed their clothes. And Moses said to the people: "Prepare for the third day; do not approach a woman."

Yahweh will come at first in a thick cloud, that the people may hear yet presumably not see him; nevertheless, on the third day he will come down upon Sinai "in the sight of all the people." Sinai will be taboo, but is this only a taboo of touch? What about seeing Yahweh? I suspect that an ellipsis, wholly characteristic of J's rhetorical strength, then intervened, again characteristically filled in by the E redactors as verses 16 and 17, and again as verse 19; but in verse 18 clearly we hear J's grand tone:

> Now Mount Sinai was all in smoke, for the Lord had come down upon it in fire; the smoke rose like the smoke of a kiln, and all the people trembled violently.

Whether people or mountain tremble hardly matters in this great trope of immanent power. Yahweh, as we know, is neither the fire nor in the fire, for the ultimate trope is the *makom*: Yahweh is the place of the world, but the world is not his place, and so Yahweh is also the place of the fire, but the fire is not his place. And so J touches the heights of his own Sublime, though himself troubled by an anxiety of representation previously unknown to him, an anxiety of touch and, for the first time, of sight:

> Yahweh came down upon Mount Sinai, on the mountain top, and Yahweh called Moses to the mountain top, and Moses went up. Yahweh said to Moses: "Go down, warn the people not to break through to gaze at Yahweh, lest many of them die. And the priests who come near Yahweh must purify themselves, lest Yahweh break forth against them." But Moses said to Yahweh: "The people cannot come up to Mount Sinai, for You warned us when You said: 'Set limits about the mountain and render it holy.' " So Yahweh said to Moses: "Go down and come back with Aaron, but do not allow the priests or the people to break through to come up to Yahweh, lest Yahweh break out against them." And Moses descended to the people and spoke to them.

However much we have grown accustomed to J, he has not prepared us for this. Never before has Yahweh, bent upon Covenant, been a potential catastrophe as well as a potential blessing. But then, certainly the difference is in the movement from an elite to a whole people. If, as I suspect, the pragmatic covenant for J was the Davidic or humanistic or theomorphic covenant, then the most salient poetic meaning here was contemporary, whether Solomonic or just after. The true covenant, without anxiety or the problematic of representation, was agonistic: with Abraham, with Jacob, with Joseph, with David, but neither with Moses nor with Solomon, and so never with the mass of the people, whether at Sinai or at J's own moment of writing. J is as elitist as Shakespeare, or as Freud; none of the three was exactly a writer on the left. Yahweh himself, in J's vision, becomes dangerously confused in the anxious expectations of at once favoring and threatening the host of the people, rather than the individuals, that he has chosen. When Moses reminds Yahweh that Sinai is off limits anyway, Yahweh evidently is too preoccupied and too little taken with Moses even to listen, and merely repeats his warning that he may be uncontrollable, even by himself.

As our text now stands, the revisionists take over, and the Commandments are promulgated. I surmise that in J's original text the Commandments, however phrased, came *after* some fragments of J that we still have in what is now Exodus 24:

> Then Yahweh said to Moses: "Come up to Yahweh, with Aaron, Nadab and Abihu, and seventy elders of Israel, and bow low but from afar. And only Moses shall come near Yahweh. The others shall not come near, and the people shall not come up with him at all.
>
> Then Moses and Aaron, Nadab and Abihu, and seventy elders of Israel went up, and they saw the God of Israel; under His feet there was the likeness of a pavement of sapphire, like the very sky for purity. Yet He did not raise His hand against the leaders of the Israelites; they beheld God, and they ate and drank.

This is again J at his uncanniest, the true Western Sublime, and so the truest challenge to a belated Longinian critic like myself. We are at Mamre again, in a sense, except that here the seventy-four who constitute an elite (of sorts) eat and drink, as did the Elohim and Yahweh at Mamre, while now Yahweh watches enigmatically, and (rather wonderfully) is watched. And again, J is proudly self-contradictory, or perhaps even dialectical, his irony being beyond my interpretive ken, whereas his Yahweh is so outrageously self-contradictory that I do not know where precisely to begin in reading the phases of this difference. But rather than entering that labyrinth – of who may or may not see Yahweh, or how, or when – I choose instead to test the one marvelous visual detail against the Second Commandment. Alas, we evidently do not have J's phrasing here, but there is a strength in the diction that may reflect an origin in J:

> You shall not make for yourself a sculptured image, or any likeness of what is in the heavens above, or on the earth below, or in the waters under the earth.

Surely we are to remember J's Yahweh, who formed the *adam* from the dust of the *adamah* and blew into his sculptured image's nostrils the breath of life. The *zelem* is forbidden to us, as our creation. But had it been forbidden to J, at least until now? And even now, does not J make for himself, and so also for us, a likeness of what is in the heavens above? The seventy-four eaters and drinkers saw with their own eyes the God of Israel, and they saw another likeness also: "under His feet there was the likeness of a pavement of sapphire, like the very sky for purity." Why precisely *this* visual image, from this greatest of writers who gives us so very few visual images, as compared to images that are auditory, dynamic, motor urgencies? I take it that J, and not the Hebrew language, inaugurated the extraordinary process of describing any object primarily by telling us not how it looked, but *how it was made*, wonderfully and fearfully made. But here J describes what is seen, not indeed Yahweh in whole or in part, but what we may call Yahweh's chosen stance.

Stance in writing is also tone, and the tone of this passage is crucial but perhaps beyond our determination. Martin Buber, as an eloquent rhetorician, described it with great vividness but with rather too much interpretive confidence in his book, *Moses*. The seventy-four representatives of Israel are personalized by this theorist of dialogical personalism:

> They have presumably wandered through clinging, hanging mist before dawn; and at the very moment they reach their goal, the swaying darkness tears asunder (as I myself happened to witness once) and dissolves except for one cloud already transparent with the hue of the still unrisen sun. The sapphire proximity of the heavens overwhelms the aged shepherds of the Delta, who have never before tasted, who have never been given the slightest idea, of what is shown in the play of early light over the summits of the mountains. And this precisely is perceived by the representatives of the liberated tribes as that which lies under the feet of their enthroned *Melek*.

Always ingenious and here refreshingly naturalistic, Buber nevertheless neglects what he sometimes recognized: J's uncanniness. Buber's motive, as he says, is to combat two opposed yet equally reductive views of Biblical theophanies: that they are either supernatural miracles or else impressive fantasies. But had J wanted us to believe that the seventy-four elders of Israel saw only a natural radiance, he would have written rather differently. The commentary of Brevard Childs is very precise: "The text is remarkable for its bluntness: 'They saw the God of Israel.'" Childs adds that from the Septuagint on to Maimonides there is a consistent toning down of the statement's directness. Surely the directness is realized yet more acutely if we recall that this is Yahweh's only appearance in the Hebrew Bible where he *says* absolutely nothing. J's emphasis is clear: the seventy-four are on Sinai to eat and drink in Yahweh's presence, while they stare at him, and he presumably stares right back. But that confronts us with the one visual detail J provides: "under His feet there was the likeness of a pavement of sapphire, like the very sky for purity." J gives us a great trope, which all commentary down to the scholarly present weakly misreads by literalization. J, himself a strong misreader of tradition, demands strong misreadings, and so I venture one here. Let us forget all such notions as Yahweh standing so high up that he seems to stand on the sky, or the old fellows never having seen early light in the mountains before. J is elliptical always; that is crucial to his rhetorical stance. He is too wily to say what you would see, if you sat there in awe, eating and drinking while you saw Yahweh. Indeed, we must assume that Yahweh is sitting, but nothing whatsoever is said about a throne, and J after all is not Isaiah or Micaiah ben Imlah or Ezekiel or John Milton. As at Mamre, Yahweh sits upon the ground, and yet it is as though the sky were beneath his feet. May not this drastic reversal of perspective represent a vertigo of vision on the part of the seventy-four? To see the God of Israel is to see as though the world had been turned upside down. And that indeed Yahweh *is* seen, *contra* Buber, we can know through J's monitory comment: "Yet He did not raise His hand against the leaders of the Israelites; they beheld God, and they ate and drank." The sublimity is balanced *not* by a Covenant meal, as all the scholars solemnly assert, but by a picnic on Sinai.

That this uncanny festivity contradicts Yahweh's earlier warnings is not J's confusion, nor something produced by his redactors, but is a dramatic confusion that J's Yahweh had to manifest if his blessing was to be extended from elite individuals to an entire people. Being incommensurate, Yahweh cannot be said to have thus touched his limits, but in the little more that J wrote Yahweh is rather less lively than he had been. His heart, as J hints, was not with Moses but with David, who was to come. J's heart, I venture as I close, was also not with Moses, nor even with Joseph, as David's surrogate, and not really with Yahweh either. It was with Jacob at the Jabbok, obdurately confronting death in the shape of a time-obsessed nameless one from among the Elohim. Wrestling heroically to win the temporal blessing of a new name, Israel—that is uniquely J's own agon.

KENNETH BURKE

The First Three Chapters of Genesis: Principles of Governance Stated Narratively

Imagine that you wanted to say, "The world can be divided into six major classifications." That is, you wanted to deal with "the principles of Order," beginning with the natural order, and placing man's socio-political order with reference to it. But you wanted to treat of these matters in *narrative* terms, which necessarily involve *temporal* sequence (in contrast with the cycle of terms for "Order," that merely cluster about one another, variously implying one another, but in no one fixed sequence).

Stated narratively (in the style of Genesis, *Bereshith*, Beginning), such an idea of principles, or "firsts" would not be stated simply in terms of classification, as were we to say "The first of six primary classes would be such-and-such, the second such-and-such" and so on. Rather, a completely narrative style would properly translate the idea of six classes or categories into terms of time, as were we to assign each of the classes to a separate "day." Thus, instead of saying "And that completes the first broad division, or classification, of our subject-matter," we'd say: "And the evening and the morning were the first day" (or, more accurately, the "One" Day). And so on, through the six broad classes, ending "last but not least," on the category of man and his dominion.

Further, a completely narrative style would *personalize* the principle of classification. This role is performed by the references to God's creative fiat, which from the very start infuses the sheerly natural order with the verbal principle (the makings of that "reason" which we take to be so essential an aspect of human personality).

Logologically, the statement that God made man in his image would be translated as: The principle of personality implicit in the idea of the first creative

From *The Rhetoric of Religion: Studies in Logology.* © 1961 by Kenneth Burke. The University of California Press, 1970.

fiats, whereby all things are approached in terms of the word, applies also to
the feeling for symbol-systems on the part of the human animal, who would
come to read nature as if it were a book. Insofar as God's words infused the
natural order with their genius, and insofar as God is represented as speaking
words to the first man and woman, the principle of human personality (which
is at the very start identified with *dominion*) has its analogue in the notion
of God as a super-person, and of nature as the act of such a super-agent. (That
is, we take symbol-using to be a distinctive ingredient of "personality.")

Though technically there is a kind of "proto-fall" implicit in the principle
of divisiveness that characterizes the Bible's view of the Creation, and though
the principle of subjection is already present (in the general outlines of a
government with God at its head, and mankind as subject to his authority
while in turn having dominion over all else in the natural realm), the Covenant
(as first announced in the first chapter) is necessarily Edenic, in a state of
"innocence," since no negative command has yet been pronounced. From the
dialectical point of view (in line with the Order-Disorder pair) we may note
that there is a possibility of "evil" implicit in the reference to all six primary
classifications as "good." But in all three points (the divisiveness, the order of
dominion, and the universal goodness) the explicit negative is lacking. In fact,
the nearest approach to an outright negative (and that not of a moralistic,
hortatory sort) is in the reference to the "void" (*bohu*) which preceded God's
classificatory acts. Rashi says that the word translated as "formless" (*tohu*) "has
the meaning of astonishment and amazement." Incidentally, in connection with
Gen. 1:29, *The Interpreter's Bible* suggests another implicit negative, in that the
explicit permitting of a vegetarian diet implies that Adam may *not* eat flesh.

In the first chapter of Genesis, the stress is upon the creative fiat as a means
of classification. It says in effect, "What hath God wrought (by his Word)?"
The second chapter's revised account of the Creation shifts the emphasis to
matters of dominion, saying in effect, "What hath God ordained (by his words)?"
The seventh "day" (or category), which is placed at the beginning of the second
chapter, has a special dialectical interest in its role as a transition between the
two emphases.

In one sense, the idea of the Sabbath is implicitly a negative, being conceived
as antithetical to all the six foregoing categories, which are classifiable together
under the single head of "work," in contrast with this seventh category, of "rest."
That is, work and rest are "polar" terms, dialectical opposites. (In his *Politics*,
Aristotle's terms bring out this negative relation explicitly, since his word for
business activity is *ascholein*, that is, "*not* to be at leisure," though we should
tend rather to use the negative the other way round, defining "rest" as "not
to be at work.")

This seventh category (of rest after toil) obviously serves well as transition between Order (of God as principle of origination) and Order (of God as principle of sovereignty). *Leisure* arises as an "institution" only when conditions of dominion have regularized the patterns of *work*. And fittingly, just after this transitional passage, the very name of God undergoes a change (the quality of which is well indicated in our translations by a shift from "God" to "Lord God." Here, whereas in 1:29, *God* tells the man and woman that the fruit of "every tree" is permitted them, the *Lord God* (2:17) notably revises thus: "But of the tree of the knowledge of good and evil, thou shalt not eat of it: for in the day that thou eatest thereof thou shalt surely die." Here, with the stress upon governance, enters the negative of command.

When, later, the serpent tempts "the woman" (3:4), saying that "Ye shall not surely die," his statement is proved partially correct, to the extent that they did not die on the day on which they ate of the forbidden fruit. In any case, 3:19 pronounces the formula that has been theologically interpreted as deriving mankind's physical death from our first parents' first disobedience: "In the sweat of thy face shalt thou eat bread, till thou return unto the ground; for out of it wast thou taken: for dust thou art, and unto dust shalt thou return."

The Interpreter's Bible denies there is any suggestion that man would have lived forever had he not eaten of the forbidden fruit. Chapter 3, verse 20 is taken to imply simply that man would have regarded death as his natural end, rather than as "the last fearful frustration." Thus, the fear of death is said to be "the consequence of the disorder in man's relationships," when they are characterized "by domination" (along with the fear that the subject will break free of their subjection). This seems to be at odds with the position taken by the Scofield Bible which, in the light of Paul's statements in Rom. 5:12–21 ("by one man sin entered the world, and death by sin"—and "by one man's offence death reigned by one") interprets the passage as meaning that "physical death" is due to a "universal sinful *state*, or nature" which is "our heritance from Adam."

It is within neither our present purpose nor our competency to interpret this verse theologically. But here's how it would look logologically:

First, we would note that in referring to "disorder" and "domination," *The Interpreter's Bible* is but referring to "Order" and "Dominion," as seen from another angle. For a mode of domination is a mode of dominion; and a socio-political order is by nature a ziggurat-like structure which, as the story of the Tower makes obvious, can stand for the principle of Disorder.

If we are right in our notion that the idea of Mortification is integral to the idea of Dominion (as the scrupulous subject must seek to "slay" within himself whatever impulses run counter to the authoritative demands of sovereignty), then all about a story of the "first" dominion and the "first" disobedience there should hover the theme of the "first" mortification.

But "mortification" is a weak term, as compared with "death." And thus, in the essentializing ways proper to the narrative style, this stronger, more dramatic term replaces the weaker, more "philosophic" one. "Death" would be the proper narrative-dramatic way of saying "Mortification." By this arrangement, the natural order is once again seen through the eyes of the socio-political order, as the idea of mortification in the toil and subjection of Governance is replaced by the image of death in nature.

From the standpoint sheerly of imagery (once the idea of mortification has been reduced to the idea of death, and the idea of death has been reduced to the image of a dead body rotting back into the ground), we now note a kind of "imagistic proto-fall," in the pun of 2:7, where the Lord God is shown creating man (*adham*) out of the ground (*adhamah*). Here would be an imagistic way of saying that man in his physical nature is essentially but earth, the sort of thing a body becomes when it decays; or that man is *first of all* but earth, as regards his place in the sheerly natural order. You'd define in narrative or temporal terms by showing what he came from. But insofar as he is what he came from, then such a definition would be completed in narrative terms by the image of his return to his origins. In this sense, the account of man's forming (in 2:7) ambiguously lays the conditions for his "return" to such origins, as the Lord God makes explicit in Gen. 3:19, when again the subject is the relation between *adham* and the *adhamah*: "For dust thou art, and unto dust shalt thou return." Here would be a matter of sheer imagistic consistency, for making the stages of a narrative be all of one piece.

But the death motif here is explicitly related to another aspect of Order or Dominion: the sweat of toil. And looking back a bit further, we find that this severe second Covenant (the "Adamic") also subjected woman to the rule of the husband—another aspect of Dominion. And there is to be an eternal enmity between man and the serpent (the image, or narrative personification, of the principle of Temptation, which we have also found to be intrinsic to the motives clustering about the idea of Order).

Logologically, then, the narrative would seem to be saying something like this: Even if you begin by thinking of death as a merely natural phenomenon, once you come to approach it in terms of conscience-laden *mortification* you get a new slant on it. For death then becomes seen, in terms of the socio-political order, as a kind of *capital punishment*. But something of so eschatological a nature is essentially a "first" (since "ends," too, are principles—and here is a place at which firsts and lasts meet, so far as narrative terms for the defining of essences are concerned). Accordingly death in the natural order becomes conceived as the fulfillment or completion of mortification in the socio-political order, but with the difference that, as with capital punishment in the sentencing of transgressions against sovereignty, it is not in itself deemed wholly "redemptive," since it needs further modifications, along the lines of placement in an undying Heavenly Kingdom after death. And this completes the pattern of Order: the symmetry of the socio-political (*cum* verbal), the natural, and the supernatural.

ROBERT ALTER

Sacred History and the Beginnings
of Prose Fiction

The Hebrew Bible is generally perceived, with considerable justice, as sacred history, and both terms of that status have often been invoked to argue against the applicability to the Bible of the methods of literary analysis. If the text is sacred, if it was grasped by the audiences for whom it was made as a revelation of God's will, perhaps of His literal words, how can one hope to explain it through categories developed for the understanding of such a fundamentally secular, individual, and aesthetic enterprise as that of later Western literature? And if the text is history, seriously purporting to render an account of the origins of things and of Israelite national experience as they actually happened, is it not presumptuous to analyze these narratives in the terms we customarily apply to prose fiction, a mode of writing we understand to be the arbitrary invention of the writer, whatever the correspondences such a work may exhibit with quotidian or even historical reality? In a novel by Flaubert or Tolstoy or Henry James, where we are aware of the conscious fashioning of a fictional artifice, sometimes with abundant documentation from the writer's notebooks and letters, it is altogether appropriate to discuss techniques of characterization, shifts of dialogue, the ordering of larger compositional elements; but we are not coercing the Bible into being "literature" by attempting to transfer such categories to a set of texts that are theologically motivated, historically oriented, and perhaps to some extent collectively composed?

At least some of these objections will be undercut by recognizing, as several recent analysts have argued, that history is far more intimately related to fiction than we have been accustomed to assume. It is important to see the common ground shared by the two modes of narrative, ontologically and formally, but

From *The Art of Biblical Narrative.* © 1981 by Robert Alter. Basic Books, 1981.

it also strikes me as misguided to insist that writing history is finally identical with writing fiction. The two kinds of literary activity obviously share a whole range of narrative strategies, and the historian may seem to resemble the writer of fiction in employing, as in some ways he must, a series of imaginative constructs. Yet there remains a qualitative difference, for example, between G. M. Trevelyan's portrait of Robert Walpole, which, though an interpretation and so in some degree an imaginative projection, is closely bound to the known historical facts, and Fielding's Jonathan Wild, a character that alludes satirically to Walpole but clearly has its own dynamics as an independent fictional invention.

The case of the Bible's sacred history, however, is rather different from that of modern historiography. There is, to begin with, a whole spectrum of relations to history in the sundry biblical narratives, as I shall try to indicate later, but none of these involves the sense of being bound to documentable facts that characterizes history in its modern acceptation. It is often asserted that the biblical writer is bound instead to the fixed materials, whether oral or written, that tradition has transmitted to him. This is a claim difficult to verify or refute because we have no real way of knowing what were the precise contents of Hebrew tradition around the beginning of the first millennium B.C.E. A close inspection, however, of the texts that have been passed down to us may lead to a certain degree of skepticism about this scholarly notion of the tyrannical authority of ancient tradition, may lead us, in fact, to conclude that the writers exercised a good deal of artistic freedom in articulating the traditions at their disposal.

As odd as it may sound at first, I would contend that prose fiction is the best general rubric for describing biblical narrative. Or, to be more precise, and to borrow a key term from Herbert Schneidau's speculative, sometimes questionable, often suggestive study, *Sacred Discontent*, we can speak of the Bible as *historicized* prose fiction. To cite the clearest example, the Patriarchal narratives may be composite fictions based on national traditions, but in the writers' refusal to make them conform to the symmetries of expectation, in their contradictions and anomalies, they suggest the unfathomability of life in history under an inscrutable God. "What we are witnessing in Genesis, and in parts of the David story," Schneidau observes, "is the birth of a new kind of historicized fiction, moving steadily away from the motives and habits of the world of legend and myth." This generalization can, I think, be extended beyond Genesis and the David story to most of biblical narrative, even where, as in parts of the Book of Kings, an abundance of legendary material is evident. Because the central thesis of Schneidau's book is the rebellion of biblical literature against the pagan world-view, which is locked into an eternal cyclical movement, his stress falls on the historicizing, though the fiction deserves equal attention. Indeed, as we shall have occasion to see, it may often be more precise to describe what happens in biblical narrative as fictionalized history, especially when we move into the period of the Judges and Kings. But before we pursue the theme of either history or fiction, we should pause over the prose component of prose fiction, which is far more than a matter of convenience in classification for the librarian.

It is peculiar, and culturally significant, that among ancient peoples only Israel should have chosen to cast its sacred national traditions in prose. Among many hazily conceived literary terms applied to the Bible, scholars have often spoken of it as the "national epic" of ancient Israel, or, more specifically, they have conjectured about an oral Creation epic and Exodus epic upon which the authors of the Pentateuch drew. But, as the Israeli Bible scholar Shemaryahu Talmon has shrewdly argued, what by all appearance we have in the Bible is, quite to the contrary, a deliberate avoidance of epic, and the prose form of Hebrew narrative is the chief evidence for this avoidance:

> The ancient Hebrew writers purposefully nurtured and developed prose narration to take the place of the epic genre which by its content was intimately bound up with the world of paganism, and appears to have had a special standing in the polytheistic cults. The recitation of the epics was tantamount to an enactment of cosmic events in the manner of sympathetic magic. In the process of total rejection of the polytheistic religions and their ritual expressions in the cult, epic songs and also the epic genre were purged from the repertoire of the Hebrew authors.

What is crucial for the literary understanding of the Bible is that this reflex away from the polytheistic genre had powerfully constructive consequences in the new medium which the ancient Hebrew writers fashioned for their monotheistic purposes. Prose narration, affording writers a remarkable range and flexibility in the means of presentation, could be utilized to liberate fictional personages from the fixed choreography of timeless events and thus could transform storytelling from ritual rehearsal to the delineation of the wayward paths of human freedom, the quirks and contradictions of men and women seen as moral agents and complex centers of motive and feeling.

The underlying impulse of this whole portentous transition in literary modes is effectively caught, though with certain imprecisions I shall try to correct, by Herbert Schneidau in an anthropological generalization that nicely complements Talmon's historical proposal. Schneidau speaks of a "world of linked analogies and correspondences" manifested in the primitive imagination and

in the divinitory mode of expression. "A cosmology of hierarchical continuities, as in mythological thought, exhibits strong metaphorical tendencies. The
enmeshing and interlocking of structures are coherently expressed in poetic
evocation of transferable, substitutable qualities and names. In this world,
movement tends to round itself into totalization, impelled by the principle of
closure." In contrast to this mythological world dominated by metaphor,
Schneidau sees metonymy—the linking of things through mere contact rather
than through likeness, as in metaphor—with its point-to-point movement
suggesting the prosaic modes of narrative and history, as the key to the literature
of the Bible. Because it is a literature that breaks away from the old cosmic
hierarchies, the Bible switches from a reliance on metaphor to a reliance on
metonymy. Schneidau attempts to summarize this whole contrast in an
aphorism: "Where myth is hypotactic metaphors, the Bible is paratactic
metonymies." That is, where myth involves a set of equivalencies arranged
in some system of subordination, the Bible offers a series of contiguous terms
arranged in sequence without a clear definition of the link between one term
and the next.

This general comparison provides an important insight into the innovative
nature of the Bible's literary enterprise, but some of the concepts invoked are
a little misleading. There are, to begin with, a good many ancient Near Eastern
narratives which are sophisticated, fundamentally secular literary works, though
for Schneidau as for Talmon the mythological poems would appear to be the
paradigm of pagan literature from which the Bible swerves. The paradigmatic
function of this particular kind of pre-Israelite narrative may well justify the
stress on the Hebrew literary rejection of myth, but other terms that Schneidau
adopts remain problematic. Hypotaxis and parataxis may be logically coor-
dinated with metaphor and metonymy respectively, but in actual syntactic
patterns, the Near Eastern mythological verse narratives would appear to be
mainly paratactic, while biblical narrative prose exhibits a good deal of variation
from parataxis to hypotaxis, according to the aims of the writer and the
requirements of the particular narrative juncture. Roman Jakobson's schematic
distinction, moreover, between metaphor and metonymy fits the case under
discussion only in a loose figurative sense because actual metaphor (rather than
inferable metaphysical "correspondences") is by no means predominant in the
extant ancient Near Eastern mythological epics. Schneidau's most valuable
perception, in any case, is not dependent on these terms, for his main point
is the vigorous movement of biblical writing away from the stable closure of
the mythological world and toward the indeterminacy, the shifting causal
concatenations, the ambiguities of a fiction made to resemble the uncertainties
of life in history. And for that movement, I would add, the suppleness of prose

as a narrative medium was indispensable, at least in the Near Eastern setting.

One final qualification should be added to this instructive if somewhat overdrawn opposition between myth and "historicized fiction." Different cultures often take different routes to what is substantially the same end; and if one moves beyond the ancient Fertile Crescent to the Greek sphere, one can find in sophisticated mythographic verse-narratives, such as Hesiod and the mythological episodes in Homer, a good deal in the treatment of motive, character, and causation that is analogous to the biblical sense of indeterminacy and ambiguity. The Hebrew writers, however, made a special virtue in this regard out of the newly fashioned prose medium in which they worked, and this deserves closer attention than it has generally received.

As an initial illustration of how the modalities of prose fiction operate in biblical narrative, I should like to consider a passage from the so-called primeval history, the creation of Eve (Gen. 2). It may serve as a useful test case because with its account of origins, its generalized human figures, its anthropomorphic deity, and the Mesopotamian background of the version of creation in which it occurs, it has been variously classified by modern commentators as myth, legend, and folklore, and would seem quite unlike what we usually think of as artfully conceived fiction. In the immediately preceding verse, one recalls, God had warned Adam under the penalty of death not to eat from the Tree of Knowledge. Man's response to this injunction is not recorded. Instead, the narrative moves on—perhaps making that hiatus itself a proleptic intimation of the link between Adam's future mate and the seizing of forbidden knowledge—to an expression in direct speech of God's concern for the solitary condition of His creature:

> 18. The Lord God said, "It is not good for man to be alone. I shall make him an aid fit for him." 19. And the Lord God formed from the earth every beast of the field and every bird of the sky and He brought them to the man to see what he would call them; and whatever the man called a living creature would be its name. 20. The man called names to all the cattle and the birds of the sky and to every beast of the field, but for the man no fit aid was found. 21. And the Lord God cast a deep slumber upon the man and he slept; and He took one of his ribs and closed up the flesh at that place. 22. And the Lord God fashioned the rib he had taken from the man into a woman and He brought her to the man. 23. The man said:
>
> > This one at last
> > bone of my bones

> This one shall be called woman
> for from man was this one taken.

24. Thus does a man leave his father and mother and cling to his woman, and they become one flesh. 25. And the two of them were naked, the man and his woman, and they were not ashamed.

The usual taxonomic approach to the Bible would explain the whole passage as a piece of ancient folklore, an etiological tale intended to account for the existence of woman, for her subordinate status, and for the attraction she perennially exerts over man. The inset of formal verse (a common convention in biblical narrative for direct speech that has some significantly summarizing or ceremonial function) in fact looks archaic, and could conceivably have been a familiar etiological tag in circulation for centuries before the making of this passage. Folkloric traditions may very well be behind the text, but I don't think that in themselves they provide a very satisfactory sense of the artful complex which the writer has shaped out of his materials. Our first ancestors of course cannot be allowed much individuality and so they are not exactly "fictional characters" in the way that later figures in Genesis like Jacob and Joseph and Tamar will be. Nevertheless, the writer, through a subtle manipulation of language and narrative exposition, manages to endow Adam and Eve with a degree of morally problematic interiority one would hardly expect in a primitive folktale explaining origins. Before we look at some of the details, we might contrast the general impression of this passage with the account of the creation of mankind (there is no separate creation of woman) in the *Enuma Elish*, the Babylonian creation epic. The god Marduk, after triumphing over the primeval mother Tiamat, announces:

> Blood I will mass and cause bones to be.
> I will establish a savage, "man" shall be his name.
> Verily, savage-man I will create.
> He shall be charged with the service of the gods
>   That they might be at ease.

Marduk shares with the God of Israel the anthropomorphic métier of a sculptor in the medium of flesh and bone, but man in the Akkadian verse narrative is merely an object acted upon, his sole reason for existence to supply the material wants of the gods. Humanity is conceived here exclusively in terms of ritual function—man is made in order to offer sacrifices to the gods—and so the highly differentiated realms of history and moral action are not intimated in the account of man's creation. This is a signal instance of what Schneidau means by humanity's being locked into a set of fixed hierarchies in the mythological world-view. Man so conceived cannot be the protagonist of prose fiction: the appropriate narrative medium is that of mythological epic, in which the stately progression of parallelistic verse—in fact, predominantly paratactic and unmetaphorical here—emphatically rehearses man's eternal place in an absolute cosmic scheme. (Of course, few mythological epics will correspond so neatly to these notions of fixity and closure. But the model of the *Enuma Elish* is decisive for our text because it reflects the prevalent norm of sacred narrative with which the Hebrew writer was breaking.) If we now return to Genesis 2, we can clearly see how the monotheistic writer works not only with very different theological assumptions but also with a radically different sense of literary form.

In contrast to the hortatory diction of Marduk and his fellow members of the Babylonian pantheon, God expresses His perception of man's condition and His own intention with a stark directness: "It is not good for man to be alone. I shall make him an aid fit for him." (His utterance, nevertheless, is close enough to a scannable verse of complementary parallelism to give it a hint of formal elevation.) Then there occurs a peculiar interruption. We have been conditioned by the previous version of cosmogony to expect an immediate act of creation to flow from the divine utterance that is introduced by the formula, "And God said." Here, however, we must wait two verses for the promised creation of a helpmate while we follow the process of man giving names to all living creatures. These verses (Gen. 2:19–20) are marked, as a formal seal of their integration in the story, by an envelope structure, being immediately preceded by the thematically crucial phrase, *'ezer kenegdo* (literally, "an aid alongside him") and concluding with that same phrase. A concise comment on these two verses in the classical Midrash nicely reflects their strategic utility: "He made them pass by in pairs. He said, 'Everything has its partner but I have no partner' " (*Bereshit Rabba* 17:5). What is especially interesting about this miniature dramatization in the Midrash is where it might have come from in the text, for the literary insights of the midrashic exegetes generally derive from their sensitive response to verbal clues—in the recurrence of a key-word, the nuanced choice of a particular lexical item, significant sound-play, and so forth. Here, however, it seems that the Midrash is responding not to any particular word in the passage but to an aspect of the text continuum which today we would call a strategy of narrative exposition. Eve has been promised. She is then withheld for two carefully framed verses while God allows man to perform his unique function as the bestower of names on things. There is implicit irony in this order of narrated events. Man is superior to all other living creatures because only he can invent language, only he has the level of consciousness that makes him capable of linguistic ordering. But this very consciousness makes him aware of his solitude in contrast to the rest of the zoological kingdom. (It is, perhaps, a solitude mitigated but not entirely removed by the creation of woman, for that creation takes place through the infliction of a kind of wound on him, and afterward, in historical time, he will pursue her, strain to become "one flesh" with her, as though to regain a lost part of himself.) The contrast between mateless man calling names to a mute world of mated creatures is brought out by a finesse of syntax not reproducible in translation. Verse 20 actually tells us that man gave names "to all cattle . . . to birds . . . to beast . . . to the man," momentarily seeming to place Adam in an anaphoric prepositional series with all living creatures. This incipient construal is then reversed by the verb "did not find," which sets man in opposition to all that has preceded. One could plausibly argue, then, that the Midrash was not merely indulging in a flight of fancy when it imagined Adam making that confession of loneliness as he named the creatures passing before him.

When God at last begins to carry out His promise at the beginning of verse 21, man, with the intervention of divine anaesthetic, is reduced from a conscious agent to an inert object acted upon, for the moment much like man in the *Enuma Elish*. The thematic difference, of course, is that this image of man as passive matter is bracketed on both sides by his performances as master of language. As soon as the awakened man discovers woman, he proceeds—as natural births elsewhere in the Bible are regularly followed by the ceremony of naming—to name her, adopting the formal emphasis of a poem. The poem (verse 23), whether or not it was the writer's original composition, fits beautifully into the thematic argument of his narrative. Written in a double chiastic structure, it refers to the woman just being named by an indicative, *zot*, "this [feminine] one," which is the first and last word of the poem in the Hebrew as well as the linchpin in the middle. Man names the animals over whom he has dominion; he names woman, over whom he ostensibly will have dominion. But in the poem, man and his bone and flesh are syntactically surrounded by this new female presence, a rhetorical configuration that makes perfect sense in the light of their subsequent history together.

The explanatory verse 24, which begins with "thus" *('al-ken)*, a fixed formula for introducing etiological assertions, might well have been part of a proverbial statement adopted verbatim by the writer, but even if this hypothesis is granted, what is remarkable is the artistry with which he weaves the etiological utterance into the texture of his own prose. The splendid image of desire fulfilled and, by extension, of the conjugal state—"they become one flesh"—is both a vivid glimpse of the act itself and a bold hyperbole. The writer, I would suggest, is as aware of the hyperbolic aspect of the image as later Plato will be when in *The Symposium* he attributes to Aristophanes the notion that lovers are the bifurcated halves of a primal self who are trying to recapture that impossible primal unity. For as soon as the idea of one flesh has been put forth (and "one" is the last word of the verse in the Hebrew), the narration proceeds as follows: "And the two of them were naked, the man and his woman, and they were not ashamed." After being invoked as the timeless model of conjugal oneness, they are immediately seen as two, a condition stressed by the deliberately awkward and uncharacteristic doubling back of the syntax in the appositional phrase, "the man and his woman"—a small illustration of how the flexibility of the prose medium enables the writer to introduce psychological distinctions, dialectical reversals of thematic direction, that would not have been feasible in the verse narratives of the ancient Near East. So the first man and woman are now two, vulnerable in their twoness to the temptation of the serpent, who will be able to seduce first one, and through the one, the other: naked (*'arumim*), unashamed, they are about to be exposed to the most cunning (*'arum*) of the beasts of the field, who will give them cause to feel shame.

From this distance in time, it is impossible to determine how much of this whole tale was sanctified, even verbally fixed, tradition; how much was popular lore perhaps available in different versions; how much the original invention of the writer. What a close reading of the text does suggest, however, is that the writer could manipulate his inherited materials with sufficient freedom and sufficient firmness of authorial purpose to define motives, relations, and unfolding themes, even in a primeval history, with the kind of subtle cogency we associate with the conscious artistry of the narrative mode designated prose fiction. (Here and in what follows, I assume when I say "conscious artistry" that there is always a complex interplay between deliberate intention and unconscious intuition in the act of artistic creation; but the biblical writer is no different from his modern counterpart in this regard.) Throughout these early chapters of Genesis, Adam and Eve are not the fixed figures of legend or myth but are made to assume contours conceived in the writer's particularizing imagination through the brief but revealing dialogue he invents for them and through the varying strategies of presentation he adopts in reporting their immemorial acts.

Let me hasten to say that in giving such weight to fictionality, I do not mean to discount the historical impulse that informs the Hebrew Bible. The God of Israel, as so often has been observed, is above all the God of history: the working out of His purposes in history is a process that compels the attention of the Hebrew imagination, which is thus led to the most vital interest in the concrete and differential character of historical events. The point is that fiction was the principal means which the biblical authors had at their disposal for realizing history. Under scrutiny, biblical narrative generally proves to be either fiction laying claim to a place in the chain of causation and the realm of moral consequentiality that belongs to history, as in the primeval history,

the tales of the Patriarchs and much of the Exodus story, and the account
of the early Conquest, or history given the imaginative definition of fiction,
as in most of the narratives from the period of the Judges onward. This
schema, of course, is necessarily neater than the persistently untidy reality of
the variegated biblical narratives. What the Bible offers us is an uneven continuum and a constant interweaving of factual historical detail (especially, but
by no means exclusively, for the later periods) with purely legendary "history";
occasional enigmatic vestiges of mythological lore; etiological stores; archetypal
fictions of the founding fathers of the nation; folktales of heroes and wonder-
working men of God; verisimilar inventions of wholly fictional personages
attached to the progress of national history; and fictionalized versions of known
historical figures. All of these narratives are presented as history, that is, as
things that really happened and that have some significant consequence for
human or Israelite destiny. The only evident exceptions to this rule are Job,
which in its very stylization seems manifestly a philosophic fable (hence the
rabbinic dictum, "There was no such creature as Job; he is a parable") and Jonah,
which, with its satiric and fantastic exaggerations, looks like a parabolic
illustration of the prophetic calling and of God's universality.

Despite the variegated character of these narratives, composed as they were
by many different hands over a period of several centuries, I would like to
attempt a rough generalization about the kind of literary project they constitute.
The ancient Hebrew writers, as I have already intimated, seek through the
process of narrative realization to reveal the enactment of God's purposes in
historical events. This enactment, however, is continuously complicated by
a perception of two, approximately parallel, dialectical tensions. One is a tension
between the divine plan and the disorderly character of actual historical events,
or, to translate this opposition into specifically biblical terms, between the divine
promise and its ostensible failure to be fulfilled; the other is a tension between
God's will, His providential guidance, and human freedom, the refractory nature
of man.

If one may presume at all to reduce great achievements to a common
denominator, it might be possible to say that the depth with which human
nature is imagined in the Bible is a function of its being conceived as caught
in the powerful interplay of this double dialectic between design and disorder,
providence and freedom. The various biblical narratives in fact may be usefully
seen as forming a spectrum between the opposing extremes of disorder and
design. Toward the disorderly end of things, where the recalcitrant facts of
known history have to be encompassed, including specific political movements,
military triumphs and reversals, and the like, would be Judges, Samuel, and
Kings. In these books, the narrators and on occasion some of the personages

˙struggle quite explicitly to reconcile their knowledge of the divine promise with their awareness of what is actually happening in history. At the other end of the spectrum, near the pole of design, one might place the Book of Esther. This post-exilic story, which presents itself as a piece of political history affecting the main diaspora community, is in fact a kind of fairytale — the lovely damsel, guided by a wise godfather, is made queen and saves her people — richly embellished with satiric invention; its comic art departs from historical verisimilitude in ways that pre-exilic Hebrew narrative seldom does, and the story demonstrates God's providential power in history with a schematic neatness unlike that of earlier historicized fiction in the Bible.

Somewhere toward the middle of this spectrum would be Genesis, where the sketchiness of the known historical materials allows considerable latitude for the elucidation of a divine plan, with, however, this sense of design repeatedly counterbalanced by the awareness of man's unruly nature, the perilous and imperious individuality of the various human agents in the divine experiment. Individuality is played against providential design in a rather different fashion in the Book of Ruth. Ruth, Naomi, and Boaz are fictional inventions, probably based on no more than names, if that, preserved in national memory. In the brief span of this narrative, they exhibit in speech and action traits of character that make them memorable individuals in a way that the more schematically conceived Esther and Mordecai are not. But in their plausible individuality they also become exemplary figures, thus earning themselves a place in the national history; Ruth, through her steadfastness, and Boaz, through his kindness and his adherence to the procedures of legitimate succession, make themselves the justified progenitors of the line of David. The Book of Ruth, then, which we might place near Genesis toward the pole of design in our imaginary spectrum, is, because of its realistic psychology and its treatment of actual social institutions, a verisimilar historicized fiction, while the Book of Esther seems more a comic fantasy utilizing pseudo-historical materials.

Let me risk a large conjecture, if only because it may help us get a clearer sighting on the phenomenon we are considering. It may be that a sense of some adequate dialectical tension between these antitheses of divine plan and the sundry disorders of human performance in history served as an implicit criterion for deciding which narratives were to be regarded as canonical. It would be an understatement to say we possess only scanty information about the now lost body of uncanonical ancient Hebrew literature, but the few hints which the Bible itself provides would seem to point in two opposite directions. On the one hand, in Kings we are repeatedly told that details skimped in the narrative at hand can be discovered by referring to the Chronicles of the Kings of Judea and the Chronicles of the Kings of Israel. Those books, one may assume, were excluded from the authoritative national tradition and hence not preserved because they were court histories, probably partisan in character, and erred on the side of the cataloguing of historical events without an informing vision of God's design working through history. On the other hand, brief and enigmatic allusion with citation is made in Numbers, Joshua, and Samuel to the Book of Yashar and the Book of the Battles of Yahweh. The latter sounds as though it was a list of military triumphs with God as principal actor; the former, to judge by the two fragments quoted (Josh. 10:13; 2 Sam. 1:18–19), was probably a verse narrative, perhaps a martial epic with miraculous elements. I would venture to guess that both books were felt to be too legendary, too committed to the direct narrative tracing of God's design, without a sufficient counterweight of the mixed stuff of recognizable historical experience.

Let us direct our attention now to the Bible's historical narratives proper in order to understand more concretely what is implied by the fictional component in describing them as historicized fiction. The large cycle of stories about David, which is surely one of the most stunning imaginative achievements of ancient literature, provides an instructive central instance of the intertwining of history and fiction. This narrative, though it may have certain folkloric embellishments (such as David's victory over Goliath), is based on firm historical facts, as modern research has tended to confirm: there really was a David who fought a civil war against the house of Saul, achieved undisputed sovereignty over the twelve tribes, conquered Jerusalem, founded a dynasty, created a small empire, and was succeeded by his son Solomon. Beyond these broad outlines, it is quite possible that many of the narrated details about David, including matters bearing on the complications of his conjugal life and his relations with his children, may have been reported on good authority.

Nevertheless, these stories are not, strictly speaking, historiography, but rather the imaginative reenactment of history by a gifted writer who organizes his materials along certain thematic biases and according to his own remarkable intuition of the psychology of the characters. He feels entirely free, one should remember, to invent interior monologue for his characters; to ascribe feeling, intention, or motive to them when he chooses; to supply verbatim dialogue (and he is one of literature's masters of dialogue) for occasions when no one but the actors themselves could have had knowledge of exactly what was said. The author of the David stories stands in basically the same relation to Israelite history as Shakespeare stands to English history in his history plays. Shakespeare was obviously not free to have Henry V lose the battle of Agincourt, or to allow someone else to lead the English forces there, but, working from the hints of historical tradition, he could invent a kind of *Bildungsroman* for the young Prince Hal; surround him with invented characters that would serve as foils, mirrors, obstacles, aids in his development; create a language and a psychology for the king which are the writer's own achievement, making out of the stuff of history a powerful projection of human possibility. That is essentially what the author of the David cycle does for David, Saul, Abner, Joab, Jonathan, Absalom, Michal, Abigail, and a host of other characters.

One memorable illustration among many of this transmutation of history into fiction is David's great confrontation with Saul at the cave in the wilderness of Ein Gedi (1 Sam. 24). The manic king, one recalls, while in pursuit of the young David, has gone into a cave to relieve himself, where by chance David and his men have taken refuge. David sneaks up to Saul and cuts off a corner of his robe. Then he is smitten with remorse for having perpetrated this symbolic mutilation on the anointed king, and he sternly holds his men in check while the unwitting Saul walks off from the cave unharmed. Once the king is at a distance, David follows him out of the cave. Holding the excised corner of the robe, he hails Saul and shouts out to his erstwhile pursuer one of his most remarkable speeches, in which he expresses fealty and reverence to the Lord's anointed one, disavows any evil intention toward him (with the corner of the robe as evidence of what he could have done but did not do), and proclaims his own humble status: "After whom did the king of Israel set out?" he says in verse-like symmetry, "After whom are you chasing? After a dead dog, after a single flea?" (1 Sam. 24:15).

At the end of this relatively lengthy speech, the narrator holds us in suspense for still another moment by choosing to preface Saul's response with a chain of introductory phrases: "And it came to pass when David finished speaking these words, that Saul said"—and then what he says has a breathtaking brevity after David's stream of words, and constitutes one of those astonishing reversals that make the rendering of character in these stories so arresting: " 'Is it your voice, David, my son?' and Saul raised his voice and wept" (1 Sam. 24:17). The point is not merely that the author has made up dialogue to which he could have had no "documentary" access; Thucydides, after all, does that as a stylized technique of representing the various positions maintained by different historical personages. In the biblical story the invented dialogue is an expression of the author's imaginative grasp of his protagonists as distinctive moral and psychological figures, of their emotion-fraught human intercourse dramatically conceived; and what that entire process of imagination essentially means is the creation of fictional character.

As elsewhere in biblical narrative, the revelation of character is effected with striking artistic economy: the specification of external circumstances, setting, and gesture is held to a bare minimum, and dialogue is made to carry a large part of the freight of meaning. To David's impassioned, elaborate rhetoric of self-justification, Saul responds with a kind of choked cry: "Is it your voice, David, my son?" Perhaps he asks this out of sheer amazement at what he has just heard, or because he is too far off to make out David's face clearly, or because his eyes are blinded with tears, which would be an apt emblem of the condition of moral blindness that has prevented him from seeing David as he really is. In connection with this last possibility, one suspects there is a deliberate if approximate echo of the blind Isaac's words to his son Jacob (after asking, "Who are you my son?" [Gen. 27:18] Isaac proclaims, "The voice is the voice of Jacob" [Gen. 27:22]). The allusion, which complicates the meaning of the present encounter between an older and a younger man in a number of ways, is not one that a historical Saul would have been apt to make on the spot, but which a writer with the privilege of fictional invention could brilliantly contrive for this shadow-haunted king whose own firstborn son will not reign after him.

Perhaps it might be objected that the David stories are merely the exception that proves the rule—a sunburst of imaginative literary activity in a series of historical books which are, after all, chronicles of known events variously embroidered with folklore and underscored for theological emphasis. Let us consider, then, a passage from that long catalogue of military uprisings, the Book of Judges, where no serious claims could be made for complexity of characterization or for subtlety of thematic development, and see if we can still observe the modalities of prose fiction in what is told and how it is told. I should like to take the story of the assassination of Eglon, King of Moab, by Ehud, the son of Gera (Judg. 3). In the absence of convincing evidence to the contrary, let us assume the historical truth of the story, which seems plausible enough: that a tough, clever guerrilla leader named Ehud, from the tribe of Benjamin (known for its martial skills), cut down Eglon more or less in the manner described, then mustered Israelite forces in the hill country of Ephraim for a successful rebellion, which was followed by a long period of relief from Moabite domination. Only the formulaic number of twice forty at the end ("And the land was quiet eighty years" [Judg. 3:30]) would patently appear not to correspond to historical fact. Where, then, in this succinct political chronicle, is there room to talk about prose fiction? Here is how the main part of the story reads:

> 15. The Israelites cried out to the Lord, and he raised up a cham-
> pion for them, Ehud the son of Gera the Benjaminite, a left-
> handed man. Now the Israelites sent tribute through him to Eglon,
> King of Moab. 16. Ehud made himself a double-edged dagger a
> *gomed* long and strapped it under his garments on his right thigh.
> 17. He brought the tribute to Eglon, King of Moab—and this

Eglon was a very stout man. 18. And it came about that after he had finished presenting the tribute, he dismissed the people who had carried it. 19. And he had come from Pesilim near Gilgal. Then he said, "A secret word I have for you, King." "Silence!" he replied, and all his attendants went out. 20. Ehud came to him as he was sitting in his cool upper chamber all alone, and Ehud said, "A word of God I have for you," and he rose from his seat. 21. And Ehud reached with his left hand and took the dagger from his right thigh and thrust it into Eglon's belly. 22. The hilt went in after the blade and the fat closed over the blade, for he did not withdraw the dagger from the belly and [the filth burst out]. 23. Ehud came out through the vestibule, closing the doors of the upper chamber on him and locking them. 24. He had just gone out when the courtiers came and saw that the doors were locked. "He is just relieving himself in the cool chamber," they said. 25. They waited a long time, and still he did not open the doors of the chamber. So they took the key and opened them, and, look, their lord was sprawled on the floor, dead.

It will be observed at once that the detailed attention given here to the implement and technique of killing, which would be normal in the *Iliad*, is rather uncharacteristic of the Hebrew Bible. One may assume that Ehud's bold resourcefulness in carrying out this assassination, which threw the Moabites into disarray and enabled the insurrection to succeed, was remarkable enough for the chronicler to want to report it circumstantially. Each of the details, then, contributes to a clear understanding of just how the thing was done (clearer, of course, for the ancient audience than for us since we no longer know much about the floor plan of the sort of Canaanite summer residence favored by Moabite kings and therefore may have a little difficulty in reconstructing Ehud's entrances and exits). The left-handed Benjaminite warriors were known for their prowess, but Ehud also counts on his left-handedness as part of his strategy of surprise: a sudden movement of the left hand will not instantaneously be construed by the king as a movement of a weapon hand. Ehud also counts on the likelihood that Eglon will be inclined to trust him as a vassal bringing tribute and that the "secret" he promises to confide to the king will thus be understood as a piece of intelligence volunteered by an Israelite collaborator. The dagger or short sword (*herev*) is of course strapped to Ehud's right thigh for easy drawing with the left hand; it is short enough to hide under his clothing, long enough to do Eglon's business without the killer's having to be unduly close to his victim, and double-edged to assure the lethalness of one quick thrust. Eglon's encumbrance of fat will make him

an easier target as he awkwardly rises from his seat, and perhaps Ehud leaves
the weapon buried in the flesh in order not to splatter blood on himself, so
that he can walk out through the vestibule unsuspected and make his escape.
One commentator [Yehezkel Kaufmann, *The Book of Judges* (Hebrew), Jerusalem, 1968] has ingeniously proposed that even the sordid detail of the release
of the anal sphincter in the death spasm has its role in the exposition of the
mechanics of the assassination: the courtiers outside, detecting the odor, assume
that Eglon has locked the door because he is performing a bodily function,
and so they wait long enough to enable Ehud to get away safely.

Yet if all this is the scrupulous report of a historical act of political terrorism, the writer has given his historical material a forceful thematic shape
through a skillful manipulation of the prose narrative medium. What emerges
is not simply a circumstantial account of the Moabite king's destruction but
a satiric vision of it, at once shrewd and jubilant. The writer's imagination
of the event is informed by an implicit etymologizing of Eglon's name, which
suggests the Hebrew *'egel*, calf. The ruler of the occupying Moabite power
turns out to be a fatted calf readied for slaughter, and perhaps even the epithet
bari, "stout," is a play on *meri*, "fatling," a sacrificial animal occasionally bracketed
with calf. Eglon's fat is both the token of his physical ponderousness, his
vulnerability to Ehud's sudden blade, and the emblem of his regal stupidity.
Perhaps it may also hint at a kind of grotesque feminization of the Moabite
leader: Ehud "comes to" the king, an idiom also used for sexual entry, and
there is something hideously sexual about the description of the dagger-thrust.
There may also be a deliberate sexual nuance in the "secret thing" Ehud brings
to Eglon, in the way the two are locked together alone in a chamber, and
in the sudden opening of locked entries at the conclusion of the story.

Ehud's claim to have a secret message for the king is accepted immediately
and without qualification by Eglon's confidential "Silence!" (or perhaps one
might translate the onomatopoeic term as *sssh!*), the Moabite either failing to
notice that Ehud has brusquely addressed him as "King" without the polite
"My lord" (*'adoni*) or construing this omission simply as evidence of Ehud's
urgency. When the two are alone and Ehud again turns to Eglon, he drops
even the bare title, flatly stating, "A word of God I have for you." This statement is a rather obvious but nevertheless effective piece of dramatic irony:
the secret thing—the Hebrew term *davar*, can mean word, message, or thing—
hidden beneath Ehud's garment is in fact the word of God that the divinely
"raised" Benjaminite champion is about to bring home implacably to the
corpulent king. Hearing that the promised political secret is actually an oracle,
Eglon rises, perhaps in sheer eagerness to know the revelation, perhaps as an
act of accepted decorum for receiving an oracular communication, and now
Ehud can cut him down.

The courtiers' erroneous assumption that their bulky monarch is taking his leisurely time over the chamber pot is a touch of scatological humor at the expense of both king and followers, while it implicates them in the satiric portrayal of the king's credulity. This last effect is heightened by the presentation of their direct speech at the end of verse 24, and the switch of the narrative to their point of view in verses 23 and 24. Let me retranslate these clauses literally to reproduce the immediate effect of seeing the scene through their eyes that one experiences in the Hebrew: "The courtiers came and saw, look, the doors of the upper chamber are locked. . . . They waited a long time and, look, he's not opening the doors of the upper chamber, and they took the keys and opened them, and, look, their lord is sprawled on the floor, dead." The syntax of the concluding clause nicely follows the rapid stages of their perception as at last they are disabused of their illusion: first they see their king prostrate, and then they realize, climactically, that he is dead. An enemy's obtuseness is always an inviting target for satire in time of war, but here the exposure of Moabite stupidity has a double thematic function: to show the blundering helplessness of the pagan oppressor when faced with a liberator raised up by the all-knowing God of Israel, and to demonstrate how these gullible Moabites, deprived of a leader, are bound to be inept in the war that immediately ensues.

In fact, great numbers of the Moabites are slaughtered at the fords of the Jordan, the location of the debacle perhaps suggesting that they allowed themselves to be drawn into an actual ambush, or at any rate, that they foolishly rushed into places where the entrenched Israelites could hold them at a terrific strategic disadvantage. Ehud's assassination of Eglon, then, is not only connected causally with the subsequent Moabite defeat but it is also a kind of emblematic prefiguration of it. The link between the regicide and the war of liberation is reinforced by two punning verbal clues. Ehud thrusts (*tq'*) the dagger into Eglon's belly (verse 21), and as soon as he makes good his escape (verse 27), he blasts the ram's horn—the same verb, *tq'*—to rally his troops. The Israelites kill 10,000 Moabites, "everyone a lusty man and a brave man" (verse 29), but the word for "lusty," *shamen*, also means "fat," so the Moabites are "laid low [or subjugated] under the hand of Israel" (verse 30) in a neat parallel to the fate of their fat master under the swift left hand of Ehud. In all this, as I have said, it is quite possible that the writer faithfully represents the historical data without addition or substantive embellishment. The organization of the narrative, however, its lexical and syntactic choices, its small shifts in point of view, its brief but strategic uses of dialogue, produce an imaginative re-enactment of the historical event, conferring upon it a strong attitudinal definition and discovering in it a pattern of meaning. It is perhaps less historicized fiction than fictionalized history—history in which the feeling and the meaning of events are concretely realized through the technical resources of prose fiction.

To round out this overview of the spectrum of fictional modalities in the Bible's sacred history, I should like to return to Genesis for a concluding illustration—this time, from the patriarchal narratives, which, unlike the story of the first ancestors of mankind, are firmly linked to Israelite national history. The linkage, to be sure, would appear to be more the writers' attribution than the result of any dependable historical traditions. Many modern scholars have assumed that the patriarchs are the invented figures of early Hebrew folklore elaborated on by later writers, particularly in order to explain political arrangements among the twelve tribes generations after the Conquest. But even if one follows the inclination of some contemporary commentators to see a historical kernel in many of these tales, it is obvious that, in contrast to our examples from Judges and the David story, the authors, writing centuries after the supposed events, had scant historical data to work with. To what degree they believed the various traditions they inherited were actually historical is by no means clear, but if caution may deter us from applying a term like "invention" to their activity, it still seems likely that they exercised a good deal of shaping power over their materials as they articulated them. The point I should like to stress is that the immemorial inventions, fabrications, or projections of folk tradition are not in themselves fiction, which depends on the particularizing imagination of the individual writer. The authors of the patriarchal narratives exhibit just such an imagination, transforming archetypal plots into the dramatic interaction of complex, probingly rendered characters. These stories are "historicized" both because they are presented as having a minute causal relation to known historical circumstances and because (as Schneidau argues) they have some of the irregular, "metonymic" quality of real historical concatenation; they are fiction because the national archetypes have been made to assume the distinctive lineaments of individual human lives.

Biblical narrative in fact offers a particularly instructive instance of the birth of fiction because it often exhibits the most arresting transitions from generalized statement, genealogical lists, mere summaries of characters and acts, to defined scene and concrete interaction between personages. Through the sudden specifications of narrative detail and the invention of dialogue that individualizes the characters and focuses their relations, the biblical writers give the events they report a fictional time and place.

Let us consider a single succinct example, Esau's selling of the birthright to Jacob (Gen. 25):

> 27. As the lads grew up, Esau became a skilled hunter, a man of
> the field, and Jacob was a mild man, who kept to his tents. 28.
> Isaac loved Esau because he had a taste for game, but Rebekah loved

Jacob. 29. Once when Jacob was cooking a stew, Esau came in from the field, famished. 30. Esau said to Jacob, "O, give me a swallow of this red red stuff for I am famished."—Thus is his name called Edom. 31. Jacob said, "First sell your birthright to me." 32. And Esau said, "Look, I am at the point of death, so what good to me is a birthright?" 33. And Jacob said, "Swear to me first," and he swore to him and sold his birthright to Jacob. 34. Then Jacob gave Esau bread and lentil stew, and he ate and he drank and he rose and he went off and Esau spurned the birthright.

Now Esau or Edom and Jacob or Israel are the eponymous founders of two neighboring and rival peoples, as the text has just forcefully reminded us in the oracle preceding their birth ("Two nations are in your womb./Two peoples apart while still in your belly./One people will outdo the other,/The older will serve the younger." [Gen. 25:23]). The story of the two rival brothers virtually asks us to read it as a political allegory, to construe each of the twins as an embodiment of his descendants' national characteristics, and to understand the course of their struggle as an outline of their future national destinies. The ruddy Esau, hungry for the red stew, is the progenitor of Edom, by folk etymology associated with 'adom, the color red, so that the people are given a kind of national emblem linked here with animality and gross appetite. This negative characterization is probably sharpened, as E. A. Speiser has proposed, by a borrowing from Near Eastern literary tradition: the red Esau, born with "a mantle of hair all over," would appear to allude to Enkidu of the Akkadian Gilgamesh Epic, whose birth is described in just this manner, and who is also an uncouth man of the field. What happens, however, when the story is read entirely as a collision of national archetypes is strikingly illustrated by the commentaries of the early rabbis who—tending to interpret Edom as the typological forerunner of Rome—are relentless in making Esau out to be a vicious brute, while Jacob the tent-dweller becomes the model of pious Israel pondering the intricacies of God's revelation in the study of the Law. The anachronism of such readings concerns us less than the way they project onto the text, from their national-historical viewpoint, a neat moral polarity between the brothers. The text itself, conceiving its personages in the fullness of a mature fictional imagination, presents matters rather differently, as even this brief passage from the larger Jacob–Esau story will suggest.

The episode begins with a schematic enough contrast between Esau the hunter and the sedentary Jacob. This apparently neat opposition, however, contains a lurking possibility of irony in the odd epithet *tam* attached to Jacob in verse 27. Most translators have rendered it, as I have, by following the immediate context, and so have proposed something like "mild," "plain," or even "retiring" as an English equivalent. Perhaps this was in fact one recognized meaning of the term, but it should be noted that *all* the other biblical occurrences of the word—and it is frequently used, both in adjectival and nominative forms—refer to innocence or moral integrity. A little earlier in Genesis (20:5–6) Abraham professed the "innocence of his heart" *(tom-levav)*; in contrast to this collocation, Jeremiah will announce (Jer. 17:9) that the "heart is treacherous" (*'aqov ha-lev*), using the same verbal root that Esau sees in Jacob's name (*Ya 'aqov*) as an etymological signature of his treachery. This usage opens the possibility that we are dealing here with recognized antonyms, both of them commonly bound in idiomatic compounds to the word for heart. Jacob, *Ya 'aqov*, whose name will soon be interpreted as the one who deceives (the Hebrew could be construed as "he will deceive"), is about to carry out an act if not of deception at least of shrewd calculation, and the choice of an epithet suggesting innocence as an introduction to the episode is bound to give us pause, to make us puzzle over the moral nature of Jacob—an enigma we shall still be trying to fathom twenty chapters later when he is an old man worn by experience, at last reunited with his lost son Joseph and received in the court of Pharaoh.

The next verse (Gen. 25:28) provides an almost diagrammatic illustration of the Bible's artful procedure of variously stipulating or suppressing motive in order to elicit moral inferences and suggest certain ambiguities. Isaac's preference for Esau is given a causal explanation so specific that it verges on satire: he loves the older twin because of his own fondness for game. Rebekah's love for Jacob is contrastively stated without explanation. Presumably, this would suggest that her affection is not dependent on a merely material convenience that the son might provide her, that it is a more justly grounded preference. Rebekah's maternal solicitude, however, is not without its troubling side, for we shall soon see a passive and rather timid Jacob briskly maneuvered about by his mother so that he will receive Isaac's blessing. This brief statement, then, of parental preferences is both an interesting characterization of husband and wife and an effectively reticent piece of exposition in the story of the two brothers.

The twins then spring to life as fictional characters when the narration moves into dialogue (Gen 25:30–33). Biblical Hebrew, as far as we can tell, does not incorporate in direct speech different levels of diction, deviations from standard grammar, regional or class dialects; but the writers, even in putting "normative" Hebrew in the mouths of their personages, find ways of differentiating spoken language according to character. Esau asks for the stew with a verb used for the feeding of animals (*hil'it*)—one might suggest the force of the locution in English by rendering it as "let me cram my maw"—and, all inarticulate appetite, he cannot even think of the word for stew but only points to it pantingly, calling it "this red red stuff." His explanation, however, "for I am famished," is factually precise, as it echoes verbatim what the narrator has just told us. In the first instance, that is, Esau does not choose an exaggeration, like that of verse 32, but states his actual condition: a creature of appetite, he is caught by the pangs of a terrible appetite. Esau speaks over the rumble of a growling stomach with the whiff of the cooking stew in his nostrils. Jacob speaks with a clear perception of legal forms and future consequences, addressing his brother twice in the imperative—"First sell . . . swear to me first"—without the deferential particle of entreaty, na, that Esau used in his own initial words to his twin. When Jacob asks Esau to sell the birthright, he withholds the crucial "to me" till the end of his proposal with cautious rhetorical calculation. Fortunately for him, Esau is too absorbed in his own immediate anguish—"I am at the point of death"— to pay much attention to Jacob's self-interest. After the transaction is completed, as we move back from dialogue to uninterrupted narration, Esau's precipitous character is mirrored stylistically in the rapid chain of verbs—"and he ate and he drank and he rose and he went off"—that indicates the uncouth dispatch with which he "spurned," or held in contempt, his birthright.

What is one to make of this vivid fictional realization of the scene in regard to its evident national-historical signification? The two are not really at cross-purposes, but certain complications of meaning are introduced in the process of fictional representation. Esau, the episode makes clear, is not spiritually fit to be the vehicle of divine election, the bearer of the birthright of Abraham's seed. He is altogether too much the slave of the moment and of the body's tyranny to become the progenitor of the people promised by divine covenant that it will have a vast historical destiny to fulfill. His selling of the birthright in the circumstances here described is in itself proof that he is not worthy to retain the birthright.

As the author, however, concretely imagines Jacob, what emerges from the scene is more than simple Israelite (and anti-Edomite) apologetics. Jacob is a man who thinks about the future, indeed, who often seems worried about the future, and we shall repeatedly see him making prudent stipulations in legal or quasi-legal terms with God, with Laban, with his mysterious adversary, about future circumstances. This qualifies him as a suitable bearer of the birthright: historical destiny does not just happen; you have to know how to make it happen, how to keep your eye on the distant horizon of present events. But this quality of wary calculation does not necessarily make Jacob more appealing as a character, and, indeed, may even raise some moral questions about him. The contrast in this scene between the impetuous, miserably famished

Esau and the shrewdly businesslike Jacob may not be entirely to Jacob's advantage, and the episode is surely a little troubling in light of the quality of "innocence" which the narrator has just fastened as an epithet to the younger twin. His subsequent stealing of his blind father's blessing by pretending to be Esau (Gen. 27) sets him in a still more ambiguous light; and the judgment that Jacob has done wrong in taking what is, in a sense, his, is later confirmed in the narrative, as Umberto Cassuto and other commentators have noted: Jacob becomes the victim of symmetrical poetic justice, deceived in the blindness of the night by having Leah passed off on him as Rachel, and rebuked in the morning by the deceiver, his father-in-law Laban: "It is not done thus in our region to give the younger daughter before the firstborn" (Gen. 29:26).

If one insists on seeing the patriarchal narratives strictly as paradigms for later Israelite history, one would have to conclude that the authors and redactor of the Jacob story were political subversives raising oblique but damaging questions about the national enterprise. Actually, there may be some theological warrant for this introduction of ambiguities into the story of Israel's eponymous hero, for in the perspective of ethical monotheism, covenantal privileges by no means automatically confer moral perfection, and that monitory idea is perhaps something the writers wanted to bring to the attention of their audiences. I do not think, though, that every nuance of characterization and every turning of the plot in these stories can be justified in either moral-theological or national-historical terms. Perhaps this is the ultimate difference between any hermeneutic approach to the Bible and the literary approach that I am proposing: in the literary perspective there is làtitude for the exercise of pleasurable invention for its own sake, ranging from "microscopic" details like sound-play to "macroscopic" features like the psychology of individual characters.

This need not imply a blurring of necessary distinctions between sacred and secular literature. The biblical authors are of course constantly, urgently conscious of telling a story in order to reveal the imperative truth of God's works in history and of Israel's hopes and failings. Close attention to the literary strategies through which that truth was expressed may actually help us to understand it better, enable us to see the minute elements of complicating design in the Bible's sacred history. But it also seems to me important to emphasize that the operation of the literary imagination develops a momentum of its own, even for a tradition of writers so theologically intent as these. Genesis is not *Pale Fire*, but all fiction, including the Bible, is in some sense a form of play. Play in the sense I have in mind enlarges rather than limits the range of meanings of the text. For the classics of fiction, ancient and modern, embody in a vast variety of modes the most serious playfulness, endlessly discovering how the permutations of narrative conventions, linguistic properties, and imaginatively constructed personages and circumstances can crystalize subtle and abiding truths of experience in amusing or arresting or gratifying ways. The Bible presents a kind of literature in which the primary impulse would often seem to be to provide instruction or at least necessary information, not merely to delight. If, however, we fail to see that the creators of biblical narrative were writers who, like writers elsewhere, took pleasure in exploring the formal and imaginative resources of their fictional medium, perhaps sometimes unexpectedly capturing the fullness of their subject in the very play of exploration, we shall miss much that the biblical stories are meant to convey.

Representations of Reality
in Homer and the Old Testament

The genius of the Homeric style becomes [especially] apparent when it is compared with an equally ancient and equally epic style from a different world of forms. I shall attempt this comparison with the account of the sacrifice of Isaac, a homogeneous narrative produced by the so-called Elohist. The King James version translates the opening as follows (Gen. 22:1): "And it came to pass after these things, that God did tempt Abraham, and said to him, Abraham! and he said, Behold, here I am." Even this opening startles us when we come to it from Homer. Where are the two speakers? We are not told. The reader, however, knows that they are not normally to be found together in one place on earth, that one of them, God, in order to speak to Abraham, must come from somewhere, must enter the earthly realm from some unknown heights or depths. Whence does he come, whence does he call to Abraham? We are not told. He does not come, like Zeus or Poseidon, from the Aethiopians, where he has been enjoying a sacrificial feast. Nor are we told anything of his reasons for tempting Abraham so terribly. He has not, like Zeus, discussed them in set speeches with other gods gathered in council; nor have the deliberations in his own heart been presented to us; unexpected and mysterious, he enters the scene from some unknown height or depth and calls: Abraham! It will at once be said that this is to be explained by the particular concept of God which the Jews held and which was wholly different from that of the Greeks. True enough—but this constitutes no objection. For how is the Jewish concept of God to be explained? Even their earlier God of the desert was not fixed in form and content, and was alone; his lack of form, his lack of local

From *Mimesis: The Representation of Reality in Western Literature.* © 1953 by Princeton University Press. Princeton University Press, 1981.

habitation, his singleness, was in the end not only maintained but developed even further in competition with the comparatively far more manifest gods of the surrounding Near Eastern world. The concept of God held by the Jews is less a cause than a symptom of their manner of comprehending and representing things.

This becomes still clearer if we now turn to the other person in the dialogue, to Abraham. Where is he? We do not know. He says, indeed: Here I am — but the Hebrew word means only something like "behold me," and in any case is not meant to indicate the actual place where Abraham is, but a moral position in respect to God, who has called to him — Here am I awaiting thy command. Where he is actually, whether in Beersheba or elsewhere, whether indoors or in the open air, is not stated; it does not interest the narrator, the reader is not informed; and what Abraham was doing when God called to him is left in the same obscurity. To realize the difference, consider Hermes' visit to Calypso, for example, where command, journey, arrival and reception of the visitor, situation and occupation of the person visited, are set forth in many verses; and even on occasions when gods appear suddenly and briefly, whether to help one of their favorites or to deceive or destroy some mortal whom they hate, their bodily forms, and usually the manner of their coming and going, are given in detail. Here, however, God appears without bodily form (yet he "appears"), coming from some unspecified place — we only hear his voice, and that utters nothing but a name, a name without an adjective, without a descriptive epithet for the person spoken to, such as is the rule in every Homeric address; and of Abraham too nothing is made perceptible except the words in which he answers God: *Hinne-ni*, Behold me here — with which, to be sure, a most touching gesture expressive of obedience and readiness is suggested, but it is left to the reader to visualize it. Moreover the two speakers are not on the same level: if we conceive of Abraham in the foreground, where it might be possible to picture him as prostrate or kneeling or bowing with outspread arms or gazing upward, God is not there too: Abraham's words and gestures are directed toward the depths of the picture or upward, but in any case the undetermined, dark place from which the voice comes to him is not in the foreground.

After this opening, God gives his command, and the story itself begins: everyone knows it; it unrolls with no episodes in a few independent sentences whose syntactical connection is of the most rudimentary sort. In this atmosphere it is unthinkable that an implement, a landscape through which the travelers passed, the serving-men, or the ass, should be described, that their origin or descent or material or appearance or usefulness should be set forth in terms of praise; they do not even admit an adjective: they are serving-men, ass, wood, and knife, and nothing else, without an epithet; they are there to serve the end which God has commanded; what in other respects they were, are, or will be, remains in darkness. A journey is made, because God has designated the place where the sacrifice is to be performed; but we are told nothing about the journey except that it took three days, and even that we are told in a mysterious way: Abraham and his followers rose "early in the morning" and "went unto" the place of which God had told him; on the third day he lifted up his eyes and saw the place from afar. That gesture is the only gesture, is indeed the only occurrence during the whole journey, of which we are told; and though its motivation lies in the fact that the place is elevated, its uniqueness still heightens the impression that the journey took place through a vacuum; it is as if, while he traveled on, Abraham had looked neither to the right nor to the left, had suppressed any sign of life in his followers and himself save only their footfalls.

Thus the journey is like a silent progress through the indeterminate and the contingent, a holding of the breath, a process which has no present, which is inserted, like a blank duration, between what has passed and what lies ahead, and which yet is measured: three days! Three such days positively demand the symbolic interpretation which they later received. They began "early in the morning." But at what time on the third day did Abraham lift up his eyes and see his goal? The text says nothing on the subject. Obviously not "late in the evening," for it seems that there was still time enough to climb the mountain and make the sacrifice. So "early in the morning" is given, not as an indication of time, but for the sake of its ethical significance; it is intended to express the resolution, the promptness, the punctual obedience of the sorely tired Abraham. Bitter to him is the early morning in which he saddles his ass, calls his serving-men and his son Isaac, and sets out; but he obeys, he walks on until the third day, then lifts up his eyes and sees the place. Whence he comes, we do not know, but the goal is clearly stated: Jeruel in the land of Moriah. What place this is meant to indicate is not clear—"Moriah" especially may be a later correction of some other word. But in any case the goal was given, and in any case it is a matter of some sacred spot which was to receive a particular consecration by being connected with Abraham's sacrifice. Just as little as "early in the morning" serves as a temporal indication does "Jeruel in the Land of Moriah" serve as a geographical indication; and in both cases alike, the complementary indication is not given, for we know as little of the hour at which Abraham lifted up his eyes as we do of the place from which he set forth—Jeruel is significant not so much as the goal of an earthly journey, in its geographical relation to other places, as through its special election, through its relatiòn to God, who designated it as the scene of the act, and therefore it must be named.

In the narrative itself, a third chief character appears: Isaac. While God and Abraham, the serving-men, the ass, and the implements are simply named, without mention of any qualities or any other sort of definition, Isaac once receives an appositive; God says, "Take Isaac, thine only son, whom thou lovest." But this is not a characterization of Isaac as a person, apart from his relation to his father and apart from the story; he may be handsome or ugly, intelligent or stupid, tall or short, pleasant or unpleasant—we are not told. Only what we need to know about him as a personage in the action, here and now, is illuminated, so that it may become apparent how terrible Abraham's temptation is, and that God is fully aware of it. By this example of the contrary, we see the significance of the descriptive adjectives and digressions of the Homeric poems; with their indications of the earlier and as it were absolute existence of the persons described, they prevent the reader from concentrating exclusively on a present crisis; even when the most terrible things are occurring, they present the establishment of an overwhelming suspense. But here, in the story of Abraham's sacrifice, the overwhelming suspense is present; what Schiller makes the goal of the tragic poet—to rob us of our emotional freedom, to turn our intellectual and spiritual powers (Schiller says "our activity") in one direction, to concentrate them there—is effected in this Biblical narrative, which certainly deserves the epithet epic.

We find the same contrast if we compare the two uses of direct discourse. The personages speak in the Bible story too; but their speech does not serve, as does speech in Homer, to manifest, to externalize thoughts—on the contrary, it serves to indicate thoughts which remain unexpressed. God gives his command in direct discourse, but he leaves his motives and his purpose unexpressed; Abraham, receiving the command, says nothing and does what he has been told to do. The conversation between Abraham and Isaac on the way to the place of sacrifice is only an interruption of the heavy silence and makes it all the more burdensome. The two of them, Isaac carrying the wood and Abraham with fire and a knife, "went together." Hesitantly, Isaac ventures to ask about the ram, and Abraham gives the well-known answer. Then the text repeats: "So they went both of them together." Everything remains unexpressed.

It would be difficult, then, to imagine styles more contrasted than those of these two equally ancient and equally epic texts. On the one hand, externalized, uniformly illuminated phenomena, at a definite time and in a definite place, connected together without lacunae in a perpetual foreground; thoughts and feeling completely expressed; events taking place in leisurely fashion and with very little of suspense. On the other hand, the externalization of only so much of the phenomena as is necessary for the purpose of the narrative, all else left in obscurity; the decisive points of the narrative alone are emphasized, what lies between is nonexistent; time and place are undefined and call for interpretation; thoughts and feeling remain unexpressed, are only suggested by the silence and the fragmentary speeches; the whole, permeated with the most unrelieved suspense and directed toward a single goal (and to that extent far more of a unity), remains mysterious and "fraught with background."

I will discuss this term in some detail, lest it be misunderstood. I said [elsewhere] that the Homeric style was "of the foreground" because, despite much going back and forth, it yet causes what is momentarily being narrated to give the impression that it is the only present, pure and without perspective. A consideration of the Elohistic text teaches us that our term is capable of a broader and deeper application. It shows that even the separate personages can be represented as possessing "background"; God is always so represented in the Bible, for he is not comprehensible in his presence, as is Zeus; it is always only "something" of him that appears, he always extends into depths. But even the human beings in the Biblical stories have greater depths of time, fate, and consciousness than do the human beings in Homer; although they are nearly always caught up in an event engaging all their faculties, they are not so entirely immersed in its present that they do not remain continually conscious of what has happened to them earlier and elsewhere; their thoughts and feelings have more layers, are more entangled. Abraham's actions are explained not only by what is happening to him at the moment, nor yet only by his character (as Achilles' actions by his courage and his pride, and Odysseus' by his versatility and foresightedness), but by his previous history; he remembers, he is constantly conscious of, what God has promised him and what God has already accomplished for him—his soul is torn between desperate rebellion and hopeful expectation; his silent obedience is multilayered, has background. Such a problematic psychological situation as this is impossible for any of the Homeric heroes, whose destiny is clearly defined and who wake every morning as if it were the first day of their lives: their emotions, though strong, are simple and find expression instantly.

How fraught with background, in comparison, are characters like Saul and David! How entangled and stratified are such human relations as those between David and Absalom, between David and Joab! Any such "background" quality of the psychological situation as that which the story of Absalom's death and its sequel (2 Sam. 18 and 19, by the so-called Jahvist) rather suggests than expresses, is unthinkable in Homer. Here we are confronted not merely with the psychological processes of characters whose depth of background is veritably abysmal, but with a purely geographical background too. For David is absent from the battlefield; but the influence of his will and his feelings continues to operate, they affect even Joab in his rebellion and disregard for the consequences of his actions; in the magnificent scene with the two messengers, both the physical and psychological background is fully manifest, though the latter is never expressed. With this, compare, for example, how Achilles, who sends Patroclus first to scout and then into battle, loses almost all "presentness" so long as he is not physically present. But the most important thing is the "multilayeredness" of the individual character; this is hardly to be met with in Homer, or at most in the form of a conscious hesitation between two possible courses of action; otherwise, in Homer, the complexity of the psychological life is shown only in the succession and alternation of emotions; whereas the Jewish writers are able to express the simultaneous existence of various layers of consciousness and the conflict between them.

The Homeric poems, then, though their intellectual, linguistic, and above all syntactical culture appears to be so much more highly developed, are yet comparatively simple in their picture of human beings; and no less so in their relation to the real life which they describe in general. Delight in physical existence is everything to them, and their highest aim is to make that delight perceptible to us. Between battles and passions, adventures and perils, they show us hunts, banquets, palaces and shepherds' cots, athletic contests and washing days—in order that we may see the heroes in their ordinary life, and seeing them so, may take pleasure in their manner of enjoying their savory present, a present which sends strong roots down into social usages, landscape, and daily life. And thus they bewitch us and ingratiate themselves to us until we live with them in the reality of their lives; so long as we are reading or hearing the poems, it does not matter whether we know that all this is only legend, "make-believe." The oft-repeated reproach that Homer is a liar takes nothing from his effectiveness, he does not need to base his story on historical reality, his reality is powerful enough in itself; it ensnares us, weaving its web around us, and that suffices him. And this "real" world into which we are lured, exists for itself, contains nothing but itself; the Homeric poems conceal nothing, they contain no teaching and no secret second meaning. Homer can be analyzed, as we have essayed to do here, but he cannot be interpreted. Later allegorizing trends have tried their arts of interpretation upon him, but to no avail. He resists any such treatment; the interpretations are forced and foreign, they do not crystallize into a unified doctrine. The general considerations which occasionally occur (in our episode, for example, v. 360: that in misfortune men age quickly) reveal a calm acceptance of the basic facts of human existence, but with no compulsion to brood over them, still less any passionate impulse either to rebel against them or to embrace them in an ecstasy of submission.

It is all very different in the Biblical stories. Their aim is not to bewitch the senses, and if nevertheless they produce lively sensory effects, it is only because the moral, religious, and psychological phenomena which are their sole concern are made concrete in the sensible matter of life. But their religious intent involves an absolute claim to historical truth. The story of Abraham and Isaac is not better established than the story of Odysseus, Penelope, and Euryclea; both are legendary. But the Biblical narrator, the Elohist, had to believe in the objective truth of the story of Abraham's sacrifice—the existence of the sacred ordinances of life rested upon the truth of this and similar stories. He had to believe in it passionately; or else (as many rationalistic interpreters believed and perhaps still believe) he had to be a conscious liar—no harmless liar like Homer, who lied to give pleasure, but a political liar with a definite end in view, lying in the interest of a claim to absolute authority.

To me, the rationalistic interpretation seems psychologically absurd; but even if we take it into consideration, the relation of the Elohist to the truth of his story still remains a far more passionate and definite one than is Homer's relation. The Biblical narrator was obliged to write exactly what his belief in the truth of the tradition (or, from the rationalistic standpoint, his interest in the truth of it) demanded of him—in either case, his freedom in creative or representative imagination was severely limited; his activity was perforce reduced to composing an effective version of the pious tradition. What he produced, then, was not primarily oriented toward "realism" (if he succeeded in being realistic, it was merely a means, not an end); it was oriented toward truth. Woe to the man who did not believe it! One can perfectly well entertain historical doubts on the subject of the Trojan War or of Odysseus' wanderings, and still, when reading Homer, feel precisely the effects he sought to produce; but without believing in Abraham's sacrifice, it is impossible to put the narrative of it to the use for which it was written. Indeed, we must go even further. The Bible's claim to truth is not only far more urgent than Homer's, it is tyrannical—it excludes all other claims. The world of the Scripture stories is not satisfied with claiming to be a historically true reality—it insists that it is the only real world, is destined for autocracy. All other scenes, issues, and ordinances have no right to appear independently of it, and it is promised that all of them, the history of all mankind, will be given their due place within its frame, will be subordinated to it. The Scripture stories do not, like Homer's, court our favor, they do not flatter us that they may please us and enchant us—they seek to subject us, and if we refuse to be subjected we are rebels.

Let no one object that this goes too far, that not the stories, but the religious doctrine, raises the claim to absolute authority; because the stories are not, like Homer's, simply narrated "reality." Doctrine and promise are incarnate in them and inseparable from them; for that very reason they are fraught with "background" and mysterious, containing a second, concealed meaning. In the story of Isaac, it is not only God's intervention at the beginning and the end, but even the factual and psychological elements which come between, that are mysterious, merely touched upon, fraught with background; and therefore they require subtle investigation and interpretation, they demand them. Since so much in the story is dark and incomplete, and since the reader knows that God is a hidden God, his effort to interpret it constantly finds something new to feed upon. Doctrine and the search for enlightenment are inextricably connected with the physical side of the narrative—the latter being more than simple "reality"; indeed they are in constant danger of losing their own reality, as very soon happened when interpretation reached such proportions that the real vanished.

If the text of the Biblical narrative, then, is so greatly in need of interpretation on the basis of its own content, its claim to absolute authority forces it still further in the same direction. Far from seeking, like Homer, merely to make us forget our own reality for a few hours, it seeks to overcome our reality: we are to fit our own life into its world, feel ourselves to be elements in its structure of universal history. This becomes increasingly difficult the further our historical environment is removed from that of the Biblical books; and if these nevertheless maintain their claim to absolute authority, it is inevitable that they themselves be adapted through interpretative transformation. This was for a long time comparatively easy; as late as the European Middle Ages it was possible to represent Biblical events as ordinary phenomena of contemporary life, the methods of interpretation themselves forming the basis for such a treatment. But when, through too great a change in environment and through the awakening of a critical consciousness, this becomes impossible, the Biblical claim to absolute authority is jeopardized; the method of interpretation is scorned and rejected, the Biblical stories become ancient legends, and the doctrine they had contained, now dissevered from them, becomes a disembodied image.

As a result of this claim to absolute authority, the method of interpretation spread to traditions other than the Jewish. The Homeric poems present a definite complex of events whose boundaries in space and time are clearly delimited; before it, beside it, and after it, other complexes of events, which do not depend upon it, can be conceived without conflict and without difficulty. The Old Testament, on the other hand, presents universal history: it begins with the beginning of time, with the creation of the world, and will end with the Last Days, the fulfilling of the Covenant, with which the world will come to an end. Everything else that happens in the world can only be conceived as an element in this sequence; into it everything that is known about the world, or at least everything that touches upon the history of the Jews, must be fitted as an ingredient of the divine plan; and as this too became possible only by interpreting the new material as it poured in, the need for interpretation reaches out beyond the original Jewish-Israelitish realm of reality—for example to Assyrian, Babylonian, Persian, and Roman history; interpretation in a determined direction becomes a general method of comprehending reality; the new and strange world which now comes into view and which, in the form in which it presents itself, proves to be wholly unutilizable within the Jewish religious frame, must be so interpreted that it can find a place there. But this process nearly always also reacts upon the frame, which requires enlarging and modifying. The most striking piece of interpretation of this sort occurred in the first century of the Christian era, in consequence of Paul's mission to the Gentiles: Paul and the Church Fathers reinterpreted the entire Jewish tradition as a succession of figures prognosticating the appearance of Christ, and assigned the Roman Empire its proper place in the divine plan of salvation. Thus while, on the one hand, the reality of the Old Testament presents itself as complete truth with a claim to sole authority, on the other hand that very claim forces it to a constant interpretative change in its own content; for millennia it undergoes an incessant and active development with the life of man in Europe.

The claim of the Old Testament stories to represent universal history, their insistent relation—a relation constantly redefined by conflicts—to a single and hidden God, who yet shows himself and who guides universal history by promise and exaction, gives these stories an entirely different perspective from any the Homeric poems can possess. As a composition, the Old Testament is incomparably less unified than the Homeric poems, it is more obviously pieced together—but the various components all belong to one concept of universal history and its interpretation. If certain elements survived which did not immediately fit in, interpretation took care of them; and so the reader is at every moment aware of the universal religio-historical perspective which gives the individual stories their general meaning and purpose. The greater the separateness and horizontal disconnection of the stories and groups of stories in relation to one another, compared with the *Iliad* and the *Odyssey*, the stronger is their general vertical connection, which holds them all together and which is entirely lacking in Homer. Each of the great figures of the Old Testament, from Adam to the prophets, embodies a moment of this vertical connection. God chose and formed these men to the end of embodying his essence and will—yet choice and formation do not coincide, for the latter proceeds gradually, historically, during the earthly life of him upon whom the choice has fallen. How the process is accomplished, what terrible trials such a formation inflicts, can be seen from our story of Abraham's sacrifice. Herein lies the reason why the great figures of the Old Testament are so much more fully developed, so much more fraught with their own biographical past, so much more distinct as individuals, than are the Homeric heroes. Achilles and Odysseus are splendidly described in many well-ordered words, epithets cling to them, their emotions are constantly displayed in their words and deeds—but they have no development, and their life-histories are clearly set forth once and for all. So little are the Homeric heroes presented as developing or having developed, that most of them—Nestor, Agamemnon, Achilles—appear to be of an age fixed from the very first. Even Odysseus, in whose case the long lapse of time and the many events which occurred offer so much opportunity for biographical development, shows almost nothing of it. Odysseus on his return is exactly the same as he was when he left Ithaca two decades earlier. But what a road, what a fate, lie between the Jacob who cheated his father out of his blessing and the old man whose favorite son has been torn to pieces by a wild beast!— between David the harp player, persecuted by his lord's jealousy, and the old king, surrounded by violent intrigues, whom Abishag and Shunnamite warmed in his bed, and he knew her not! The old man, of whom we know how he has become what he is, is more of an individual than the young man; for it is only during the course of an eventful life that men are differentiated into full individuality; and it is this history of a personality which the Old Testament presents to us as the formation undergone by those whom God has chosen to be examples. Fraught with their development, sometimes even aged to the verge of dissolution, they show a distinct stamp of individuality entirely foreign to the Homeric heroes. Time can touch the latter only outwardly, and even that change is brought to our observation as little as possible; whereas the stern hand of God is ever upon the Old Testament figures; he has not only made them once and for all and chosen them, but he continues to work upon them, bends them and kneads them, and, without destroying them in essence, produces from them forms which their youth gave no grounds for anticipating. The objection that the biographical element of the Old Testament often springs from the combination of several legendary personages does not apply; for this combination is a part of the development of the text. And how much wider is the pendulum swing of their lives than that of the Homeric heroes! For they are bearers of the divine will, and yet they are fallible, subject to misfortune and humiliation—and in the midst of misfortune and in their humiliation their acts and words reveal the transcendent majesty of God. There is hardly one of them who does not, like Adam, undergo the deepest humiliation—and hardly one who is not deemed worthy of God's personal intervention and personal inspiration. Humiliation and elevation go far deeper and far higher than in Homer, and they belong basically together. The poor beggar Odysseus is only masquerading, but Adam is really cast down, Jacob really a refugee, Joseph really in the pit and then a slave to be bought and sold. But their greatness, rising out of humiliation, is almost superhuman and an image of God's greatness. The reader clearly feels how the extent of the pendulum's swing is connected with the intensity of the personal history—precisely the most extreme circumstances, in which we are immeasurably forsaken and in despair, or immeasurably joyous and exalted, give us, if we survive them, a personal stamp which is recognized as the product of a rich existence, a rich development. And very often, indeed generally, this element of development gives the Old Testament stories a historical character, even when the subject is purely legendary and traditional.

Homer remains within the legendary with all his material, whereas the material of the Old Testament comes closer and closer to history as the narrative proceeds; in the stories of David the historical report predominates. Here too, much that is legendary still remains, as for example the story of David and Goliath; but much—and the most essential—consists in things which the narrators knew from their own experience or from firsthand testimony. Now the difference between legend and history is in most cases easily perceived by a reasonably experienced reader. It is a difficult matter, requiring careful historical and philological training, to distinguish the true from the synthetic or the biased in a historical presentation; but it is easy to separate the historical from the legendary in general. Their structure is different. Even where the legendary does not immediately betray itself by elements of the miraculous, by the repetition of well-known standard motives, typical patterns and themes, through neglect of clear details of time and place, and the like, it is generally quickly recognizable by its composition. It runs far too smoothly. All crosscurrents, all friction, all that is casual, secondary to the main events and themes, everything unresolved, truncated, and uncertain, which confuses the clear progress of the action and the simple orientation of the actors, has disappeared. The historical event which we witness, or learn from the testimony of those who witnessed it, runs much more variously, contradictorily, and confusedly; not until it has produced results in a definite domain are we able, with their help, to classify it to a certain extent; and how often the order to which we think we have attained becomes doubtful again, how often we ask ourselves if the data before us have not led us to a far too simple classification of the original events! Legend arranges its material in a simple and straightforward way; it detaches it from its contemporary historical context, so that the latter will not confuse it; it knows only clearly outlined men who act from few and simple motives and the continuity of whose feelings and actions remains uninterrupted. In the legends of martyrs, for example, a stiff-necked and fanatical persecutor stands over against an equally stiff-necked and fanatical victim; and a situation so complicated—that is to say, so real and historical—as that in which the "persecutor" Pliny finds himself in his celebrated letter to Trajan on the subject of the Christians, is unfit for legend. And that is still a comparatively simple case. Let the reader think of the history which we are ourselves witnessing; anyone who, for example, evaluates the behavior of individual men and groups of men at the time of the rise of National Socialism in Germany, or the behavior of individual peoples and states before and during the last war, will feel how difficult it is to represent historical themes in general, and how unfit they are for legend; the historical comprises a great number of contradictory motives in each individual, a hesitation and ambiguous groping on the part of groups; only seldom (as in the last war) does a more or less plain situation, comparatively simple to describe, arise, and even such a situation is subject to division below the surface, is indeed almost constantly in danger of losing its simplicity; and the motives of all the interested parties are so complex that the slogans of propaganda can be composed only through the crudest simplification—with the result that friend and foe alike can often employ the same ones. To write history is so difficult that most historians are forced to make concessions to the technique of legend.

It is clear that a large part of the life of David as given in the Bible contains history and not legend. In Absalom's rebellion, for example, or in the scenes from David's last days, the contradictions and crossing of motives both in individuals and in the general action have become so concrete that it is impossible to doubt the historicity of the information conveyed. Now the men who composed the historical parts are often the same who edited the older legends too; their peculiar religious concept of man in history, which we have attempted to describe above, in no way led them to a legendary simplification of events; and so it is only natural that, in the legendary passages of the Old Testament, historical structure is frequently discernible—of course, not in the sense that the traditions are examined as to their credibility according to the methods of scientific criticism; but simply to the extent that the tendency to a smoothing down and harmonizing of events, to a simplification of motives, to a static definition of characters which avoids conflict, vacillation, and development, such as are natural legendary structure, does not predominate in the Old Testament world of legend. Abraham, Jacob, or even Moses produces a more concrete, direct, and historical impression than the figures of the Homeric world—not because they are better described in terms of sense (the contrary is the case) but because the confused, contradictory multiplicity of events, the psychological and factual cross-purposes, which true history reveals, have not disappeared in the representation but still remain clearly perceptible. In the stories of David, the legendary, which only later scientific criticism makes recognizable as such, imperceptibly passes into the historical; and even in the legendary, the problem of the classification and interpretation of human history is already passionately apprehended—a problem which later shatters the framework of historical composition and completely overruns it with prophecy; thus the Old Testament, in so far as it is concerned with human events, ranges through all three domains: legend, historical reporting, and interpretative historical theology.

Connected with the matters just discussed is the fact that the Greek text seems more limited and more static in respect to the circle of personages involved in the action and to their political activity. In the recognition scene with which we began, there appears, aside from Odysseus and Penelope, the housekeeper Euryclea, a slave whom Odysseus' father Laertes had bought long before. She, like the swineherd Eumaeus, has spent her life in the service of Laertes' family; like Eumaeus, she is closely connected with their fate, she loves them and shares their interests and feelings. But she has no life of her own, no feelings of her own; she has only the life and feelings of her master. Eumaeus too, though he still remembers that he was born a freeman and indeed of a noble house (he was stolen as a boy), has, not only in fact but also in his own feeling, no longer a life of his own, he is entirely involved in the life of his masters. Yet these two characters are the only ones whom Homer brings to life who do not belong to the ruling class. Thus we become conscious of the fact that in the Homeric poems life is enacted only among the ruling class— others appear only in the role of servants to that class. The ruling class is still so strongly patriarchal, and still itself so involved in the daily activities of domestic life, that one is sometimes likely to forget their rank. But they are unmistakably a sort of feudal aristocracy, whose men divide their lives between war, hunting, marketplace councils, and feasting, while the women supervise the maids in the house. As a social picture, this world is completely stable; wars take place only between different groups of the ruling class; nothing ever pushes up from below. In the early stories of the Old Testament the patriarchal condition is dominant too, but since the people involved are individual nomadic or half-nomadic tribal leaders, the social picture gives a much less stable impression; class distinctions are not felt. As soon as the people completely emerges—that is, after the exodus from Egypt—its activity is always discernible, it is often in ferment, it frequently intervenes in events not only as a whole but also in separate groups and through the medium of separate individuals who come forward; the origins of prophecy seem to lie in the irrepressible politico-religious spontaneity of the people. We receive the impression that the movements emerging from the depths of the people of Israel-Judah must have been of a wholly different nature from those even of the later ancient democracies—of a different nature and far more elemental.

With the more profound historicity and the more profound social activity of the Old Testament text, there is connected yet another important distinction from Homer: namely, that a different conception of the elevated style and of the sublime is to be found here. Homer, of course, is not afraid to let the realism of daily life enter into the sublime and tragic; [the] episode of the scar is an example, we see how the quietly depicted, domestic scene of the foot-washing is incorporated into the pathetic and sublime action of Odysseus' homecoming. From the rule of the separation of styles which was later almost universally accepted and which specified that the realistic depiction of daily life was incompatible with the sublime and had a place only in comedy or, carefully stylized, in idyl—from any such rule Homer is still far removed. And yet he is closer to it than is the Old Testament. For the great and sublime events in the Homeric poems take place far more exclusively and unmistakably among the members of a ruling class; and these are far more untouched in their heroic elevation than are the Old Testament figures, who can fall much lower in dignity (consider, for example, Adam, Noah, David, Job); and finally, domestic realism, the representation of daily life, remains in Homer in the peaceful realm of the idyllic, whereas, from the very first, in the Old Testament stories, the sublime, tragic, and problematic take shape precisely in the domestic and commonplace: scenes such as those between Cain and Abel, between Noah and his sons, between Abraham, Sarah, and Hagar, between Rebekah, Jacob, and Esau, and so on, are inconceivable in the Homeric style. The entirely different ways of developing conflicts are enough to account for this. In the Old Testament stories the peace of daily life in the house, in the fields, and among the flocks, is undermined by jealousy over election and the promise of a blessing, and complications arise which would be utterly incomprehensible to the Homeric heroes. The latter must have palpable and clearly expressible reasons for their conflicts and enmities, and these work themselves out in free battles; whereas, with the former, the perpetually smouldering jealousy and the connection between the domestic and the spiritual, between the paternal blessing and the divine blessing, lead to daily life being permeated with the stuff of conflict, often with poison. The sublime influence of God here reaches so deeply into the everyday that the two realms of the sublime and the everyday are not only actually unseparated but basically inseparable.

MEIR STERNBERG

The Wooing of Rebekah

"Men work together," I told him from the heart,
"Whether they work together or apart."
    —ROBERT FROST, "The Tuft of Flowers"

POINT OF VIEW AND ITS BIBLICAL CONFIGURATION

The Bible teaches more than one general lesson about narration. Far from a technical choice, point of view has emerged as an ideological crux and force, none the less artful for being thus engaged. And far from a matter of who speaks or sees what, I shall now proceed to argue, it always forms a combination of perspectives—such as the divine, the quasi-divine or narratorial, and the human views of Saul's anointment or Pharaoh's affliction. Curiously, some theoretical approaches to point of view are akin to biblical geneticism in fragmenting the text into bits of discourse and seeking to assign each to its appropriate originator. That the object is to identify the internal rather than the historical sources of transmission only renders this exercise in atomism all the more ill-judged; and its pursuit among so-called structuralists flies in the face of the very notion of structure as a network of relations.

For one thing, whatever else point of view may be or do, it entails a relation between subject and object, perceiving mind and perceived reality. In this sense, all speakers (or viewers) figure as interpreters, their speech deriving from a process of interpretation and reflecting or betraying an interpretive construct that they would regard as the world and others might dismiss as a lie or illusion. Discourse renders a world from a certain viewpoint. The whole text accordingly unfolds as a threefold complex—with the most variable interplay between discourse, world, and perspective—whose disentanglement by the reader forms

From *The Poetics of Biblical Narrative.* © 1985 by Meir Sternberg. Indiana University Press, 1985.

neither a luxury nor a technicality but the very condition of making sense. Who stands behind this piece of language and what does it project? From what viewpoint does that action or description unfold, and why? Can the perceiver be identified and evaluated by the field of perception? Where does the subject end and the object begin? Is this particular reflector ironic or ironized, reliable or biased or even mendacious, or in short, how does his interpretation stand to the text's and ours? These are among the typical questions arising throughout.

Nor is any of the questions resolvable out of context. As well as interacting with all other components, point of view itself forms a system of perspectival relations—one constant, most variable, all mutually defining. Briefly, as I argued elsewhere, narrative communication involves no fewer than four basic perspectives: the author who fashions the story, the narrator who tells it, the audience or reader who receives it, and the characters who enact it. Where the narrator is practically identical with the author, as in Homer or Fielding or indeed the Bible, the discourse therefore operates with three basic relationships that constitute the point of view: between narrator and characters, narrator and reader, reader and characters. Of these relationships, the first alone normally remains constant in its inequality, opposing the omniscient and reliable narrator to his essentially fallible agents. Whereas the two others are amenable to free variation: what the reader knows and how well he judges, for instance, depend on the narrator's strategy of telling. Whether or not he takes us into his confidence will make an enormous difference to the reading, including our ability to identify or discriminate the perspectives of the dramatized observers and correct their subjective distortions of the implied world and world view. But regardless of narrative strategy, if we are to make any sense of the text— to distinguish one refracting medium from another, opinion from fact, shadow from substance, commitment from irony—we must perform these reconstructive operations as best we can. And we can only perform them by making inferences about the different perspectives in relation to one another and above all to the supreme authority that figures as the contextual measure of their validity. A judgment cannot be located along a scale of reliability, nor a description pronounced objective or subjective, nor a character stamped as ignorant or knowing, nor a reading follow an ironic or straight line—except by reference to the contextual norm embodied in the all-authoritative narrator. Which is to say that a text cannot even be decomposed into its perspectival parts without having been recomposed into a coherent whole, an orchestration of voices and a hierarchy of interpretations.

Given these universals of structure and reading, the marks distinguishing each narrative lie in its treatment of the variable factors and relationships. And here the biblical configuration of point of view has quite a few claims to originality. Most notable is its knocking down of the usually impassable barriers separating authoritative teller from fallible characters to admit God to the position of superperceiver as well as superagent. The reasons having already been discussed, we may now focus on the consequences for the overall art of perspective.

Again, the usual theoretical models and taxonomies fail to apply here. For, as with every structure worthy of the name, the displacement of a part launches a chain reaction that transforms the whole set of relations characterizing omniscient narrative. Where the general model of omniscience in literature dispenses with one of the basic perspectives by virtually equating the author with the narrator, the Bible introduces a new perspective by dissociating God from the characters and aligning him with the narrator. (Within an inspirational framework, God himself even becomes the author of the book as well as of its plot, without forfeiting his agentlike status.) In so doing, as if to complicate matters further and sharpen the peculiarity of the maneuver, the narrative undermines the normal correlation between a viewpoint's mode of existence (within or without the world) and level of authority (nonprivileged or privileged respectively). Like all commonsensical linkages, this norm may hold in the Bible for the godlike narrator (detached and privileged) as well as for the earthly cast (involved and nonprivileged) but, what is ideologically appropriate, not for divinity itself.

The lines of demarcation are thus redrawn to establish a novel fourfold pattern, involving two assorted and roughly symmetrical couples: the elevated superhumans on the one hand and the erring humans on the other. God existentially inside while perspectivally above the world, the reader wedded in some degree to his fellow men: this structure of point of view acts as a constant reminder of their respective positions in the scheme of things. From this unpromising premise, and not so much despite as because of its theological bearing, there also springs an intricate, flexible, and challenging art of perspective, to which the Wooing of Rebekah in Genesis 24 affords a good introduction.

THE WOOING

Positions and Discrepancies Established

(1) Abraham was old, advanced in years; and the Lord had blessed Abraham in everything. (2) And Abraham said to his servant, the oldest of his house, who ruled over everything that he had, Put thy hand, pray, under my thigh, (3) and I will make thee swear by the Lord, the God of heaven and the God of the earth, that

thou shalt not take a wife for my son from the daughters of the Canaanites, among whom I dwell; (4) but to my native land [*el artsi ve'el moladeti*] shalt thou go and take a wife for my son, for Isaac. (5) And the servant said to him, Perhaps the woman may not be willing to follow me to this land; shall I then lead thy son back to the land from which thou camest? (6) And Abraham said to him, Take care that thou dost not lead my son back there. (7) The Lord, the God of heaven, who took me from my father's house and from the land of my birth [*erets moladeti*], and who spoke to me and swore to me, saying, To thy offspring will I give this land, he will send his angel before thee and thou shalt take a wife for my son from there. (8) And if the woman is not willing to follow thee, then thou wilt be free of this oath of mine; only thou shalt not lead my son back there. (9) So the servant put his hand under the thigh of Abraham his master and swore to him concerning this matter.

This is a scene to which the reader has been looking forward for some time, and not merely because the original audience must have known, as every schoolboy now does, that Isaac married Rebekah. The accidentals of the extratextual knowledge brought to the reading are standardized by the internal knowledge built into the reading process. And since narrative tact as well as poetics rules out the baldness of an overt foreshadowing, this internalization takes a form subtle enough to keep even the knowledgeable reader occupied, yet determinate enough to enlighten the less informed.

It is the analogy between Abraham's two sons that first anticipates the marital theme. Ishmael's career shows three landmarks: late birth (Gen. 16:16), mortal danger averted by a timely divine intervention (21:14–19), and marriage to a compatriot of his Egyptian mother's (21:21). Isaac having likewise gone through the first two stages (21:1–8; 22:1–12), the third is now due by compositional logic. That expectation even gains further point from the tightening of the analogy toward the final stage. The divine promise "I will make him a great nation" (21:18), which came between Ishmael's ordeal and his marriage, now recurs with redoubled force after the sacrificial binding of Isaac: "I will indeed bless thee and I will multiply thy offspring as the stars of heaven and the sand on the seashore, and thy offspring shall possess the gate of his enemies" (22:17). The fulfillment of this promise—significantly echoed at both the beginning (24:7) and the end (24:60) of our tale—again requires a bride. And indeed, as if on cue, she or at least her name makes an immediate entrance:

After these things, it was told to Abraham, Behold, Milcah too
has borne sons, to Nahor thy brother: Uz his firstborn, Buz his
brother, Kemuel the father of Aram, Kesed, Hazo, Pildash, Yidlaf,
and Bethuel. And Bethuel begot Rebekah. These eight Milcah bore
to Nahor, Abraham's brother. And his concubine, whose name was
Reumah, also bore Tebah, Tahash, and Ma'acah.

(22:20–24)

This material could hardly seem less promising: a bare genealogical list of
supernumeraries, with none but remote antiquarian value. Yet even catalogues
bring grist to the Bible's mill, and the lump of history gets assimilated to the
art of the personal story. Inserted under the guise of family news, this digression
assumes new shape and meaning in context. The genealogical list falls into
analogical pattern, the chronological parataxis ("After these things") stiffens into
causal sequence, the retrospect turns round its face to become a prospection.
Juxtaposed with God's blessing and placed in structural correspondence to
Ishmael's marriage, the report virtually names the bride-to-be. Not, however,
in a manner so transparent as to destroy the pleasures of inference. That is
why Rebekah gets tucked away in the middle, and a rival candidate, Ma'acah,
occupies a far more prominent position. But the camouflage arrests and amuses
rather than misleads even the unforewarned reader. Ma'acah is clearly a red
herring: a concubine's daughter, in a cycle where mixed descent has played
such an unsettling role, she might be a good match for Ishmael but hardly
for Abraham's heir. And Rebekah's obtrusive presence amply makes up for
her unobtrusive location. In a list supposed to enumerate the "sons" that
"Milcah too has borne"—the allusion to Sarah in "too" interprets *banim* as "sons"
rather than "children"—why include a female who is not even a daughter? Of
Nahor's presumably numerous descendants, moreover, Rebekah is the only
grand-daughter mentioned. And as if to italicize the clue, her mention is at
once followed by a summative numbering ("These eight Milcah bore to Nahor")
that pointedly excludes her. The coherence of that item, the signals imply,
must be sought along lines other than genealogical.

The indirections that culminate in this miniature guess-who puzzle, then,
serve as a built-in anticipation, elevating the reader to a vantage post from
which he identifies Rebekah as the God-appointed bride. But does Abraham,
the dramatized recipient of the family news, share this foreknowledge? It is
interesting that, where we might expect him to name Rebekah, he does not
even direct his servant to her family. This strange failure has often been missed,
due to the common fallacy of hindsight reading and specifically a misreading

of verse 4. The point needs to be established, therefore, as the groundwork of the tale's play of viewpoints and its overall sense.

It is a fact that the faithful servant does not at all approach the family on arrival, but stops at the well to contrive a test that opens the field to every girl in the town. Indeed, he does not depart for Nahor's house in the first place: his destination is given rather as "Mesopotamia, the city of Nahor." (This reference need not even be to a person but to the place that figures as Nakhur in the Mari tablets.) And the servant's proceeding not only reflects but follows his instructions. Note that Abraham, far from pronouncing the name that is trembling on *our* lips, starts with a general characterization of the bride required and a negative characterization at that: "not from the daughters of the Canaanites, among whom I dwell." And as the dialogue begins so does it proceed and end—with the negative feature of Canaan looming larger than any positive attraction of Mesopotamia, let alone any specific Mesopotamian. Hence the harping on the spatial opposition between "here" and "there" that depersonalizes the whole transaction. In case the woman refuses to settle in "this land," the servant asks, shall Isaac join her "in the land from which thou camest?" No, Abraham insists, he must not return "there": God, who promised my offspring "this land," will see to it that you bring a woman "from there." Yet whatever happens, there is no question of Isaac's settling "there." Which clearly means that, destined to inherit the land, Isaac must on no account marry among those doomed to disinheritance; but since Mesopotamia's recommendation lies in not being Canaan, it would lose all appeal were Isaac to disinherit himself by emigrating. The historical process launched by Abraham's call must no more be reversed by his son's repatriation than subverted by local intermarriage.

No wonder, therefore, that Abraham frames the scenario in the widest ethno-geographical terms; that he makes no mention of his brother Nahor, perhaps even in a deliberate attempt to bring home his point and minimize the danger of emigration; that he impersonalizes the bride into "a woman." He acts from a sense of national destiny rather than from family feeling or nostalgia for his old country. And the servant, who would otherwise appear a disobedient fool or knave, jeopardizing if not sabotaging his mission by his failure to make a beeline for the family address, simply observes his terms of reference.

Within these terms of reference, accordingly, the direction *el artsi ve'el moladeti telekh* in verse 4 does not bear the meaning "thou shalt go to my land and to my kindred," assigned to it by most translators and exegetes. It rather forms a hendiadys signifying "thou shalt go to the land of my kindred/birth" or "to my native land," precisely like the *erets moladeti* of verse 7. In the context of the Abraham saga, as it happens, *moledet* refers to an entity larger than the family anyway. God's very first address to Abraham, "Go forth from thy land and thy *moledet* and thy father's house to the land that I will show thee" (12:1), marks an ascending order of specificity where *moledet* falls between country and kindred. Given the otherwise symmetrical relations between the divinely ordered exodus ("go forth from") and the humanly ordered return ("go to"), moreover, Abraham's omission of the specific "father's house" from the reversed scenario would make little sense were it not for its perfect congruity with the impersonal spirit of the "here–there" opposition. In retrospect, indeed, we note that when the servant rewrites history to cajole the relatives into believing that Abraham expressly directed him to them, he thrice replaces in transmission Abraham's original "land and *moledet*" by "father's house and family" (38, 40, 41). The version revised after the event to narrow down the field only highlights the generality of the original intention.

By the time the servant puts his hand under his master's thigh, therefore, the tale has already established a fourfold (and practically, threefold) structure of point of view, with marked and gradated discrepancies in awareness. God (who promised) and the narrator (who anticipated the fulfillment) stand together at one pole, their supernatural knowledge going with absolute control. The opposite pole is occupied by the patriarch and his envoy, their powers so humanly limited that they can no more foresee than ensure the outcome: to them the issue remains open against their desire, its concrete terms to be disclosed only in historical embodiment, its resolution problematic and fraught with danger. In between stands the reader, privileged enough to foreknow the end as determinate and happy even beyond the characters' dreams, but reduced to ignorance in all that concerns the route leading up to the providential end.

This conforms to the Bible's favorite system of perspectival relations, serving to reconcile the claims of art and ideology into a happy ideological art. God, omniscient and omnipotent by doctrinal fiat, will prove so in dramatic terms as the action translates his implicit will and pledge into the stuff of history: the premise lays the ground for the demonstration and the demonstration vindicates and inculcates the premise—which sounds poor logic but makes excellent rhetoric in the telling. At the same time as the narrator exploits his authority to dramatize and glorify God's, God's own powers invest the compositional foreshadowing-by-analogy with such force as to enable the narrator to canalize interest into the desired grooves without compromising his art of indirection. In turn, the characters' limited knowledge, governed by the realistic norm, first establishes a sharp opposition between the natural and the supernatural spheres and then motivates a progressive discovery of God's benevolent control. The reader's intermediate position, finally, guarantees his awareness of God's superintendence, while leaving the movement from promise to fulfillment dark enough to sustain interest and allow the demonstration to work itself out in human terms. Given the initial sense of divine providence, the interplay of character and event may develop with impunity.

Typical in essentials, this perspectival scheme yet manifests some variables. Above all, the Bible does not often effect such a severance between the informational and the normative axes of point of view. Considered by themselves, the informational tensions might be expected to generate powerful irony at the expense of the least knowing, the dramatis personae. But we actually experience little irony, because the discrepancies in awareness are tempered by parity in values: knowledge of principles always redeems in the Bible any lacunae in the knowledge of facts and contingencies; though not, as evildoers find out the hard way, vice versa. Thus, the implied reader shares—if only by artful courtesy—the narrator's world view. But so does Abraham, who, ignorant of all details and personalities, is still confident that God "will send his angel" to look after them. And so, it progressively emerges, does his servant, who speaks and acts for him throughout as a like-minded ambassador. As he sets out, therefore, the variations between the nondivine perspectives yet go with the question common to all fellow-believers: *How* will God manage the affair?

The Movement from Divergence to Convergence of Perspectives

(10) The servant took ten camels of the camels of his master and went, with all kinds of goods from his master in his hand; and he arose and went to Mesopotamia, to the city of Nahor. (11) And he made the camels kneel down outside the city by the well of water at evening time, the time when the women come out to draw water. (12) And he said, O Lord, God of my master Abraham, make things go well for me this day and show kindness to my master Abraham. (13) Behold, I am standing by the spring of water, and the daughters of the men of the city are coming out to draw water. (14) The maiden to whom I shall say, Pray let down thy pitcher that I may drink, and who will say, Drink, and I shall water thy camels too—let her be the one whom thou hast appointed for thy servant Isaac. (15) Before he had finished speaking, and behold, Rebekah came out, who was born to Bethuel the son of Milcah, the wife of Nahor, Abraham's brother, with her pitcher upon her shoulder. (16) And the maiden was very good-looking, a virgin, and no man had known her. She went down to the spring and filled her pitcher and came up. (17) And the servant ran towards her and said, Pray give me a little water to drink from thy pitcher.

(18) And she said, Drink, my lord; and she made haste and lowered her pitcher onto her hand and let him drink. (19) And when she had finished letting him drink, she said, I shall draw for thy camels too, until they have finished drinking. (20) And she made haste and emptied her pitcher into the trough, and ran again to the well to draw, and she drew for all his camels. (21) And the man stood wondering at her, keeping silent to learn whether the Lord had prospered his journey or not. (22) And when the camels had finished drinking, the man took a gold ring, half a shekel in weight, and two bracelets for her hands, ten gold shekels in weight. (23) And he said, Whose daughter art thou? Pray tell me. Is there room in thy father's house for us to spend the night? (24) And she said to him, I am the daughter of Bethuel the son of Milcah, whom she bore to Nahor. (25) And she said to him, We have both straw and provender in plenty, also room to spend the night in. (26) And the man bowed his head and worshipped the Lord. (27) And he said, Blessed be the Lord, the God of my master Abraham, who has not withheld his kindness and his truth from my master. I being on a journey, the Lord has led me to the house of my master's brothers.

Thrown on his own devices on arrival, the servant leaves nothing to chance, as his mandate entitled him to do, but takes a twofold initiative that weds good sense to piety. Of the eligible young women in the city, he will not settle for less than the best. So, appealing to God to bless his principle of choice, he improvises a shrewd character test. What touchstone could be more appropriate than the reception of a wayfarer to determine a woman's fitness to marry into the family of the paragon of hospitality? And it is a stiff test, too, since it would require far more than common civility to volunteer to water "ten" thirsty camels. (Note how this initially descriptive, realistic-looking feature now gains actional and thematic value as well: from a measure of Abraham's wealth, it transforms into a measure of his daughter-in-law's worthiness to enjoy it.)

The perfection of the initiative thus continues to moderate the irony threatened by the discrepancies in foreknowledge. Yet these discrepancies make for variance even in the application of the perfect yardstick. What to the servant is a character test of a prospective bride is to the reader a retrospective (and exhilarating) characterization of Rebekah. Having already been cast in the bridal role, how can she fail to pass with flying colors?

Indeed, her entrance could hardly be more auspicious. Where a folktale would first stage two or three abortive trials, in the interests of variety and retardation and contrastive portrayal, the Bible brings on the appointed winner at once. Not that it spurns the effects yielded by a drawn-out process—we shall see them all generated by oblique means. Rather, the narrative's primary concern is to show God at his invisible work, and any serialization of the test would upset the balance between human ingenuity and divine control. Far from delayed, therefore, the girl shows up even "before he had finished speaking." She is, literally, God's answer (in the medium of plot) to the servant's prayer; and so in fact do both he and we view her. However, we reach that conclusion with much greater certitude, thanks to a sudden widening of the informational discrepancy to our advantage. Though the new development seems to emerge from the servant's viewpoint ("and behold!"), the narrator smuggles into the report three facts inaccessible to any human observer. It is by his privilege and for our benefit alone that the text reveals the water-drawer's name ("Rebekah"), her lineage ("born to Bethuel," etc., to jog the memory of forgetful readers), and, most hidden and reassuring, her morals ("a virgin," etc.). Less favored, the dramatized spectator is also less reassured. The timing is perfect, the good looks a welcome bonus, but what about the character? Only the test can show.

The test does, of course, show. But it performs this role beyond anyone's expectations and with a consummate art that has been mistaken by hard-line geneticists for patchwork and by their modern heirs for "an original narrative prolixity . . . made wordier still by subsequent transmission," with the extenuating circumstance that "the repetitiveness which we occasionally find a bit overwhelming was not so sensed by the authors and editors of the Bible." [Bruce Vawter, *On Genesis: A New Reading* (Doubleday, 1977)]. It is only by the grace of what I called the Bible's foolproof composition that such extreme underreaders yet manage to grasp the essentials of plot and judgment, without suffering anything worse than boredom. If "we" find anything overwhelming, it is not at all the repetitiveness but the fireworks of repetition.

The variations in the passage from wish to fulfillment have a random look, since they manifest the wildest heterogeneity: changes in wording, in continuity, in specification. Below the surface, however, all this formal variety combines into functional unity. All the variations go to dramatize a single point: that the young woman's performance surpasses even the most optimistic expectations. Thus, the increased specificity largely derives from the references to haste that punctuate the narrative: "she made haste and lowered her pitcher . . . she made haste and lowered her pitcher into the trough . . . she ran again to the well." This spontaneous dispatch bears more than the obvious complimentary implications for character and judgment. It echoes nothing less than Abraham's model hospitality, "He ran to meet them . . . Abraham made haste into the tent . . . Abraham ran to the tent . . . he made haste to prepare it" (18:2–7); and the elevating analogy stamps her as worthy of the patriarch himself. Hence also another rise in particularity, from the envisaged "drawing" of water to its actual enactment, "she went down to the spring and filled her pitcher and came up." This meticulous picture of the girl descending empty and then ascending loaded suggests what an arduous chore the drawing of water is, literally uphill work, even in normal conditions; how exhausting when one goes down and up at a run; how interminable when one has to provide for a whole caravan; and all (another recurrent detail) with one little pitcher.

The watering must have taken quite a while; and this is further stressed in verse 21 by the description of the man as "wondering at her, keeping silent to learn whether the Lord had prospered his journey or not," otherwise oddly interpolated between two mentions of her performance. In temporal terms, this discontinuous repetition marks a sequence of "action → regression → progression," and in terms of point of view, a shift from our perspective to the servant's. The reader, who knows that the maiden is destined to complete the service she has undertaken, needs no special telling that "she drew for all his camels." But while she is breaking her back for him, the internal observer can hardly believe what she has already done and only hope ("or not" is for him still on the cards) that she will get through with her task. The descriptive realism, in short, renders the well scene anything but an idyllic encounter: the emphasis rather falls on the correlation between the volunteer's physical labor and moral worth.

That she does more than could be expected becomes doubly impressive in view of the fact that he asks for less. The envisioned request "Pray lower thy pitcher that I may drink" drops to "Pray give me a little water to drink from thy pitcher." So it is she who prolongs the sip into a full-sized drink, just as she thinks of supporting the pitcher for the drinker's convenience and adds the deferential "my lord" in addressing what is to the narrator "the servant" or at most "the man." As for the camels, everyone hopes of course that she will offer to "water" them, but the scope of her initiative again surprises the covert as well as the dramatized observer: "For thy camels too I will draw, *until they have finished drinking*." And however formidable the undertaking, she means exactly what she says, as the narrator underlines through another subtle (in Hebrew, even punning) repetition with variation. "She drew for *all* his camels" (*kol*, full number) and "the camels *finished* drinking" (*killu*, full belly).

Only at one point, the very outset, does the variation in performance give real cause for concern. Where expected to respond "Drink and I shall water thy camels too," she actually stops halfway through: "Drink, my lord." Even the stoutest heart will miss a beat at this. Is she the type that will oblige at request but offer nothing beyond? Does she overlook the camels thoughtlessly or deliberately? Is it one thing to "lower" a pitcher for a single man and quite another to exhaust oneself on behalf of his thirsty beasts? Owing to the discrepancies in information, these gaps must have troubled the servant even more than the reader: our perplexity about Rebekah may well have been his despair of the first candidate. He may already have written her off when, upon the girl's delivering the second part as well, and to more than perfection, it all turns out to be a false alarm.

In retrospect we discover that the narrator has mixed a little mischief with serious business to extraordinary effect. The mischief consists in retarding the plot with a view to heightened suspense. But the retardation is more cunning and multifunctional than it looks. In playing on our fears, it also serves to insinuate by the backstairs of composition the abortive trial that a folktale would introduce by the front door of the action. Due to our initial ignorance of her personality, Rebekah assumes for a moment the features and fate of a heroine who, if not an utter washout, does not come up to matriarchal standard. Her unfolding thus spread or distributed over two stages, she functions as a two-in-one. Rebekah-of-the-first-half ("Drink, my lord") enriches the plot by indirection and makes the real Rebekah shine by contrast. Far from gratuitous, still less detrimental, the false alarm proves salutary: this is often the case with the piecemeal and tortuous emergence of literary character, and Rebekah affords us the first example of the Bible's command of this art of (temporary or, elsewhere, permanent) ambiguity. We appreciate her true self all the more for not being allowed to take its virtues for granted.

This contrast-in-sequence is enhanced, moreover, by surprise as well as suspense and relief. Not Rebekah's behavior and character alone but even her motives prove contrary to our initial fears. If she responds by installments, it is only because she will not lump together man and beast. Only after she has "finished letting him drink" does she express her readiness to do the same for the camels. Just as she began by injecting into her speech the deferential "my lord," so does she end by showing more tact than could be foreseen or perhaps even required. What threatened failure reveals itself as another God-sent bonus and blessing. She has certainly earned the costly gifts presented to her on the spot.

That the servant must have shared much of our experience (apprehension, enlightenment, character inference) marks a shift in perspectival design and relations. What we have been tracing amounts to a twofold movement that is integral to the Bible's dynamics of point of view. One movement consists in a process of illumination within each of the limited perspectives—the reader's and the hero's—that brings them closer by degrees to the static pole of the omniscient. At this stage, though still not so privileged as God and the narrator themselves, each of the human observers has gained considerable insight into the disposition of things. Relatively, of course, the servant has made more progress since the outset, but that is in keeping with another feature of the strategy. If the first dynamics consists in a progressive narrowing of informational discrepancies vis-à-vis the omniscient, the second involves a convergence of the restricted viewpoints themselves. Having been launched from different starting points along the scale of knowledge, they are then propelled forward not only in the same direction but also at a pace variable enough to allow the one behind to overtake and keep more or less abreast of the one who got a head start.

The narrative began by conferring on the reader an informational advantage over master and servant, through oblique pointers to Rebekah. Abraham then fades out, and the plot traces the envoy's route to knowledge and success. On arrival, his initiative commands personal admiration and doctrinal assent but, as formerly with the master, it is not at once rewarded with enlightenment. On the contrary, his ignorance relative to the reader deepens owing to the narrator's un-evenhanded treatment of Rebekah's entrance; and the resultant discrepancy leads to further variations in the response to her conduct, dooming the less informed observer to lowered understanding and heightened suspense. The test once under way, however, the two viewpoints begin to converge. Not only do we experience much of his alarm at the threat of failure, but he attains to much of our knowledge when all ends well.

Regarding ignorance and knowledge alike, to be sure, this new alignment is not yet perfect, nor, as a matter of principle, will it ever evolve into strict identity. Apart from all contingencies, it makes an essential difference that, though equally concerned to penetrate appearances and unravel mysteries by way of interpretation, the servant is not a "reader" in the sense that we are. Like all figural interpreters, he directly confronts a world that we receive through the mediation of an artful teller and text. He exercises interpretation on the world of objects; we, on a web of words that projects such a world. And whatever the similarity between these worlds, notably in divine control, each still retains its features and constraints vis-à-vis the interpreter: each, in my earlier formulation, remains a distinct semiotic system, with its own medium, communicator, addressee, and rules of decipherment.

Thus, the servant's knowledge is regulated by God, ours by the narrator, and the two omniscients operate with different means even to the same end. In the absence of explicit foretelling, as here, the reader's foreknowledge and expectations derive from probabilities beyond the agent's ken. The structural anticipations of Rebekah relate far more to the logic (arrangement, coherence, conventions) of the text than of the world; and even if noticed, would hardly

carry the same weight for "real life" interpreters as for one facing a verbal artifice. Or consider even the latent parallels between Rebekah's and Abraham's
hospitality. The rationale of the test implies that the servant may also have
detected them, but only in general outline: since he observes events not words,
he could not have been affected by the linguistic echoes of "haste" that clinch
the analogy for us. In general—and the following chapters will come back to
this key issue —the poetics of the narrative is reserved for the reader's viewpoint
and interpretive operations.

Moreover, the dramatized interpreter and his interpreting are themselves
part of the represented world and accordingly, like everything else, objects of
the reader's interpretation. This builds into the pattern an ironic discrepancy
in our favor. But the irony can be sharpened ad hoc, as with Samuel the anointer,
through the manipulation of specific perspectival disparities; or it can be
attenuated and even neutralized ad hoc, through the reduction of such variations to the point of denying the reader any sense of superiority—not at least
beyond that inherent in the position of secretly watching and eavesdropping
on a character who goes about his business unaware of being made a show
of. Hence the significance of our tale's early alignment of the normative viewpoints and, along the informational axis, its movement from initial tensions
to relative harmony. Both go a long way toward bridging the distance between
the observers with their distinct posts and sources and procedures of observation. In line with this movement, the ensuing dialogue not only brings them
closer but also, though holding far more disclosures and surprises for the servant
than for the reader, makes a two-level discovery scene, where he recognizes
a set of factors and we applaud his recognitions.

Far from being looked down on for his ignorance of the recipient's identity,
the ambassador further endears himself to us by covering Rebekah with gold,
because it is exactly his unawareness of the fact that clinches his awareness
of the principle: the young woman has earned the gifts, since nothing counts
like personal merit. The factual discrepancy itself then gets bridged in the
dialogue scene. What is more, the girl's speech affords another chance for
perspectival convergence in the observation of her exquisite manners, whose
finer points would hardly be lost on an Oriental and a great man's steward
at that. She answers the questions in the order but, with the same regard for
decorum, not always in the terms in which they are posed. "Whose daughter
art thou?" receives the straightforward answer, "I am the daughter of Bethuel,"
where the omission of her own name spares the questioner, at whatever cost
to ego, a detail in which he expressed no interest. But to the inquiry about
"room in thy father's house for us to spend the night" she diplomatically replies
by stating the objective facilities for hospitality, without extending even to a
munificent stranger the invitation that is not hers to extend.

No sooner has this model bride crowned her performance than the reader finds his sentiments and reasoning voiced by the servant, who takes none of the credit for himself but puts it all where it is ideologically due. He does the right thing on the right grounds. Since in a God-directed world there is no room for coincidence, the encounter with Abraham's grandniece must be an act of providence. (He has started, we recall, with the believer's shibboleth, "Make things go well for me," or in literal paradox, "devise an accident for me.") This declaration of faith thus crowns the meeting of the reader's early anticipation, formed by appeal to the poetic coherence of the text, and the character's later recognition, anchored in the doctrine of the existential coherence of the world. And since the biblical text itself largely depends for its coherence on the assumption of divine control—the narrator playing providence only in God's name and to God's glory—the man's simple piety reinforces rather than just parallels our more complex interpretation.

New Tensions and Final Resolution

Among its other roles, the next phase seals this marriage of true minds:

> (28) The maiden ran and told her mother's household about these things. (29) Now Rebekah had a brother whose name was Laban; and Laban ran out to the man, to the spring. (30) And on seeing the ring and the bracelets on his sister's hands, and on hearing the words of Rebekah his sister, saying, Thus and so did the man speak to me, he went to the man; and behold, he was standing by the camels at the spring. (31) And he said, Come, O blessed of the Lord; why dost thou stand outside? I have prepared the house, and room for the camels. (32) And the man came into the house, and he ungirded the camels and gave straw and provender for the camels and water to wash his feet and the feet of the men who were with him. (33) Then food was set before him to eat, and he said, I will not eat until I have spoken my piece. And he said, Speak.

In terms of plot structure, this episode clearly performs a bridging function. The second movement of the action having been completed with the discovery of the bride, the logic of causality now requires the servant's arrival at the house to launch the movement that will end in the departure for Canaan with the family's blessing. And since protocol forbids the girl's inviting him herself, the narrator packs her off home to summon a higher authority, embodied in Laban. For a causal link between highlights, however, the episode certainly looks overtreated, unrolling at a leisurely pace and with circumstantial detail associated

with the Homeric rather than the biblical style. It looks even more so from
the reader's vantage point, since foreknowledge presses for a quick transition
to the business at hand. Of course, the lingering heightens our expectancy.
Yet judged by the economies of biblical narrative, suspense alone does not
justify the extent of the retardation – as noted at the foregoing stage – still less
the minutiae that compose it. This sense of excess indicates a search for tighter
and less obvious coherence.

The whole passage gains intelligibility from its implications for character
and perspective. These not only elaborate but also parallel the overt plot
function in that they likewise work backward and forward at the same time,
linking antecedents to consequents. Thus, the dispatch with which Rebekah
fulfills her plot assignment ("ran" not "went") rounds off her characterization
by giving us an insight into her mind: it suggests more than ordinary goodwill
to the stranger and lessens the fear that she may refuse to follow him. No
sooner have we gathered that the obstacles if any will come from the family,
than Laban enters the picture: his immediate role in the plot (as host) motivates
his portrayal in anticipation of his ultimate role (as guardian).

That portrayal itself looks back to the young woman's, just as it looks
ahead to the negotiation scene. Laban's "running" follows so hard upon Rebekah's
as to give him the benefit of all the favorable effects associated with her haste
throughout: the whole family, it seems, is a credit to Abraham. No later than
the next verse, however, this carry-over impression proves misleading. The
initial similarity turns into contrast as the narrator doubles back in time from
the hospitable action ("he ran") to its ulterior motive (the sight of "the ring
and the bracelets"). And when the action resumes ("he went"), we find the
contrast settled through an inside view in free indirect style ("and behold") where
"the camels" prominently figure, as indeed they are to do twice again in relation
to Laban's solicitude. Accordingly, even his pious address to the stranger as
"blessed of the Lord" sounds an ironic note, sharpened by unwitting allusion
to God's promise to "bless" Abraham by multiplying his descendants (22:17)
and to Abraham's being "blessed in everything" (24:1). Ignorant of antecedents
and identities, Laban twists this charged phrase into homage to material blessing.

This sequential shift in portrayal repeats the technique through which
Rebekah's figure and mind have been unfolded, and insinuates anew the theme
of the abortive test. But its point lies in reversing the earlier movement (verses
18–19) from unfavorable to favorable impression. While Laban's initial
correspondence to Rebekah somewhat dims her virtues by suggesting a family
portrait, the sudden about-face highlights her singularity more than ever before:
she shines in contrast to what her analogue actually is as well as to what she
herself might have been. And while the initial correspondence bodes good for

the servant's endeavors in the coming negotiations, its breakdown-and-reversal intensifies suspense by disclosing the kind of people he has to deal with. The indirect revelation of character through details in excess of plot exigencies thus affects our understanding and expectations of the plot itself.

This new disturbing element, however, consolidates the recent perspectival alliance between reader and ambassador. To start with, our relations with him and with Laban have developed in opposed directions. Laban has our approval as long as he seems to rush out on instinct, but he forfeits it as soon as it transpires that his bustle was prompted by knowledge of the traveler's wealth. The disclosure of informational parity here not only fails to ensure but actively unsettles his normative alignment with the reader: this makes a telling opposition to the process whereby our moral bond with the servant has counteracted (and foretold the decrease in) informational imparity. Principle always outranks fact, whether considered as dimensions of the Bible's epistemology or its structure of point of view. And in providing a negative illustration of this scale, Laban serves to draw us yet closer to the servant as well as to Rebekah.

Again, not that the two viewpoints perfectly coincide. The insight afforded us into Laban's mind is, as privileged *and* compositional disclosure, beyond the servant's reach; just as the opacity of the servant's own mind puts his current thoughts beyond ours. We are still due for some of those surprises that keep biblical man somewhat less—or, aesthetically, more—than a known quantity even on the closest acquaintance. Yet the emergence of a new, threatening viewpoint reinforces our sense of familiarity and solidarity with the old. While the family is still in the dark, moreover, we are privy to the servant's predicament and intentions, share his hopes and to a lesser extent his fears, and, judging from his past performance with its combination of ingenuity and faith, can even hazard an informed guess as to his general tactics. In retrospect, of course, even the remaining gaps and discrepancies vanish. But hindsight is an aid to rather than a condition of our involvement, inference, irony at the expense of the unknowing. Of all listeners, we alone are in a position to appreciate his maneuvers and motives throughout an address where he rarely speaks straight [For expository convenience I divided the speech into its tactical blocks, but it may be well to read it as a whole first]:

(34) And he said, I am Abraham's servant. (35) The Lord has abundantly blessed my master and he has become great; he has given him sheep and cattle, silver and gold, manservants and maidservants, camels and asses. (36) And Sarah my master's wife bore a son to my master after reaching old age, and he has given him everything he has.

The materialistic exordium shows that the speaker had no need of our privileges to take Laban's measure. The harping on wealth and status begins as early as the formal self-identification, "I am Abraham's servant." For by identifying himself in these self-effacing terms, as though he did not have so much as a name of his own, he at once transfers to his master all the benefits of the impressive entrance: the costly gifts, the ten loaded camels, and "the men who were with him" (their mention reserved for the arrival at the house to suggest the family's viewpoint). It is not he who is "blessed of the Lord," the servant indeed goes on to emphasize in pointed and corrective allusion to Laban's form of address, but Abraham: "The Lord has abundantly blessed my master." So much so, that all they have observed amounts only to a fraction of this blessing. "Sheep and cattle, silver and gold, manservants and maidservants, camels and asses": the items in full view ("gold," "manservants," "camels") are so interspersed as to command belief in their unseen mates; and, against the background of the narrator's shorthand (e.g., 13:2), the range of the catalogue signals the dramatized speaker's reluctance to leave much to his audience's imagination. The opening verse thus marks a steady progression in the inducement of the thought, "If such are his servants, how great must the master be!"

Immediately thereafter, however, the speaker passes to another branch of family news, or so his unforewarned auditors may think. From our vantage point, we easily trace the connection: the next step in the softening-up process is to introduce the prospective bridegroom, display his eligibility, and transfer to him in turn the aura of material blessing. All this gets accomplished without giving the show away. Isaac, the hidden subject of the discourse, comes in only as grammatical object—first of Sarah's "bearing" and then of Abraham's "giving." He even remains nameless, his presence thus subordinated (indeed like Rebekah's on her first appearance amid Nahor's descendants) to the heading of good news about familiar relatives. The audience will be caught all the more effectively if led to believe that they are forming their own conclusions. Hence the sandwiching of the "son" between two otherwise overspecific references to his parents: born by "Sarah the wife of my master" (a reminder of her legal status) to "my master" (harking back to the wealth and establishing legitimacy). Hence also "when she was old," an indication of time ostensibly meant to provoke cheers for the mother but in fact calculated to recommend the son. If she was old at the time, then he is still young now; and if she bore him by a miracle, then he must be blessed and is certainly the only heir. (No mention of Ishmael, naturally.) Indeed, the bland tempter proceeds, his father has already "given him everything he has." This anticipates matters a bit, since Abraham makes over his property to Isaac (in these very words) only before his death (25:5). But since the present company cannot know, the intention may pass for the deed.

The man's art lies not so much in the slight stretching of the facts as in their thorough insinuation. And to mask his drift, the persuader varies his technique from the first step to the second. Abraham's riches can be safely painted in the most glowing colors, under the cover story of "You will be happy to learn that." But when it comes to his deficiency of children, that pretext would hardly serve. Therefore the speaker so wraps up the topic as to invite the deduction that the parent's misfortune is the son's good fortune: to let the thought "What a catch!" steal into the audience's mind before they find him actually offered to them on a hard condition.

> (37) And my master made me swear, saying, Thou shalt not take a wife for my son from among the daughters of the Canaanites in whose land I dwell. (38) But to my father's house shalt thou go and to my kindred, and take a wife for my son. (39) And I said to my master, Perhaps the woman will not follow me. (40) And he said to me, The Lord, before whom I walk, will send his angel with thee and prosper thy journey, and thou shalt take a wife for my son from my kindred and from my father's house. (41) Then shalt thou be clear of my oath, when thou comest to my kindred; and if they will not give thee, thou shalt be clear of my oath.

To the unsuspecting materialist, it would indeed prove a catch with a catch. Since Abraham's condition is too operational to be much watered down, the rhetoric addresses itself to pressing for its acceptance. And having already made the most of the worldly blandishments, it now shifts its focus to the familial. What appeared so far the object of a report becomes the frame of reference for an appeal, from one branch of the family to another and with a view to maintaining their kinship. To maximize the force of that appeal, its original terms (verses 3–8) are deftly remolded in quotation, by assorted means but to a single end. The most decisive (and frequent) variation consists in replacing Abraham's "to my native land [el artsi ve'el moladeti] shalt thou go" by "to my father's house and to my kindred," with the result that the ethno-geographical opposition between Canaanite and non-Canaanite transforms into the sentimental opposition between nonfamily and family. Rebekah's guardians would obviously find it much harder to reject a proposal of marriage addressed to them as kinsmen than as Mesopotamians, let alone non-Canaanites. Recast into such positive terms, moreover, the geography takes on a flattering aspect; and to allay its terrors even further, the (mis)quoter personalizes each of Abraham's spatial references to "there" into "my kindred," so as to substitute a tie of blood for a sense of distance.

This crucial variation launches the attack that others either cover or carry forward. Of the preventive measures, the most salient is of course the omission of all reference to the possibility originally raised by the servant ("Shall I then lead thy son back to the land from which thou camest?") and ruled out by his master. While even a negative mention might put ideas into the family's head, silence dismisses them as unthinkable—hence also the elision of Abraham's own exodus *from* Mesopotamia, in a speech that otherwise leans so heavily on past associations as to play down all unfamiliar factors, including the bridegroom himself. Note how "a wife for my son, for Isaac" contracts into "a wife for my son," so as to minimize the threat of the unknown.

Other variations, however, pile on the pressure. It is with this offensive intent that the contingency originally envisaged as "Perhaps the woman may not be willing to follow me" now reappears as "Perhaps the woman will not follow me." The shift from subjective cause ("not willing") to objective result ("not follow") presumably reflects the servant's confidence in the young woman and certainly covers a wider range of obstacles, with family veto at their head. And then we find the shift completed and the implication voiced in Abraham's reply. In retelling, it not only fails to glance at any reluctance on the girl's part but throws the responsibility square on her guardians. "If they will not give thee," in disregard for family claims and heavenly guidance, then "thou shalt be clear of my oath."

With this spot of moral blackmail, so final-sounding in form and message alike, the whole audience (this time, the reader included) might expect the address to close. In fact, however, it brings one line of persuasion to a climax only to usher in another:

> (42) And I came today to the spring and said, O Lord, the God of my master Abraham, if thou wilt prosper the journey on which I go, (43) behold, I am standing by the spring of water; the maiden to whom I shall say, Pray give me to drink a little water from thy pitcher, (44) and who will say to me, Drink thou and for thy camels I will draw too—may she be the woman whom God has appointed for my master's son. (45) Before I had finished speaking in my heart, and behold, Rebekah came out with her pitcher upon her shoulder, and she went down to the spring and drew. And I said to her, Pray give me to drink. (46) And she made haste and lowered her pitcher from her shoulder, and said, Drink, and thy camels I shall water too. I drank, and the camels she watered too. (47) And I asked her and said, Whose daughter art thou? And she said, The daughter of Bethuel, the son of Nahor, whom Milcah bore to him. And I put a ring on her nose and the bracelets on her hands. (48) And I bowed my head and worshipped the Lord and blessed the Lord,

who has led me by the true way to take my master's brother's daughter for his son.

The speaker has yet another weapon, skillfully reserved for the last. Again, bringing it to bear marks not so much a shift of ground as of focus and emphasis. The opening itself, we recall, introduced three themes—or, in terms of rhetoric, pressure points—with family bond and divine blessing subordinated to the dominant note of material fortune. The second stage then took up and elaborated the argument from kinship, while still keeping God's involvement in active reserve through Abraham's mention of "the angel" appointed to oversee the mission. Now this reserve force takes over, its pressure judged (correctly, it transpires) best qualified to clinch the issue. Success depends on bringing home the impression that God has been in control all along, perceptibly so ever since Abraham took the initiative.

As the reader knows, this happens to be the literal truth. But truth, alas, does not always have the ring of truth. Just as Abraham's original instructions would not sound flattering enough to the audience, so might the original encounter with the young woman seem too coincidental to establish divine stage-managing. If completely unforeseen, the coincidence that the true believer would read as all the more providential is liable to strike the outsider, let alone an interested party, as the operation of chance. Therefore the servant, like many novelists after him, resorts to invention in order to give the truth a more truthlike appearance. Having just edited Abraham's orders in the interests of moral and sentimental pressure, he now turns the revised version to ideological account: God has realized Abraham's wishes in leading his envoy to the family. The surprise of the encounter is diminished, so that its persuasiveness may increase.

Hence this stage also forms yet another landmark in the development of perspectival relations. The reader's alliance with the servant against the family has so far operated along the informational axis of point of view. Equally in the know about all that has passed since the first scene in Canaan, we have been equally alive (and well-disposed) to the liberties he takes with the facts in repeating them to the ignorant decision-makers: the omission of Ishmael, the premature transfer of property, the delayed disclosure of the reason for the embassy, or the variance between the ambassador's statement and the patriarch's commission. Our initial opposition in viewpoint to the servant has modulated all the way into an alignment against a new opposition exposed to dramatic coaxing and irony. At the back of our minds, to be sure, there has lurked from the start the memory that this new party no more shares the allies' faith than their knowledge. But the ideological division gains point so gradually that one hardly notices its relevance as such. In sequence, the family first appears as an obstacle to patriarchal destiny, but not necessarily for theological reasons; then Laban shows his true colors, but his character still lends itself to ethical as distinct from doctrinal judgment; then the servant shortens Abraham's reference to "the Lord, the God of heaven" into "the Lord" *tout court*, as if to broaden the common ground with idolaters, but how much pressure will this change of terms bear? Only with the overall shift of emphasis at the present stage does this divergence come into the open—though for our eyes only—and the opposition perceptibly extends to the ideological axis of perspective as well. Privilege and true belief now go together, as do their opposites, and the drawing of the line all along the perspectival front explains the servant's last wave of attack. He can manipulate the family because they are his informational inferiors; and he must manipulate them because they are his ideological inferiors. According to their lights, the unvarnished truth would not carry enough weight to induce them to part with Rebekah. It therefore needs refashioning *ad hominem* into a narrative so smooth and well-made as to bespeak divine composition in their own terms. The semiotics of the plot has to be made intelligible to a meaner intelligence.

This secret motive inferred, the new variations in retelling fall into rhetorical pattern. Given the revised instructions, the first problem is to justify the entire well episode. If directed to the family, why didn't the envoy go straight to the family? To forestall this query, he leaves out the sentence "and the daughters of the men of the city came out to draw water" from the quotation of his prayer to God on arrival. With the original range of choice excised, what remains by implication is an appeal for divine guidance in choosing the right kinswoman. It would do him little good to turn to the family without knowing for whose hand to ask; and who except God could do the pinpointing?

Indeed, he proceeds, he had scarcely finished speaking before Rebekah appeared: here he follows events closely enough, but not without recomposition. In divergence from his own viewpoint at the time, he refers to the (then anonymous) girl as "Rebekah," to give an impression of old familiarity with her name and strengthen the sense of her predestination ("It is this Rebekah, here, whom God has appointed!"). For the same reason, he avoids all mention of the temporary doubt and suspense produced by her failure to volunteer service for the camels: despite the triumphant resolution, nothing must complicate the symmetry between his forecast and her performance. If the believer's heavenly plus may look a minus to others, then even scoring is indicated. Nor does the speaker say a word about her good looks, and even her exertions on his behalf assume the telegraphic form "the camels she watered too." This apparent ingratitude no doubt suggests the common bargaining technique of doing less than justice to coveted goods. But it also has a strategic significance, as part of the general depreciation of human in favor of divine agency. The less specified the girl's actions, the more impressive the correspondence between plan and fulfillment; and the less transparent the girl's virtues to the eyes of the beholder, the more visible God's hand.

The well scene loses its original balance, in short, to become less of a character test and more of a manifestation of divine choice. In the interests of the same rhetorical strategy, after all, the servant in his reportorial role cheerfully plays down his own ingenuity in devising the test and his confidence in its results. Reversing the original order, he now puts the inquiry "Whose daughter art thou?" *before* the bestowal of the gifts, as though he would not commit himself as long as there remained the slightest doubt about the alignment of human wishes with divine disposition. And in the ensuing report of his thanksgiving, he appropriately describes the happy coincidence in terms of God's having led him not "to the house of my master's brothers" but "to take my master's brother's daughter for his son."

> (49) Now therefore, if you will deal kindly and truly with my master, tell me; and if not, tell me and I will turn to the right or to the left. (50) And Laban and Bethuel answered and said, The thing issues from the Lord; we cannot speak to thee bad or good. (51) Behold, Rebekah is before thee. Take her and go, and let her be the wife of thy master's son, as the Lord has spoken. (52) When the servant heard their words, he bowed himself to the ground before the Lord.

The course of events becomes so self-explanatory in remodeling that the artificer will not spoil the effect by pointing the moral. Instead, he gathers the human and the divine threads of persuasion into "Now therefore, if you will deal kindly and truly with my master, tell me." Compared with the neutral "If you consent," to which it operationally amounts, the phrasing is so loaded and slanted as to deter noncompliance. On the one hand, the allusion to the recent divine guidance "by the true way" insinuates the meaning "If you will do as God has done" or even the more threatening rhetorical question "Will you go against God?" On the other hand, just as a Fielding's address to "the sagacious reader" punishes dissent with the stigma of witlessness, so is the servant's wording calculated to brand refusal as an offense against morality. Still—and now comes the final pressure—if they do refuse, "I will turn to the right or to the left": I will take my suit elsewhere, to relatives more mindful of God and humanity, kinship and wealth.

Small wonder, then, that Laban and Bethuel declare in response that "the thing issues from the Lord; we cannot speak to thee bad or good." Where God has "spoken" through the design of events, there remains little room for human speech. Nor is it surprising that, though the material and familial considerations must have had some effect, the narrator makes the kinsmen single out the act of providence. Their world picture falls short of the monotheism common to all the Hebrew observers; their morality leaves something to be desired; their knowledge, thanks to the servant's inventiveness, is certainly deficient; and the consent wrung from them, as their subsequent dilatoriness shows, not quite wholehearted even after the event. These manifold discrepancies in viewpoint, whose reconstruction forms much of the business and pleasure of reading, retain their distancing and characterizing force. Yet their imperfect vision also enters into the final movement toward convergence and harmony. Like all the other limited participants—the reader included—the Mesopotamians undergo a process of discovery that brings home to them God's management of the world.

ROLAND BARTHES

The Struggle with the Angel:
Textual Analysis of Genesis 32:22-32

(22) And he rose up that night, and took his two wives, and his two women servants, and his eleven sons, and passed over the ford Jabbok. (23) And he took them, and sent them over the brook, and sent over that he had. (24) And Jacob was left alone; and there wrestled a man with him until the breaking of the day. (25) And when he saw that he prevailed not against him, he touched the hollow of his thigh; and the hollow of Jacob's thigh was out of joint as he wrestled with him. (26) And he said, Let me go, for the day breaketh. And he said, I will not let thee go, except thou bless me. (27) And he said unto him, What is thy name? And he said, Jacob. (28) And he said, Thy name shall be called no more Jacob, but Israel: for as a prince hast thou power with God and with men, and hast prevailed. (29) And Jacob asked him, and said, Tell me, I pray thee, thy name. And he said, Wherefore is it thou dost ask after my name? And he blessed him there. (30) And Jacob called the name of the place Peniel: for I have seen God face to face, and my life is preserved. (31) And as he passed over Penuel the sun rose upon him, and he halted upon his thigh. (32) Therefore the children of Israel eat not of the sinew which shrank, which is upon the hollow of the thigh, unto this day: because he touched the hollow of Jacob's thigh in the sinew that shrank.

The clarifications—or precautionary remarks—which will serve as an introduction to the following analysis will in fact be largely negative. First of all,

From *Image, Music, Text.* © 1977 Roland Barthes. Translation © 1977 by Stephen Heath. Hill & Wang, 1977.

it must be said that I shall not be giving any preliminary exposition of the principles, perspectives and problems of the structural analysis of narrative. That analysis is not a science nor even a discipline (it is not taught), but, as part of the newly developing semiology, it nevertheless represents an area of research which is becoming well known, so much so that to set out its prolegomena on the occasion of every fresh analysis would be to run the risk of producing an impression of useless repetition. Moreover, the structural analysis presented here will not be very pure. I shall indeed be referring in the main to the principles shared by all those semiologists concerned with narrative and, to finish, I shall even show how the piece under discussion lends itself to an extremely classic and almost canonical structural analysis, this orthodox consideration (orthodox from the point of view of the structural analysis of narrative) is all the more justified in that we shall be dealing with a mythical narrative that may have entered writing (entered Scripture) via an oral tradition. At the same time, however, I shall allow myself every so often (and perhaps continuously on the quiet) to direct my investigations towards an analysis with which I am more at home, textual analysis ("textual" is used with reference to the contemporary theory of the *text*, this being understood as production of *signifiance* and not as philological object, custodian of the Letter). Such an analysis endeavours to "see" each particular text in its difference — which does not mean in its ineffable individuality, for this difference is "woven" in familiar codes; it conceives the text as taken up in an *open* network which is the very infinity of language, itself structured without closure; it tries to say no longer *from where* the text comes (historical criticism), nor even *how* it is made (structural analysis), but how it is unmade, how it explodes, disseminates — by what coded paths it *goes off*. Finally, the last of these precautionary remarks and intended to forestall any disappointment, there is no question in what follows of a methodological confrontation between structural or textual analysis and exegesis, this lying outside my competence. I shall simply analyse the text of Genesis 32 (traditionally called "Jacob's struggle with the angel") as though I were at the first stage of a piece of research (which is indeed the case). What is given here is not a "result" nor even a "method" (which would be too ambitious and would imply a "scientific" view of the text that I do not hold), but merely a "way of proceeding."

I. SEQUENTIAL ANALYSIS

Structural analysis embraces roughly three types or three objects of analysis, or again, if one prefers, comprises three tasks. 1) The inventorization and classification of the "psychological," biographical, characterial and social attributes of the characters involved in the narrative (age, sex, external qualities, social situation or position of importance, etc.). Structurally, this is the area of indices (notations, of infinitely varied expression, serving to transmit a signified—as, for example, "irritability," "grace," "strength"—which the analyst names in his metalanguage; it being understood that the metalinguistic term may very well not figure directly in the text—as indeed is generally the case—which will not employ "irritability" or "grace" or whatever. If one establishes a homology between narrative and (the linguistic) sentence, then the indice corresponds to the adjective, to the *epithet* (which, let us not forget, was a figure of rhetoric). This is what we might call *indicial analysis*. 2) The inventorization and classification of the *functions* of the characters; what they do according to their narrative status, in their capacity as subject of an action that remains constant: the Sender, the Seeker, the Emissary, etc. In terms of the sentence, this would be the equivalent of the *present participle* and is that *actantial analysis* of which A. J. Greimas was the first to provide the theory. 3) The inventorization and classification of the *actions*, the plane of the *verbs*. These narrative actions are organized in sequences, in successions apparently ordered according to a pseudo-logical schema (it is a matter of a purely empirical, cultural logic, a product of experience—even if ancestral—and not of reasoning). What we have here is thus *sequential analysis*.

Our text lends itself, if in fact briefly, to indicial analysis. The contest it describes can be read as an indice of Jacob's strength (attested in other episodes of the chronicle of this hero's exploits) and that indice leads towards an anagogical meaning which is the (invincible) strength of God's Elect. Actantial analysis is also possible, but as the text is essentially made up of seemingly contingent actions it is better to work mainly on a sequential (or actional) analysis of the episode, being prepared in conclusion to add one or two remarks concerning the actantial. I shall divide the text (without, I think, forcing things) into three sequences: 1. the Crossing, 2. the Struggle, 3. the Namings.

1. *The Crossing* (vv. 22–24). Let us straightaway give the schema of the sequences of this episode, a schema which is twofold or at least, as it were, "strabismic" (what is at stake here will be seen in a moment):

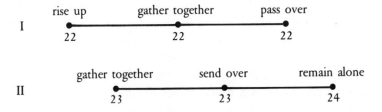

It can be noted at once that structurally *rise up* is a simple *operator for beginning*;

one might say, putting things quickly, that by *rise up* is to be understood not only that Jacob starts moving but also that the discourse *gets underway*. The beginning of a narrative, of a discourse, of a text, is an extremely sensitive point—*where to begin?* The *said* must be torn from the *not-said*, whence a whole rhetoric of beginning *markers*. The most important thing, however, is that the two sequences (or sub-sequences) seem to be in a state of redundancy (which is perhaps usual in the discourse of the period: a piece of information is given and then repeated; but the rule here is reading, not the historical and philological determination of the text: we are reading the text not in its "truth" but in its "production"—which is not its "determination"). Paradoxically moreover (for redundancy habitually serves to homogenize, to clarify and assure a message), when read after two millennia of Aristotelian rationalism (Aristotle being the principal theoretician of classic narrative) the redundancy of the two sub-sequences creates an abrasion, a grating of readability. The sequential schema, that is, can be read in two ways: 1) Jacob himself crosses over the ford—if need be after having made several trips back and forth—and thus the combat takes place on the left bank of the flood (he is coming from the North) *after he has definitively crossed over*; in this case, *send over* is read *cross over himself*; 2) Jacob sends over but does not himself cross over; he fights on the right bank of the Jabbok *before crossing over*, in a rearguard position. Let us not look for some *true* interpretation (perhaps our very hesitation will appear ridiculous in the eyes of the exegetes); rather, let us consume two different pressures of readability: 1) if Jacob remains alone *before* crossing the Jabbok, we are led towards a "folkloric" reading of the episode, the mythical reference then being overwhelming which has it that a trial of strength (as for example with a dragon or the guardian spirit of a river) must be imposed on the hero *before* he clears the obstacle, *so that*—once victorious—he can clear it; 2) if on the contrary Jacob having crossed over (he and his tribe), he remains alone on the good side of the flood (the side of the country to which he wants to go), then the passage is without structural finality while acquiring on the other hand a reli-gious finality: if Jacob is alone, it is no longer to settle the question of and obtain the crossing but in order that he be *marked* with solitude (the familiar *setting apart* of the one chosen by God). There is a historical circumstance which increases the undecidability of the two interpretations. Jacob's purpose is to return home, to enter the land of Canaan: given this, the crossing of the River Jordan would be easier to understand than that of the Jabbok. In short, we are confronted with the crossing of a spot that is neutral. The crossing is crucial if Jacob has to win it over the guardian of the place, indifferent if what is important is the solitude, the mark of Jacob. Perhaps we have here the tangled trace of two stories, or at least of two narrative instances: the one, more "archaic" (in the simple stylistic sense of the term), makes of the crossing itself an ordeal; the other, more "realist," gives a "geographical" air to Jacob's journey by mentioning the places he goes through (without attaching any mythical value to them).

If one carries back on to this twofold sequence the pattern of subsequent events, that is the Struggle and the Naming, the dual reading continues, coherent to the end in each of its two versions. Here again is the diagram:

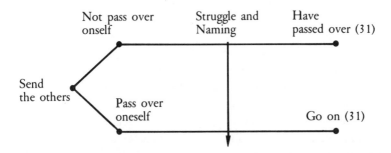

If the Struggle stands between the "not pass over" and the "have passed over" (the folklorizing, mythical reading), then the mutation of the Names corresponds to the very purpose of every etymological saga; if on the contrary the Struggle is only a stage between a position of immobility (of meditation, of election) and a movement of setting off again, then the mutation of the Name has the value of a spiritual rebirth (of "baptism"). All of which can be summarized by saying that in this first episode there is sequential readability but cultural ambiguity. No doubt the theologian would grieve at this indecision while the exegete would acknowledge it, hoping for some element of fact or argument that would enable him to put an end to it. The textual analyst, judging by my own impression, savours such *friction* between two intelligibilities.

2. *The Struggle* (vv. 24–29). For the second episode we have once again to start from a complication (which is not to say a doubt) of readability — remember that textual analysis is founded on *reading* rather than on the objective structure of the text, the latter being more the province of structural analysis. This complication stems from the interchangeable character of the pronouns which refer to the two opponents in the combat: a style which a purist would describe as *muddled* but whose lack of sharpness doubtless posed no problem for Hebrew syntax. Who is "a man"? Staying within verse 25, is it "a man" who does not succeed in getting the better of Jacob or Jacob who cannot prevail over this someone? Is the "he" of "he prevailed not against him" (25) the same as the "he" of "And he said" (26)? Assuredly everything becomes clear in the

end but it requires in some sort a retroactive reasoning of a syllogistic kind: you have vanquished God. He who is speaking to you is he whom you vanquished. Therefore he who is speaking to you is God. The identification of the opponents is oblique, the readability is *diverted* (whence occasionally commentaries which border on total misunderstanding; as for example: "He wrestles with the Angel of the Lord and, thrown to the ground, obtains from him the certainty that God is with him").

Structurally, this amphibology, even if subsequently clarified, is not without significance. It is not in my opinion (which is, I repeat, that of a reader today) a simple complication of expression due to an unpolished, archaizing style; it is bound up with a paradoxical structure of the contest (paradoxical when compared with the stereotypes of mythical combat). So as to appreciate this paradox in its structural subtlety, let us imagine for a moment an endoxical (and no longer paradoxical) reading of the episode: A wrestles with B but fails to get the better of him; to gain victory at all costs, A then resorts to some exceptional strategy, whether an unfair and forbidden blow (the forearm chop in wrestling matches) or a blow which, while remaining within the rules, supposes a secret knowledge, a "dodge" (the "ploy" of the Jarnac blow [In 1547 Guy de Jarnac won a duel by an unexpected thrust which hamstrung his opponent]). *In the very logic of the narrative* such a blow, generally described as "decisive," brings victory to the person who administers it: the emphatic mark of which this blow is structurally the object cannot be reconciled with its being ineffective—by the very god of narrative it *must* succeed. Here, however, the opposite occurs: the decisive blow fails; A, who gave the blow, is not the victor; which is the structural paradox. The sequence then takes an unexpected course:

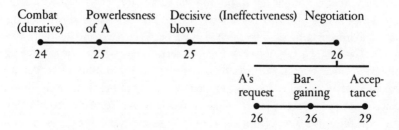

It will be noted that A (it matters little from the point of view of the structure if this be *someone, a man, God* or *the Angel*) is not strictly speaking vanquished but *held in check*. For this to be seen as a defeat, the adjunction of a *time limit* is needed: this is the breaking of day ("for the day breaketh" 26), a notation which picks up verse 24 ("until the breaking of day") but now in the explicit context of a mythical structure. The theme of the nocturnal combat is structurally justified by the fact that at a certain moment, fixed in advance (as is the rising of the sun, as is the duration of a boxing match), the rules of the combat will no longer obtain, the structural play will come to an end, as too the supernatural play (the "demons" withdraw at dawn). Thus we can see that it is within a quite "regular" combat that the sequence sets up an unexpected readability, a logical surprise: the person who has the knowledge, the secret, the special ploy, is nevertheless defeated. The sequence itself, however actional, however anecdotal it may be, functions to *unbalance* the opponents in the combat, not only by the unforeseen victory of the one over the other, but above all (let us be fully aware of the *formal* subtlety of this surprise) by the illogical, *inverted*, nature of the victory. In other words (and here we find an eminently structural term, well known to linguists), the combat, as it is reversed in its unexpected development, *marks* one of the combatants: the weakest defeats the strongest, *in exchange for which* he is marked (on the thigh).

It is plausible (moving somewhat away from pure structural analysis and approaching textual analysis, vision *without barriers* of meanings) to fill out this schema of the mark (of the disequilibrium) with contents of an ethnological kind. The structural meaning of the episode, once again, is the following: a situation of balance (the combat at its outset) — and such a situation is a prerequisite for any marking (ascesis in Ignatius of Loyola for instance functions to establish the *indifference* of the will which allows the manifestation of the divine mark, the choice, the election) — is disturbed by the unlikely victory of one of the participants: there is an inversion of the mark, a counter-mark. Let us turn then to the family configuration. Traditionally, the line of brothers is in principle evenly balanced (they are all situated on the same level in relation to the parents); this equality of birth is normally unbalanced by the right of primogeniture: the eldest is marked. Now in the story of Jacob, there is an inversion of the mark, a counter-mark: it is the younger who supplants the elder (Gen. 27:36), taking his brother by the heel in order to reverse time; it is Jacob, the younger brother, who marks himself. Since Jacob has just obtained a mark in his struggle with God, one can say in a sense that A (God) is the substitute of the elder brother, once again beaten by the younger. The conflict with Esau is *displaced* (every symbol is a *displacement*; if the "struggle with the angel" is symbolic, then it has displaced something). Commentary — for which I am insufficiently equipped — would at this point doubtless have to widen the interpretation of the *inversion of the mark*, by placing it either in a historico-economic context — Esau is the eponym of the Edomites and there were economic ties between the Edomites and the Israelites; figured here per-

haps is an overthrow of the alliance, the start of a new league of interests? — or
in the field of the symbolic (in the psychoanalytical sense of the term) — the
Old Testament seems to be less the world of the Fathers than that of the
Enemy Brothers, the elder are ousted in favour of the younger; in the myth
of the Enemy Brothers Freud pointed to the theme of *the smallest difference*:
is not the blow on the thigh, on the thin sinew, just such a *smallest difference*?
Be that as it may, in this world God marks the young, acts against nature:
his (structural) function is to constitute a *counter-marker*.

To conclude discussion of this extremely rich episode of the Struggle, of
the Mark, I should like to add a remark as semiologist. We have seen that
in the binary opposition of the combatants, which is perhaps the binary
opposition of the Brothers, the younger is marked both by the reversal of the
anticipated distribution of strengths and by a bodily sign, the touch on the
thigh, the halting (not without recalling Oedipus, Swollen Foot, the Lame One).
A mark is creative of meaning. In the phonological representation of language,
the "equality" of the paradigm is unbalanced in favour of a marked element
by the presence of a trait absent from its correlative and oppositional term.
By marking Jacob (Israel), God (or the Narrative) permits an anagogical
development of meaning, creates the formal operational conditions of a new
"language," the election of Israel being its "message." God is a logothete, a founder
of a language, and Jacob is here a "morpheme" of the new language.

3. *The Namings or Mutations* (vv. 27–32). The object of the final sequence is the exchange of names, that is to say the promotion of new statuses,
new powers. Naming is clearly related to Blessing: to bless (to accept the
homage of a kneeling suppliant) and to name are both suzerain acts. There
are two namings:

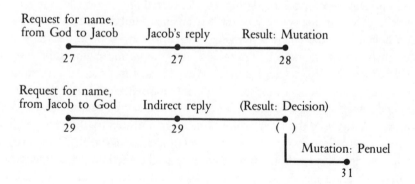

The mutation bears on Names, but in fact it is the entire episode which functions
as *the creation of a multiple trace* — across Jacob's body, the status of the Brothers,

Jacob's name of the place, the kind of food (creation of an alimentary taboo: the whole story can also be interpreted *a minimo* as the mythical foundation of a taboo). The three sequences that have been analysed are homological; what is in question in each is a *change*—of place, parental line, name, alimentary rite; all this keeping very close to an activity of language, a transgression of the rules of meaning.

Such is the sequential (or actional) analysis of our text. As has been seen, I have tried to remain always on the level of the structure, that is to say of the systematic correlation of the terms denoting an action. If I have chanced to mention certain possible meanings, the purpose has not been to discuss the probability of those meanings but rather to show how the structure "disseminates" contents—which each reading can make its own. My object is not the philological or historical document, custodian of a truth to be discovered, but the volume, the *signifiance* of the text.

II. STRUCTURAL ANALYSIS

The structural analysis of narrative being in part already constituted (by Propp, Lévi-Strauss, Greimas, Bremond), I wish to conclude—putting myself even more in the background—by confronting the text under discussion with two modes of structural analysis so as to demonstrate the interest of these two modes, though my own work has a somewhat different orientation: Greimas's actantial analysis and Propp's functional analysis.

1. *Actantial analysis.* The actantial grid worked out by Greimas [See especially A. J. Greimas, *Sémantique structurale* and *Du Sens*]—to be used, as he himself says, with prudence and flexibility—divides the characters, the actors, of a narrative into six formal classes of actants, defined by what they do according to narrative status and not by what they are psychologically (thus one actant may combine several characters just as a single character may combine several actants; an actant may also be figured by an inanimate entity). The "struggle with the angel" forms a very familiar episode in mythical narratives: the overcoming of an obstacle, the Ordeal. As far as the particular episode is concerned (things might perhaps be different over the whole set of Jacob's exploits), the actants are "filled" as follows: Jacob is the *Subject* (subject of the demand, the quest, the action); the *Object* (of the same demand, quest, action) is the crossing of the guarded and forbidden place, the flood, the Jabbok; the *Sender*, who sets in circulation the stake of the quest (namely the crossing of the flood), is obviously God; the *Receiver* is Jacob again (two actants are here present in a single figure); the *Opponent* (the one or ones who hinder the Subject in his quest) is God himself (it is he who, mythically, guards the crossing); the *Helper* (the one or ones who aid the Subject) is Jacob who provides help

to himself through his own, legendary, strength (an indicial trait, as was noted).

The paradox, or at very least the anomic nature of the formulation, can be seen at once: that the subject be confounded with the receiver is banal; that the subject be his or her own helper is less usual (it generally occurs in "voluntarist" narratives or novels); but that the sender be the opponent is very rare and there is only one type of narrative that can present this paradoxical form – narratives relating an act of blackmail. If the opponent were only the (provisional) holder of the stake, then of course there would be nothing extraordinary: it is the opponent's role to have and defend ownership of the object that the hero wants to obtain (as with the dragon guarding a place to be crossed). Here however, as in every blackmail, God, at the same time that he guards the flood, also dispenses the mark, the privilege. The actantial form of the text is thus far from conciliatory: structurally, it is extremely audacious – which squares well with the "scandal" represented by God's defeat.

2. *Functional analysis.* Propp was the first to establish the structure of the folktale, by dividing it into its *functions* or narrative acts. [V. Propp, *Morphology of the Folktale.* Unfortunately, the word "function" is always ambiguous; at the beginning of the present piece we used it to define actantial analysis which assesses characters by their roles in the action (precisely their "function"); in Propp's terminology, there is a shift from character to the action itself, grasped in its *relations* to the actions surrounding it.] The functions, according to Propp, are stable elements, limited in number (some thirty or so) and always identical in their concatenation, even if occasionally certain functions are absent from this or that narrative. It so happens – as will be seen in a moment – that our text fulfills perfectly a section of the functional schema brought to light by Propp who would have been unable to imagine a more convincing application of his discovery.

In a preparatory section of the folktale (as analysed by Propp) there necessarily occurs an absence of the hero, something already the case in the tale of Jacob: Isaac sends Jacob far from his homeland to Laban (Gen. 28:2, 5). Our episode effectively begins at the fifteenth of Propp's narrative functions and can be coded in the following manner, showing at each stage the striking parallelism between Propp's schema and the Genesis narrative:

Propp and the folktale	*Genesis*
15. Transference from one place to another (by bird, horse, ship, etc.)	Set out from the North, from the Aramaeans, from the house of Laban, Jacob journeys home, to his father's house (29:1, Jacob sets out)

16. Combat between the Villain and the Hero	This is the sequence of the Struggle (32:24–27)
17. The hero is branded, "marked" (generally it is a matter of a mark on the body, but in other cases it is simply the gift of a jewel, of a ring)	Jacob is marked on the thigh (32:25 – 32)
18. Victory of the Hero, defeat of the Villain	Jacob's victory (32:26)
19. Liquidation of the misfortune or lack: the misfortune or lack had been established in the initial absence of the Hero: this absence is repaired	Having succeeded in crossing Penuel (32:31), Jacob reaches Schechem in Canaan (33:18)

There are other parallels. In Propp's function 14, the hero acquires the use of a magical object; for Jacob this talisman is obviously the blessing that he surprises his blind father into giving him (Gen. 27). Again, function 29 represents the transfiguration of the hero (for example, the Beast transformed into a handsome nobleman); such a transfiguration seems to be present in the changing of the Name (Gen. 32:28) and the rebirth it implies. The narrative model stamps God with the role of the Villain (his *structural* role—it is not a question of a psychological role); the fact is that a veritable folktale stereotype can be read in the Genesis episode—the difficult crossing of a ford guarded by a hostile spirit. A further similitude between episode and tale is that in both cases character motivations (their reasons for acting) go unnoted, the ellipsis of such notations being not a stylistic element but a pertinent structural characteristic of the narration. Structural analysis in the strict sense of the term would thus conclude emphatically that the "struggle with the angel" is a true fairytale, since according to Propp all fairytales belong to the same structure, the one he described.

So we can see that what might be called the structural exploitation of the episode is very possible and even imperative. Let me indicate in conclusion, however, that what interests me most in this famous passage is not the "folkloristic" model but the abrasive frictions, the breaks, the discontinuities of readability, the juxtaposition of narrative entities which to some extent run free from an explicit logical articulation. One is dealing here (this at least is for me the savour of the reading) with a sort of *metonymic montage*: the themes (Crossing, Struggle, Naming, Alimentary Rite) are *combined*, not "developed." This abruptness, this asyndetic character of the narrative is well expressed by Hosea 12:3-4:

> "He took his brother by the heel in the womb / / and by his strength he had power with God."

Metonymic logic is that of the unconscious. Hence it is perhaps in that direction that one would need to pursue the present study, to pursue the reading of the text—its dissemination, not its truth. Evidently, there is a risk in so doing of weakening the episode's economico-historical force (certainly existent, at the level of the exchanges of tribes and the questions of power). Yet equally in so doing the symbolic explosion of the text (not necessarily of a religious order) is reinforced. The problem, the problem at least posed for me, is exactly to manage not to reduce the Text to a signified, whatever it may be (historical, economic, folkloristic or kerygmatic), but to hold its *signifiance* fully open.

HAROLD BLOOM

Wrestling Sigmund: Three Paradigms for Poetic Originality

I begin with a parable, rather than a paradigm, but then I scarcely can distinguish between the two. The parable is Bacon's, and I have brooded on it before, as part of a meditation upon the perpetual (shall we say obsessive?) belatedness of strong poetry:

> The children of time do take after the nature and malice of the father. For as he devoureth his children, so one of them seeketh to devour and suppress the other, while antiquity envieth there should be new additions, and novelty cannot be content to add but it must deface.

I doubt that I have been able to add much to that dark observation of Bacon's, but I want again to swerve from it towards my own purposes. I don't read the ghastly image of malicious time devouring us as irony or allegory, but rather as sublime hyperbole, because of the terrible strength of the verb, "devouring." Time is an unreluctant Ugolino, and poems, as I read them, primarily are deliberate lies against that devouring. Strong poems reluctantly know, not Freud's parodistic Primal History Scene (*Totem and Taboo*) but what I have called the Scene of Instruction. Such a scene, itself both parable and paradigm, I have shied away from developing, until now, probably because of my own sense of trespass, my own guilt at having become a Jewish Gnostic after and in spite of an Orthodox upbringing. But without developing such a notion, I cannot go further, and so I must begin with it here.

We all choose our own theorists for the Scene of Instruction, or rather,

From *The Breaking of the Vessels*. © 1982 by The University of Chicago. The University of Chicago Press, 1982.

as Coleridge would have said, we do not find their texts, but are found by them. More often than not, these days, the theorists that advanced sensibilities are found by are the German language fourfold of Marx, Nietzsche, Freud, and Heidegger, but the inevitable precursor for formulating a Scene of Instruction has to be Kierkegaard, allied to Marx and Heidegger, involuntarily, by his antithetical relationship to Hegel. It may be that any Scene of Instruction has to be, rather like Derrida's Scene of Writing, more an unwilling parody of Hegel's quest than of Freud's. But I am content with a misprision of Kierkegaard, while being uneasily aware that his "repetition" is a trope that owes more than he could bear to the Hegelian trope of "mediation."

To talk about paradigms, however parabolically, in the context of poetry and criticism, is to engage the discourse of "repetition," in Kierkegaard's rather than Freud's sense of that term. I haven't ever encountered a useful discursive summary of Kierkegaard's notion, and I myself won't try to provide one, because Kierkegaard's idea of repetition is more trope than concept, and tends to defeat discursiveness. His little book *Repetition* is subtitled "An Essay in Experimental Psychology," but "experimental" there is the crucial and tricky term, and modifies "psychology" into an odd blend of psychopoetics and theology. Repetition, we are told first, "is recollected forwards" and is "the daily bread which satisfies with benediction." Later, the book's narrator assures us that "repetition is always a transcendence," and indeed is "too transcendent" for the narrator to grasp. The same narrator, Constantine Constantius, wrote a long open letter against a Hegelian misunderstanding of his work, which insisted that true or anxious freedom willed repetition: "it is the task of freedom to see constantly a new side of repetition." Each new side is a "breaking forth," a "transition" or "becoming," and therefore a concept of happening, and not of being. If repetition, in this sense, is always a transition or a crossing, then the power of repetition lies in what its great American theorist, Emerson, called the shooting of a gap or the darting to an aim. Kierkegaard, unlike Emerson, was a Christian, and so his repetition cannot be only a series of transitions; eternity becomes true repetition.

But if we are more interested in poetry than in eternity, we can accept a limited or transitional repetition. We can say, still following the aesthetic stage in Kierkegaard, that Wallace Stevens *is* the repetition of Walt Whitman, or that John Ashbery *is* the repetition of Stevens. In this sense, repetition means the re-creation or revision of a paradigm, but of what paradigm? When a strong poet revises a precursor, he re-enacts a scene that is at once a catastrophe, a romance, and a transference. All three paradigms technically are tainted, though favorably from the perspective of poetry. The catastrophe is also a creation; the romance is incestuous; the transference violates taboo and its ambivalences.

Are these three categories or one? What kind of a relational or dialectical event is at once creatively catastrophic, incestuously romantic, and ambivalently a metaphor for a trespass that *works*?

For an instance, I go back to the example of Wallace Stevens, still the poet of our moment. When I was a youngster, the academy view of Stevens was that of a kind of hothouse exquisite, vaguely perfumed, Ronald Firbank grown fat, and transmogrified into a Pennsylvania Dutchman practising insurance in Hartford, Connecticut. Now, in 1981, this vision has its own archaic charm, but thirty years ago it filled me with a young enthusiast's fury. I remember still the incredulous indulgence displayed by one of the masters of Yale New Criticism, now heartbreakingly mourned by me, when I read an essay in his graduate seminar suggesting that the seer of Hartford was the true ephebe of Walt Whitman, one of the roughs, an American. Stevens himself, a few miles up the road then, would have denied his own poetic father, but that after all is the most ancient of stories. I cite here again a small poem by the sane and sacred Walt that even Stevens confesses he had pondered deeply. The poem is called "A Clear Midnight":

> This is thy hour O Soul, thy free flight into the wordless,
> Away from books, away from art, the day erased, the lesson done,
> Thee fully forth emerging, silent, gazing, pondering the themes thou
>   lovest best,
> Night, sleep, death and the stars.

The Whitmanian soul, I take it, is the Coleridgean moon, the Arab of *Notes toward a Supreme Fiction*. Perhaps the ocean would have been redundant had it been lined up with night, sleep, and death, instead of "the stars," since moon and the tides are so intimately allied in the most pervasive of feminine tropes. We don't need the ocean anyway, since the moon as mother of the months is always the mother proper, Whitman's and our "fierce old mother," moaning for us to return whence we came. The mother's face is the purpose of the poem, as Keats told us implicitly, and Stevens in so many words. But the purpose of the poem, for the poet *qua* person, is Kenneth Burke's purpose, and not my own. The poet *qua* poet is my obsessive concern, and the Scene of Instruction creates the poet as or in a poet.

The Scene of Instruction in Stevens is a very belated phenomenon, and even Whitman's origins, despite all his mystifications, are shadowed by too large an American foreground. A better test for my paradigms is provided by the indubitable beginning of a canonical tradition. The major ancient possibilities are the Yahwist, the strongest writer in the Bible, and Homer. Beside them we can place Freud, whose agon with the whole of anteriority is the largest and most intense of our century. Because Freud has far more in common with the Yahwist than with Homer, I will confine myself here to the two Jewish writers, ancient and modern.

I want to interpret two difficult and haunting texts, each remarkable in several ways, but particularly as a startling manifestation of originality. One goes back to perhaps the tenth century before the Common Era; the other is nearly three thousand years later, and comes in our own time. The first is the story of Wrestling Jacob, and tells how Jacob achieved the name Israel, in Gen. 32:23–32, the author being that anonymous great writer, fully the equal of Homer, whom scholars have agreed to call by the rather Kafkan name of the letter J, or the Yahwist. The second I would call, with loving respect, the story of Wrestling Sigmund, and tells how Freud achieved a theory of the origins of the human sexual drive. As author we necessarily have the only possible modern rival of the Yahwist, Freud himself, the text being mostly the second of the *Three Essays on the Theory of Sexuality*.

Here is the text of Jacob's encounter with a daemonic being, as rendered literally by E. A. Speiser in the Anchor Bible:

> In the course of that night he got up and, taking his two wives, the two maidservants, and his eleven children, he crossed the ford of the Jabbok. After he had taken them across the stream, he sent over all his possessions. Jacob was left alone. Then some man wrestled with him until the break of dawn. When he saw that he could not prevail over Jacob, he struck his hip at its socket, so that the hip socket was wrenched as they wrestled. Then he said, "Let me go, for it is daybreak." Jacob replied, "I will not let you go unless you bless me." Said the other, "What is your name?" He answered, "Jacob." Said he, "You shall no longer be spoken of as Jacob, but as Israel, for you have striven with beings divine and human, and have prevailed." Then Jacob asked, "Please tell me your name." He replied, "You must not ask my name." With that, he bade him goodby there and then.
>
> Jacob named the site Peniel, meaning, "I have seen God face to face, yet my life has been preserved." The sun rose upon him just as he passed Penuel, limping on his hip.

I shall enhance my reputation for lunatic juxtapositions by citing next to this Sublime passage a cento of grotesque passages from Freud, the first two being from the second *Essay*, "Infantile Sexuality," and the third from *Essay* III, but summarizing the argument of the second *Essay*:

> It was the child's first and most vital activity, his sucking at his

mother's breast, or at substitutes for it, that must have familiarized him with this pleasure. The child's lips, in our view, behave like an *erotogenic zone*, and no doubt stimulation by the warm flow of milk is the cause of the pleasurable sensation. The satisfaction of the erotogenic zone is associated, in the first instance, with the satisfaction of the need for nourishment. To begin with, sexual activity props itself upon functions serving the purpose of self-preservation and does not become independent of them until later. No one who has seen a baby sinking back satiated from the breast and falling asleep with flushed cheeks and a blissful smile can escape the reflection that this picture persists as a prototype of the expression of sexual satisfaction in later life. The need for repeating the sexual satisfaction now becomes detached from the need for taking nourishment.

Our study of thumb-sucking or sensual sucking has already given us the three essential characteristics of an infantile sexual manifestation. At its origin it props itself upon one of the vital somatic functions; it has as yet no sexual object, and is thus *auto-erotic*; and its sexual aim is dominated by an *erotogenic zone*.

At a time at which the first beginnings of sexual satisfaction are still linked with the taking of nourishment, the sexual instinct has a sexual object outside the infant's own body in the shape of his mother's breast. It is only later that he loses it, just at the time, perhaps, when he is able to form a total idea of the person to whom the organ that is giving him satisfaction belongs. As a rule the sexual drive then becomes auto-erotic, and not until the period of latency has been passed through is the original relation restored. There are thus good reasons why a child sucking at his mother's breast has become the prototype of every relation of love. The finding of an object is in fact a re-finding of it.

Wrestling with a divine being or angel is rather a contrast to sucking at one's mother's breast, and achieving the name Israel is pretty well unrelated to the inauguration of the sexual drive. All that the Yahwist's and Freud's breakthroughs have in common is that they *are* breakthroughs, difficult to assimilate because these curious stories are each so *original*. But before I explore that common difficulty, I need to give a commentary upon each of these passages. What is the nature of Jacob's agon, and what does it mean to see Freud's own agon as being central to his theory of sexual origins?

To consider the Yahwist as being something other than a religious writer would be as eccentric as to consider Freud a religious writer despite himself. But who sets the circumferences? All the academies, from the Academy of Ezra through the Academies of Alexandria on down to our own institutions, have in common their necessity for consensus. The Yahwist may have written to persuade, but he remains hugely idiosyncratic when compared either to the Elohist, who probably came a century after him, or to the much later Priestly Author, who may have belonged to the age of Ezra and the Return from Babylon, some six centuries after the Yahwist. E and P are far more normative than J, and far less original, in every meaning of "original." But I want to specify a particular aspect of J's originality, and it is one that I have never seen discussed as such. We are familiar, since the work of Nietzsche and of Burckhardt, with the ancient Greek concept of the agonistic, but we scarcely recognize an ancient Hebrew notion of agon, which is crucial throughout J's writing. J is an *unheimlich* writer, and perhaps the greatest master of the literary Sublime in what has become Western tradition. But J is also the most remarkable instance of what Blake meant, when in *The Marriage of Heaven and Hell* he characterized the history of all religions as choosing forms of worship from poetic tales. J's poetic tales of Yahweh and the Patriarchs are now so much the staple of Judaism and Christianity, and have been such for so long, that we simply cannot read them. Yet they were and are so original that there is quite another sense in which they never have been read, and perhaps cannot be read. If we allowed them their strangeness, then their uncanniness would reveal that tradition never has been able to assimilate their originality.

Yahweh appears to Abraham by the terebinths of Mamre; Abraham sits at the entrance of his tent as the day grows hot. He looks up, sees three men, one of them Yahweh, whom he recognizes, and invites them for an immediate meal. Yahweh and his angels devour rolls, curd, milk, and roast calf, while Abraham stands nearby. Yahweh then prophesies that Sarah, well past a woman's periods, will have a son. Sarah, listening behind Yahweh's back, at the tent entrance, laughs to herself. Yahweh, offended, asks rhetorically if anything is too much for him. Poor, frightened Sarah says she didn't laugh, but Yahweh answers: "Yes, you did."

What can we do with a Yahweh who sits on the ground, devours calf, is offended by an old woman's sensible derision, and then walks on to Sodom after being argued down by Abraham to a promise that he will spare that wicked city if he finds just ten righteous among the inhabitants? The silliest thing we can do is to say that J has an anthropomorphic concept of god. J doesn't have a concept of Yahweh; indeed we scarcely can say that J even has a conceptual image of Yahweh. J is nothing of a theologian, and everything of a storyteller, and his strong interest is personality, particularly the personality of Jacob. J's interest in Yahweh is intense, but rather less than J's concern for Jacob, because Jacob is cannier and more agonistic even than Yahweh. Yahweh just about *is* the uncanny for J; what counts about Yahweh is that he is the source of the Blessing, and the Blessing is the aim of the agon, in total distinction from the Greek notion of agon.

The contest among the Greeks was for the foremost place, whether in chariot racing, poetry, or civic eminence. The subtle and superb Jacob knows only one foremost place, the inheritance of Abraham and of Isaac, so that tradition will be compelled to speak of the God of Abraham, the God of Isaac, the God of Jacob, the God of Judah. The Blessing means that the nation shall be known as Israel, the name that Jacob wins as agonist, and that the people shall be known as Jews after Judah, rather than say as Reubens, if that first-born had been chosen. Such a blessing achieves a pure temporality, and so the agon for it is wholly temporal in nature, whereas the Greek agon is essentially spatial, a struggle for the foremost place, and so for place, and not a mastery over time. That, I take it, is why temporality is at the center of the nightlong wrestling between Jacob and some nameless one among the Elohim, and I am now ready to describe that most significant of J's visions of agon.

I quote again Speiser's literal version of J's text:

> In the course of that night he got up and, taking his two wives, the two maidservants, and his eleven children, he crossed the ford of the Jabbok. After he had taken them across the stream, he sent over all his possessions. Jacob was left alone. Then some man wrestled with him until the break of dawn. When he saw that he could not prevail over Jacob, he struck his hip at its socket, so that the hip socket was wrenched as they wrestled. Then he said, "Let me go, for it is daybreak." Jacob replied, "I will not let you go unless you bless me." Said the other, "What is your name?" He answered, "Jacob." Said he, "You shall no longer be spoken of as Jacob, but as Israel, for you have striven with beings divine and human, and have prevailed." Then Jacob asked, "Please tell me your name." He replied, "You must not ask my name." With that, he bade him good-by there and then.
>
> Jacob named the site Peniel, meaning, "I have seen God face to face, yet my life has been preserved." The sun rose upon him just as he passed Penuel, limping on his hip.

So great is the uncanniness of this that we ought to approach J with a series of questions, rather than rely upon any traditional or even modern scholarly commentary whatsoever. Jacob has left Laban, and is journeying home, uneasily expecting a confrontation with his defrauded brother Esau. On the night before this dreaded reunion, Jacob supervises the crossing, into the land of the Blessing, of his household and goods. But then evidently he crosses back over the Jabbok so as to remain alone at Penuel in Transjordan. Why? J does not tell us, and instead suddenly confronts Jacob and the reader with "some man" who wrestles with Jacob until the break of dawn. About this encounter, there is nothing that is other than totally surprising. J's Jacob has been an agonist literally from his days in Rebecca's womb, but his last physical contest took place in that womb, when he struggled vainly with his twin Esau as to which should emerge first, Esau winning, but dragging out his tenacious brother, whose hand held on to his heel. Popular etymology interpreted the name Jacob as meaning "heel." Craft and wiliness have been Jacob's salient characteristics, rather than the physical strength evidently displayed in this nocturnal encounter. Yet that strength is tropological, and substitutes for the spiritual quality of persistence or endurance that marks Jacob or Israel.

Who is that "man," later called one of the Elohim, who wrestles with Jacob until dawn? And why should they wrestle anyway? Nothing in any tradition supports my surmise that this daemonic being is the Angel of Death, yet such I take him to be. What Jacob rightly fears is that he will be slain by the vengeful Esau on the very next day. Something after all is curiously negative and even fearful about Jacob's opponent. Rabbinical tradition explains this strange being's fear of the dawn as being an angel's pious fear lest he be late on Yahweh's business, but here as so often the Rabbis were weak misreaders of J. Everything about the text shows that the divine being's dread of daybreak is comparable to Count Dracula's, and only the Angel of Death is a likely candidate among the Elohim for needing to move on before sunrise. This wrestling match is not a ballet, but is deadly serious for both contestants. The angel lames Jacob permanently, yet even this cannot subdue the patriarch. Only the blessing, the new naming Israel, which literally means "May God persevere," causes Jacob to let go even as daylight comes. Having prevailed against Esau, Laban and even perhaps against the messenger of death, Jacob deserves the agonistic blessing. In his own renaming of the site as Peniel, or the divine face, Jacob gives a particular meaning to his triumphal declaration that: "I have seen one of the Elohim face to face, and yet my life has been preserved." Seeing Yahweh face to face was no threat to Abraham's life, in J's view, but it is not Yahweh whom Jacob has wrestled to at least a standstill. I think there is no better signature of J's sublimity than the great sentence that ends the episode, with its powerful implicit contrast between Israel and the fled angel. Here is Jacob's true epiphany: "The sun rose upon him just as he passed Penuel, limping on his hip."

If there is an aesthetic originality in our Western tradition beyond interpretive assimilation, then it inheres in J's texts. We do not know Homer's precursors any more than we know J's, yet somehow we can see Homer as a revisionist, whereas J seems more unique. Is this only because Homer has been misread even more strongly than J has? The prophet Hosea is our first certain interpreter of wrestling Jacob, and Hosea was a strong poet, by any standards, yet his text is not adequate to the encounter he describes. But Hosea's Yahweh was a rather more remote entity than J's, and Hosea did not invest himself as personally in Jacob as J seems to have done. What interpretive paradigm can help us read Jacob's contest strongly enough to be worthy of the uncanniness of J, an author who might be said impossibly to combine the antithetical strengths of a Tolstoy and a Kafka?

I recur to the distinction between the Hebrew temporal Sublime agon and the Greek spatial striving for the foremost place. Nietzsche, in his notes for the unwritten "untimely meditation" he would have called *We Philologists*, caught better even than Burckhardt the darker aspects of the Greek agonistic spirit:

> The agonistic element is also the danger in every development; it overstimulates the creative impulse. . . .
>
> The greatest fact remains always the precociously panhellenic HOMER. All good things derive from him; yet at the same time he remained the mightiest obstacle of all. He made everyone else superficial, and that is why the really serious spirits struggled against him. But to no avail. Homer always won.
>
> The destructive element in great spiritual forces is also visible here. But what a difference between Homer and the Bible as such a force!
>
> The delight in drunkenness, delight in cunning, in revenge, in envy, in slander, in obscenity—in everything which was *recognized* by the Greeks as human and therefore built into the structure of society and custom. The wisdom of their institutions lies in the lack of any gulf between good and evil, black and white. Nature, as it reveals itself, is not denied but only *ordered*, limited to specified days and religious cults. This is the root of all spiritual freedom in the ancient world; the ancients sought a moderate release of natural forces, not their destruction and denial.
>
> [translated by William Arrowsmith]

Whatever Nietzsche means by "the Bible" in that contrast to Homer, he is not talking accurately about J, the Bible's strongest writer. Not that J, with his obsessive, more-than-Miltonic sense of temporality, essentially agrees with

Homer upon what constitutes spiritual freedom; no, perhaps J is further from
Homer in that regard than even Nietzsche states. J does not discourse in good
and evil, but in blessedness and unblessedness. J's subject, like Homer's, is strife,
including the strife of gods and men. And drunkenness, delight in cunning,
in revenge, in envy, in slander, in obscenity are at least as much involved in
the expression of J's exuberance as they are of Homer's. But J's temporal nature
is not Homer's spatial realm, and so the agonistic spirit manifests itself very
differently in the linguistic universes of these two masters. In Homer, the gods
transcend nature spatially, but Yahweh's transcendence is temporal. The overcoming of nature by means of the Blessing must be temporal also. Jacob's
temporal victory over one of the Elohim is a curious kind of creative act which
is one and the same as Jacob's cunning victories over Esau and Laban. In Greek
terms this makes no sense, but in ancient Hebrew thinking this corresponds
to that vision in which Yahweh's creation of the world, his rescue of the Israelites
at the Red Sea, and the return of his people from Babylon are all one creative
act on his part. Thorleif Boman defines the Hebrew word for eternity, *olam*,
as meaning neither otherworldliness nor chronological infinity but rather time
without boundaries. Something like that is the prize for which agonists strive
in J. When Jacob becomes Israel, the implication is that his descendants also
will prevail in a time without boundaries.

That Jacob is, throughout his life, an agonist, seems beyond dispute, and
certainly was the basis for Thomas Mann's strong reading of J's text in the
beautiful *Tales of Jacob* volume which is the glory of Mann's Joseph tetralogy.
Yet distinguishing Hebrew from Greek agon is not much beyond a starting
point in the interpretation of the recalcitrant originality of J's text. Whoever
it is among the Elohim, the angel fears a catastrophe, and vainly inflicts a crippling wound upon Jacob, averting one catastrophe at the price of another.
And yet, as agonists, the angel and Jacob create a blessing, the name of Israel,
a name that celebrates the agonistic virtue of persistence, a persistence into
unbounded temporality. That creation by catastrophe is one clear mark of this
encounter. Another is the carrying across from Jacob's struggles in earlier life,
veritably in the womb, his drive to have priority, where the carrying across
is as significant as the drive. If the drive for priority is a version of what Freud
has taught us to call family romance, then the conveyance of early zeal and
affect into a later context is what Freud has taught us to call transference.

Catastrophe creation, family romance, and transference are a triad equally
central to J and to Freud, and in some sense Freud's quest was to replace J
and the other biblical writers as the legitimate exemplar of these paradigms.
Ambivalence is the common element in the three paradigms, if we define
ambivalence strictly as a contradictory stance mixing love and hate towards

a particular object. Before returning to Wrestling Jacob, I want to cite the most shocking instance of Jahweh's ambivalence in the Hebrew Bible, an ambivalence manifested towards his particular favorite, Moses. The text is Exod. 4:24–26, translated literally:

> Yahweh encountered Moses when Moses camped at night on his way [to Egypt] and Yahweh sought to kill Moses. So Zipporah [Moses' wife] cut off her son's foreskin with a flint and touched Moses on his legs with it, saying: "Truly you are a bridegroom of blood to me." And when Yahweh let Moses alone, she added, "A bridegroom of blood due to the circumcision."

Confronted by this passage, normative interpretation has been very unhappy indeed, since in it the uncanny of originality has gone beyond all limits. Indeed only Gnostics, ancient and modern, could be happy with this text, in which the agonistic seems truly to have crossed over into a really shocking divine murderousness. Whoever it was among the Elohim, even if the Angel of Death, Jacob undauntedly confronted an agonist. Yet Zipporah is even more courageous in her rescue of Moses. Perhaps the Hebraic concept of agon is more extensive even than I have indicated. Consider, though only briefly, the opening of Psalm 19, which I cite in the extraordinary King James version:

> The heavens declare the glory of God; and the firmament showeth his handiwork.
> Day unto day uttereth speech, and night unto night showeth knowledge.
> There is no speech nor language, where their voice is not heard.
> Their line is gone out through all the earth, and their words to the end of the world. In them hath he set a tabernacle for the sun,
> Which is as a bridegroom coming out of his chamber, and rejoiceth as a strong man to run a race.
> His going forth is from the end of the heaven, and his circuit unto the ends of it: and there is nothing hid from the heat thereof.

That marvelous fifth verse reverberates in Spenser, Shakespeare, Milton, and Wordsworth, and is the most curiously Pindaric moment in the Bible, with the Hebrew agonistic vision coinciding just this once with the Greek. But against whom is this rejoicing bridegroom of a sun contending? Not with God but with man, must be the answer. The Psalmist is far more normative than the Yahwist. Who could conceive of a Psalm in the uncanny mode of the Yahwist? One way of arriving at a reading of Wrestling Jacob's night encounter is to contrast it with the characteristic stances and attitudes of the poets of Psalms confronting their Maker. Voices in the Psalms do not demand blessings; they implore. The sun emerges from his chamber like a bridegroom, and rejoicing at his own skill as an agonist, but the sun reflects the glory of God. It is not God's glory but Israel's, meaning Jacob just transformed into Israel, which is celebrated so sublimely by the Yahwist:

> The sun rose upon him just as he passed Penuel, limping on his hip.

What allies Freud to the Yahwist is this agonistic Sublime, as manifested in the power of the uncanny, in what cannot be rendered normative. We might think of the school of Ego Psychology, of Heinz Hartmann, Lowenstein, Kris, and Erikson, as being Psalmists in relation to Freud-as-Yahwist, an analogy that could be continued by describing Lacan and his school as Gnostics. Scenes of Instruction like the agon of Jacob or Yahweh's night attack upon Moses are akin to Freud's fantasies of catastrophe, because the outrage to normative sensibilities is beyond assimilation. Even our difficulties in recovering the uncanny originality of J are matched by our difficulties in acknowledging how peculiar and extreme a writer Freud sometimes compels himself to be, for reasons nearly as unknowable as the Yahwist's motives.

Wittgenstein, who resented Freud, and who dismissed Freud as a mythologist, however powerful, probably was too annoyed with Freud to read him closely. This may explain Wittgenstein's curious mistake in believing that Freud had not distinguished between the Primal Scene and the somewhat later Primal Scene fantasy. Freud's "Primal Scene" takes place in the beginning, when an infant sees his parents in the act of love, without in any way understanding that sight. Memory, according to Freud, holds on to the image of copulation until the child, between the ages of three and five, creates the Primal Scene fantasy, which is an Oedipal reverie. One of my former students, Cathy Caruth, caught me in making this same error, so that in my literary transformation of Freud into the Primal Scene of Instruction, I referred to such a Primal Scene as being at once oral and written. I would clarify this now by saying that the "oral" scene is the topos or Primal Scene proper, the negative moment of being influenced, a perpetually lost origin, while the "written" scene is the trope or Primal Scene fantasy. This means, in my terms, that in a poem a topos or rhetorical commonplace is *where* something can be *known*, but a trope or inventive turning is *when* something is desired or *willed*. Poems, as I have written often, are verbal utterances that cannot be regarded as being simply linguistic entities, because they manifest their will to utter *within* traditions of uttering, and as soon as you will that "within," your mode is discursive and topological as well as linguistic and tropological. As a Primal Scene, the Scene of Instruction is a Scene of Voicing; only when fantasized or troped does it become a Scene of Writing.

That Scene of Voicing founds itself upon the three models of family romance, transference, and catastrophe creation, and here I assert no novelty in my own formulation, since Dryden for one deals with the family romance of poets in his *Preface to Fables, Ancient and Modern*, with poetic transference in stating his preference for Juvenal over Horace in his *Discourse Concerning . . . Satire*, and even with a kind of catastrophe creation in his *Parallel Betwixt Poetry and Painting*. Dryden's mastery of dialectical contrasts between related poets seems to me now as good a guide for an antithetical practical criticism as I can find. Dryden is dialectical both in the open sense that Martin Price expounds, an empirical testing by trial and error, and also in the antithetical sense in which his description of one poet always points back to the contrasting poet from whom the critic is turning away.

What Dryden and the English tradition cannot provide is a third sense of critical dialectic, which in Freudian or Hegelian terms is the problematic notion of the overdetermination of language, and the consequent underdetermination of meaning. Hegelian terms do not much interest me, even in their Heideggerian and deconstructive revisions, since they seem to me just too far away from the pragmatic workings of poetry. Catastrophe creation, whether in its explicit Gnostic and Kabbalistic versions, or its implicit saga in the later Freud, contributes a model for distinguishing between the meaning of things in non-verbal acts, and the meaning of words in the linguistic and discursive acts of poetry. By uttering truths of desire within traditions of uttering, the poetic will also gives itself a series of overdetermined names. Gnosis and Kabbalah are attempts to explain how the overdetermination of Divine names has brought about an underdetermination of Divine meanings, a bringing about that is at once catastrophe and creation, a movement from fullness to emptiness.

Freud is not only the powerful mythologist Wittgenstein deplored, but also *the* inescapable mythologist of our age. His claims to science should be shrugged aside forever; that is merely his mask. Freudian literary criticism I remember comparing to the Holy Roman Empire: not holy, or Roman, or an empire; not Freudian, or literary, or criticism. Any critic, theoretical or practical, who tries to *use* Freud ends up being used *by* Freud. But Freud has usurped the role of the mind of our age, so that more than forty years after his death we have no common vocabulary for discussing the works of the spirit except what he gave us. Philosophers, hard or soft, speak only to other philosophers; theologians mutter only to theologians; our literary culture speaks to us in the language of Freud, even when the writer, like Nabokov or Borges, is violently anti-Freudian. Karl Kraus, being Freud's contemporary, said that psychoanalysis itself was the disease of which it purported to be the cure. We come after, and we must say that psychoanalysis itself is the culture of which it purports to be the description. If psychoanalysis and our literary culture no longer can be distinguished, then criticism is Freudian whether it wants to be or not. It relies upon Freudian models even while it pretends to be in thrall to Plato, Aristotle, Coleridge, or Hegel, and all that I urge is that it achieve a clearer sense of its bondage.

Freudian usurpation as a literary pattern is uniquely valuable to critics because it is *the* modern instance of poetic strength, of the agonistic clearing-away of cultural rivals, until the Freudian tropes have assumed the status of priority, while nearly all precedent tropes seem quite belated in comparison. When we think of earliness we now think in terms of primal repression, of the unconscious, of primary process, and of the drives or instincts, and all these are Freud's figurative language in his literary project of representing the civil wars of the psyche. The unconscious turns out alas not to be structured like *a* language, but to be structured like *Freud's* language, and the ego and superego, in their conscious aspects, are structured like Freud's own texts, for the very good reason that they *are* Freud's texts. We have become Freud's texts, and the *Imitatio Freudi* is the necessary pattern for the spiritual life in our time.

Ferenczi, a great martyr of that *Imitatio*, urged us in his apocalyptic *Thalassa*

> to drop once and for all the question of the beginning and end
> of life, and conceive the whole inorganic and organic world as a
> perpetual oscillating between the will to live and the will to die
> in which an absolute hegemony on the part of either life or death
> is never attained . . . it seems as though life had always to end
> catastrophically, even as it began, in birth, with a catastrophe.

Ferenczi is following yet also going beyond Freud's apocalyptic *Beyond the Pleasure Principle*, where the Nirvana Principle or Death Drive is described as an *"urge inherent in organic life to restore an earlier state of things"* which the living entity has been obliged to abandon under the pressure of external disturbing forces." Such an urge, Freud insists, takes priority over the Pleasure Principle, and so *"the aim of all life is death."* Three years later, in *The Ego and the Id*, Freud speculated upon the two aboriginal catastrophes dimly repeated in every human development under the illstarred dominance of the death-drive. Our curious pattern of sexual development, particularly the supposed latency period between the ages of five and twelve, is related to those great cataclysms when all the cosmos became ice and again when the oceans went dry and life scrambled up upon the shore. These are Freud's scientist versions of the Gnostic escapades of the Demiurge, or the great trope of the Breaking of the Vessels in the Lurianic Kabbalah.

But why should Freud have been haunted by images of catastrophe, however creative? It is not, I think, hyperbolic to observe that, for the later Freud, human existence is quite as catastrophic a condition as it was for Pascal and for Kierkegaard, for Dostoevsky and for Schopenhauer. There is a crack in everything that God has made, is one of Emerson's dangerously cheerful apothegms. In Freud, the fissure in us between primary process and secondary process insures that each of us is her or his own worst enemy, exposed endlessly to the remorseless attacks of the superego, whose relation to the hapless ego is shockingly like the Gnostic vision of the relation of Yahweh to human beings.

The horror of the family romance, as Freud expounds it, is one version of this human fissure, since the child attempts to trope one of the stances of freedom, yet makes the parents into the numinous shadows that Nietzsche called ancestor gods. As a revision of the Primal Scene, the family romance's falsification shows us that Oedipal fantasies are only ironies, or beginning moments merely, for truly strong poets and poems. This limitation makes the family romance a model neither catastrophic nor creative enough, and gives us the necessity for advancing to another model, the psychoanalytic transference, whose workings are closer to the dialectical crises of poetic texts.

The Freudian transference, as I have attempted to demonstrate elsewhere, depends for its pattern upon the sublimely crazy myth that Freud sets forth in *Totem and Taboo*. Briefly and crudely, the totem is the psychoanalyst and the taboo is the transference. All the ambivalences of the Oedipal situation are transferred from the individual's past to the analytical encounter, and the agon thus threatens to act out again the erotic defeat and tragedy of every psyche whatsoever. Against this threat, Freud sought to muster the strength of what he called "working through" but his beautiful late essay, "Analysis Terminable and Interminable," confesses that the benign powers of the totemic analyst tend to be confounded by the malign intensity of each patient's fantasy-making power. Working-through is replaced by repetition, and so by the death drive, which deeply contaminates all repressive defenses. This mutual contamination of drive and defense is the clearest link between Freud's visionary cosmos and the arena of Post-Enlightenment poetry. Contamination is not a trope but the necessary condition of all troping (or all defending); another word for contamination here might be "blurring" or even "slipping." There may be boundaries between the ego and the id, but they blur always in the transference situation, just as poet and precursor slip together in the Scene of Instruction or influence relationship.

I am suggesting that neither my use of Freud's images of Oedipal ambivalence, nor those images themselves, are generally read strongly enough. Identification in the Oedipal agon is not the introjection of the paternal superego but rather is a violent narcissistic metamorphosis. I rely here upon a formulation by the psychoanalyst Joseph H. Smith:

> The poet as poet is taken over by a power with which he has chosen to wrestle. It is not essentially a matter of passivity. The experience of a negative moment that coincides with the negative moment of a precursor is to be understood as an achieved catastrophe. It reaches beyond the ordinary understanding of oedipal identification to those primal internalizations which are and yet cannot be because no boundary is yet set across which anything could be said to be internalized. They are, rather, boundary-establishing phenomena which presuppose the possibility of internalization proper. But who is to say that there is not such a reestablishment of boundaries even in oedipal identifications?.

I would go further than Smith in suggesting that every ambivalent identification with another self, writer or reader, parent or child, is an agon that makes ghostlier the demarcations between self and other. That blurring or slipping creates, in that it restores the abyss in the Gnostic sense, where the abyss is the true, alien godhead that fell away into time when the Demiurge sickened to a catastrophic false creation. The transference shakes the foundations of the ego more authentically than the family romance does, even though the transference is an artificial Eros and the family romance a natural one. After all, the transference, like a poem, is a lie against time, a resistance that must be overcome if we are to accept unhappy truth. Let us call a transference a kind of parody of a Sublime poem, since the taboo protects the totem analyst from the patient, yet no taboo can protect a precursor poet from the fresh strength or daemonic counter-sublime of an authentic new poet. To call a transference a parody of a poem is to suggest that catastrophe creations and family romances are also parodies of poetic texts. How can a parody be a model or paradigm for interpretation? We are accustomed to thinking of poems as parodies of prior poems, or even as parodies of paradigms. Yet reversing the order gets us closer, I am convinced, to the actualities of poetic interpretation.

Yeats wrote that "Plato thought nature but a spume that plays/Against a ghostly paradigm of things." Freud thought of nature very differently, yet he had his own version of a transcendentalism, in what he called "reality testing." Yet his paradigms for object attachments play uncanny tricks upon nature, or perhaps rely upon the uncanny tricks that nature seems to play with human sexuality. I go back here to the passages I quoted from the *Three Essays on the Theory of Sexuality* earlier in this chapter. The child sucking at his mother's breast becomes the paradigm for all sexual pleasure in later life, and Freud asserts that to begin with, sexual activity props itself upon the vital function of nourishment by the mother's milk. Thumb-sucking and the sensual smacking of the lips then give Freud the three characteristics of infantile sexual manifestation. These are: (1) propping, at the origin, upon a vital somatic function; (2) auto-eroticism, or the lack of a sexual object; (3) domination of sexual aim by an erotogenic zone; here, the lips. It is at this point in his discussion that Freud makes one of his uncanniest leaps, relying upon his extraordinary trope of *Anlehnung* or propping (or anaclisis, as Strachey oddly chose to translate it). While the propping of the sexual drive upon the vital order still continues, the sexual drive finds its first object outside the infant's body in the mother's breast, and in the milk ensuing from it. Suddenly Freud surmises that just at the time the infant is capable of forming a total idea of the mother, quite abruptly the infant loses the initial object of the mother's breast, and tragically is thrown back upon auto-eroticism. Consequently, the sexual drive has no proper object again until after the latency period has transpired, and adolescence begins. Hence that dark and infinitely suggestive Freudian sentence: "The finding of an object is in fact a re-finding of it."

Thus human sexuality, alas, on this account has not had, from its very origins, any real object. The only real object was milk, which belongs to the vital order. Hence the sorrows and the authentic anguish of all human erotic quest, hopelessly seeking to rediscover an object, which never was the true object anyway. All human sexuality is thus tropological, whereas we all of us desperately need and long for it to be literal. As for sexual excitation, it is merely what Wrestling Sigmund terms a marginal effect (*Nebenwirkung*), because it reflects always the propping process, which after all has a double movement, of initial leaning, and then deviation or swerving. As Laplanche says, expounding Freud: "Sexuality in its entirety is in the slight deviation, the *clinamen* from the function." Or as I would phrase it, our sexuality is in its very origins a misprision, a strong misreading, on the infant's part, of the vital order. At the crossing (Laplanche calls it a "breaking or turning point") of the erotogenic zones, our sexuality is a continual crisis, which I would now say is not so much mimicked or parodied by the High Romantic crisis poem, but rather our sexuality itself is a mimicry or parody of the statelier action of the will which is figured forth in the characteristic Post-Enlightenment strong poem.

I call Freud, in the context of these uncanny notions, "Wrestling Sigmund," because again he is a poet of Sublime agon, here an agon between sexuality and the vital order. Our sexuality is like Jacob, and the vital order is like that one among the Elohim with whom our wily and heroic ancestor wrestled, until he had won the great name of Israel. Sexuality and Jacob triumph, but at the terrible expense of a crippling. All our lives long we search in vain, unknowingly, for the lost object, when even that object was a *clinamen* away from the true aim. And yet we search incessantly, do experience satisfactions, however marginal, and win our real if limited triumph over the vital order. Like Jacob, we keep passing Penuel, limping on our hips.

How can I conclude? Paradigms are not less necessary, but more so, when the power and the originality of strong poets surpass all measure, as Freud and the Yahwist go beyond all comparison. Sexuality, in Freud's great tropological vision, is at once a catastrophe creation, a transference, and a family romance. The blessing, in the Yahwist's even stronger vision, is yet more a catastrophe creation, a transference, a family romance. Those strategems of the spirit, those stances and attitudes, those positions of freedom, or ratios of revision and crossings, that I have invoked as aids to reading strong poems of the Post-Enlightenment, are revealed as being not wholly inadequate to the interpretation of the Yahwist and of Freud. So I conclude with the assertion that strength demands strength. If we are to break through normative or weak misreadings of the Yahwist and of Freud, of Wordsworth and Whitman and Stevens, then we require strong paradigms, and these I have called upon agonistic tradition to provide.

ROBERT POLZIN

The Second Address of Moses:
Deuteronomy 5:1b–28:68

The reporting context of [Deuteronomy] 4:41–43 provides a concluding frame to Moses' first address, while 4:44–5:1a constitutes the introductory frame to Moses' second, main address. Like the introduction to Moses' first address (1:1–5), the author's framing context here situates the words of Moses in space and time, giving the circumstances in which Moses' reported speech was uttered. These details selectively repeat information found in the previously reported speech of Moses.

The core of the second address is the so-called Deuteronomic lawcode (12:1–26:15). Before I undertake my central task of examining those utterances within this second address whose phraseological, psychological, and temporal composition have an important bearing on our understanding of the ideological composition of the book, I want to give an illustration of the various ways in which the surface planes of an utterance may be related to its deeper ideological plane within the overall composition of a work.

Certain aspects of utterances' phraseological, temporal, or psychological composition may affect their deeper ideological point of view; other aspects may not. Deut. 5:1–5 illustrates both cases. The first few verses of Moses' second address offer us a good example of how variation on the plane of phraseology, or on another surface plane, in some cases is concurrent with a shift in point of view on the ideological plane, yet in other cases is not. The terminology employed here is drawn from Uspensky (1973). Basic to his approach are the following points:

    i. The most basic point of view of a work is *ideological* or evaluative; it comprises that system of viewing the world according to which the work is

From *Moses and the Deuteronomist: A Literary Study of the Deuteronomic History* (Part One). ©
1980 by Robert Polzin. The Seabury Press and Harper & Row, 1980.

conceptually unified. It is the "ultimate semantic authority" of a work, in
Bakhtin's terms. Often this level is the least accessible to formalization, for its
analysis relies to a degree on intuitive understanding.

ii. The *phraseological* plane appears to be coextensive with "the plane of
expression" in Hjelmslev's terms (1961), or similar to the signifier aspect of
the verbal sign in de Saussure's terms (1966). Since Uspensky makes the point
that this plane is often the only one on which we can detect changes in the
author's position, I think it is safe to infer that this plane refers to the surface
of the text in general and to the opposition there of reported to reporting
speech in particular, and that the other surface planes refer to specific aspects
of the phraseological plane which are considered important enough by Uspensky
to merit the designation of a special term.

iii. The *spatio-temporal* plane involves the location in time and space from
whose perspective an author, narrator, or character speaks in a work. In
Deuteronomy the temporal plane has more relevance than the spatial plane.
As this analysis of Deuteronomy is meant to illustrate, the multiplicity of
temporal points of view in a work is often quite complex.

iv. The *psychological* plane involves whether the author or narrator describes what a person says or does from a point of view that is internal or
external to the person described, to the person speaking, or to the person or
persons spoken to. If, for example, an author transmits information that is
generally not accessible to the normal onlooker, he is taking an internal
psychological point of view. Most often, these psychological elements are
conveyed by distinct phraseological elements of a text.

v. It is to be emphasized once again that the composition of a work on
one plane may or may not concur with its composition on another plane.

We may now proceed to 5:1-5, in which Moses speaks to Israel (italics
added):

> Hear, O Israel, the statutes and the ordinances which *I* speak in
> *your* hearing this day, and *you* shall learn them and be careful to
> do them. (2) The LORD *our* God made a covenant with *us* in Horeb.
> (3) Not with *our* fathers did the LORD make this covenant, but with
> *us*, who are all of *us* here alive this day. (4) The LORD spoke with
> *you* face to face at the mountain, out of the midst of the fire, (5) while
> *I* stood between the LORD and *you* at that time, to declare to *you*
> the word of the LORD; for *you* were afraid because of the fire, and
> *you* did not go up into the mountain.

There is a clear phraseological alternation in Moses' utterances here between
an "I vs. you" form in vv. 1, 4 and 5, and an "our/us" form in verses 2 and

3. One might well ask whether a shift is thereby indicated on other surface planes as well. Also do these surface shifts involve an ideological shift as well?

It is easy to see that this phraseological shift also involves a change of perspective on the psychological plane. Moses alternates his point of view between one who presents himself as above his hearers in special knowledge and one who emphasizes shared experiences with his fellow Israelites. The choice of the "I vs. you" form indicates a distinction between speaker and listener, and Moses thereby speaks from the position of his self-consciousness as declarer-teacher of God's word. The use of the "our/us" form indicates no such distinction, and emphasizes a shared status between speaker and hearer. The *teacher* imparts knowledge which his hearers are not presumed to know; the *fellow Israelite* speaks of matters experienced in common with his hearers. The shift involves an overt presentation of the prophetic status of Moses as opposed to a status shared with his fellow Israelites. The question naturally arises whether this phraseological/psychological shift in perspective necessarily indicates, at this point, a shift on the ideological plane as well, especially since we have by now discovered in the book hints of an ideological dialogue that does involve the question of Moses' unique status.

. . . This phraseological shift from the "I vs. you" form to the "our/us" form does not *necessarily* involve utterances belonging to differing ideologies. Let us see why this is so.

In 4:1–28, which emphasizes retributive justice and the nonuniqueness of Moses, Moses exhorts the Israelites not to forget "the covenant of the LORD your God, which he made with you" (4:23). On the other hand, in the second part of the chapter, which emphasizes grace, free election, and the uniqueness of Israel (4:29–39), Moses reminds the people that God will not "forget the covenant with your fathers which he swore to them" (4:31). When we add to this the information found in 5:2–3, namely, that the covenant made "with us in Horeb" was "not with our fathers," we are able, thus far in our reading of the book, to come to two conclusions about the concurrence of the phraseological and the ideological planes of 5:1–5:

i. It is clear from chapters 4 and 5 that the phraseological distinction between "covenant with you" and "covenant with your fathers" in chapter 4, and "covenant in Horeb" and "covenant with our fathers" in chapter 5 involves an ideological distinction as well. A speaker's overt identification with the covenant made at Horeb indicates an ideological point of view *concentrating* on retributive justice and the nonuniqueness of Moses and Israel. On the other hand, a speaker's identification with the covenant made with our/your fathers seems to involve an ideological viewpoint *centering* on mercy, grace, and the unique statuses of Moses and Israel.

ii. Nevertheless, *either* covenant is spoken of as:

"with *you*" (4:23) or "with *us*" (5:2):   Horeb Covenant
"with *your* fathers" (4:31) or "with
our fathers" (5:3):   Patriarchal Covenant

We can see immediately that the retributive ideology can alternate between the "I vs. you" form and the "our/us" form. For example, the retributive voice alternates between an "I vs. you" form in 4:23 and an "our/us" form in 5:2–3. This voice, therefore, may be exercising the same phraseological shift within chapter 5 itself which it does between chapters 4 and 5. Although chapters 4 and 5 do not give us enough information, we may assume that the ideological voice of grace or mercy also speaks in both the "I vs. you" and the "our/us" tones. Therefore, in 5:1–5 the phraseological alternation between the "I vs. you" and the "our/us" forms has significance on the psychological plane but not necessarily on the ideological plane.

An inference can be drawn from the preceding analysis: since the phraseological shift of the forms we have been discussing (between "your" and "our") involves a psychological shift but not necessarily an ideological one, both voices of the basic dialogue about Moses' unique status as prophet of God appear to be in general agreement at least concerning Moses' role as one who both declares (*l*e*haggîd*) and teaches (*l*e*lammed*) God's word. Moreover, both voices seem to be in agreement that this prophetic role does not inhibit them from describing Moses as speaking from the point of view of his self-perception as an Israelite, sharing the same knowledge and experience as his fellow Israelites. *The conflict over Moses' unique role centers rather on whether there could ever be another prophet like him.* As we by now have seen in a number of different contexts, the Deuteronomist's constant and obvious exaltation of Moses paradoxically contributes to the ultimate exaltation of the one who quotes him throughout the Book of Deuteronomy, the Deuteronomic narrator himself.

THE SURFACE COMPOSITION OF THE SECOND MOSAIC ADDRESS

1. Whereas Moses' first address is, by more than half, *his* reporting of speech in *direct* discourse, over half of his second address, i.e., the lawcode of chapters 12–26, consists of his reporting of speech in a manner other than by direct discourse. More specifically, if we limit ourselves to Moses' reporting of God's words, Moses' utterances shift between addresses from a concentration on reporting God's words in direct discourse to a concentration on reporting them in a manner that largely destroys the contours which heretofore have distinguished God's words from Moses'. The importance of this distinction

in depicting Moses in his practice of reporting the word of God is great. Since the Deuteronomic lawcode is phrased as a direct address of Moses to the people, it is this compositional fact that makes it much more difficult to decide, with any clear-cut boundaries, which utterances are meant to represent the reported speech of God, which are the commenting and responding reactions of Moses himself, and which utterances combine both.

In Moses' first address it was much easier to distinguish between Moses' *declaring* God's word and his *teaching* or *interpreting* that word. Thus, that address divided itself neatly into chapters 1 to 3 on one hand (Moses the *maggîd*) and chapter 4 on the other (Moses the *mᵉlammed*). In the second address, these two Mosaic functions are much more synthetically combined. This is true in the Mosaic utterances that frame the lawcode: chapters 5:1–11:32 and 26:16–28:68 contain proportionately far fewer quotations of God in direct discourse than the first address; this is also true of the Deuteronomic lawcode itself which quotes the LORD in direct discourse only in 17:16b and 18:17–20.

These two functions of Moses' role as mouthpiece of God—to declare and to interpret his word—correspond neatly to aspects of how we receive or accept another speaker's speech. On the one hand, the basic tendency in reacting to another's speech "may be to maintain its integrity and authenticity; a language may strive to forge hard and fast boundaries for reported speech." On the other hand, the basic tendency might be to infiltrate "reported speech with authorial retort and commentary in deft and subtle ways . . . to obliterate its boundaries."

For example, large, clear-cut blocks of reported speech in direct discourse normally will be indicative of the first tendency, and Moses' first address illustrates this situation. On the other hand, his second address, with its wholesale shift away from the reporting of God's words in direct discourse, together with its abundance of commentary and response, illustrates the second tendency. When we couple these facts with the authoritative source of the utterances Moses is reporting (*God* spoke them), we see that there is an immediate build-up in the phraseological composition of the book concerning Moses' status as a mouthpiece of God. In the first address, Moses is depicted mostly as reporting God's word by respecting the clear-cut boundaries of that speech through the predominant use of direct discourse; in the second address, reports of God's word in direct discourse almost completely disappear. God is only quoted in direct discourse nine times in twenty-four chapters: 5:6–21, 28–31; 9:12, 13–14, 23; 10:1–2, 11; 17:16; 18:17–20. Most of these cases occur in Moses' reporting context. Given the tendency of the second address to synthesize reporting and reported voices, these few direct utterances seem therefore to have an important function which we will attempt to identify below.

Other aspects of the second address's phraseological composition can be mentioned here. Moses is described as framing the reported words of God by means of his reporting utterances of 5:1–11:32 and 26:16–28:68. One can analyze the speech of a *character* of a work in the same way as one analyzes the speech of an author or a narrator of a work. Just as we . . . are now analyzing the reported utterances of [Deuteronomy's] hero, Moses, so in turn each of Moses' addresses may be analyzed from the point of view of the *reporting* utterances of Moses as well as from the point of view of the *reported* utterances they contain. Within the second address, Moses' reporting frames are to the lawcode of 12–26 what in the book itself the narrator's reporting frames are to all of Moses' addresses contained therein. Stated in this way, we can see that the over-all composition of Deuteronomy is one in which we read how Moses is described as declaring and interpreting the word of God as a panoramic preview of how the Deuteronomic narrator will describe and interpret the word of Moses in Joshua–2 Kings.

2. There is an aspect of the second address which confirms our interpretation of Moses' more intense depiction there as declarer and interpreter of God's words. Although the phrases "God of *our* fathers" or "*our* God" appear at least twenty-three times in the book, we find them only once in the lawcode, which overwhelmingly prefers the "I vs. you" form, and therefore the lawcode predominantly employs phrases such as "your God." Thus, although Moses' utterances are many times longer in the second address than in the first, the first address describes Moses as using the "our" form eleven times, but only twice does he directly use this form in the second address. This is an indication of a psychological shift between the two addresses. Moses at chapter 5 leaves off speaking to his audience sometimes as a fellow Israelite, and henceforth (apart from 5:2 and 6:4) speaks only from the viewpoint of his role as teacher, insofar as the "I vs. you" and "our/us" forms are concerned.

The predominant *psychological* viewpoint of the second address is immediately set up by the content of chapter 5, whose main intent is to describe the circumstances that led to the privileged information Moses transmits in his utterances. All the Israelites heard the voice of God giving the ten words, but only Moses, at the elders' request and God's command, hears God's further words to be reported to the rest of the people. This is the main psychological perspective of the second address.

The second address's *temporal* composition is predominantly future-oriented, just as the first address was predominantly past-oriented. The temporal orientation of the second address is divided up into utterances that address the context of Israel's *immediate* future in the land (the lawcode), and utterances that describe the *distant* future of punishment and devastation (e.g., chapter

28). The immediate past is sometimes addressed, as in chapter 5 and in chapters 9 and 10. But even in these cases, it appears to be an opportunity to draw some concrete lesson about the future that is motivating Moses' references. Thus chapter 5 prepares us for Moses' authoritative pronouncement of the lawcode; and chapters 9 and 10 describe past circumstances that explain why God will allow a disobedient people to possess the land.

THE IDEOLOGICAL PROBLEMS OF THE SECOND ADDRESS

At first reading, Moses' second address would seem to contradict the tentative conclusion we reached as a result of our analysis of his first address [elsewhere]. The conclusion reached there was that the Deuteronomic voice which tends to emphasize the uniqueness of Moses or Israel tends also to emphasize hope through the grace and mercy of God, whereas those utterances that appear to diminish Moses' or Israel's unique status tend also to emphasize law and God's retributive justice. But Moses' second address is filled with utterance upon utterance that exalt and emphasize Moses' and Israel's unique statuses. The cumulative effect of these statements appears to be that there will never be another prophet like Moses and that no nation has enjoyed such a special status with the LORD as Israel. And all this in the unremitting context of God's retributive justice and covenant of law with Israel. This context appears to contradict the tentative conclusions we reached in our analysis of the first address.

It is no surprise that this address, which contains an extensive lawcode of fifteen chapters, would be dominated by an ideological voice concerned above all with retributive justice and a covenant of law, rather than with mercy and a covenant of grace. What *is* surprising is that such a block of material, so obviously dominated in this way, also succeeds by a number of interlocking devices in diminishing the unique statuses of Moses and Israel at the same time as it unceasingly employs utterances that seem to exalt them. This paradox is what we want to describe from a compositional point of view. The easier part of our task will be to describe how extensively the unique statuses of Moses and Israel are advanced in the second address. (The frequency and intensity of Moses' rhetoric concerning God's retributive justice is so great in the second address that it will be assumed in the following discussion.)

The obvious way in which Moses' unique status vis-à-vis other prophets is not only underlined but also advanced in the second address is by Moses' account of his commissioning by God in chapter 5. Whereas in the first address Moses only states that the LORD had commanded him to teach the Israelites commandments and ordinances (e.g., 4:5), here at the beginning of his second address he describes the circumstances which led up to this command and reports the actual command in direct discourse. After the people approach Moses and request him to "hear all that the LORD our God will say; and speak to us all that the LORD our God will say" (5:27), God tells Moses:

> "I have heard the words of this people, which they have spoken to you; they have rightly said all that they have spoken. Oh that they had such a mind as this always, to fear me and to keep all my commandments, that it might go well with them, and with their children forever! Go and say to them, 'Return to your tents.' But you, stand here by me, and I will tell you all the commandments and the statutes and the ordinances which you shall teach them, that they may do them in the land which I give them to possess."
> (5:28-31)

The point is clear: after hearing the voice of God speak the words of the decalogue, the people fear that they cannot hear more and live. God agrees with this position and commands Moses to teach the people all the command- ments, statutes, and ordinances he will tell him. The lawcode is precisely a report of Moses' teaching the people what God had told him. Moses did not in fact die as they thought they would had they heard the words of God which *he* had heard.

The rest of the words of Moses in Deuteronomy, coming before chapter 12 and after chapter 26, comprise what Moses said to prepare the people to hear the word of God contained within the lawcode, and subsequently to spell out for them its implications. 5:22-31 comprises Moses' account of how God commissioned him to speak the central words of the book, the "Mosaic" lawcode of chapters 12-26. 5:28-31 are the authenticating words of God that show the basis for the unique teaching role Moses enjoys in the Book of Deuteron- omy. Through them we see why "there has not arisen a prophet since in Israel like Moses, whom the LORD knew face to face" (34:10). These words are most directly explained by what Moses says and does through and in his second address. And within this second address, Deuteronomy 5 contains Moses' account of the vision that authenticates the central role he plays in the book, just as Isaiah 6 does with respect to the rest of that book.

Utterances advancing Israel's unique status are also abundantly present in the second address. The following is representative:

> For you are a people holy (*qds* = "set apart") to the LORD your God; the LORD your God has chosen you to be a people for his own possession out of all the peoples that are on the face of the earth.
> (7:6)

What is clear, therefore, about the utterances of the second address is their frequent insistence on the unique statuses of Moses and Israel. But there *are* a few utterances that seem to challenge the main position of the address. A direct challenge to Moses' unique status as teacher of Israel is launched directly at the *source* of Moses' central role in the book, the authenticating utterance of God in 5:28–31. For Moses repeats his account of this divine utterance within the lawcode itself in 18:17–20. This account of the divine commissioning uses Moses' words against himself, as it were, by revealing that *another* "Moses" is part of the package; *his* commission also is to report to the people God's word:

> And the LORD said to me, "They have rightly said all that they have spoken. I will raise up for them a prophet like you from among their brethren; and I will put my words in his mouth, and he shall speak to them all that I command him. And whoever will not give heed to my words which he shall speak in my name, I myself will require it of him."
>
> (18:17–18)

A challenge to all the many utterances about Israel's unique status seems to be found in 9:4–5:

> Do not say in your heart, after the LORD your God has thrust the Anakim out before you, "It is because of my righteousness that the LORD has brought me in to possess this land"; *whereas it is because of the wickedness of these nations that the LORD is driving them out before you*. Not because of your righteousness or the uprightness of your heart are you going in to possess their land; *but because of the wickedness of these nations the LORD your God is driving them out from before you*, and that he may confirm the word which the LORD swore to your fathers, to Abraham, to Isaac, and to Jacob.
>
> (emphasis added)

This passage, perhaps not as directly contradictory as 18:17–18, via-à-vis Moses, still casts a shadow on all the many overt statements about God's special treatment of Israel, especially those found in chapters 9 and 10. The special relationship proposed by Moses is to be interpreted against a universal situation in which the ultimate motive for God's giving of the land to Israel is retributive in nature, i.e., to punish for *their* sins the nations dispossessed by Israel. *And what happened to those nations will happen, therefore, to the Israelites also when they disobey God.* It seems, after all, that Israel is no different from the other nations who in the past also have enjoyed God's blessings (for they *do* possess the land which Israel is to take). Israel is simply benefiting from *their* disobedience just as other nations will benefit from Israel's disobedience. And as we shall soon see, the statement about the word sworn to the fathers, and the ideological position it represents, is effectively neutralized by the retributive statements that precede it.

Although 18:17–20 and 9:4–5 are each in its own way a powerful attack on the overtly preponderant message of the second address, it will be hard to take them seriously, and easy to treat them as clumsy additions to the book, unless it can be shown that these two explicit statements coincide exactly with other aspects of the surface composition of the second address. A careful compositional analysis of the phraseological, temporal, and psychological planes of the second address will show in fact that the overt exaltation of Moses and Israel is paradoxically accompanied by a subtle but effective campaign which aims at diminishing their unique roles. We will see how the second address is the central stage in which, as the book develops, one voice progressively gets louder in its portrayal of Moses' and Israel's unique divine election, at the same time as *another* voice, in quiet opposition to the first, is progressively and ever more effectively challenging those statuses. The first voice is a disguised servant of the second.

THE INTERRELATIONSHIPS BETWEEN THE SURFACE AND DEEP COMPOSITION OF MOSES' SECOND ADDRESS

1. Since the surface planes of the second address seem to result in a point of view that overwhelmingly advances a covenant of retributive justice as the broad context for the depiction of Moses as *the* prophet of an Israel that has been especially chosen by Yahweh, it might be helpful to review how this viewpoint is built up in the second address, and where there are utterances and compositional devices that seem to oppose or alter the predominant position expressed there.

If we begin by examining the broad context of God's retributive justice, which is so predominant in this address that we have not felt it necessary to quote illustrative examples, we shall see that the surface composition of this address does nevertheless contain a number of utterances that do not seem to fit into this broad context. Most of these utterances invoke the oath or covenant which God swore to the fathers, usually in connection with the gift of the land. Consider the following:

> that the LORD may turn the fierceness of his anger, and show you
> mercy, and have compassion on you and multiply you, as he swore
> to your fathers.
>
> (13:17b)

Here is an utterance that speaks of a God of mercy and compassion rather than of strict retribution. But such an idea is immediately colored by the following verse:

> if you obey the voice of the LORD your God, keeping all his
> commandments which I command you this day, and doing what
> is right in the sight of the LORD your God.
>
> (13:18)

One way, therefore, of neutralizing the utterance dealing with the idea of an apparently unconditional covenant made with the fathers is to prefix it with, or immediately add to it, an utterance that invokes a necessary condition of obedience. So that when Moses states,

> You shall remember the LORD your God for it is he who gives you
> power to get wealth; that he may confirm his covenant which he
> swore to your fathers, as at this day,
>
> (8:18)

he immediately follows it with:

> And if you forget the LORD your God and go after other gods and
> serve them and worship them, I solemnly warn you this day that
> you shall surely perish.
>
> (8:19)

Or consider the pattern of preceding an utterance that invokes the promise made to the fathers with an utterance demanding the necessary precondition of obedience:

> All the commandment which I command you this day you shall
> be careful to do, that you may live and multiply and go in and
> possess the land which the LORD swore to give to your fathers.
>
> (8:1)

Besides the texts just mentioned, we may cite as further examples 6:3, 10–15, 23–24; 7:6–11, 12–13; 10:11–13, 15–17; 11:8–9, 20–21; 12:1; 13:17–18; 26:14–15. This pattern attempts to effect a synthesis of the covenant with the fathers and the covenant at Horeb, and to make the latter a precondition for the former. Obedience thereby becomes a condition of God's apparently unconditional oath to the fathers.

We now see more clearly what our analysis of 4:1–40 and 5:1–5 tentatively indicated: the distinction between the convenant with the fathers and the covenant at Horeb is absolutely basic to the ideological tension within the book. The presence in an utterance in Deuteronomy of a phrase such as "the

God of our fathers" or "the covenant made with the fathers" or "the oath which God swore to the fathers" brings with it associations of mercy, grace, and divine election that are at odds with the ultimate viewpoint of the book on the justice of God. Whenever such concepts are brought to mind by these phrases, the basic evaluative stance of the book finds it necessary to neutralize them either by an overt bracketing of them with controlling retributive statements or else by an insinuation that the covenant at Horeb is *somehow* a necessary condition for the fulfillment of the unconditional oath and covenant God swore to the fathers.

This last point brings up the only other major tradition threatening the predominantly retributive nature of the second address: in spite of Israel's disobedience at Horeb, God still gave them the land. Chapters 9 and 10 deal primarily with this topic, and the Deuteronomic voice of retribution succeeds in transforming this merciful act of the LORD into an act of justice by means of two short verses. 9:4–5 effectively neutralizes God's merciful gift of the land by putting it in the wider context of his just punishment of the wicked nations Israel will dispossess. These verses illustrate very well the paradoxical situation in which the Deuteronomist found himself: the oath to the fathers and Israel's disobedience at Horeb were too much a part of his heritage completely to ignore in his account. He therefore had to invoke both ideas within a broader context of retribution that effectively renders powerless the threat they posed to his basic position.

When we recognize the pattern of apparently admitting the unconditional covenant with the fathers, but actually neutralizing its troublesome features in the ways we have just outlined, we see also that the unique status of Israel, so unlike the other nations, is also effectively undermined. No matter how often the second address refers to Israel's special status, as in 7:6, the basic attitude of this address is epitomized in passages such as:

> Like the nations that the LORD makes to perish before you, so shall you perish, because you would not obey the voice of the LORD your God.
>
> (8:20)

If the second address consistently and overtly counters any utterance threatening the retributive justice of God, and therefore emphasizes that Israel is ultimately not unique among the other nations, this means that such a strategy is carried out upon the surface composition of this address. We may say, therefore, that the phraseological, psychological, and temporal planes of the address largely concur with its deeper ideological plane, insofar as the conditional nature of God's covenant and Israel's relatively nonunique status are concerned.

When it comes to the question of *Moses'* role as outlined in the second address, it seems that its surface composition almost never concurs with its deep ideological plane. As we described above, the overt viewpoint of the address is one which consistently emphasizes Moses' unique role as God's greatest mouthpiece. It is important now to see how the surface composition in this regard is subtly but effectively undermined by the "ultimate semantic authority" of the book, so that Moses' role in this address even helps to neutralize the voice of the unique election of Israel and the unconditional promise made to the fathers. We must now turn to the lawcode itself.

2. The phraseological composition of the lawcode contained in the second address presents us with the book's most sustained example of the voice that exalts Moses' unique authority. Whereas Moses quoted the ten commandments of the LORD in direct discourse, that is, God was allowed to speak to the Israelites directly, here in the lawcode it is *Moses* who speaks in direct address to the Israelites concerning "the statutes and laws that you shall be careful to observe in the land which the LORD, the God of your fathers, is giving you to occupy as long as you live on earth" (12:1). The practical effect of this compositional device is to raise the authority of the Mosaic voice to a position almost indistinguishable from that of the voice of God. Conversely, in this address the direct voice of God is almost totally silenced. Not that the distinction between God's word and Moses' goes unrecognized here. Rather it seems to be the effect of this most obvious compositional aspect of the lawcode to obliterate the practical importance of the distinction between God's word and Moses'. We hope to see how this device serves the basic ideological stance of the book.

Through Moses' reporting style, we have the promulgation of a lawcode in which a maximum amount of reporting response and commentary (Moses'? the Deuteronomist's?) has been allowed openly to infuse what we may describe as the reported speech of God, insofar as Deuteronomy 5 characterizes the lawcode. What we normally would have expected, and up to this point indeed have found in the book, the Deuteronomist now deliberately avoids. That is, except for parts of the frame-break of 10:6–9, Moses' speech heretofore has been characterized by a reverence for the word of God that always made clear on the surface of the text when he was *reporting* the speech of the LORD and when he was retorting and commenting upon it. This contrast between the subordinate style of Moses' first address and the supremely authoritative promulgation of the lawcode contained in his second address raises for us a central compositional aspect of our analysis of this book. What effect upon the reader's perception of Moses, the hero of this book, does such a shift accomplish? There can be no doubt that the Deuteronomist utilizes this device to manipulate the responses of his intended audience; the nature of this manipulation is crucial here. I want now to attempt to characterize in some detail how and to what degree our perception of Moses is thereby affected. The importance of this topic lies in the intimate connection between the respective roles of the narrator and the hero of this book, and in the compositional means whereby, as we have already seen, the Deuteronomist programs his audience's perception of his narrator by directing their continuing confrontations with the hero of this part of his history.

We can use the conclusions of our analysis of Moses' first address to help us solve the puzzle surrounding the sudden compositional shift embodied in the lawcode. We saw above that the basic compositional structure of Moses' first address mirrors that of the Deuteronomic History. That is, just as the first address neatly divided itself into a Moses who factually reports *God's* words in direct discourse (Deut. 1–3), then analyzes and evaluates their significance for the subsequent history of Israel (Deut. 4), so also the Deuteronomic History neatly divides itself into a narrator who first factually reports *Moses'* words in direct discourse (Deut.), and then himself analyzes and evaluates their significance in the subsequent history of his people (Josh.–2 Kings).

But the strategy of the Deuteronomist does not, of course, end with the first address. If Moses can first report God's words, then interpret their significance for his audience, so also can the Deuteronomic narrator. But Moses' authority and preeminence can be, indeed must be, advanced to accomplish the purposes of the author apparent in the composition of the book. The overall message of Deuteronomy seems to me to be based on the following: as Moses authoritatively conveyed and interpreted the word of God, so the narrator authoritatively conveys and interprets the words of Moses; as Moses teaches, so does the narrator. The first stage of this strategy, the first address, is to show Moses first reporting, then commenting on God's words; the second stage, that is, the second address and especially the lawcode, has Moses both reporting and interpreting God's words *at one and the same time and in such a way as to make it impossible to distinguish which parts of the lawcode represent reported speech of God and which represent the reporting speech of Moses*. In the first address, "the explicitness and inviolability of the boundaries between authorial and reported speech reach the utmost limits," to quote Voloshinov's words from another context. In the second address, Moses' reporting speech "strives to break down the self-contained compactness of the reported speech, to resolve it, to obliterate its boundaries" (ibid). What the Deuteronomist is gradually obliterating, as his narrator's long report of Moses' various addresses advances, is the distinction between the teaching authority of his hero and that of his narrator. The second address, and the Mosaic lawcode that is central to it and the Book of Deuteronomy itself, is the crucial stage in the Deuteronomist's over-all plan.

The Deuteronomic History, and the Book of Deuteronomy as its panoramic preview, vibrate with the following hermeneutic ratio: as the word of God is to the word of Moses, so the word of Moses is to the word of the Deuteronomic narrator. So that the supreme blurring of the words of God and of Moses in the lawcode serves the same purpose as the other devices of the Deuteronomist we have seen [elsewhere] that overtly exalted the unique status of Moses: it contributes toward a subtle but powerful exaltation of the authority of the narrator's words to such an extent that when the narrator is ready to speak in his own voice so as to make the distinction between his words and Moses' practically irrelevant (Josh.–2 Kings), the reader will have been already prepared for this by the hypostasis of the divine-Mosaic words of the lawcode.

3. An example of how the Deuteronomist constitutes his narrator's prophetic authority, whether the latter is busy on the surface of the text exalting Moses' unique authority or denying it, is found in the juxtaposition of two apparently opposed statements within the lawcode, dealing with the activity and authenticity of prophets: 13:1–6 on the one hand and 18:15–22 on the other.

The lawcode begins in chapter 12 with those familiar laws dealing with the centralization of worship, and turns in chapter 13 to the question of how enticers to apostasy are to be treated once Israel inhabits the land. The chapter begins with the admonition:

> Everything that I command you shall be careful to do; you shall not add to it or take from it.
>
> (13:1)

Moses immediately details what is to be done in the event that such enticers are prophets or dreamers (*nābî'* or *holēm*). Even if their signs or portents come true, "you shall not listen to the words of that prophet or that dreamer of dreams" (13:4); he "shall be put to death" (13:6). Chapter 18 also deals with the question of prophets:

> For these nations, which you are about to dispossess, give heed to soothsayers and to diviners; but as for you, the LORD your God has not allowed you to do so. The LORD your God will raise up for you a prophet like me from among you, from your brethren— him you shall heed—just as you desired of the LORD your God at Horeb on the day of the assembly.
>
> (18:14–16)

Then, in order to further authenticate his own words, Moses reports God's words in a manner that is uncharacteristic of the entire lawcode, that is, through direct discourse:

> And the LORD said to me, "They have rightly said all that they have spoken. I will raise up for them a prophet like you from among their brethren; and I will put my words in his mouth, and he shall speak to them all that I command him."
>
> (18:17–18)

How will the Israelites recognize a prophet *not* sent by God so that they may put him to death?:

> when a prophet speaks in the name of the LORD, if the word does not come to pass or come true, that is a word which the LORD has not spoken; the prophet has spoken it presumptuously, you need not be afraid of him.
>
> (18:22)

The contrast between these two pericopes dealing with words spoken by a prophet in the name of the LORD could not be greater. Both deal ultimately with the status of the very lawcode of which they are a part, and each appears to provide a different explanation of that status. We want therefore to deal with these two pericopes not according to the question of true or false prophecy in general, but in relation to the very prophetic words of Moses of which they are a part in the lawcode. They seem to offer differing if not contradictory instructions concerning whether the lawcode itself is to be accepted as utterly unique or simply fundamental for successive words of the LORD.

13:1–6, with its command in verse 1 not to add or take away anything from the lawcode, cannot be interpreted to show Moses being reported as forever closing off any words of God to Israel subsequent to the lawcode itself. God will again speak as he repeatedly is reported doing throughout the rest of Deuteronomy (e.g., 31:16–21; 32:49–52), and throughout the rest of the Deuteronomic History. But what we do have in 13:1 (as well as in its preceding version in 4:2) appears to be the prohibition of any prophetic speech that blurs the boundaries between God's word and man's interpretation as thoroughly and as authoritatively as Moses is described as doing in the lawcode itself, where direct command of God and Mosaic comment or retort are so interwoven that it is impossible to distinguish *on the surface of the lawcode's text* what belongs to the reporting speech of Moses and what belongs to the reported speech of God. In other words, 13:1, in its present context within the lawcode, forbids subsequent reports of the word of God which synthesize reported speech, retort, and commentary as thoroughly as is the case with the lawcode. What is contained in this prohibition is the promulgation of an *authoritarian dogmatism* that centralizes control over the Mosaic lawcode by forbidding any further authoritative addition to or commentary upon it. The ironic thrust of this verse should not be ignored: this dogmatism expresses itself and provides for self-legitimization through and within prophetic discourse whose surface style is directly contrary to its own authoritarian tyranny. Disregarding its own fundamental synthesis of reporting (Moses') and reported (God's) speech, 13:1 expressly forbids the subordination of the lawcode either to a reporting context that authoritatively reports or comments from without, or to a revisionary process that would, by addition or subtraction, alter it from within. *What Moses could do with God's word, man may not do with Moses' word, which itself has become indistinguishable from God's word.* And it is precisely in this light that 18:14–22 appears so amazingly contradictory to 13:1–6. For we now have to deal with a mandate within the lawcode that provides for a legitimate revisionary process vis-à-vis the lawcode itself.

In relating the lawcode to its context within the second address, we can see very clearly that the divine utterance directly quoted by Moses in 5:28–31 authenticates his central teaching role in Deuteronomy, just as that same utterance, requoted by Moses with necessary modifications in 18:17–20, authenticates the Deuteronomic narrator's teaching role in his history. It will be instructive to set down sections of these two pericopes side by side. They represent Moses twice relating the same incident, and presumably the same utterance of God responding to the people's request for an intermediary to convey God's words to them:

5:23–31	18:16–19
Moses:	*Moses:*
all the heads of your tribes and the elders came to me and said, ". . . Why should we now risk death? for this great fire will devour us. If we hear the voice of the LORD our God again we shall die."	There you said,
	"Let us not hear again the voice of the LORD our God, nor see this great fire again or we shall die."
When the LORD heard these words which you spoke to me, he said, "I have heard what	Then the LORD said to me,

| this people has said to you: every word they have spoken is right. | What they have said is right. |
| but you yourself stand here beside me, and I will set forth to you all the commandment, the statutes and laws which you shall teach them to observe in the land which I am giving them to occupy." | I shall raise up for them a prophet like you, one of their own race, and I will put my words in his mouth. He shall convey all my commands to them, and if anyone does not listen to the words which he will speak in my name I will require satisfaction from him." |

Moses is described therefore as appealing to the same occasion and to the same divine utterance to authenticate both his own prophetic role and that of "a prophet like him." If we ask ourselves what specific laws, commandments, and statutes Moses is empowered by the commission of 5:31 to set forth, we are led by the very clarity of the phraseological composition of the book to answer: the laws and statutes introduced by the words of 12:1, "These are the statutes and laws" and concluded by 26:16, "This day the LORD your God commands you to keep these statutes and laws." But when we ask what precise words are meant when God says in 18:18, "and I will put my words into his mouth. He shall convey all my commands to them," the answer is not quite so straightforward. Historical critical answers would typically understand 18:14–22 as a later exegesis of an older tradition used anew to provide authentication either for a succession of prophets or else for the coming of a single "eschatological" prophetic mediator. Thus, we are told, the "words" referred to in 18:18 would be those announced by a later anonymous prophet or prophets, truly commissioned by God. We are supposed to find here some kind of an attempt to authenticate the office of prophecy in Israel. My analysis will avoid such examples of historical exegesis not only because of their diachronic implications (I want to ask more elementary literary questions first), but also because they appear to me to be so general in their thrust that specific relationships between 18:14–22 and the rest of Deuteronomy and the Deuteronomic History are unable to be articulated.

There appear to me to be quite specific words which are referred to in 18:18. The words which the prophet like Moses is to speak to the Israelites are precisely twofold: just as Moses first relates the commandments of God in direct discourse (most often in the first address and most pointedly in the second address with the reporting of the decalogue) and then abruptly shifts to a much more authoritative manner of reporting that obliterates, with the exception of a few functionally important instances, the distinction between the divine reported and Mosaic reporting speech (the lawcode of 12–26), so also the prophet like Moses first relates the words of God/Moses in direct discourse (Deut) and then abruptly shifts to a much more authoritative manner of reporting that erases the distinction between the words of God/Moses and his own (Josh.–2 Kings). The "prophet like Moses" is the narrator of the Deuteronomic History, and through him, the Deuteronomist himself. The Deuteronomist uses Moses to explain by a hortatory lawcode the wide-ranging implications of the decalogue; this same author will soon be using the Deuteronomic narrator to explain in an exemplary history the wide-ranging implications of that lawcode.

Using this hypothesis, we can be very precise concerning the words of God referred to in 18:14–22. The very clarity of the phraseological composition of the history allows us to see that these words begin with the narrator's report in Josh. 1:1; "After the death of Moses, the servant of the Lord, the Lord said to Joshua, the son of Nun, his assistant . . . " and end with the final words of 2 Kings 25:30.

An important aspect therefore of the phraseological composition of the Deuteronomic History is highlighted by the following ratio: the decalogue of Deuteronomy 5:6–21 is to the lawcode of 12:2–26:15 as the directly quoted words of Moses in Deuteronomy are to the words of the narrator in Joshua–2 Kings. Concerning the laws and statutes *directly* quoted by Moses in 5:6–21 we are told that all the Israelites heard God's voice out of the darkness (5:23), and thus Moses' quoting of these laws at this point in the narrative is not described as presenting anything new to his audience. Similarly, we may assume that a great proportion of the Mosaic words found in Deuteronomy are presented as traditions known to most Israelites, not just to that privileged prophet of God who has risen up after Moses. Concerning, however, the laws and statutes reported by Moses in 12–26, we are explicitly told in chapter 5 that only Moses had gone near to listen to all these words of the Lord. His prophetic function is here at one and the same time to declare and to interpret God's word (*maggîd* and *mᵉlammed*). Without him, the Israelites are described as being unwilling and unable either to know or understand God's further word. Similarly, with the beginning of the Book of Joshua, we are presented with a narrator who has taken over the *maggîd* and *mᵉlammed* roles of Moses in such a way that he speaks with as much authority as Moses. The message he proclaims is as authoritative and necessary in relation to the previous book as Moses' lawcode was in relation to the covenantal decalogue that preceded its promulgation.

4. It is precisely at this point that our comparison of the two texts that constitute respectively the prophetic offices of Moses and the Deuteronomic narrator, vis-à-vis the lawcode and Joshua–2 Kings, reveals a difference between what God is quoted by Moses as telling him in 5:23–31 and what God is requoted by Moses as telling him in 18:16–19 – a crucial difference that may shed light on the apparent contradiction between 18:15–22 and 13:1–6; that is, the latter seems to forbid any subsequent prophetic activity that would either add to or take away anything from the "further words of God" embodied in the lawcode, while the former seems to sanction it.

Immediately after Moses quotes God's words predicting another prophet like himself, he adds a negative criterion for distinguishing the false from the true prophet: "When the word spoken by the prophet in the name of the LORD is not fulfilled and does not come true, it is not a word spoken by the LORD. The prophet has spoken presumptuously; do not hold him in awe" (18:22). It follows therefore that the people are to hold in awe and recognize the authority of the prophet whose word *does* come true. But when we look at Moses' previous reporting of these words of God in 5:23–31 and its surrounding context, we find not even a hint concerning the possibility that Moses might presume "to utter in my name what I have not commanded him." That there is no consideration of such a situation is entirely appropriate since the Book of Deuteronomy presents its hero's authority as *already* established, whereas we have seen in countless ways and in some detail how the book's primary function is precisely to establish the authority of the Deuteronomic narrator, its "author." It is against the background of these two pericopes that the monumental historiographic work of Joshua–2 Kings is seen in the clearest light. It is the narrator's claim that his monumental work, by the very wealth and accuracy of its historical interpretation, is a true explanation of the various events that shaped Israel's life from their incursion into the land to their exile out of the land. If Moses is depicted in the lawcode as formulating the laws, statutes, and commandments of the LORD in great detail, and only outlining the subsequent history of Israel in general terms (e.g., at the end of his first and second address), the narrator formulates the word of the LORD from another perspective: he puts the laws, statutes, and commandments of the LORD in the background of his own discourse by placing them in the mouth of Moses, and focuses his own discourse on establishing in great detail how the subsequent history of Israel is illuminated by such a background.

The status of the Deuteronomic History as the further words of Moses is directly challenged by 13:1. Not only is this pericope followed by a law relating to apostasy that negates the negative criterion found in 18:21–22, it is also preceded by a commandment forbidding apostasy; 12:29–31. It is as if Moses were depicted as stating in 13:1 that to add to or subtract from these further words of the LORD is tantamount to preaching apostasy since the word of God will have been altered *internally* by adding on spurious laws or withholding genuine ones, or *externally* by presuming to comment on or interpret these sacred and immutable words of the LORD. To alter the word of God is to follow other gods and to entice Israel to follow other gods. *The penalty is death (13:6) even if the (false) prophet offers a sign or a portent that comes true (13:3).*

The command of 13:1 (as well as of 4:2 of which it is a reiteration) is in fact a hermeneutic anomaly within Deuteronomy. This would not be so were the lawcode formulated as the word of the LORD quoted in direct discourse, so that the "I" of this command referred to the LORD himself. Here in the lawcode, the "I" of the command of 13:1 is the direct word of Moses himself and there is no way one can distinguish between the reporting "I" of Moses and the reported "I" of the LORD. Moreover, there is nothing within the lawcode that enables one to separate the reported words of the LORD from the commenting and responding words of Moses. In such a situation, where statute, commentary, and response are interwoven throughout the entire lawcode by the leveling speech of Moses, *the very words of Moses as interpretation of the further words of the LORD may not be added to or taken away from.* Deut. 13:1 is totally at odds with 18:16–19 since the latter provides for an authoritative revision of the lawcode through the "further words" of the prophet whom God would raise up after Moses. The hermeneutic dilemma posed by 13:1 lies in the fact that it both validates and invalidates the subsequent pericope of 18:14–22. Deut. 13:1a commands Israel to "observe everything I command you." Therefore, the command to listen to and obey the prophet coming after Moses must be observed. However, 13:1b commands that "you must not add anything to it, nor take anything away from it." Thus, the command to listen to and obey the prophet coming after Moses must not be observed since this would be adding to or taking something away from what Moses commands. How are we to disentangle ourselves from the hermeneutic snare of 13:1 in which the right hand giveth and the left hand taketh away?

There seem to be two compositional pointers that may set us in the right direction in interpreting this pair of conflicting pericopes. First, the word of the LORD expressed in direct discourse in chapter 18 has the crucial function of authenticating the role of the Deuteronomic narrator vis-à-vis his history. The "I" of 18:18–20 is directly that of the LORD. On the other hand, the "I" of 13:1 directly refers to Moses. It may be therefore that we are listening once more to that dialogue between two voices that we have [described elsewhere] in other sections of Deuteronomy. Both voices are here on the surface of the text, both voices are in obvious conflict with one another, and it is only by a close compositional analysis that we can come to some conclusion about the relative strength of each voice. In 13:1 we undoubtedly hear the voice that has all along exalted the unique status of Moses as prophet vis-à-vis Israel. As such, it fits in with the content of the entire lawcode, except that of 18:14–22. But even here within the phraseological composition of the two conflicting commands, there is an indication that the voice represented by 18:14–22 has subordinated the voice found in 13:1 and throughout most of the lawcode. For, whereas in 13:1 it is only Moses speaking directly who seems to be exalting his unique role, in 18:18–20 it is (atypically in the lawcode) God who directly denies the unique role attributed to Moses throughout the greater part of the surface of the text.

Second, the very *content* of 13:1 is contradicted by the *composition* of Deuteronomy itself. For if 13:1 forbids anything to be added to or taken away from a lawcode that is as much commentary and response to divine legislation as it is divine legislation itself, then the very setting of this lawcode within the immediate context of the surrounding reported words of Moses (especially 6:20–25) and within the larger context of the reporting words of the narrator both in Deuteronomy and in Joshua–2 Kings effectively neutralizes the command of 13:1 and subordinates the voice for which it stands to another voice that has taken over these words for its own purposes.

What we seem to have in 12:29–13:6 are the words of an argument that threatens, even under the penalty of death, the very existence of the enterprise carried through by the Deuteronomist. Taken at face value, this pericope supports an understanding of Israelite law and religion that is rooted in an attitude toward the divine word which we have called *authoritarian dogmatism*. Taken to its logical conclusion, this voice is the voice of a religious tyranny that allows no room for subsequent revision or revitalization of God's word. However, such a tyrannical voice is devastatingly neutralized in its very proclamation by the varied compositional strategies we have been noting. First, its content is contradicted by the context into which the Deuteronomist has placed the lawcode: Deuteronomy is an interpretation—a putting into perspective—of a lawcode in which is found the command not to interpret it. Second, its content is contradicted by a subsequent portion of the lawcode in such a way that, whereas Moses is described as saying no one may follow him as supreme interpreter of God's word, he is then described as quoting God in direct discourse to the effect that a prophet *will indeed* come after him. Third, and perhaps most important, the Deuteronomist has stilled this voice at the same time as he has allowed it to speak *simply by constructing the entire lawcode according to a surface style that directly contradicts this voice's own authoritarian tyranny*. How better to focus on the absurdity of forbidding any ongoing process of interpreting the word of God than by putting such a prohibition within a lawcode whose basic style already inextricably combines word of God with commentary and response to that word?

13:1–6 as representative of other dogmatic utterances like it in Deuteronomy is not just contrary to an isolated pericope following later in the lawcode, it is in fact subjected to a multifaceted compositional attack. This onslaught insures that its readers will ultimately reject its claims as quickly as they are made. The style of the prohibition has been deliberately fashioned to override and submerge its content. To believe that Moses could have spoken as directly as he is characterized as doing in the lawcode of Deuteronomy is, in terms of both style and substance, the means by which the Deuteronomist prepares his audience to accept as authoritative the subsequent books of his history.

THE SECOND ADDRESS: A SUMMARY CONCLUSION

Our discussion of Deuteronomy 5–26 was introduced by a general treatment of its ideological problems and by an illustration of how surface phenomena of the text, elements on its phraseological, psychological, or temporal planes, may or may not concur with what is happening on its ideological plane. Our analysis of the address itself revealed that whether its utterances were busy promoting the retributive justice of God or his great mercy, whether the uniqueness of Moses or Israel was being defended or attacked, *all* of the utterances were subordinated to a dominant ideological point of view that tended to diminish the status both of Israel and Moses, within the broad context of God's retributive justice. Thus, whether the *content* of an utterance advocates God's consuming justice, as is the case with most of the utterances of this address dealing with this matter, or rather God's ever gracious mercy, as in the majority of statements in chapters 9 and 10 which describe how God decided to give Israel the land in spite of their disobedience, everything in the utterance serves in one way or another to bolster the predominantly retributive nature of God's dealings with Israel. For example, the content of 9:4–5 shows that the subject of God's mercy is explicitly subordinated to his more basic desire for justice: to punish the nations whom Israel will dispossess. Similarly, when the phraseological *composition* of the second address is obviously promoting the unique status of Moses, by giving him the authority to teach God's commandment, laws, and statutes in the form of a direct address to Israel rather than by reporting God's words in direct discourse as he did with the decalogue, this phraseological device, although it is an advance over Moses' first address as an illustration of his authority, still is at the service of a subtle and complicated ideology. This ultimate semantic authority diminishes Moses' unique authority either by means of the reporting frame-breaks of chapters 10 and 27 or else by means of directly contradictory utterances such as 18:17–21. A commandment as troubling to it as 13:1 even highlights the basic paradox of the lawcode's diction: the more exalted Moses' speech is, the less exalted it becomes. Finally, the hint of a far distant future offering mercy for Israel, which is found in the *conclusion* to Moses' first address, is swallowed up by the absolutely merciless conclusion of the second address.

Most of the direct quotations of God in the second address also have an essential connection with the ideological composition of the book. That the decalogue is reported in direct discourse in 5:6–21 illustrates the main distinction of the chapter that whereas God's ten words were heard by the people, God's further words, chapters 12–26, are known only through Moses' mediation. This characterizes Moses as a model of the teacher of God's words that the narrator will become in Joshua-2 Kings. The divine utterance in 5:28–31 authenticates Moses' central teaching role in the book, just as 18:17–20 authenticates the narrator's teaching role in the history he presents to us. The divine words directly quoted in chapters 9 and 10 document Israel's immediate idolatrous disobedience at Horeb and God's merciful decision to give them the land in spite of this, and prepare the way for the Deuteronomist's perceptive insight that even in respect of the covenant of Horeb there is an element of unconditionality. Only with the direct divine utterance of 17:16 are we unable to suggest a clear-cut connection with the main ideological stance of the second address.

We see, then, how the overt content, composition, or conclusion of this address of Moses may at points promote or deny God's justice or mercy, diminish or enhance Israel's and Moses' unique roles. But in all cases, the ultimate semantic authority of the book is busy "taking over" these overt positions in the service of a dominating point of view that is ceaselessly a softening, rather than a rejection, of an unconditional covenant between God and Israel, and a diminution, for varying reasons, of the unique status of Israel and of their prophet Moses.

The overriding voice of the Book of Deuteronomy is against an immutable orthodoxy that would petrify the living word of God. If the word of God, expressed by Moses in Moab, is not absolutely immutable, neither is the promise made to our fathers. Here we can see from another angle the inner connection between the themes of the uniqueness of Moses and of Israel and the God of mercy and grace. If the terms of the covenant God made with the Israelites at Horeb are subject to revision at least in the sense of subsequent interpretation, then the same has to be said about the promise God made to our fathers. This promise made to the elect of Israel must not be so unconditionally understood that it provides a rigid guarantee of mercy in the face of widespread disobedience to God's law. On the one hand, whenever the election of Israel and the promise made to our fathers is invoked in the second address, these tendencies toward a comfortable security are generally neutralized by the overriding retributive justice of the covenant made at Horeb. On the other hand, whenever the authoritative status of Moses threatens to overwhelm the second address, this tendency is generally neutralized by the *critical traditionalism* inherent in Moses' style of reporting God's words in the lawcode. These two aspects of the composition of the second address help us see more clearly than in the first address how and why the themes of Moses' and Israel's unique statuses are bound up with the question of the ultimate justice or mercy of God.

Both the dominant voice of retributive justice and the subordinate voice of mercy heard throughout the second address embrace the traditions centering on the promise made to the fathers as well as the covenant made in Horeb. But the voice of mercy wants these two traditions to be understood according to an immutable and authoritarian dogmatism that apparently aimed at preserving the blessings of the elect of God at all costs. Thus, when it is allowed to appeal so often to the promise made to the fathers in the first address, and less often to this theme in the second address, its inclination to focus on the unconditional nature of God's promised blessing can be felt by the reader. When it is allowed to appeal to the conditional covenant at Horeb, its inclination is to focus on the immutable nature of the blessing that follows obedience to the law. Even through the reflecting voice of the Deuteronomist who has taken it over, it can still be heard to proclaim a religion that cuts beneficially both ways: "If you obey God, the covenant at Horeb ensures blessing; if you receive, as you must, the promise made to the fathers, then you must not have disobeyed God, or at least God's mercy has prevailed."

The voice of retributive justice on the other hand rearranges the relationship between these two traditions so that even when the merciful acts of God may not be denied, they are put in the perspective of God's justice. The polemic between these two voices does not involve the denial either of divine election or of God's mercy and justice. Each voice accepts all three traditions. Nor do they disagree about the element of unconditionality emphasized in the promise made to the fathers and the element of conditionality evident in the Mosaic covenant. The issue rather is whether these traditions are to be interpreted so dogmatically that they are absolutely immutable and incapable of varying interpretive emphases from age to age. The creative solution of the dominant voice of the second address of Moses is to admit an element of unconditionality in the Horeb covenant (e.g., chapters 9 and 10 in which Israel is promised the land even though she was disobedient) and to require an element of conditionality in the promise made to the fathers (e.g., by always surrounding such references with the unremitting condition of obedience).

The dominant voice of retribution wins out in the second address because it concentrates on exposing the authoritarian dogmatism implicit in the opposing voice. The ultimate semantic authority of the Book of Deuteronomy, as we have so far discovered it, proclaims an attitude toward the word of God that claims the right to emphasize now one aspect, viz., judgment, now another aspect, viz., mercy, of God's relationship with Israel, *depending on the situation in which they find themselves*. This right recognizes in the word of God a critical traditionalism and a revisionary capability that the opposing voice of the book tends to disallow. Whatever hints there were in the first address of a real ideological dialogue have faded away in the second address. A *monologic* Deuteronomic voice, characterized by a deep sense of critical traditionalism, appears to be in full control as the third address of Moses begins.

MARTIN BUBER

Job

In the actual reality of the catastrophe, "honest and wicked" (Job 9:22) are destroyed together by God, and in the outer reality the wicked left alive knew how to assert themselves successfully in spite of all the difficulties; "they lived, became old, and even thrived mightily" (21:7), whereas for the pious, endowed with weaker elbows and more sensitive hearts, their days "were swifter than a weaver's shuttle, and were spent without hope" (7:6); "the robbers' tents are peaceful, and they that anger God have secure abodes" (12:6), whereas the upright is "become a brother of jackals" (30:29). This is the experience out of which the Book of Job was born, a book opposed to the dogmatics of Ezekiel, a book of the question which then was new and has persisted ever since.

I cannot ascribe this book—which clearly has only slowly grown to its present form—in its basic kernel to a time later (or earlier) than the beginning of the exile. Its formulations of the question bear the stamp of an intractable directness—the stamp of a first expression. The world in which they were spoken had certainly not yet heard the answers of Psalm 73 or Deutero-Isaiah. The author finds before him dogmas in process of formation, he clothes them in grand language, and sets over against them the force of the new question, the question brought into being out of experience; in his time these growing dogmas had not yet found their decisive opponents. The book, in spite of its thorough rhetoric—the product of a long-drawn-out literary process—is one of the special events in world literature, in which we witness the first clothing of a human quest in form of speech.

It has rightly been said [Johannes Hempel, *Die althebräische Literatur* (1930)] that behind the treatment of Job's fate in this discussion lie "very bitter experiences of a supra-individual kind." When the sufferer complains, "He breaks

From *On the Bible: Eighteen Studies.* © 1968 by Schocken Books, Inc.

me around, and I am gone" (Job 19:10), this seems no longer the complaint of a single person. When he cries, "God delivers me to the wicked, and hurls me upon the hands of the evil-doers" (16:11), we think less of the sufferings of an individual than of the exile of a people. It is true it is a personal fate that is presented here, but the stimulus to speaking out, the incentive to complaint and accusation, bursting the bands of the presentation, are the fruit of supra-personal sufferings. Job's question comes into being as the question of a whole generation about the sense of its historic fate. Behind this "I," made so personal here, there still stands the "I" of Israel.

The question of the generation, "Why do we suffer what we suffer?" had from the beginning a religious character; "why?" here is not a philosophical interrogative asking after the nature of things, but a religious concern with the acting of God. With Job, however, it becomes still clearer; he does not ask, "Why does God *permit* me to suffer these things?" but "Why does God *make* me suffer these things?" That everything comes from God is beyond doubt and question; the question is, How are these sufferings compatible with His godhead?

In order to grasp the great inner dialectic of the poem, we must realize that here not two, but four answers stand over against each other; in other words, we find here four views of God's relationship to man's sufferings.

The first view is that of the Prologue to the book which, in the form in which it has reached us, cannot have come from an ancient popular book about Job, but bears the stamp of a poetic formation. The popular view of God, however, stands here apparently unchanged. It is a God allowing a creature, who wanders about the earth and is subject to Him in some manner, the "Satan," that is the "Hinderer" or "Adversary," to "entice" Him (2:3)—the verb is the same as is used in the story of David being enticed by God or Satan to sin—to do all manner of evil to a God-fearing man, one who is His "servant" (1:8; 2:3), of whose faithfulness God boasts. This creature entices the deity to do all manner of evil to this man, only in order to find out if he will break faith, as Satan argues, or keep it according to God's word. The poet shows us how he sees the matter, as he repeats in true biblical style the phrase "gratuitously." In order to make it clear whether Job serves him "gratuitously" (1:9), that is to say, not for the sake of receiving a reward, God smites him and brings suffering upon him, as He Himself confesses (2:3), "gratuitously," that is to say, without sufficient cause. Here God's acts are questioned more critically than in any of Job's accusations, because here we are informed of the true motive, which is one not befitting to deity. On the other hand man proves true as man. Again the point is driven home by the frequent repetition of the verb *barekh*, which means both real blessing and also blessing of dismissal, departure (1:5; 11, 2:5, 9): Job's wife tells him, reality itself tells him to "bless" God, to dismiss Him, but he bows down to God and "blesses" Him, who has allowed Himself to be enticed against him "gratuitously." This is a peculiarly dramatic face-to-face meeting, this God and this man. The dialogue poem that follows contradicts it totally: there the man is another man, and God another God.

The second view of God is that of the friends. This is the dogmatic view of the cause and effect in the divine system of requital: sufferings point to sin. God's punishment is manifest and clear to all. The primitive conception of the zealous God is here robbed of its meaning: it was YHVH, God of Israel, who was zealous for the *covenant* with His *people*. Ezekiel had preserved the covenant faith, and only for the passage of time between covenant and covenant did he announce the unconditional punishment for those who refused to return in penitence; this has changed here, in an atmosphere no longer basically historical, into the view of the friends, the assertion of an all-embracing empirical connection between sin and punishment. In addition to this, for Ezekiel, it is true, punishment followed unrepented sin, but it never occurred to him to see in all men's sufferings the avenging hand of God; and it is just this that the friends now proceed to do: Job's sufferings testify to his guilt. The inner infinity of the suffering soul is here changed into a formula, and a wrong formula. The first view was that of a small mythological idol, the second is that of a great ideological idol. In the first the faithful sufferer was true to an untrue God, who permitted his guiltless children to be slain; whereas here man was not asked to be true to an incalculable power, but to recognize and confess a calculation that his knowledge of reality contradicts. There man's faith is attacked by fate, here by religion. The friends are silent seven days before the sufferer, after which they expound to him the account book of sin and punishment. Instead of his God, for whom he looks in vain, his God, who had not only put sufferings upon him, but also had "hedged him in" until "His way was hid" from his eyes (3:23), there now came and visited him on his ash heap *religion*, which uses every art of speech to take away from him the God of his soul. Instead of the "cruel" (30:21) and living God, to whom he clings, religion offers him a reasonable and rational God, a deity whom he, Job, does not perceive either in his own existence or in the world, and who obviously is not to be found anywhere save only in the very domain of religion. And his complaint becomes a protest against a God who withdraws Himself, and at the same time against His false representation.

The third view of God is that of Job in his complaint and protest. It is the view of a God who contradicts His revelation by "hiding His face" (13:24). He is at one and the same time fearfully noticeable and unperceivable (9:11), and this hiddenness is particularly sensible in face of the excessive presence of the "friends," who are ostensibly God's advocates. All their attempts to cement the rent in Job's world show him that this is the rent in the heart of the world. Clearly the thought of both Job and the friends proceeds from the question about justice. But unlike his friends, Job knows of justice only as a human activity, willed by God, but opposed by His acts. The truth of being just and the reality caused by the unjust acts of God are irreconcilable. Job cannot forego either his own truth or God. God torments him "gratuitously" (9:17; it is not without purpose that here the word recurs, which in the Prologue Satan uses and God repeats); He "deals crookedly" with him (19:6). All man's supplications will avail nothing: "there is no justice" (19:7). Job does not regard himself as free from sin (7:20; 14:16 f.), in contradistinction to God's words about him in the Prologue (1:8; 2:3). But his sin and his sufferings are incommensurable. And the men, who call themselves his friends, suppose that on the basis of their dogma of requital they are able to unmask his life and show it to be a lie. By allowing religion to occupy the place of the living God, He strips off Job's honor (19:9). Job had believed God to be just and man's duty to be to walk in His ways. But it is no longer possible for one who has been smitten with such sufferings to think God just. "It is one thing, therefore I spake: honest and wicked He exterminates" (9:22). And if it is so, it is not proper to walk in His ways. In spite of this, Job's faith in justice is not broken down. But he is no longer able to have a *single faith* in God and in justice. His faith in justice is no longer covered by God's righteousness. He believes now in justice in spite of believing in God, and he believes in God in spite of believing in justice. But he cannot forego his claim that they will again be united somewhere, sometime, although he has no idea in his mind how this will be achieved. This is in fact meant by his claim of his rights, the claim of the solution. This solution must come, for from the time when he knew God Job *knows* that God is not a Satan grown into omnipotence. Now, however, Job is handed over to the pretended justice, the account justice of the friends, which affects not only his honor, but also his faith in justice. For Job, justice is not a scheme of compensation. Its content is simply this, that one must not cause suffering gratuitously. Job feels himself isolated by this feeling, far removed from God and men. It is true, Job does not forget that God seeks just such justice as this from man. But he cannot understand how God himself violates it, how He inspects His creature every morning (7:18), searching after his iniquity (10:6), and instead of forgiving his sin (7:21) snatches at him stormily (9:17)—how He, being infinitely superior to man, thinks it good to reject the work of His hands (10:3). And in spite of this Job knows that the friends, who side with God (13:8), do not contend for the true God. He has recognized before this the true God as the near and intimate God. Now he only experiences Him through suffering and contradiction, but even in this way he does experience God. What Satan designed for him and his wife in the Prologue, recommended to him more exactly, that he should "bless" God, dismiss Him, and die in the comfort of his soul, was for him quite impossible. When in his last long utterance he swears the purification oath, he says: "As God lives, who has withdrawn my right" (27:2). God lives, and He bends the right. From the burden of this double, yet single, matter Job is able to take away nothing, he cannot lighten his death. He can only ask to be confronted with God. "Oh that one would hear me!" (31:35)—men do not hear his words, only God can be his hearer. As his motive he declares that he wants to reason with the deity (13:3); he knows he will carry his point (13:18). In the last instance, however, he merely means by this that God will again become present to him. "Oh that I knew where I might find Him!" (23:3). Job struggles against the remoteness of God, against the deity who rages and *is silent*, rages and "hides His face," that is to say, against the deity who has changed for him from a nearby person into a sinister power. And even if He draw near to him again only in death, he will again "see" God (19:26) as His "witness" (16:19) against God Himself, he will see Him as the avenger of his blood (19:25), which must not be covered by the earth until it is avenged (16:18) by God on God. The absurd duality of a truth known to man and a reality sent by God must be swallowed up somewhere, sometime, in a unity of God's presence. How will it take place? Job does not know this, nor does he understand it; he only believes in it. We may certainly say that Job "appeals from God to God" [A. S. Peake, *The Problem of Suffering* (1904)], but we cannot say that he rouses himself against a God "who contradicts His own innermost nature" [F. Baumgaertel, *Der Hiobdialog* (1933)], and seeks a God who will conduct Himself toward him "as the requital dogma demands." By such an interpretation the sense of the problem is upset. Job cannot renounce justice, but he does not hope to find it, when God will find again "His inner nature" and "His subjection to the norm," but only when God will appear to him again. Job believes now, as later Deutero-Isaiah (Isa. 45:15) did under the influence of Isaiah (8:17), in "a God that hides Himself." This hiding, the eclipse of the divine light, is the source of his abysmal despair. And the abyss is bridged the moment man "sees," is permitted to see again, and this becomes a new foundation. It has been rightly said that Job is more deeply rooted in the primitive Israelite view of life than his dogmatic friends. There is no true life for him but that of a firmly established covenant between God and man; formerly he lived in this covenant and received his righteousness from it, but now God has disturbed it. It is the dread of the faithful "remnant" in the hour of the people's catastrophe that here finds its personal expression. But this dread is suggestive of the terror that struck Isaiah as he stood on the threshold of the cruel mission laid upon him—"the making fat and heavy." His words "How long?" are echoed in Job's complaint. How long will God hide His face? When shall we be allowed to see Him again? Deutero-Isaiah expresses (40:27) the despairing complaint of the faithful remnant which thinks that because God hides Himself, Israel's "way" also "is hid" from Him, and He pays no attention to it, and the prophet promises that not only Israel but all flesh shall see Him (40:5).

The fourth view of God is that expressed in the speech of God Himself. The extant text is apparently a late revision, as is the case with many other sections of this book, and we cannot restore the original text. But there is no doubt that the speech is intended for more than the mere demonstration of the mysterious character of God's rule in nature to a greater and more comprehensive extent than had already been done by the friends and Job himself; for more than the mere explanation to Job: "Thou canst not understand the secret of any thing or being in the world, how much less the secret of man's fate." It is also intended to do more than teach by examples taken from the world of nature about the "strange and wonderful" character of the acts of God, which contradict the whole of teleological wisdom, and point to the "playful riddle of the eternal creative power" as to an "inexpressible positive value" [Rudolf Otto, *Das Heilige*, 23–25 (1936)]. The poet does not let his God disregard the fact that it is a matter of *justice*. The speech declares in the ears of man, struggling for justice, another justice than his own, a divine justice. Not *the* divine justice, which remains hidden, but *a* divine justice, namely that manifest in creation. The creation of the world is justice, not a recompensing and compensating justice, but a distributing, a giving justice. God the Creator bestows upon each what belongs to him, upon each thing and being, insofar as He allows it to become entirely itself. Not only for the ·sea (Job 38:10), but for every thing and being God "breaks" in the hour of creation "His boundary," that is to say, He cuts the dimension of this thing or being out of "all," giving it its fixed measure, the limit appropriate to this gift. Israel's ancient belief in creation, which matured slowly only in its formulations, has here reached its completion: it is not about a "making" that we are told here, but about a "founding" (38:4), a "setting" (38:5, 9 f.), a "commanding" and "appointing" (38:12). The creation itself already means communication between Creator and creature. The just Creator gives to all His creatures His boundary, so that each may become fully itself. Designedly man is lacking in this presentation of heaven and earth, in which man is shown the justice that is greater than his, and is shown that he with his justice, which intends to give to everyone what is due to him, is called only to emulate the divine justice, which gives to everyone what he is. In face of such divine teaching as this it would be indeed impossible for the sufferer to do aught else than put "his hand upon his mouth" (40:4), and to confess (42:3) that he had erred in speaking of things inconceivable for him. And nothing else could have come of it except this recognition – if he had heard only a voice "from the tempest" (38:1; 40:6). But the voice is the voice of *Him who answers*, the voice of Him that "heard" (31:35), and appeared so as to be "found" of him (23:3). In vain Job had tried to penetrate to God through the divine remoteness; now God draws near to him. No more does God hide Himself, only the storm cloud of His sublimity still shrouds Him, and Job's eye "sees" Him (42:5). The absolute power has for human personality's sake become personality. God offers Himself to the sufferer who, in the depth of his despair, keeps to God with his refractory complaint; He offers Himself to him as an answer. It is true, "the overcoming of the riddle of suffering can only come from the domain of revelation" [W. Eichrodt, *Theologie des Alten Testaments*, III (1939)], but it is not the revelation in general that is here decisive, but the particular revelation to the individual: the revelation as an *answer* to the individual sufferer concerning the question of his sufferings, the self-limitation of God to a person, answering a person.

The *way* of this poem leads from the first view to the fourth. The God of the first view, the God of the legend borrowed by the poet, works on the basis of "enticement"; the second, the God of the friends, works on the basis of purposes apparent to us, purposes of punishment or, especially in the speeches of Elihu which are certainly a later addition, of purification and education; the third, the God of the protesting Job, works against every reason and purpose; and the fourth, the God of revelation, works from His godhead, in which every reason and purpose held by man are at once abolished and fulfilled. It is clear that this God, who answers from the tempest, is different from the God of the Prologue; the declaration about the secret of divine action would be turned into a mockery if the fact of that "wager" was put over against it. But even the speeches of the friends and of Job cannot be harmonized with it. Presumably the poet, who frequently shows himself to be a master of irony, left the Prologue, which seems completely opposed to his intention, unchanged in content in order to establish the foundation for the multiplicity of views that follows. But in truth the view of the Prologue is meant to be ironical and unreal; the view of the friends is only logically "true" and demonstrates to us that man must not subject God to the rules of logic; Job's view is real, and therefore, so to speak, the negative of truth; and the view of the voice speaking from the tempest is the supralogical truth of reality. God justifies Job: he has spoken "rightly" (42:7), unlike the friends. And as the poet often uses words of the Prologue as motive words in different senses, so also here he makes God call Job as there by the name of His "servant," and repeat it by way of emphasis four times. Here this epithet appears in its true light. Job, the faithful rebel, like Abraham, Moses, David, and Isaiah, stands in the succession of men so designated by God, a succession that leads to Deutero-Isaiah's "servant of YHVH," whose sufferings especially link him with Job.

"And my servant Job shall pray for you"—with these words God sends the friends home (42:8). It is the same phrase as that in which YHVH in the story of Abraham (Gen. 20:7) certifies the patriarch, that he is His *nabi*. It will be found that in all the pre-exilic passages, in which the verb is used in the sense of intercession (and this apparently was its first meaning), it is only used of men called prophets. The significance of Job's intercession is emphasized by the Epilogue (which, apart from the matter of the prayer, the poet apparently left as it was) in that the turning point in Job's history, the "restoration" (Job 42:10) and first of all his healing, begins the moment he prays "for his friends." This saying is the last of the reminiscences of prophetic life and language found in this book. As if to stress this connection, Job's first complaint begins (3:3 ff.) with the cursing of his birth, reminding us of Jeremiah's words (Jer. 20:14 ff.), and the first utterance of the friends is poured out in figures of speech taken from the prophetic world (4, 12 ff.), the last of which (4:16) modifies the peculiar form of revelation of Elijah's story (I Kings 19:12). Job's recollection of divine intimacy, of "the counsel of God upon his tent" (Job 29:4), is expressed in language derived from Jeremiah (Jer. 23:18, 22), and his quest, which reaches fulfillment, to "see" God, touches the prophetic experience which only on Mount Sinai were non-prophets allowed to share (Exod. 24:10, 17). Jeremiah's historical figure, that of the suffering prophet, apparently inspired the poet to compose his song of the man of suffering, who by his suffering attained the vision of God, and in all his revolt was God's witness on earth (cf. Isa. 43:12; 44:8), as God was his witness in heaven.

MARTIN BUBER

The Heart Determines: Psalm 73

What is remarkable about this poem—composed of descriptions, of a story, and of confessions—is that a man tells how he reached the true meaning of his experience of life, and that this meaning borders directly on the eternal.

For the most part we understand only gradually the decisive experiences we have in our relation with the world. First we accept what they seem to offer us, we express it, we weave it into a "view," and then think we are aware of our world. But we come to see that what we look on in this view is only an appearance. Not that our experiences have deceived us. But we had turned them to our use, without penetrating to their heart. What is it that teaches us to penetrate to their heart? Deeper experience.

The man who speaks in this psalm tells us how he penetrated to the heart of a weighty group of experiences—those experiences that show that the wicked prosper.

Apparently, then, the question is not what was the real question for Job—why the good do not prosper—but rather its obverse, as we find it most precisely, and probably for the first time, expressed in Jeremiah (12:1): "Why does the way of the wicked prosper?"

Nevertheless, the psalm begins with a prefatory sentence in which, rightly considered, Job's question may be found hidden.

This sentence, the foreword to the psalm, is

> Surely, God is good to Israel:
> To the pure in heart.

It is true that the Psalmist is here concerned not with the happiness or

---

From *On the Bible: Eighteen Studies.* © 1968 by Schocken Books, Inc.

unhappiness of the person, but with the happiness or unhappiness of Israel. But the experience behind the speeches of Job, as is evident in many of them, is itself not merely personal, but is the experience of Israel's suffering both in the catastrophe that led to the Babylonian exile and in the beginning of the exile itself. Certainly only one who had plumbed the depths of personal suffering could speak in this way. But the speaker is a man of Israel in Israel's bitter hour of need, and in his personal suffering the suffering of Israel has been concentrated, so that what he now has to suffer he suffers as Israel. In the destiny of an authentic person the destiny of his people is gathered up, and only now becomes truly manifest.

Thus the Psalmist, whose theme is the fate of the person, also begins with the fate of Israel. Behind his opening sentence lies the question "Why do things go badly with Israel?" And first he answers, "Surely, God is good to Israel," and then he adds, by way of explanation, "to the pure in heart."

On first glance this seems to mean that it is only to the impure in Israel that God is not good. He is good to the pure in Israel; they are the "holy remnant," the true Israel, to whom He is good. But that would lead to the assertion that things go well with this remnant, and the questioner had taken as his starting point the experience that things went ill with Israel, not excepting indeed this part of it. The answer, understood in this way, would be no answer.

We must go deeper in this sentence. The questioner had drawn from the fact that things go ill with Israel the conclusion that therefore God is not good to Israel. But only one who is not pure in heart draws such a conclusion. One who is pure in heart, one who becomes pure in heart, cannot draw any such conclusion. For he experiences that God is good to him. But this does not mean that God rewards him with his goodness. It means, rather, that God's goodness is revealed to him who is pure in heart: he experiences this goodness. Insofar as Israel is pure in heart, becomes pure in heart, it experiences God's goodness.

Thus the essential dividing line is not between men who sin and men who do not sin, but between those who are pure in heart and those who are impure in heart. Even the sinner whose heart becomes pure experiences God's goodness as it is revealed to him. As Israel purifies its heart, it experiences that God is good to it.

It is from this standpoint that everything that is said in the psalm about "the wicked" is to be understood. The "wicked" are those who deliberately persist in impurity of heart.

The state of the heart determines whether a man lives in the truth, in which God's goodness is experienced, or in the semblance of truth, where the fact that it "goes ill" with him is confused with the illusion that God is not good to him.

The state of the heart determines. That is why "heart" is the dominant key word in this psalm, and recurs six times.

And now, after this basic theme has been stated, the speaker begins to tell of the false ways in his experience of life.

Seeing the prosperity of "the wicked" daily and hearing their braggart speech has brought him very near to the abyss of despairing unbelief, of the inability to believe any more in a living God active in life. "But I, a little more and my feet had turned aside, a mere nothing and my steps had stumbled." He goes so far as to be jealous of "the wicked" for their privileged position.

It is not envy that he feels, it is jealousy, that it is *they* who are manifestly preferred by God. That it is indeed they is proved to him by their being sheltered from destiny. For them there are not, as for all the others, those constraining and confining "bands" of destiny; "they are never in the trouble of man." And so they deem themselves superior to all, and stalk around with their "sound and fat bellies," and when one looks in their eyes, which protrude from the fatness of their faces, one sees "the paintings of the heart," the wish-images of their pride and their cruelty, flitting across. Their relation to the world of their fellow men is arrogance and cunning, craftiness and exploitation. "They speak oppression from above" and "set their mouth to the heavens." From what is uttered by this mouth set to the heavens, the Psalmist quotes two characteristic sayings which were supposed to be familiar. In the one (introduced by "therefore," meaning "therefore they say") they make merry over God's relation to "His people." Those who speak are apparently in Palestine as owners of great farms, and scoff at the prospective return of the landless people from exile, in accordance with the prophecies: the prophet of the Exile has promised them water (Isa. 41:17 f.), and "they may drink their fill of water," they will certainly not find much more here unless they become subject to the speakers. In the second saying they are apparently replying to the reproaches leveled against them: they were warned that God sees and knows the wrongs they have done, but the God of heaven has other things to do than to concern Himself with such earthly matters: "How does God know? Is there knowledge in the Most High?" And God's attitude confirms them, those men living in comfortable security: "they have reached power," theirs is the power.

That was the first section of the psalm, in which the speaker depicted his grievous experience, the prosperity of the wicked. But now he goes on to explain how his understanding of this experience has undergone a fundamental change.

Since he had again and again to endure, side by side, his own suffering and their "grinning" well-being, he is overcome: "It is not fitting that I should make such comparisons, as my own heart is not pure." And he proceeded to purify it. In vain. Even when he succeeded in being able "to wash his hands in innocence" (which does not mean an action or feeling of self-righteousness, but the genuine, second and higher purity that is won by a great struggle of the soul), the torment continued, and now it was like a leprosy to him; and as leprosy is understood in the Bible as a punishment for the disturbed relation between heaven and earth, so each morning, after each pain-torn night, it came over the Psalmist — "It is a chastisement — why am I chastised?" And once again there arose the contrast between the horrible enigma of the happiness of the wicked and his suffering.

At this point he was tempted to accuse God as Job did. He felt himself urged to "tell how it is." But he fought and conquered the temptation. The story of this conquest follows in the most vigorous form that the speaker has at his disposal, as an appeal to God. He interrupts his objectivized account and addresses God. If I had followed my inner impulse, he says to Him, "I should have betrayed the generation of Thy sons." The generation of the sons of God! Then he did not know that the pure in heart are the children of God; now he does know. He would have betrayed them if he had arisen and accused God. For they continue in suffering and do not complain. The words sound to us as though the speaker contrasted these "children of God" with Job, the complaining "servant of God."

He, the Psalmist, was silent even in the hours when the conflict of the human world burned into his purified heart. But now he summoned every energy of thought in order to "know" the meaning of this conflict. He strained the eyes of the spirit in order to penetrate the darkness that hid the meaning from him. But he always perceived only the same conflict ever anew, and this perception itself seemed to him now to be a part of that "trouble" which lies on all save those "wicked" men — even on the pure in heart. He had become one of these, yet he still did not recognize that "God is good to Israel."

"Until I came into the sanctuaries of God." Here the real turning point in this exemplary life is reached.

The man who is pure in heart, I said, experiences that God is good to him. He does not experience it as a consequence of the purification of his heart, but because only as one who is pure in heart is he able to come to the sanctuaries. This does not mean the Temple precincts in Jerusalem, but the sphere of God's holiness, the holy mysteries of God. Only to him who draws near to these is the true meaning of the conflict revealed.

But the true meaning of the conflict, which the Psalmist expresses here only for the other side, the "wicked," as he expressed it in the opening words for the right side, for the "pure in heart," is not — as the reader of the following words is only too easily misled into thinking — that the present state of affairs is replaced by a future state of affairs of a quite different kind, in which "in the end" things go well with the good and badly with the bad; in the language of modern thought the meaning is that the bad do not truly exist, and their "end" brings about only this change, that they now inescapably experience their nonexistence, the suspicion of which they had again and again succeeded in dispelling. Their life was "set in slippery places"; it was so arranged as to slide into the knowledge of their own nothingness; and when this finally happens, "in a moment," the great terror falls upon them and they are consumed with terror. Their life has been a shadow structure in a dream of God's. God awakes, shakes off the dream, and disdainfully watches the dissolving shadow image.

This insight of the Psalmist, which he obtained as he drew near to the holy mysteries of God, where the conflict is resolved, is not expressed in the context of his story, but in an address to "his Lord." And in the same address he confesses, with harsh self-criticism, that at the same time the state of error in which he had lived until then and from which he had suffered so much was revealed to him: "When my heart rose up in me, and I was pricked in my reins, brutish was I and ignorant, I have been as a beast before Thee."

With this "before Thee" the middle section of the psalm significantly concludes, and at the end of the first line of the last section (after the description and the story comes the confession) the words are significantly taken up. The words "And I am" at the beginning of the verse are to be understood emphatically: "Nevertheless I am," "Nevertheless I am continually with Thee." God does not count it against the heart that has become pure that it was earlier accustomed "to rise up." Certainly even the erring and struggling man was "with Him," for the man who struggles for God is near Him even when he imagines that he is driven far from God. That is the reality we learn from the revelation to Job out of the storm, in the hour of Job's utter despair (30:20–22) and utter readiness (31:35–39). But what the Psalmist wishes to teach us, in contrast to the Book of Job, is that the fact of his being with God is revealed to the struggling man in the hour when—not led astray by doubt and despair into treason, and become pure in heart—"he comes to the sanctuaries of God." Here he receives the revelation of the "continually." He who draws near with a pure heart to the divine mystery learns that he is continually with God.

It is a revelation. It would be a misunderstanding of the whole situation to look on this as a pious feeling. From man's side there is no continuity, only from God's side. The Psalmist has learned that God and he are continually with one another. But he cannot express his experience as a word of God. The teller of the primitive stories made God say to the fathers and to the first leaders of the people: "I am with thee," and the word "continually" was unmistakably heard as well. Thereafter, this was no longer reported, and we hear it again only in rare prophecies. A Psalmist (23:5) is still able to say to God: "Thou art with me." But when Job (29:5) speaks of God's having been with him in his youth, the fundamental word, the "continually," has disappeared. The speaker in our psalm is the first and only one to insert it expressly. He no longer says: "Thou art with me," but "I am continually with Thee." It is not, however, from his own consciousness and feeling that he can say this, for no man is able to be continually turned to the presence of God: he can say it only in the strength of the revelation that God is continually with him.

The Psalmist no longer dares to express the central experience as a word of God; but he expresses it by a gesture of God. God has taken his right hand— as a father, so we may add, in harmony with that expression "the generation of Thy children," takes his little son by the hand in order to lead him. More precisely, as in the dark a father takes his little son by the hand, certainly in order to lead him, but primarily in order to make present to him, in the warm touch of coursing blood, the fact that he, the father, is continually with him.

It is true that immediately after this the leading itself is expressed: "Thou dost guide me with Thy counsel." But ought this to be understood as meaning that the speaker expects God to recommend to him in the changing situations of his life what he should do and what he should refrain from doing? That would mean that the Psalmist believes that he now possesses a constant oracle, who would exonerate him from the duty of weighing up and deciding what he must do. Just because I take this man so seriously I cannot understand the matter in this way. The guiding counsel of God seems to me to be simply the divine Presence communicating itself direct to the pure in heart. He who is aware of this Presence acts in the changing situations of his life differently from him who does not perceive this Presence. The Presence acts as counsel: God counsels by making known that He is present. He has led His son out of darkness into the light, and now he can walk in the light. He is not relieved of taking and directing his own steps.

The revealing insight has changed life itself, as well as the meaning of the experience of life. It also changes the perspective of death. For the "oppressed" man death was only the mouth toward which the sluggish stream of suffering and trouble flows. But now it has become the event in which God—the continually Present One, the One who grasps the man's hand, the Good One— "takes" a man.

The tellers of the legends had described the translation of the living Enoch and the living Elijah to heaven as "a being taken," a being taken away by God Himself. The Psalmists transferred the description from the realm of miracle to that of personal piety and its most personal expression. In a psalm that is related to our psalm not only in language and style but also in content and feeling, the forty-ninth, there are these words: "But God will redeem my soul from the power of Sheol, when He takes me." There is nothing left here of the mythical idea of a translation. But not only that—there is nothing left of heaven either. There is nothing here about being able to go after death into heaven. And, so far as I see, there is nowhere in the "Old Testament" anything about this.

It is true that the sentence in our psalm that follows the words "Thou shalt guide me with Thy counsel" seems to contradict this. It once seemed to me to be indeed so, when I translated it as "And afterwards Thou dost take me up to glory." But I can no longer maintain this interpretation. In the original text there are three words. The first, "afterwards," is unambiguous—"After Thou hast guided me with Thy counsel through the remainder of my life," that is, "at the end of my life." The second word needs more careful examination. For us who have grown up in the conceptual world of a later doctrine of immortality, it is almost self-evident that we should understand "Thou shalt take me" as "Thou shalt take me up." The hearer or reader of that time understood simply, "Thou shalt take me away." But does the third word, *kabod*, not contradict this interpretation? Does it not say *whither* I shall be taken, namely, to "honor" or "glory"? No, it does not say this. We are led astray into this reading by understanding "taking up" instead of "taking."

This is not the only passage in the Scriptures where death and *kabod* meet. In the song of Isaiah on the dead king of Babylon, who once wanted to ascend into heaven like the day star, there are these words (14:18): "All the kings of the nations, all of them, lie in *kabod*, in glory, every one in his own house, but thou wert cast forth away from thy sepulcher." He is refused an honorable grave because he has destroyed his land and slain his people. *Kabod* in death is granted to the others, because they have uprightly fulfilled the task of their life. *Kabod*, whose root meaning is the radiation of the inner "weight" of a person, belongs to the earthly side of death. When I have lived my life, says our Psalmist to God, I shall die in *kabod*, in the fulfillment of my existence. In my death the coils of Sheol will not embrace me, but Thy hand will grasp me. "For," as is said in another psalm related in kind to this one, the sixteenth, "Thou wilt not leave my soul to Sheol."

Sheol, the realm of nothingness, in which, as a later text explains (Eccles. 9:10), there is neither activity nor consciousness, is not contrasted with a kingdom of heavenly bliss. But over against the realm of nothing there is God. The "wicked" have in the end a direct experience of their non-being; the "pure in heart" have in the end a direct experience of the Being of God.

This sense of *being taken* is now expressed by the Psalmist in the unsurpassably clear cry, "Whom have I in heaven!" He does not aspire to enter heaven after death, for God's home is not in heaven, so that heaven is empty. But he knows that in death he will cherish no desire to remain on earth, for now he will soon by wholly "with Thee"—here the word recurs for the third time—with Him who "has taken" him. But he does not mean by this what we are accustomed to call personal immortality, that is, continuation in the dimension of time so familiar to us in this our mortal life. He knows that after death "being with Him" will no longer mean, as it does in this life, "being separated from Him." The Psalmist now says with the strictest clarity what must now be said: it is not merely his flesh that vanishes in death, but also his heart, that inmost personal organ of the soul, which formerly "rose up" in rebellion against the human fate and which he then "purified" till he became pure in heart—this personal soul also vanishes. But He who was the true part and true fate of this person, the "rock" of this heart, God, is eternal. It is into His eternity that he who is pure in heart moves in death, and this eternity is something absolutely different from any kind of time.

Once again the Psalmist looks back at the "wicked," the thought of whom had once so stirred him. Now he does not call them the wicked, but "they that are far from Thee."

In the simplest manner he expresses what he has learned: since they are far from God, from Being, they are lost. And once more the positive follows the negative, once more, for the third and last time, that "and I," "and for me," which here means "nevertheless for me." "Nevertheless for me the good is to draw near to God." Here, in this conception of the good, the circle is closed. To him who may draw near to God, the good is given. To an Israel that is pure in heart the good is given, because it may draw near to God. Surely, God is good to Israel.

The speaker here ends his confession. But he does not yet break off. He gathers everything together. He has made his refuge, his "safety," "in his Lord"—he is sheltered in Him. And now, still turned to God, he speaks his last word about the task which is joined to all this, and which he has set himself, which God has set him—"To tell of all Thy works." Formerly he was provoked to tell of the *appearance*, and he resisted. Now he knows, he has the *reality* to tell of: the works of God. The first of his telling, the tale of the work that God has performed with him, is this psalm.

In this psalm two kinds of men seem to be contrasted with each other, the "pure in heart" and "the wicked." But that is not so. The "wicked," it is true, are clearly one kind of men, but the others are not. A man is as a "beast" and purifies his heart, and behold, God holds him by the hand. That is not a kind of men. Purity of heart is a state of being. A man is not pure in kind, but he is able to be or become pure—rather he is only essentially pure when he has become pure, and even then he does not thereby belong to a kind of men. The "wicked," that is, the bad, are not contrasted with good men. The good, says the Psalmist, is "to draw near to God." He does not say that those near to God are good. But he does call the bad "those who are far from God." In the language of modern thought that means that there are men who have no share in existence, but there are no men who possess existence. Existence cannot be possessed, but only shared in. One does not rest in the lap of existence, but one draws near to it. "Nearness" is nothing but such a drawing and coming near continually and as long as the human person lives.

The dynamic of farness and nearness is broken by death when it breaks the life of the person. With death there vanishes the heart, that inwardness of man, out of which arise the "pictures" of the imagination, and which rises up in defiance, but which can also be purified.

Separate souls vanish, separation vanishes. Time that has been lived by the soul vanishes with the soul; we know of no duration in time. Only the "rock" in which the heart is concealed, only the rock of human hearts, does not vanish. For it does not stand in time. The time of the world disappears before eternity, but existing man dies into eternity as into the perfect existence.

ROBERT GORDIS

The Style of Koheleth

HIS RELIGIOUS VOCABULARY

One of the principal obstacles to the understanding of *Koheleth* [in English this book of the Bible is called *Ecclesiastes*; the name Koheleth, which means preacher or teacher in Hebrew, also designates the author or editor of the book] has been its unique style, for which readers have not been prepared, particularly since the book is in the Bible. Because of its place in the sacred canon, most readers turn to it with more devoutness than alertness, expecting to be edified rather than stimulated by its contents.

The time is long overdue for recognizing, as Ehrlich observed, that the Bible is not a collection of religious texts, but rather "a national literature upon a religious foundation" [*Kommentar zu Psalmen* (Berlin, 1905)]. Only from this point of view can the reader savor fully the vitality, color and broad humanity of the Bible and appreciate the variety in outlook, temperament and mode of expression to be found within its pages. Priest and prophet, sage and psalmist, legist and poet, rationalist and mystic, skeptic and believer, all have found their place in the Bible. The canon of Scripture was created not by a religious sect of like-minded believers, but by a people sharing a common historical experience. The Librarian of the Synagogue was therefore capable of being hospitable to contradictory and even to extreme viewpoints, with which traditional Judaism might wrestle, but which it would never obliterate.

For the religious spirit, the Bible is eternally the Revelation of God, but in no superficial and mechanical sense. The Bible must be approached in the spirit of the profound Rabbinic comment on two rival schools, "Both these and the others are the words of the Living God."

From *Koheleth–The Man and His World.* © 1951 by Robert Gordis. Bloch Publishing, 1968.

Koheleth is the product of Hebrew life and thought and must be viewed against that background, but he represents a definitely individual interpretation of the tradition he inherited, and so cannot be understood purely in terms of parallels. His style reflects the elements both of similarity and of difference which mark his relationship to his contemporaries.

. . . At the very outset it must be borne in mind that Koheleth was a linguistic pioneer. He was struggling to use Hebrew for quasi-philosophic purposes, a use to which the language had not previously been applied. A thousand years later, medieval translators like the Tibbonides, who rendered Saadiah, Maimonides, Judah Halevi and other Jewish philosophers into Hebrew, still found that the language had not yet fully developed the flexibility, precision and vocabulary necessary for the treatment of philosophic themes. Koheleth's comparative success in this respect is not the least element of his literary skill.

His task was rendered still more difficult by a third factor. Biblical Hebrew has a deceptively simple syntax, as far as the forms are concerned. But as a result, each available device possesses a large number of uses and nuances. Perhaps the principal syntactic trait of Hebrew is that it uses parataxis almost exclusively, as against the hypotaxis preferred in Indo-European languages. A study of the luxuriant variety of shades of meaning of the Biblical connective *Vav*, "and," proves highly instructive in this respect. Hence, the interpreter must often use a large variety of subordinate clauses, where Hebrew uses a simple co-ordinate clause. Nor can he always be sure that he has gauged the author's intent correctly. Another difficulty inheres in the fact that the old Semitic mood endings had all but disappeared in Biblical Hebrew, with the result that the mood of verbs can only be inferred from the context.

Classical Hebrew had only two tenses, the perfect and the imperfect, and both were concerned not with the time of the action, which might be in the past, present or future, but with the extent to which the action was looked upon as completed. As a result, the perfect was generally used to denote past action and the imperfect, future action, but this was far from universally the case. In the latest stage of Biblical Hebrew, represented by *Esther, Ezra-Nehemiah-Chronicles*, and *Koheleth*, the participle was increasingly used as a present tense, often with progressive force, a usage which became regular in Mishnaic and modern Hebrew. The infinitive was likewise utilized in a variety of ways. The vigor and succinctness of Biblical Hebrew is in large measure due to the relative paucity of adjectives and adverbs — it is preeminently a language of nouns and verbs. All these aspects of Biblical Hebrew complicate the understanding of a text in which exactness is essential. But they do not exhaust the problems of Koheleth's style, which possesses several special features.

Like other writers since his time, who were raised in a religious tradition from which they later broke away in whole or in part, Koheleth uses the language in which he was reared, and incidentally, the only one he knew, to express his own individual viewpoint. The contemporary reader will think of Ernest Renan, Anatole France and George Santayana in modern times as offering a partial analogy.

A very remarkable parallel, *mutatis mutandis*, is afforded by the philosopher Spinoza, who lived nineteen centuries after Koheleth. One of the profoundest contemporary students of Spinoza, Professor H. A. Wolfson of Harvard [*The Philosophy of Spinoza* (Cambridge, 1934)], demonstrated that Spinoza's *Ethics* has been widely misunderstood because of the failure to reckon with the author's practice of using the traditional philosophical vocabulary of his time to express his own individual and heterodox concepts. In Wolfson's words, "The *Ethics* — contrary to the generally accepted opinion — is primarily a criticism of the fundamental principles of religious philosophy which at the beginning of the Christian era were laid down by Philo and were still in vogue at the time of Spinoza in the seventeenth century. This criticism is constructed according to an old forensic device which may be described as 'yes' and 'but.' The 'yes' part is an expression of Spinoza's assent to the external formulation of some of the principles of traditional religious philosophy. The 'but' part is a statement of the special sense in which he himself is willing to use that formulation . . . It is for this reason also that the *Ethics*, in my opinion, has so often been misunderstood and so often misinterpreted." Wolfson proceeds to point out that such standard elements of the philosophical vocabulary as "substance," "mode," "attribute," "thought," "extension," "body," "soul," and "freedom," are all affirmed by Spinoza, but in senses widely at variance with those of conventional theologians and philosophers. For example, "Spinoza has no objection to adopting the vocabulary of his opponents and describing the human soul as being of divine origin."

To be sure, Koheleth was far from being a systematic thinker and technical philosopher like Spinoza, but both men had undergone a strikingly similar development. They had both been reared within the Jewish tradition, which had indeed grown in extent in the intervening centuries, though remaining basically the same — a faith in a Creator ruling His world in justice and mercy. Both thinkers had broken with this all but universally accepted pattern of belief in many respects and had developed an original world-view. Because of their background and inclination, however, both preferred to express their ideas in the terminology to which they were accustomed. As might have been expected, Spinoza even accepted certain elements of traditional beliefs, which were not a direct and logical consequence of his thought. In sum, both the skeptic of

the 3rd century B.C.E. and the heretic of the 17th century C.E. retained not
only the language and the modes of expression characteristic of their traditional
upbringing, but part of its thought-content as well.

Another striking instance of the unconventional use of traditional vocabulary
is afforded by Goethe's *Faust*. In lines 328 f. the poet writes:

> Ein guter Mensch in seinem dunklen Drange
> Ist sich des rechten Weges wohl bewusst.

Literally rendered, the passage reads: "A good man in his vague striving
is quite conscious of the right way." Yet as all commentators on the passage
have recognized, *ein guter Mensch* and *des rechten Weges* are used not in their
ordinary moral sense, but in a Goethean sense as "one who has ideals and seeks
to realize them, or in other words, possesses that 'good will' which Goethe
calls 'the foundation of right conduct.' "

In the ancient world of Koheleth, the world-view of traditional religion
was, of course, infinitely more pervasive and compelling than in Spinoza's or
Goethe's time. Hence Koheleth could not dispense with such conventional
religious and ethical terms as "sinner," "fool," "good (before God)," "the gift
of God," "God's favor, gift or will." Nor was it merely a matter of terminology.
His entire world-view found expression within this same framework.

A few instances of this tendency may be cited. Traditional morality declared
that he who fulfilled God's will would be happy. Koheleth declares that he
who is happy is fulfilling God's will:

> Indeed, every man to whom God has given wealth and possessions
> and granted the power to enjoy them, taking his share and rejoicing
> in his labor, that is the gift of God . . . for it is God who provides
> the joy in a man's heart.
>
> (5:18 f.)

The conventional Wisdom teachers call the sinner a fool. So does Koheleth,
but he reserves the right to define his terms. A sinner is he who fails to work
for the advancement of his own happiness. The Book of *Proverbs* promises
that the righteous will ultimately inherit the wealth of the evildoer:

> He who increases his wealth by usury and interest is gathering it
> for him who befriends the poor.
>
> (Prov. 28:8)

Koheleth promises the same to the man who is "pleasing to God," the man
who obeys God's will, and seeks to achieve joy:

> To the man God favors, He gives wisdom, knowledge and joy,

but to the sinner, He assigns the task of gathering and amassing,
only to hand it over at last to the man who is pleasing to God.
(2:26).

The Prophets, with unfailing insistence, call upon the people to hear the word
of God. So does Koheleth. He, too, calls upon his reader to remember God
and His purpose for man, before old age sets in and the time for joy is past:

> Remember your Creator in the days of your youth,
> Before the evil days come and the years draw near,
> Of which you will say, "I have no pleasure in them."
> (12:1)

This clothing of the hedonistic principle in religious guise is not without analogy
in Hebrew literature. The book of *Proverbs* counsels:

> Hear, my son, and be wise,
> And walk in the ways of your heart.
> (23:19)

Ben Sira, whose general moral system is conventional, makes the enjoyment
of life a duty:

> My son, if you have the means, treat yourself well,
> For there is no pleasure in the grave,
> And there is no postponement of death.
> (14:11)

The same theme is stressed elsewhere in his book (14:15–19; 30:21–23). Even
more striking are the words of the Babylonian sage, Samuel, of the 3rd century,
cited in the Talmud:

> Seize hold and eat, seize hold and drink, for this world whence
> we depart is like a wedding feast.
> (B. Erub. 54a)

Samuel's great contemporary, Rab, expresses the same sentiment in typically
religious language:

> Every man must render an account before God of all the good things
> he beheld in life and did not enjoy.
> (Jerusalem Talmud, *Kiddushin*, end)

No more perfect analogy could be found to Koheleth's words:

> Rejoice, young man, in your youth,

And let your heart cheer you in your youthful days.
Follow the impulses of your heart
And the desires of your eyes,
And know that for all this,
God will call you to account.

(11:9)

The resemblance of language is striking. The Rabbi uses the traditional term
din veḥeśbōn (lit. "judgment and reckoning"), Koheleth, the Biblical word
mišpāṭ (lit. "judgment"). Similarly, when Koheleth says, "Go, then, eat your
bread with joy and drink your wine with a glad heart, for God has already
approved your actions" (9:7), he is expressing his philosophy of life in a religious
vocabulary congenial both to his own temper and to the spirit of his age.
Koheleth's insistence that man's failure to enjoy life's blessings is a sin in the
eyes of God has its parallel in the Talmudic discussion on the Nazir, the ascetic
in Biblical times who took a vow to abstain from wine and to let his hair grow
long. In explaining the Biblical provision which enjoined him to bring a sin-
offering at the close of his Nazirate period (Num. 6:14), the Talmud declares:
"Whoever deprives himself of wine is called 'a sinner,'" adding a further
generalization, "If the Nazir, who deprived himself only of wine, is called 'a
sinner,' how much more so he who deprives himself of every blessing!"

The same attitude of opposition to asceticism is reflected in the deeply
moving story attributed to Koheleth's contemporary, the High Priest Simon
the Just, who never ate the "guilt-offering" of a Nazir who had been defiled,
except in one special instance. This was the case of a handsome, curly-headed
youth who, feeling that he was in danger of falling into sin because of his own
beauty, became a Nazir and dedicated his locks to God. Talmudic Judaism
was all but universally opposed to the institution of the Nazir because of its
own wholehearted acceptance of life's blessings. Koheleth's insistence upon the
enjoyment of life flowed from a tragic realization of the brevity of life, rather
than from an optimistic joy in a world governed by a good God, as taught
by the Rabbis. But his stylistic usage is illumined by theirs.

Moreover, Koheleth's highly personal use of conventional religious
terminology rests upon a solid foundation in Biblical Hebrew. The key word
is *ḥāṭā'*, which originally meant "miss (the goal or way), go wrong," as the
Semitic cognates clearly indicate. This non-moral meaning of the root *ḥāṭā'*,
"miss," it is interesting to note, is preserved primarily in Wisdom literature.
The more frequent meaning "sinner" is a secondary development from "miss
the path of duty, or of God, hence, sin." Finally, in accordance with a widespread
semantic process, the nouns *ḥēṭ'*, *ḥaṭṭā'th*, "sin," develop the connotation of
"the consequence of sin," hence "punishment."

In Koheleth, ḥōṭē' in its common sense of "sinner" does occur, but in each instance its meaning is made clear by the juxtaposition of rāshā', "wicked," or ṣaddīk, "righteous" (7:20; 8:12; 9:2). The meaning "punishment" occurs verbally in 5:5. Its earlier but rarer meaning occurs in 9:18, where it is synonymous with "fool." Two more passages remain, 2:26 and 7:26, which have been widely regarded as pious interpolations, because in them Koheleth foretells suffering to the "sinner." It is significant, however, that in both these passages the ḥōṭē' is contrasted, not with ṣaddīk, but with a characteristic term of his own, ṭōbh liphᵉnei hā'elōhīm, literally, "he who is good before God." Actually ḥōṭē' in these passages is used both in its non-moral sense of "fool, one who misses the right path," and in its religious connotation of "sinner," as Koheleth understands it, the man who violates God's will be failing to enjoy the blessings of God's world, as in the Talmudic parallels adduced above.

On the other hand, other words, which from their origin lack the purely intellectual non-ethical meaning which inheres in the root ḥāṭā', are used by Koheleth exclusively in their conventional moral meanings. This is true of rāshā', "wicked;" resha', "evil doing;" and ṣaddīk, "righteous."

Closely similar to Koheleth's use of ḥāṭā in terms of his own world-view is his employment of the traditional idiom yārē' elōhīm, "fearing God," which is frequent elsewhere in the Bible in the connotation of observing the moral law as the will of God. The phrase occurs in the book of Koheleth four times. The last of these is in the Epilogue, which does not emanate from our author, and so it is used here in the conventional sense. In 8:12, which is a quotation or a restatement of a conventional utterance, Koheleth uses it in its accepted meaning, and makes his meaning clear by using it in direct contrast with rāshā' in the next verse. In the two remaining passages, 5:6 and 7:18, Koheleth uses the idiom in perfect consistency with his viewpoint—"he who fears God" is he who obeys God's will by avoiding foolish actions and their consequent penalty.

An understanding of Koheleth's unique vocabulary is an essential key to the book and its message.

HIS USE OF QUOTATIONS

The second important characteristic of Koheleth's style, which has not been adequately noted in the past, with disastrous results for our understanding of the book, is his use of proverbial quotations. Sumerian, Egyptian and Akkadian literature, like the Bible and the Talmud, affords an impressive array of examples of quotations cited by writers for a variety of purposes. These quotations have been generally overlooked or misunderstood because they are cited without any introductory formula indicating their true relationship to the literary document in which they are imbedded; that no such device as quotation marks was available to the ancient writers is self-evident. To complicate matters still further, their uses fall into no less than ten categories, which are, however, related developments of the same basic technique. That any given passage is indeed a quotation must be understood by the reader, who is called upon in Semitic literature to supply not only punctuation but vocalization as well.

This widespread use of quotations is entirely comprehensible in the ancient world, in which the tradition of the past was omnipresent and age and wisdom were regarded as synonymous. Hence quotations are to be met with even in the Prophets, in spite of the fact that prophetic inspiration is essentially a unique and personal quality, the product of direct ecstatic communion with God. Though the prophet's message is not the result of study and argument, and needs no logical demonstration, for it bears its inner assurance of truth in the conviction that "thus saith the Lord," he, too, is conscious of the traditions of his predecessors.

It is, however, in Wisdom literature that quotations play the most fundamental role. Here there is no supernatural revelation, merely patient observation used as the basis of reasonable conclusions. Each generation of Sages finds in the extant proverbial literature of the past a body of truth, created by their predecessors, whose observations on life have approved themselves to their colleagues.

In particular, the unconventional Wisdom writers, to whose ranks Koheleth belonged, would have occasion to use this literary device, since their ideas were an outgrowth of the accepted doctrine of the schools and their careers continued to be closely associated with practical Wisdom. It must constantly be kept in mind that the relationship of these unconventional Wise Men to the culture of their day was essentially complex. Within their world-view were elements of the completely conventional, the modified old, and the radically new. They doubtless accepted many aspects of the practical Wisdom as expounded in the schools where they were educated and in which they themselves taught. As teachers of Wisdom they would have occasion to quote conventional proverbs or compose original sayings of their own, which were not different in form or spirit from those of their more traditionally minded colleagues. Especially in the realm of practical affairs, their standpoint would resemble that of the schools. In other areas of thought, there would be ideas that they could accept in modified form, while still others they would oppose entirely. These might be cited, as in *Koheleth*, in order to serve as the text for an ironic or negating comment, or they might occur as in *Job*, where the speaker cites the words and sentiments of his opponents in order to demolish them, or quotes the utterances of the Lord in order to submit to Him.

Before the evidence for this usage in Koheleth is set forth, several points should be made clear. The term "quotations," as used here, refers to *words which do not reflect the present sentiments of the author of the literary composition in which they are found, but have been introduced by the author to convey the standpoint of another person or situation.* These quotations include, but are not limited to, citations of previously existing literature, whether written or oral. In sum, the term refers to passages that cite the speech or thought of a subject, actual or hypothetical, past or present, which is distinct from the context in which it is embodied.

The abundance of material not only demonstrates the validity of the usage postulated for the Bible, but sheds welcome light on the variety of techniques employed. Of the ten categories of quotations noted, several do not appear in Koheleth and therefore need not be discussed here.

As a point of departure for this usage, Eccles. 4:8 may be cited:

יש אחד ואין שני גם בן ואח אין לו ואין קץ לכל עמלו גם עינו לא תשבע עשר
ולמי אני עמל ומחסר את נפשי מטובה גם זה הבל וענין רע הוא.   It is obvious
that the words ולמי אני עמל ומחסר את נפשי מטובה are not the words of
citation of a hypothetical speech and thought, an idea that *might or should have* occurred to the subject. Needless to add, a *verbum dicendi* (or quotation marks) must be supplied, and, what is more, the verb must be made to reflect the required mood:

> Here is a man alone, with no one besides him, neither son nor brother. Yet there is no end to his toil, nor is his eye ever satisfied with his wealth. *He never asks himself*, "For whom am I laboring and depriving myself of joy?" Yes, it is vanity, a bad business.

In interpreting the passage in Song of Songs 1:7 f., it has been very plausibly suggested that the second verse is a hypothetical quotation. If the beloved is forced to ask after the whereabouts of her lover, the other shepherds will try to persuade her to forget him.

איכה תרעה איכה תרביץ בצהרים   הגידה לי שאהבה נפשי
שלמה אהיה כעטיה על עדרי חבריך:
אם לא תדעי לך היפה בנשים
ורעי את גדיתיך על משכנות הרעים: צאי לך בעקבי הצאן

> Tell me, O you whom I love,
> Where do you feed and rest your flock at noon?
> Why should I be a wanderer (?)
> Among the flocks of your friends,

Who would mock me and say, if I asked about you:
"If you do not know, fairest among women,
Go forth in the tracks of the flocks
And feed your kids near the shepherds' tents."

A similar view has been proposed for Job 22:4 f., the second verse being
regarded as a hypothetical formulation by Eliphaz of the reproof God could
address to man, were He minded to do so:

המיראתך יכיחך   יבוא עמך במשפט:
הלא רעתך רבה   ואין־קץ לעונתיך

Will God reprove you because of your piety,
Enter into argument with you,
For God could say to man:
"Indeed your evil is great,
And there is no end to your sins!"

The identical usage is often to be met with in Rabbinic literature, particularly
in legal argumentation, where hypothetical considerations are frequently invoked:

Keth. 13:3 בנכסים מועטים הבנות יזונו והבנים יחזרו על הפתחים אמר
אדמון מפני שאני זכר הפסדתי.

When an inheritance is small, the daughters are to be supported
and the sons are to go begging from door to door. Admon says,
A son might argue under these circumstances, "Shall *I* suffer because
I am a male?"

Baba Metzia 35a ונהמניה לוה למלוה נמי בהא כמה היה שוה לא קים
ליה בנויה.

Let the borrower believe the lender on this point too, as to what
the pledged object is worth. "No," *the borrower could say, "The lender
is an honorable man,* but he is not familiar with its true value."

Passages such as these are not, however, quotations in the usual sense of
the term, that is to say, these passages did not have an independent literary
existence before they appeared in their present context.

Quotations of the more usual form are also frequent in Koheleth, who
would have occasion to utilize brief, pithy and widely familiar proverbs. This
trait is undoubtedly the result of his background and occupation as a Wisdom
teacher. His speculations on life did not lead him to abandon his interest in
the mundane concerns of the lower Wisdom; he merely went beyond them.

As he continued to teach the practical Wisdom to his pupils, he doubtless contributed to its literature, most of which was couched in short, pithy maxims of a realistic turn. Hence, maxims similar in both form and spirit to those in the Book of *Proverbs* are common in *Koheleth*. These are not interpolations by more conventional readers, as had been assumed. They belong, as MacDonald has well noted, to the author's method of keeping connection with the past, while leaving it behind.

Koheleth's quotations of proverbs vary in method and purpose. The several categories, which constitute one of the most characteristic marks of his style, must now be described. . . .

I. *The straightforward use of proverbial quotations*, cited to buttress an argument and therefore requiring no expansion or comment, because the writer accepts them as true.

How citations of this kind blend with the author's own words is illustrated in B. Erub. 54a, where Ben Sira 14:11–12 is cited, again without any external mark:

בני אם יש לך היטיב לך שאין בשאול תענוג ולא למות התמהמה ואם תאמר
אניח לבני חוק מי יניד לך בני אדם דומין לעשבי השדה הללו נוצצין
והללו נובלין.

While there is no formal indication, Rab begins this counsel to Rab Hamnuna with a quotation from *Ben Sira* to which he appends his own comments:

> "My son, if you have the wherewithal,
> Do good to yourself,
> For there is no pleasure in the grave,
> And no postponement of death."
> And if you say, Let me leave a portion for my son,
> Who can tell you in the grave (what will happen to it)?
> Men are like the grass of the field,
> Some sprout and others decay.

The stichs in quotation marks are cited from Ben Sira 14:11–12; the remainder is Rab's own, except for the last stich, which is a free paraphrase of Ben Sira 14:18b.

This straightforward use of quotations is common in Koheleth. Even the most unconventional thinker will recognize the value of practical counsel, such as is given in the Book of *Proverbs*. The most confirmed cynic will agree that

Through sloth the ceiling sinks,
And through slack hands the house leaks.
(Eccles. 10:18)

Or he will suggest that it is wise to diversify one's undertakings:

Send your bread upon the waters,
So that you may find it again after many days.
(Eccles. 11:1)

Exactly as in any other Wisdom book, like Proverbs and Ben Sira, the notebook of Koheleth registers these and others of a conventional mould. That these are generally excised by modern scholars like Siegfried, McNeile, Haupt and Barton, though with no unanimity, is due to a rigid view of his personality, which declares that if Koheleth be unconventional, he must be an iconoclast throughout, perpetually at war with conventional ideas.

Whether Koheleth is quoting proverbs already extant, or composing them himself, is difficult to determine. Thus in his learned and stimulating work, *The Proverb* [Cambridge, 1931], Archer Taylor observes: "We shall never know, for example, which of the Exeter Gnomes in Old English poetry are proverbial and which are the collector's moralizing in the same pattern. . . . In a dead language the means which are available are various, but not always effective or easily applied. A passage, when it varies grammatically or syntactically from ordinary usage or from the usage of the context, can be safely declared to be proverbial." He also cites countless examples of the difficulty in distinguishing folk sayings and the work of individuals, and he remarks: "Of course an individual creates a proverb and sets it in circulation. The inventor's title to his property may be recognized by all who use it or his title may be so obscured by the passage of time that only investigation will determine the source of the saying." Especially pertinent is his statement: "Biblical proverbs, and among them perhaps even those which we have discussed, may have been proverbs before their incorporation into Holy Writ."

Particularly congenial to the pessimism of Koheleth would be a statement like 7:3, which he inserts in his notebook:

"Sorrow is better than joy, for through sadness of countenance the understanding improves."

II. At times, Koheleth appears to buttress his argument with *a proverb, part of which is apposite, while the rest of the saying, though irrelevant, is quoted for the sake of completeness*, a literary practice common to writers in all ages. The use of quotation marks will serve to make the matter clear.

אל תבהל על פיך ולבך אל ימהר להוציא דבר לפני האלהים כי האלהים
בשמים ואתה על הארץ על כן יהיו דבריך מעטים: כי בא החלום ברב
ענין וקול כסיל ברב דברים:

Do not hasten to speak, nor let yourself be rushed into uttering
words before God; for God is in heaven and you are on earth —
therefore let your words be few. For "as dreams come with many
concerns, so the fool speaks with many words."

(5:1–2)

The same usage occurs in Egyptian literature. In the *Admonitions of a Prophet*,
which probably emanates from the end of the second millennium, we have
a graphic description of the widespread destruction sweeping over the social
order, with the lowly attaining to wealth and importance. In the "Second Poem,"
each stanza begins with the refrain, "Behold," a characteristic rhetorical device.
Part of this section reads as follows:

Behold, he that had no bread now possesseth a barn; (but) that
wherewith his storehouse is provided is the poverty of another.
Behold, the bald head that used no oil now possesseth jars of pleasant
myrrh.
Behold, she that had no box now possesseth a coffer.
She that looked at her face in the water now possesseth a mirror.

[A verse left incomplete.]

Behold, a man is happy when he eateth his food:

"Spend thy possessions in joy and without holding thee back!
It is good for a man to eat his food, which God assigneth to
him whom he praiseth."

The last two sentences, as Erman notes, are "a quotation from an old book"
[A. Erman, *The Literature of the Ancient Egyptians* (New York, 1927)]. They
have been introduced to buttress the argument. Actually they are not altogether
appropriate. For while the author is describing the lot of a man formerly poor,
who is now happy to have something to eat, the proverb urges the enjoyment
of life. But the use of quotations only partly relevant to the context is usual
with writers everywhere.

As Taylor has indicated, only where a characteristic fillip of style occurs
is it possible to determine whether the proverb is a quotation or indubitably
original.

Thus 11:4 seems a typical quotation, but all the earmarks of Koheleth's personality are to be seen in the ironic comment that precedes it (v. 3). His thought seems to be that the events of nature will take place without man's assistance, and that there is therefore no justification for idle gazing:

> If the clouds are filled with rain, they will empty it upon the earth;
> if a tree is blown down by the wind in the south or in the north,
> wherever it falls, there it lies. Therefore on with your work, for
> he who watches the wind will never sow and he who gapes at the
> clouds will never reap.
>
> (Eccles. 11:3–4)

Incidentally, the unity and integrity of the passage seem clear from its chiastic structure, for 3a and 4b deal with cloud and rain, while 3b and 4a are concerned with the wind uprooting a tree.

Other examples of the straightforward use of proverbs in Ecclesiastes are to be found in the collection 10:2 to 11:6, all of which may be original epigrams of Koheleth.

III. Particularly characteristic of Koheleth is *the use of proverbial quotations as a text*, on which he comments from his own viewpoint. While the Commentary should be consulted for a full discussion of all such passages, a few instances may be adduced here.

Eccles. 7:1–14 is a collection of seven Hokmah utterances, expressing conventional Wisdom teachings and linked together by the opening word *tobh*. Each proverb is amplified by a comment bearing all the earmarks of Koheleth's style and viewpoint. Thus a typically abstemious and moralizing doctrine is sounded in Eccles. 7:2a:

> Better to go to a house of mourning
> than to go to a banquet hall.

a proverb, warning against the revelry and immorality of the house of mirth. But Koheleth gives it a darker undertone:

> For that is the end of all men,
> And the living may take the lesson to heart.
>
> (Eccles. 7:2b)

Examples of this use of proverb as text with ironic comment are plentiful. Thus a proverb extols the virtues of cooperation. Koheleth approves the sentiment, but for reasons of his own:

Men say, "Two are better than one, because they have a reward in their labor." True, for if either falls, the other can lift his comrade, but woe to him who is alone when he falls, with no one else to lift him. Then also, if two sleep together, they will be warm, but how can one alone keep warm? Moreover, if some enemy attack either one, the two will stand against him, while a triple cord cannot quickly be severed.

(Eccles. 4:9–12)

The teachers of morality emphasized that love of money does not make for happiness. This idea is expanded by Koheleth through the characteristic reflection that strangers finally consume the substance of the owner, an idea to which he refers again and again (cf. 2:18 ff.; 4:7 ff.):

"He who loves money will never have enough of it and he who loves wealth will never attain it"–this is indeed vanity. For as wealth increases, so do those who would spend it, hence what value is there in the owner's superior ability, except that he has more to look upon?

(Eccles. 5:9 f.)

The Book of Proverbs counsels submission to political authority:

Fear, my son, God and king, and meddle not with those who seek change.

(Prov. 24:21)

Koheleth repeats this idea, but with his tongue in his cheek:

I say: keep the king's command, because of the oath of loyalty,

submit to the king because of your oath of fealty, but also, he adds as an afterthought:

Since the king's word is law, who can say to him, "What are you doing?"

(Eccles. 8:2–4)

because the king is powerful enough to crush you.

Similarly, to maintain oneself in an atmosphere of political tyranny and intrigue requires skill in choosing the proper occasion. That idea Koheleth appends as a comment to a perfectly moral utterance about the virtue of obedience:

"Whoever keeps his command will experience no trouble," for a wise mind will know the proper time and procedure. For everything has its proper time and procedure, man's evil being so widespread.

(Eccles. 8:5 f.)

In addition to these examples, which mirror the political conditions of Koheleth's time, we find several interesting instances of his use of conventional *Hokmah* material in the field of religious and philosophic speculation.

For example, Koheleth is not disposed to deny altogether that retribution overtakes the sinner. But, he insists, this takes place only after a long delay, which affords the wrongdoer the opportunity and the incentive to sin.

These two limitations on Divine justice are referred to in an interesting passage, 8:11–14, the center of which (vv. 12b, 13) is a quotation of the traditional view, from which Koheleth dissents:

> Because judgment upon an evil deed is not executed speedily, men's hearts are encouraged to do wrong, for a sinner commits a hundred crimes and God is patient with him, though I know the answer that "it will be well in the end with those who revere God and fear Him and it will be far from well with the sinner, who, like a shadow, will not long endure, because he does not fear God."

> Here is a vanity that takes place on the earth—there are righteous men who receive the recompense due the wicked, and wicked men who receive the recompense due the righteous. I say, this is indeed vanity.

Koheleth would undoubtedly agree with the common view that life on any terms is preferable to death. Yet his general intellectual conviction as to the futility of living impels him to a comment, which ostensibly justifies, but actually undermines, the entire proposition:

> "He who is attached to the living still has hope, for a live dog is better than a dead lion!" The living know at least that they will die, but the dead know nothing, nor have they any reward, for their memory is forgotten. Their loves, their hates, their jealousies, all have perished—never again will they have a share in all that is done under the sun.

(Eccles. 9:4–6)

This usage of a quotation cited by the author and then refuted, or at least discussed, occurs several times in the Babylonian *Complaint on the Injustice of the World*, the so-called "Babylonian Koheleth." Thus the author explicitly cites two conventional proverbs on the well-being of the righteous, which he does not accept, as the succeeding comment indicates (ll. 69–71):

A saying I wish to discuss with you:

"They go on the road to fortune, who do not think of
   murder."
"More than a mere creature is the weak one who prays
   to God."
More than any other child of man, have I been troubled
   about God's plan.

Another quotation without an introductory formula occurs in ll. 215 ff. The poet laments the prosperity and success of the wicked. He then cites the conventional proverbs which urge obedience to the god as the secret of well-being, but he then refutes them by emphasizing the unpredictability and transitoriness of God's favor:

Without God, the rogue possesses wealth,
For murder as his weapon accompanies him.
"You who do not seek the counsel of the God, what is your fortune?"
"He who bears the yoke of God, his bread is provided!"
No, seek rather a good wind of the gods.
What you have destroyed in a year, you restore in an instant,
Among men I have set offerings, changeable are the omens.

The lines in quotation marks are not indicated externally as such, but are evidently citations of accepted ideas, with which the melancholy poet is in disagreement. That lines 217 f. constitute a quotation is recognized by Ebeling, who adds the comment, "So sagen die Leute," the precise formula required in all the instances cited above.

That Sumerian Wisdom literature, still awaiting investigation, will disclose a similar use of proverbs as quotations has been affirmed by a leading Sumerologist [Prof. Samuel N. Kramer].

This literary technique has persisted from the dawn of civilization in Egypt and Mesopotamia through ancient Palestine down to modern America. We encounter it in the work of a contemporary poet, who uses a quotation, usually associated with a sentimental context, and follows it up with a blunt comment of his own [Elliott Coleman's *Twenty-seven Night Sonnets* (Milan, 1949)].

IV. *Contrasting proverbs* offer another way of contravening accepted doctrines. As is well known, proverbs frequently contradict one another, since they express the half-truths of empirical wisdom. "Fools rush in where angels

fear to tread" is opposed by the saw, "He who hesitates is lost." The beautiful
sentiment, "Absence makes the heart grow fonder," is bluntly denied by the
saying, "Out of sight, out of mind."

The compiler of *Proverbs* was aware of this tendency when he quoted these
two maxims in succession:

> Answer not a fool according to his folly, lest thou also be
> like unto him.
> Answer a fool according to his folly, lest he be wise in his
> own eyes.
>
> (Prov. 26:4–5)

Both *Job* and *Koheleth* use the same device, but for their own purposes. They
quote one proverb and then register their disagreement by citing another
diametrically opposed thereto.

No theme was dearer to the hearts of the instructors of youth than that
of the importance of hard work. Koheleth expresses his doubts on the subject
by quoting the conventional view and following it with another proverb of
opposite intent:

> "The fool folds his hands and thus destroys himself."
> "Better is a handful acquired with ease, than two hands full
> gained through toil and chasing after wind."
>
> (Eccles. 4:5, 6)

That Koheleth favors the second view is proved by its position as a refutation
after verse 5, by the characteristic phrase "vanity and chasing after wind," and
by his oft-repeated view of the folly of toil in a meaningless world.

Like all the Wise Men, conventional or otherwise, Koheleth has a prejudice
in favor of wisdom as against folly. He himself tells how the wisdom of one
poor man proved more efficacious than a mighty army. Yet he knows, too,
how little wisdom is honored for its own sake, and how one fool can destroy
the efforts of many wise men. These ideas seem to be expressed in some
reflections, consisting of brief proverbs contradicted by others:

> "Wisdom is better than strength" but "the poor man's wisdom is
> despised and his words go unheeded."
> "Wisdom is better than weapons," but "one fool can destroy
> much good."
>
> (Eccles. 9:16, 18)

Here, the latter proverbs, in which Koheleth expresses his own standpoint,
are undoubtedly of his own composition. The former proverbs, from which

he dissents, may be quotations, or, as seems more probable, original restatements by Koheleth of conventional *Hokmah* doctrines.

Koheleth's *unconventional use of a religious vocabulary* and his frequent *citation of proverbial lore* for his own special purposes are among the most unique elements of his style.

ROBERT ALTER

The Garden of Metaphor:
The Song of Songs

The Song of Songs comprises what are surely the most exquisite poems that have come down to us from ancient Israel, but the poetic principles on which they are shaped are in several ways instructively untypical of biblical verse. When it was more the scholarly fashion to date the book late, either in the Persian period (W. F. Albright) or well into the Hellenistic period (H. L. Ginsberg), these differences might have been attributed to changing poetic practices in the last centuries of biblical literary activity. Several recent analysts, however, have persuasively argued that all the supposed stylistic and lexical evidence for a late date is ambiguous, and it is quite possible, though not demonstrable, that these poems originated, whatever subsequent modifications they may have undergone, early in the First Commonwealth period.

The most likely sources of distinction between the Song of Songs and the rest of biblical poetry lie not in chronology but in genre, in purpose, and perhaps in social context. Although there are some striking love motifs elsewhere in biblical poetry—in Psalms, between man and God, in the Prophets, between God and Israel—the Song of Songs is the only surviving instance of purely secular love poetry from ancient Israel. The erotic symbolism of the Prophets would provide later ages an effective warrant for reading the Song of Songs as a religious allegory, but in fact the continuous celebration of passion and its pleasures makes this the most consistently secular of all biblical texts—even more so than Proverbs, which for all its pragmatic worldly concerns also stresses the fear of the Lord and the effect of divine justice on the here and now. We have no way of knowing the precise circumstances under which or for which

From *The Art of Biblical Poetry.* © 1985 by Robert Alter. Basic Books, 1985.

the Song of Songs was composed. A venerable and persistent scholarly theory
sees it as the (vestigial?) liturgy of a fertility cult; others—to my mind, more
plausibly—imagine it as a collection of wedding songs. What I should like to
reject at the outset is the whole quest for the "life-setting" of the poems—
because it is, necessarily, a will-o'-the-wisp and, even more, because it is a prime
instance of the misplaced concreteness that has plagued biblical research, which
naïvely presumes that the life-setting, if we could recover it, would somehow
provide the key to the language, structure, and meaning of the poems.

The imagery of the Song of Songs is a curious mixture of pastoral, urban,
and regal allusions, which leaves scant grounds for concluding whether the
poems were composed among shepherds or courtiers or somewhere in between.
References in rabbinic texts suggest that at least by the Roman period the poems
were often sung at weddings, and, whoever composed them, there is surely
something popular about these lyric celebrations of the flowering world, the
beauties of the female and male bodies, and the delights of lovemaking. The
Wisdom poetry of Job and Proverbs was created by members of what one
could justifiably call the ancient Israelite intelligentsia. Prophetic verse was
produced by individuals who belonged—by sensibility and in several signal
instances by virtue of social background as well—to a spiritual-intellectual elite.
The psalms were tied to the cult, and at least a good many of them were probably
created in priestly circles (the mimetic example of short prayers embedded in
biblical narrative suggests that ordinary people, in contradistinction to the
professional psalm-poets, may have improvised personal prayers in simple prose).
It is only in the Song of Songs that there is no one giving instruction or
exhortation, no leader or hierophant, no memorializer of national experience,
but instead the voices of two lovers, praising each other, yearning for each
other, proffering invitations to enjoy. I shall not presume to guess whether
these poems were composed by folk poets, but it is clear that their poetic idiom
is one that, for all its artistic sophistication, is splendidly accessible to the folk,
and that may well be the most plausible explanation for the formal differences
from other kinds of biblical poetry.

To begin with, semantic parallelism is used here with a freedom one rarely encounters in other poetic texts in the Bible. Since virtually the whole book
is a series of dramatic addresses between the lovers, this free gliding in and
out of parallelism—the very antithesis of the neat boxing together of matched
terms in Proverbs—may be dictated in part by the desire to give the verse the
suppleness and liveliness of dramatic speech. Thus the very first line of the
collection: "Let him kiss me with the kisses of his mouth,/for your love is
better than wine" (1:2). The relation of the second verset to the first is not
really parallelism but explanation—and a dramatically appropriate one at that,

which is reinforced by the move from third person to second: your kisses, my love, are more delectable than wine, which is reason enough for me to have declared at large my desire for them.

In many lines, the second verset is a prepositional or adverbial modifier of the first verset—a pattern we have enountered occasionally elsewhere, but which here sometimes occurs in a whole sequence of lines, perhaps as part of an impulse to apprehend the elaborate and precious concreteness of the object evoked instead of finding a matching term for it. Here, for example, is the description of Solomon's royal palanquin (3:6–10):

1	Who is this coming up from the desert	like columns of smoke,
2	Perfumed with myrrh and frankincense	of all the merchant's powders?
3	Look, Solomon's couch,	sixty warriors round it
	of the warriors of Israel,	
4	All of them skilled with sword,	trained in war,
5	Each with sword on thigh,	for terror in the nights.
6	A litter King Solomon made him	of wood from Lebanon.
7	Its posts he made of silver,	its bolster gold,
	its cushion purple wool,	
8	Its inside decked with love	by the daughters of Jerusalem.

The only strictly parallelistic lines here are 4 and 7. For the rest, the poet seems to be reaching in his second (and third) versets for some further realization of the object, of what it is like, where it comes from: What surrounds Solomon's couch? Why are the warriors arrayed with their weapons? Who is it who has so lovingly upholstered the royal litter?

Now, the picture of a perfumed cloud ascending from the desert, with a splendid palanquin then revealed to the eye of the beholder, first with its entourage, afterward with its luxurious fixtures, also incorporates narrative progression; and because the collection involves the dramatic action of lovers coming together or seeking one another (though surely not, as some have fancied, in a formal drama), narrativity is the dominant pattern in a number of the poems. Such narrativity is of course in consonance with a general principle of parallelistic verse in the Bible, as one can see clearly in single lines like this: "Draw me after you, let us run—/the king has brought me to his chambers" (1:4). The difference is that in the Song of Songs there are whole poems in which all semblance of semantic equivalence between versets is put aside for the sake of narrative concatenation from verset to verset and from line to line. I will quote the nocturnal pursuit of the lover at the beginning of chapter 3 (3:1–4), with which one may usefully compare the parallel episode in 5:2–8 that works on the same poetic principle:

1	On my bed at night	I sought the one I so love,
	I sought him, did not find him.	
2	Let me rise and go round the town	in the streets and squares
3	Let me seek the one I so love,	I sought him, did not find him.
4	The watchmen going round the town found me—	"Have you seen the one I so love?"
5	Scarce had I passed them	when I found the one I so love.
6	I held him, would not loose him	till I brought him to my mother's house,
	to the chamber of her who conceived me.	

In this entire sequence of progressive actions, the only moment of semantic equivalence between versets is in the second and third versets of the last line, and the focusing movement there from house to chamber is subsumed under the general narrative pattern: the woman first gets a tight grip on her lover (6a), then brings him to her mother's house (6b), and finally introduces him (6c) into the chamber (perhaps the same one in which she was lying at the beginning of the sequence).

This brief specimen of narrative reflects two other stylistic peculiarities of the Song of Songs. Although the collection as a whole makes elaborate and sometimes extravagant use of figurative language, when narrative governs a whole poem, as in 3:1–4 and 5:2–8, figuration is entirely displaced by the report of sequenced actions. There are no metaphors or similes in these six lines, and, similarly, in the description of the palanquin coming up from the desert to Jerusalem that we glanced at, the only figurative language is "like columns of smoke" at the beginning (where the original reading may in fact have been "*in* columns of smoke") and "decked with love" at the end (where some have also seen a textual problem). The second notable stylistic feature of our poem is the prominence of verbatim repetition. Through the rapid narrative there is woven a thread of verbal recurrences that, disengaged, would sound like this: I sought the one I so love, I sought him, did not find him, let me seek the one I so love, I sought him, did not find him, the one I so love, I found the one I so love. This device has a strong affinity with the technique of incremental repetition that is reflected in the more archaic layers of biblical poetry (the most memorable instance being the Song of Deborah). In the Song of Songs, however, such repetition is used with a degree of flexibility one does not find in the archaic poems, and is especially favored in vocative forms where the lover adds some item of enraptured admiration to the repetition: "Oh, you are fair, my darling,/oh, you are fair, *your eyes are doves*" (4:1). One finds the increment as well in the explanatory note of a challenge: "How is your lover more than another,/fairest of women,//how is your lover more than another,/*that thus you adjure us?*" (5:9). One notices that there is a sense of choreographic balance lacking in the simple use of incremental repetition because in both these lines an initial element ("my darling," "fairest of women") is subtracted as the increment is added. In any case, the closeness to incremental repetition is not necessarily evidence of an early date but might well reflect the more popular character of these love poems, folk poetry and its sophisticated derivatives being by nature conservative in their modes of expression.

The most telling divergence from quasi-synonymous parallelism in the Song of Songs is the use of one verset to introduce a simile and of the matching verset to indicate the referent of the simile: "Like a lily among brambles,/so is my darling among girls.//Like an apple tree among forest trees,/so is my lover among lads" (2:2–3). The same pattern appears, with a very different effect, in some of the riddle-form proverbs. In the Song of Songs, such a pattern makes particular sense because, more than in any other poetic text of the Bible, what is at issue in the poems is the kind of transfers of meaning that take place when one thing is represented in terms of or through the image of something else, and the "like . . . /so . . ." formula aptly calls our attention to the operation of the simile. With the exception of the continuously narrative passages I have mentioned, figurative language plays a more prominent role here than anywhere else in biblical poetry, and the assumptions about how figurative language should be used have shifted in important respects.

The fact is that in a good deal of biblical poetry imagery serves rather secondary purposes, or sometimes there is not very much of it, and in any case "originality" of metaphoric invention would not appear to have been a consciously prized poetic value. Let me propose that outside the Song of Songs one can observe three general categories of imagery in biblical poems: avowedly conventional images, intensive images, and innovative images. Conventional imagery accounts for the preponderance of cases, and the Book of Psalms is the showcase for the artful use of such stock images. Intensive imagery in most instances builds on conventional metaphors and similes, with the difference that a particular figure is pursued and elaborated through several lines or even a whole poem, so that it is given a kind of semantic amplitude or powerfully assertive pressure. Intensive imagery occurs sometimes in Psalms, fairly often in Job, and is the figurative mode par excellence of prophetic poetry. Innovative imagery is the rarest of the three categories, but it can occur from time to time in any genre of biblical verse simply because poetry is, among other things, a way of imagining the world through inventive similitude, and poets, whatever their conventional assumptions, may on occasion arrest the attention of their audience through an original or startling image. The highest concentration of innovative imagery in the Bible is evident in the Book of Job, which I would take to be not strictly a generic matter but more a reflection of the poet's particular genius and his extraordinary ability to imagine disconcerting realities outside the frame of received wisdom and habitual perception. Let me offer some brief examples of all three categories of imagery in order to make this overview of biblical figuration more concrete, which in turn should help us see more clearly the striking difference of the Song of Songs.

Stock imagery, as I have intimated, is the staple of biblical poetry, and Psalms is the preeminent instance of its repeated deployment. Here is an exemplary line: "Guard me like the apple of Your eye,/in the shadow of Your wings conceal me" (Ps. 17:8). Both the apple of the eye as something to be cherished and the shadow of wings as a place of shelter are biblical clichés, though the two elements are interestingly connected here by a motif of darkness (the concentrated dark of the pupil and the extended shadow of wings) and linked in a pattern of intensification that moves from guarding to hiding. There may be, then, a certain effective orchestration of the semantic fields of the metaphors, but in regard to the purpose of the psalm, the advantage of working with such conventional figures is that our attention tends to be guided through the metaphoric vehicle to the tenor for which the vehicle was introduced. In fact, as Benjamin Hrushovski has recently argued, there is a misleading implication of unidirectional movement in those very terms "tenor" and "vehicle," coined for critical usage by I. A. Richards some six decades ago, and when we return to the Song of Songs we will see precisely why the unidirectional model of metaphor is inappropriate. In the frequent biblical use, however, of stock imagery, the relation between metaphor and referent actually approaches that of a vehicle—that is, a mere "carrier" of meaning—to a tenor. In our line from Psalms, what the speaker, pleading for divine help, wants to convey is a sense of the tender protection he asks of God. The apple of the eye and the shading of wings communicate his feeling for the special care he seeks, but in their very conventionality the images scarcely have a life of their own. We think less about the dark of the eye and the shadow of wings than about the safeguarding from the Lord for which the supplicant prays.

Since I have pulled this line out of context, let me refer with a comment on the whole poem to the use of cliché in just one other fairly typical psalm, Psalm 94. In the twenty-three lines of this poem, which calls quite impressively on the Lord as a "God of retribution" to destroy His enemies, there are only four lines that contain any figurative language. How minimal and how conventional such language is will become clear by the quoting in sequence of these four isolated instances of figuration: "The Lord knows the designs of man,/that they are mere breath" (11); ". . . until a pit is dug for the wicked" (13); "When I thought my foot had slipped,/Your faithfulness, Lord, supported me" (18); "But the Lord is my stronghold,/and my God is my sheltering rock" (22). Pitfall, stumbling, and stronghold occur time after time in biblical poetry, and their role in this otherwise nonfigurative poem is surely no more than a minor amplification of the idea that security depends upon God. The metaphor of breath or vapor may to the modern glance seem more striking, but it is in fact such a conventional designation for insubstantiality in the Bible that modern translations that render it unmetaphorically as "futile" do only small violence to the original.

We have seen a number of instances of intensive imagery [elsewhere], but since the focus of those considerations was not on figurative language, one brief example from the prophets may be useful. Here is Deutero-Isaiah elaborating a metaphor in order to contrast the ephemerality of humankind and the power and perdurability of God (Isa. 40:6–8):

All flesh is grass,	all its faithfulness like the flower of the field.
Grass withers, flower fades	when the Lord's breath blows on them.
Grass withers, flower fades,	and the word of the Lord stands forever.

The metaphor of grass for transience is thoroughly conventional, but the poet gives it an intensive development through these three lines in the refrain-like repetition of the key phrases; the amplification of grass with flower (a vegetal figure that involves beauty and still more fragility and ephemerality, as flowers wither more quickly than grass); and in the contrast between grass and God's breath-wind-spirit (*ruaḥ*). God's power is a hot wind that makes transient growing things wither, but God's spirit is also the source of His promise to Israel, through covenant and prophecy, which will be fulfilled or "stand" (*yaqum*) forever while human things and human faithfulness vanish in the wilderness of time. One sees how a cliché has been transformed into poignantly evocative poetry, and here the frame of reference of the metaphor, ephemeral things flourishing, interpenetrates the frame of reference of Israel vis-à-vis God as the pitfalls and strongholds of Psalms do not do to the objects or ideas to which they allude.

Finally, the Job poet abundantly interweaves with such intensive developments of conventional figures forcefully innovative images that carry much of the burden of his argument. Sometimes the power of these images depends on an elaboration of their implications for two or three lines, as in this representation of human life as backbreaking day labor tolerable only because of the prospect of evening/death as surcease and recompense: "Has not man a term of service on earth,/and like the days of a hireling his days?//Like a slave he pants for the shadows,/like a hireling he waits for his wage" (Job 7:1–2). Sometimes we find a rapid flow of innovative figures that in its strength from

verset to verset seems quite Shakespearian, as in these images of the molding
of man in the womb: "Did You not pour me out like milk,/curdle me like
cheese?//With skin and flesh You clothed me,/with bones and sinews wove
me?" (Job 10:10–11). The brilliantly resourceful Job poet also offers a more
compact version of the innovative image, in which an otherwise conventional
term is endowed with terrific figurative power because of the context in which
it is set. Thus, the verb *sabo'a*, "to be satisfied" or "sated," is extremely common
in biblical usage, for the most part in literal or weakly figurative utterances,
but this is how Job uses it to denounce the Friends: "Why do you pursue me
like God,/and from my flesh you are not sated?" (Job 19:22). In context,
especially since Job has just been talking about his bones sticking to his flesh
and skin (19:20), the otherwise bland verb produces a horrific image of cannibalism, which manages to say a great deal with awesome compression about
the perverted nature of the Friends' relationship to the stricken Job.

The innovative image by its forcefulness strongly colors our perception
of its referent: once we imagine the Friends cannibalizing Job's diseased and
wasted flesh, we can scarcely dissociate the words they speak and their moral
intentions from this picture of barbaric violence. What remains relatively stable,
as in the two other general categories of biblical imagery, is the subordinate
relation of image to referent. We are never in doubt that Job's subject is the
Friends' censorious behavior toward him, not cannibalism, or the shaping of
the embryo, not cheese-making and weaving. By contrast, what makes the
Song of Songs unique among the poetic texts of the Bible is that, quite often,
imagery is given such full and free play there that the lines of semantic subordination blur, and it becomes a little uncertain what is illustration and what
is referent.

It should be observed, to begin with, that in the Song of Songs the process
of figuration is frequently "foregrounded"—which is to say, as the poet takes
expressive advantage of representing something through an image that brings
out a salient quality it shares with the referent, he calls our attention to his
exploitation of similitude, to the artifice of metaphorical representation. One
lexical token of this tendency is that the verbal root *d-m-h*, "to be like," or,
in another conjugation, the transitive "to liken," which occurs only thirty times
in the entire biblical corpus (and not always with this meaning), appears five
times in these eight brief chapters of poetry, in each instance flaunting the
effect of figurative comparison. Beyond this lexical clue, the general frequency
of simile is itself a "laying bare" of the artifice, making the operation of
comparison explicit in the poem's surface structure.

The first occurrence of this verb as part of an ostentatious simile is
particularly instructive because of the seeming enigma of the image: "To a mare

among Pharaoh's chariots/I would liken you, my darling" (1:9). Pharaoh's chariots were drawn by stallions, but the military stratagem alluded to has been clearly understood by commentators as far back as the classical Midrashim: a mare in heat, let loose among chariotry, could transform well-drawn battle lines into a chaos of wildly plunging stallions. This is obviously an instance of what I have called innovative imagery, and the poet—or, if one prefers, the speaker—is clearly interested in flaunting the innovation. The first verset gives us a startling simile, as in the first half of a riddle-form proverb; the second verset abandons semantic parallelism for the affirmation of simile making ("I would liken you" or, perhaps, "I have likened you") together with the specification in the vocative of the beloved referent of the simile. The lover speaks out of a keen awareness of the power of figurative language to break open closed frames of reference and make us see things with a shock of new recognition: the beloved in poem after poem is lovely, gentle, dovelike, fragrant, but the sexual attraction she exerts also has an almost violent power to drive males to distraction, as the equine military image powerfully suggests.

It is not certain whether the next two lines (1:10–11), which evoke the wreaths of jewels and precious metals with which the beloved should be adorned, are a continuation of the mare image (referring, that is, to ornaments like those with which a beautiful mare might be adorned) or the fragment of an unrelated poem. I would prefer to see these lines as an extension of the mare simile because that would be in keeping with a general practice in the Song of Songs of introducing a poetic comparison and then exploring its ramifications through several lines. A more clearcut example occurs in these three lines (2:8–9), which also happen to turn on the next occurrence of the symptomatic verb *d-m-h*:

> Hark! My lover, here he comes!   bounding over the mountains,
>   loping over the hills.
> My lover is like a buck   or a young stag.
> Here he stands behind our wall,   peering in at the windows,
>   peeping through the lattice.

This poem, which continues with the lover's invitation to the woman to come out with him into the vernal countryside, begins without evident simile: the waiting young woman simply hears the rapidly approaching footsteps of her lover and imagines him bounding across the hills to her home. What the middle line, which in the Hebrew begins with the verb of likening, *domeh*, does is to pick up a simile that has been pressing just beneath the verbal surface of the preceding line and to make it explicit—all the more explicit because the speaker offers overlapping alternatives of similitude, a buck *or* a young stag. The third line obviously continues the stag image that was adumbrated in the

first line and spelled out in the second, but its delicate beauty is in part a function
of the poised ambiguity as to what is foreground and what is background.
It is easy enough to picture a soft-eyed stag, having come down from the hills,
peering in through the lattice; it is just as easy to see the eager human lover,
panting from his run, looking in at his beloved. The effect is the opposite of
the sort of optical trick in which a design is perceived at one moment as a
rabbit and the next as a duck but never as both at once, because through the
magic of poetic likening the figure at the lattice is simultaneously stag and lover.
What I would call the tonal consequence of this ambiguity is that the lover
is entirely assimilated into the natural world at the same time that the natural
world is felt to be profoundly in consonance with the lovers. This perfectly
sets the stage for his invitation (2:10–13) to arise and join him in the freshly
blossoming landscape, all winter rains now gone.

A variant of the line about the buck occurs in another poem at the end
of the same chapter (2:16–17), and there is something to be learned from the
different position and grammatical use of the verb of similitude:

My lover is mine and I am his,	who browses among the lilies.
Until day breathes	and shadows flee,
Turn, and be you, my love, like a buck,	or a young stag
on the cleft mountains.	

The verb "browses," *ro'eh*, which when applied to humans means "to herd"
and would not make sense in that meaning here, requires a figurative reading
from the beginning. The only landscape, then, in this brief poem is metaphorical:
the woman is inviting her lover to a night of pleasure, urging him to hasten
to enjoy to the utmost before day breaks. The lilies and the "cleft mountains"—
others, comparing the line to 8:14, render this "mountains of spice," which
amounts to the same erotic place—are on the landscape of her body, where
he can gambol through the night. What is especially interesting in the light
of our previous examples is that the verb of similitude occurs not in the speaker's
declaration of likeness but in an imperative: "be you, my love, like [*demeh le*]
a buck." The artifice of poetry thus enters inside the frame of dramatic action
represented through the monologue: the woman tells her man that the way
he can most fully play the part of the lover is to be like the stag, to act out
the poetic simile, feeding on these lilies and cavorting upon this mount of
intimate delight.

Of the two other occurrences of the verb *d-m-h* in the Song of Songs,
one is a variant of the line we have just considered, appearing at the very end
of the book (8:14) and possibly detached from context. The other occurrence
(7:8–10) provides still another instructive instance of how this poetry rides
the momentum of metaphor:

This stature of yours is like the palm,	your breasts like the clusters.
I say, let me climb the palm,	let me hold its branches.
Let your breast be like grape clusters,	your breath like apples,
You palate like goodly wine	flowing for my love smoothly,

stirring the lips of sleepers.

The speaker first announces his controlling simile, proclaiming that his beloved's stately figure is like (*damta le*) the palm. The second verset of the initial line introduces a ramification — quite literally, a "branching out" — of the palm image or, in terms of the general poetics of parallelism, focuses it by moving from the tree to the fruit-laden boughs. The next line is essentially an enactment of the simile, beginning with "I say," which Marvin Pope quite justifiably renders as "methinks" because the verb equally implies intention and speech. The simile ceases to be an "illustration" of some quality (the stately stature of the palm tree in the woman) and becomes a reality that impels the speaker to a particular course of action: if you are a palm, what is to be done with palm trees is to climb them and enjoy their fruit. The last two lines of the poem sustain the sense of a virtually real realm of simile by piling on a series of images contiguous with the initial one but not identical with it: from clusters of dates to grape clusters, from branches to apples, from the breath of the mouth and from grapes to wine-sweet kisses.

Another reflection of the poetics of flaunted figuration that contributes to the distinctive beauty of the Song of Songs is the flamboyant elaboration of the metaphor in fine excess of its function as the vehicle for any human or erotic tenor. In terms of the semantic patterns of biblical parallelism, this constitutes a special case of focusing, in which the second or third verset concretizes or characterizes a metaphor introduced in the first verset in a way that shifts attention from the frame of reference of the referent to the frame of reference of the metaphor. Let me quote from the exquisite poem addressed to the dancing Shulamite in chapter 7 the vertical description of the woman, ascending from feet to head (7:2–6).

1	How lovely your feet in sandals,	nobleman's daughter!
2	Your curving thighs are like ornaments,	the work of a master's hand.
3	Your sex a rounded bowl —	may it never lack mixed wine!
4	Your belly a heap of wheat,	hedged about with lilies.
5	Your two breasts like two fawns,	twins of a gazelle.
6	Your neck like an ivory tower,	your eyes pools in Heshbon
	by the gate of Bat-Rabbim.	
7	Your nose like the tower of David,	looking out toward Damascus.
8	Your head on you like crimson wool,	the locks of your head like purple,

a king is caught in the flowing tresses.

This way of using metaphor will seem peculiar only if one insists upon imposing on the text the aesthetic of a later age. A prime instance of what I have called the misplaced concreteness of biblical research is that proponents of the theory of a fertility-cult liturgy have felt that the imagery of metallic ornament had to be explained as a reference to the statuette of a love goddess and the looming architectural imagery by an invoking of the allegedly supernatural character of the female addressed. This makes only a little more sense than to claim that when John Donne in "The Sunne Rising" writes, "She'is all States, and all Princes, I,/Nothing else is," he must be addressing, by virtue of the global imagery, some cosmic goddess and not sweet Ann Donne.

Our passage begins without simile for the simple technical reason that the second verset of line 1 is used to address the woman who is the subject of the enraptured description. After this point, the second (or, for the triadic lines, the third) verset of each line is employed quite consistently to flaunt the metaphor by pushing its frame of reference into the foreground. The poet sets no limit on and aims for no unity in the semantic fields from which he draws his figures, moving rapidly from artisanry to agriculture to the animal kingdom to architecture, and concluding with dyed textiles. (In the analogous vertical description of the lover, 5:10–16, the imagery similarly wanders from doves bathing in watercourses and beds of spices to artifacts of gold, ivory, and marble, though the semantic field of artifact dominates as the celebration of the male body concentrates on the beautiful hardness of arms, thighs, and loins.) There is nevertheless a tactical advantage in beginning the description with perfectly curved ornaments and a rounded bowl or goblet, for the woman's beauty is so exquisite that the best analogue for it is the craft of the master artisan, an implicit third term of comparison being the poet's fine craft in so nicely matching image with object for each lovely aspect of this body.

That implied celebration of artifice may explain in part the flamboyant elaboration of the metaphors in all the concluding versets. It should be observed, however, that the function of these elaborations changes from line to line in accordance with both the body part invoked and the position of the line in the poem. In line 2, "the work of a master's hand" serves chiefly as an intensifier of the preceding simile of ornament and as a way of foregrounding the idea of artifice at the beginning of the series. In lines 3–5, as the description moves upward from feet and thighs to the central erogenous zone of vagina, belly, and breasts, the elaborations of the metaphor in the second versets are a way of being at once sexually explicit and decorous through elegant *double entente*. That is, we are meant to be continuously aware of the sexual details referred to, but it is the wittily deployed frame of reference of the metaphor that is kept in the foreground of our vision: we know the poet alludes to the

physiology of lovemaking, but we "see" a curved bowl that never runs dry;
the wheat-like belly bordered by a hedge of lilies is an ingenious superimposi-
tion of an agricultural image on an erotic one, since lilies elsewhere are implicitly
associated with pubic hair; the bouncing, supple, symmetrical breasts are
not just two fawns but also, in the focusing elaboration, a gazelle's perfectly
matched twins.

The geographical specifications of the final versets in lines 6 and 7 have
troubled many readers. It seems to me that here, when the poet has moved
above the central sexual area of the body, he no longer is impelled to work
out a cunning congruity between image and referent by way of *double entente*,
and instead he can give free rein to the exuberance of figurative elaboration
that in different ways has been perceptible in all the previous metaphors. If,
as his eye moves to neck and face, the quality of grandeur rather than supple
sexual allure is now uppermost, there is a poetic logic in the speaker's expand-
ing these images of soaring architectural splendor and making the figurative
frame of reference so prominent that we move from the dancing Shulamite
to the public world of the gate at Bat-Rabbim and the tower of Lebanon looking toward Damascus. As the lover's gaze moves up from the parts of the
body usually covered and thus seen by him alone to the parts generally visible,
it is appropriate that the similes for her beauty should be drawn now from
the public realm. In a final turn, moreover, of the technique of last-verset
elaboration, the triadic line 8 introduces an element of climactic surprise: the
Shulamite's hair having been compared to brilliantly dyed wool or fabric, we
discover that a king is caught, or bound, in the tresses (the Hebrew for this
last term is a little doubtful, but since the root suggests running motion, the
reference to flowing hair in context seems probable). This amounts to a strong
elaboration of a relatively weak metaphor, and an elaboration that subsumes
the entire series of images that has preceded: the powerful allure of sandaled
feet, curving thighs, and all the rest that has pulsated through every choice
of image now culminates in the hair, where at last the lover, through the self-
designation of king, introduces himself into the poem, quite literally inter-
involves himself with the beloved ("a king is caught in the flowing tresses").
Up till now, she has been separate from him, dancing before his eager eye.
Now, after a climactic line summarizing her beauty (7:7), he goes on to imagine
embracing her and enjoying her (7:8–10, the climbing of the palm tree that
I quoted earlier). It is a lovely illustration of how the exuberant metaphors
carry the action forward.

Such obtrusions of metaphorical elaboration are allied with another
distinctive mode of figuration of these poems, in which the boundaries between
figure and referent, inside and outside, human body and accoutrement or natural

setting, become suggestively fluid. Let me first cite three lines from the brief poem at the end of Chapter 1 (1:12–14):

While the king was on his couch,	my nard gave off its scent.
A sachet of myrrh is my lover to me,	between my breasts he lodges.
A cluster of cypress is my lover to me,	in the vineyards of Ein Gedi.

The first line is without figuration, the woman simply stating that she has scented her body for her lover. But the immediately following metaphoric representation of the lover as a sachet of myrrh—because he nestles between her breasts all night long—produces a delightful confusion between the literal nard with which she has perfumed herself and the figurative myrrh she cradles in her lover. Thus the act and actors of love become intertwined with the fragrant paraphernalia of love. The third line offers an alternative image of a bundle of aromatic herbs and then, in the second verset, one of those odd geographical specifications like those we encountered in our preceding text. I have not followed the New [Jewish Publication Society] and Marvin Pope in translating the second verset as "from the vineyards," because it seems to me that the Hebrew has an ambiguity worth preserving. Presumably the metaphor is elaborated geographically because the luxuriant oasis at Ein Gedi was especially known for its trees and plants with aromatic leaves, and so the specification amounts to a heightening of the original assertion. At the same time the initial Hebrew particle *be*, which usually means "in," leaves a teasing margin for imagining that it is not the cypress cluster that *comes from* Ein Gedi but the fragrant embrace of the lovers that takes place *in* Ein Gedi. Though this second meaning is less likely, it is perfectly consistent with the syntax of the line, and the very possibility of this construal makes it hard to be sure where the metaphor stops and the human encounter it represents begins. There is, in other words, an odd and satisfying consonance in this teasing game of transformations between the pleasure of play with language through metaphor and the pleasure of love play that is the subject of the lines. That same consonance informs the beautiful poem that takes up all of chapter 4, ending in the first verse of chapter 5. It will provide an apt concluding illustration of the poetic art of the Song of Songs.

1	Oh, you are fair, my darling,	oh, you are fair, your eyes are doves.
2	Behind your veil, your hair like a flock of goats	streaming down Mount Gilead.
3	Your teeth are like a flock of ewes	coming up from the bath,
4	Each one bearing twins,	none bereft among them.
5	Like the scarlet thread your lips,	your mouth is lovely.
6	Like a pomegranate-slice your brow	behind your veil.

7   Like the tower of David your   built in rows.
    neck,
8   A thousand shields are hung on   all the heroes' bucklers.
    it,
9   Your two breasts are like two   twins of the gazelle,
    fawns,
                    browsing among the lilies.
10 Until day breathes   and shadows flee
11 I'll betake me to the mount of   and to the hill of frankincense.
    myrrh
12 You are all fair, my darling,   there's no blemish in you.
13 With me from Lebanon, bride,   with me from Lebanon, come!
14 Descend from Amana's peak,   from the peak of Senir and Hermon,
15 From the dens of lions,   from the mounts of panthers.
16 You ravish my heart, bride,   you ravish my heart with one glance
                                           of your eyes,
                    with one gem of your necklace.
17 How fair your love, my sister   how much better your love than wine.
    bride, and
          and the scent of your ointments than any spice!
18 Nectar your lips drip, bride,   honey and milk under your tongue,
          and the scent of your robes like Lebanon's scent.
19 A locked garden, my sister and   a locked pool, a sealed-up spring.
    bride,
20 Your groove a grove of   with luscious fruit,
    pomegranates
                    cypress with nard.
21 Nard and saffron, cane and   with all aromatic woods,
    cinnamon,
22 Myrrh and aloes,   with all choice perfumes.
23 A garden spring,   a well of fresh water,
          flowing from Lebanon.
24 Stir, north wind,   come, south wind,
25 Breathe on my garden,   let its spices flow.
26 "Let my lover come to his garden,   and eat its luscious fruit."
27 I've come to my garden, my sister   I've plucked my myrrh with my spice,
    and bride,
28 Eaten my honeycomb with my   drunk my wine with my milk.
    honey,
29 "Eat, friends, and drink,   be drunk with love."

As elsewhere in the Song of Songs, the poet draws his images from whatever semantic fields seem apt for the local figures—domesticated and wild animals, dyes, food, architecture, perfumes, and the floral world. Flamboyant elaboration of the metaphor, in which the metaphoric image takes over the foreground, governs the first third of the poem (ll. 2–4, 7–9), culminating in the extravagant picture of the woman's neck as a tower hung with shields. The very repetition of *ke* ("like"), the particle of similitude, half a dozen times through these initial lines, calls attention to the activity of figurative comparison as it is being carried out. There is a certain witty ingenuity with which the elaborated metaphors are related to the body parts: twin-bearing, newly washed ewes to two perfect rows of white teeth and, perhaps, shields on the tower walls recalling the layered rows of a necklace.

What I should like to follow out more closely, however, is the wonderful transformations that the landscape of fragrant mountains and gardens undergoes from line 11 to the end of the poem. The first mountain and hill—rarely has a formulaic word-pair been used so suggestively—in line 11 are metaphorical, referring to the body of the beloved or, perhaps, as some have proposed, more specifically to the *mons veneris*. It is interesting that the use of two nouns in the construct state to form a metaphor ("mount of myrrh," "hill of frankincense") is quite rare elsewhere in biblical poetry, though it will become a standard procedure in postbiblical Hebrew poetry. The naturalness with which the poet adopts that device here reflects how readily objects in the Song of Songs are changed into metaphors. The Hebrew for "frankincense" is *levonah*, which sets up an intriguing *faux raccord* with "Lebanon," *levanon*, two lines down. From the body as landscape—an identification already adumbrated in the comparison of hair to flocks coming down from the mountain and teeth to ewes coming up from the washing—the poem moves to an actual landscape with real rather than figurative promontories. If domesticated or in any case gentle animals populate the metaphorical landscape at the beginning, there is a new note of danger or excitement in the allusion to the lairs of panthers and lions on the real northern mountainside. The repeated verb "ravish" in line 16, apparently derived from *lev*, "heart," picks up in its sound (*libavtini*) the interecho of *levonah* and *levanon* and so triangulates the body-as-landscape, the external landscape, and the passion the beloved inspires.

The last thirteen lines of the poem, as the speaker moves toward the consummation of love intimated in lines 26–29, reflect much more of an orchestration of the semantic fields of the metaphors: fruit, honey, milk, wine, and, in consonance with the sweet fluidity of this list of edibles, a spring of fresh flowing water and all the conceivable spices that could grow in a well-irrigated garden. Lebanon, which as we have seen has already played an important role in threading back and forth between the literal and figurative landscapes, continues to serve as a unifier. The scent of the beloved's robes is like Lebanon's scent (l. 18), no doubt because Lebanon is a place where aromatic trees grow, but also with the suggestion, again fusing figurative with literal, that the scent of Lebanon clings to her dress because she has just returned from there (ll. 13–15). "All aromatic woods" in line 21 is literally in the Hebrew "all the trees of *levonah*," and the echo of *levonah-levanon* is carried forward two lines later when the locked spring in the garden wells up with flowing water (*nozlim*, an untranslatable poetic synonym for water) from Lebanon—whether because Lebanon, with its mountain streams, is the superlative locus of fresh running water, or because one is to suppose some mysterious subterranean feed-in from the waters of wild and mountainous Lebanon to this cultivated garden. In either case, there is a suggestive crossover back from the actual landscape to a metaphorical one. The garden at the end that the lover enters—and to "come to" or "enter" often has a technical sexual meaning in biblical Hebrew—is the body of the beloved, and one is not hard put to see the physiological fact alluded to in the fragrant flowing of line 25 (the same root as *nozlim* in line 23) that precedes the enjoyment of luscious fruit.

What I have just said, however, catches only one side of a restless dialectic movement of signification and as such darkens the delicately nuanced beauty of the poem with the shadow of reductionism. For though we know, and surely the original audience was intended to know, that the last half of the poem conjures up a delectable scene of love's consummation, this garden of aromatic plants, wafted by the gentle winds, watered by a hidden spring, is in its own right an alluring presence to the imagination before and after any decoding into a detailed set of sexual allusions. The poetry by the end becomes a kind of self-transcendence of *double entente*: the beloved's body is, in a sense, "represented" as a garden, but it also turns into a real garden, magically continuous with the mountain landscape so aptly introduced at the midpoint of the poem.

It is hardly surprising that only here in biblical poetry do we encounter such enchanting interfusions between the literal and metaphorical realms, because only here is the exuberant gratification of love through all five senses the subject. Prevalent preconceptions about the Hebrew Bible lead us to think of it as a collection of writings rather grimly committed to the notions of covenant, law, solemn obligation, and thus the very antithesis of the idea of play. There is more than a grain of truth in such preconceptions (one can scarcely imagine a Hebrew Aristophanes or a Hebrew *Odyssey*), but the literary art of the Bible, in both prose narrative and poetry, reflects many more elements of playfulness than might meet the casual eye. Only in the Song of Songs, however, is the writer's art directed to the imaginative realization of a world of uninhibited self-delighting play, without moral conflict, without the urgent context of history and nationhood and destiny, without the looming perspectives of a theological world-view. Poetic language and, in particular, its most characteristic procedure, figuration, are manipulated as pleasurable substance: metaphor transforms the body into spices and perfumes, wine and luscious fruit, all of which figurative images blur into the actual setting in which the lovers enact their love, a natural setting replete with just those delectable things. There is a harmonious correspondence between poem and world, the world exhibiting the lovely tracery of satisfying linkages that characterizes poetry itself. In the fluctuating movement from literal to figurative and back again, both sides of the dialectic are enhanced: the inventions of the poetic medium become potently suffused with the gratifying associations of the erotic, and erotic longing and fulfillment are graced with the elegant aesthetic form of a refined poetic art.

YEHOSHUA GITAY

The Place and Function
of the Song of the Vineyard
in Isaiah's Prophecy

When a song is introduced in Isa. 5:1ff., the form of Isaiah's prophetic address is changed. The song, at first reading, does not seem complicated, but a closer reading reveals a complex use of language. Scholars are divided concerning their aesthetic appreciation of the song. There is a tone of excitement: "The fugitive rhythm, the musical euphony, the charming assonances . . . [are] impossible to reproduce" (Delitzsch). On the other hand, a contrasting judgment stresses the prosaic, uninspiring side: "[Isaiah's] words are not a song because his language here is the simplest" (Ehrlich). Furthermore, scholars disagree about the interpretation of the song: parable, allegory, fable? There is growing suspicion about the authenticity and authorship of the text. It will be my goal to shed some light on the structure of the song, its rhetoric, its stylistic quality, and above all to point out the function and role of the song in the book of Isaiah.

Isa. 5:1 introduces a term that defines the nature of the discourse: a "song," a genre not unfamiliar to Isaiah's audience. The prophet has employed songs in his addresses in at least two other cases: 23:16 and 26:1ff. Isa. 23:16 is significant for our analysis because of the exact use of the term "song": Isaiah seems here to quote a popular song, "the song of the harlot." (The parable of the farmer in 28:24ff. is also important, but it is not the same type of song as the song of the vineyard, and there is no specific use of the word "song.")

A brief look at Isaiah's songs in 23:16 and 26:1ff. reveals a specific style that differs from the surrounding context: we notice a chain of verbs tied

From *Isaiah and His Audience: The Structure and Meaning of Isaiah 1-12*. © 1986 by Yehoshua Gitay. Indiana University Press, 1986.

together in a series of very short sentences of two words in 23:16, and, again, a series of pairs structured as *puns* in 26:1ff.; both are characteristic phenomena of biblical songs or poems.

However, the song we are discussing differs from its "sisters" in Isaiah in regard to the genre and its function. It is not a mimic satirical song, but an *example* (*māšāl*), and I deliberately choose this word for its wide definition, for reasons which I shall specify below. We are informed explicitly that the vineyard is just an example (v. 7). As the prophet interprets, the vineyard is Israel. The song deals, in fact, with the relationship between Israel and God.

Thus Isa. 5:1–7 is more than just a song. A survey of biblical scholarship concerning the definition of the genre of 5:1ff. indicates a certain confusion. Critics incline to utilize three, supposedly unidentified definitions of the song of the vineyard: parable, fable, and allegory. We should realize, however, that the differences are, in fact, not crucial. The word parable is derived from the Greek *parabolē*: to compare, to contrast. "Fable" (*confabulatio* in Latin, to "converse") is defined usually as a short story that centers around a moral lesson. The simple story presents the problem and indicates a solution. Of course, one may make specific distinctions between parable, which has only one point of comparison, and allegory, in which every detail is significant. We can say that parable asks for decision, whereas allegory seeks to instruct. But both parable and allegory are partial synonyms. Concerning allegory, we may indicate that it is a story intended by the author to convey a hidden meaning, which has to be perceived. Various literary forms may be regarded as special types of allegory, in that they narrate one coherent set of circumstances, which signify a second order of correlated meanings. The fable, on the other hand, is a short story that exemplifies a moral thesis or a principle of human behavior; usually in its conclusion either the narrator or one of the characters states the moral in the form of an *epigram*; animals and plants in fables act like the human types they represent.

An example (*māšāl*) is designed not as an end in itself but as a vehicle. The task of defining the exact type or genre is less important than the function of this literary type. In other words, what is the relationship between the story and the audience, or what is the impact of the story on the audience?—these are, in fact, the significant questions that concern the critic.

Let me explain the issue by the following remark:

> A literary work has two poles: the artistic and the aesthetic. The artistic pole is the author's text and the aesthetic [pole] is the realization accomplished by the reader. . . . As the reader passes through the various perspectives offered by the text and relates the different views and patterns to one another he sets the work in

motion, and so sets himself in motion, too. . . . Practically every discernible structure in fiction has this two-sidedness: it is verbal and affective. . . . Any description of the interaction between the two must therefore incorporate both the structure of the effects (the text) and that of response (the reader).

(W. Iser, *The Act of Reading*)

In short, the issues of function and perception are our major subject of inquiry. A text such as our *māšāl* is not independent and its structure and form is designed according to the audience's condition and perception. The fundamental question is, therefore, the "why." Why do speakers, or writers insert parables or stories into their discourses?

I shall demonstrate the function of the story by two illustrations. The first is Nathan's parable in 2 Sam. 12. It is obvious that Nathan does not seek to teach David a new lesson or to provide him with fresh information. The purpose is self-awareness, a moral conclusion that David is unable to reach independently, as the king is not ready to react responsively to a straight criticism.

The second illustration is cited in Martin Buber's *Tales of the Hasidim*. He tells a story about Rabbi Jacob Joseph, a vigorous opponent of Hasidim. One morning he found the gate of the synagogue closed; it was still locked an hour after it should have been opened, and no one had shown up. He was told that the people, on their way to prayer, had stopped to listen to the wonderful stories a stranger was telling. "Bring him to me!" the Rabbi ordered. They brought the Baal Shem. "What do you think you are doing! Keeping the people from prayer!" Rabbi, the Baal Shem said calmly: "Anger does not become you. Let me tell you a story." "Once I drove cross-country with three horses— a bay, a piebald, and a white horse. And not one of them could neigh. Then I met a peasant coming toward me and he called: slacken the reins! So I slackened the reins, and then all three horses began to neigh." The Rabbi could say nothing for emotion. "Do you understand?" "I do," said the Rabbi who burst into tears and wept for a long time. He realized that never before has he learnt how to weep.

Thus, by describing "what," not "why," and the particular rather than the general, parables are potentially a useful device for imitating acts of self-confrontation in listeners.

The *māšāl*, we may summarize, is used effectively in religious discourse in a context of changing attitudes, but above all and most significantly, it provokes an act of self-confrontation and confronting not only in belief, but the very sense of self and way of life.

Now, what is it, the critic should ask, that the listeners of the song of the vineyard are not ready to confront directly, hence causing the speaker to employ a specific rhetorical strategy, the *māšāl*? It is disappointing that Isaiah's scholarship does not address the issue of the argumentative context, that is, the situation that gave birth to the song. There are two basic reasons for this failure: the search for short and sporadic units isolated from a broad context, and the focus on form while the issue of effect is neglected. That is to say, we need to search the condition, the polemic background against which the song has been recited. In this respect, it should be noted that a parable, a story, may be commonly known, but it still must be applied to a particular social moment, which means that it is not sufficient just to know the literal meaning of Nathan's parable or the Baal Shem's: the point is to try to reconstruct the condition, the argumentative or rhetorical situation that caused the employment of the parable.

But first let me comment that, as a rule, parables are relatively brief, and this brevity allows such tales to be woven easily into interpersonal dialogue and public discourse. Now the biblical school that argues for an exilic composition or post-exilic composition of the song of the vineyard, considers the story as an apologetic or theodition composition, whose aim is to justify the catastrophe, the fall of Jerusalem in 587 B.C.E. We should realize, in response, that there is no specific literary ground for rejecting the authenticity of the song. The motif of the vineyard as a symbol of Judah and Jerusalem is often employed by Isaiah. The *māšāl* corresponds, for instance, with 3:14 as the vineyard in both cases stands for the nation, and the issue is God's judgment. The characteristic verb *b'r* ("ravaged") appears in both texts. (5:5, 3:14). Furthermore, the close relationship between God and Israel is expressed figuratively in terms of vineyard in 27:2–4 as well, and God in both texts is the one who takes care of the vineyard. (For the motif, see also Jer. 2:21).

I have already mentioned Isaiah's strategy of employing specific songs in his discourse. I may add, that the technique of starting with a defined familiar genre, e.g., lament (1:21), and then switching to a judgment—"therefore"—(1:24), is utilized in our song as well: "My beloved had a vineyard" (5:1) and later: "Now then . . . judge" (5:3).

The rhetorical strategy of the example is common to Isaiah. The point is that whatever the goals of the rhetorician are, his tropes must persuade persons of the truth of his position. Most often this truth is not presented as a known fact, but through a semantic movement or transformation of meaning, as a "revelation," or new comprehension about the nature of things. No additional previously unknown elements are added to the listeners' knowledge of the empirical characteristics of things; rather the listeners are led to see their natures through their relationships. In the book of Isaiah the technique is employed persuasively at least twice: 1:2–3 and 5:1–7.

Comparing Israel to domestic animals whose behavior is anticipated, Isaiah, in 1:2–3, demonstrates without further explanation the absurdity of Israel's behavior. A similar rhetorical strategy is practiced in 5:1–7. In both instances the audience is confronted concretely and particularly, since, we recall, it is easier to refute a general conception than a specific one. There are scholars who doubt the possibility that such a serious religious thinker as Isaiah would be able to tell stories or sing songs. The argument is that the audience would disregard such a performance. Consequently, if we seek to defend the authenticity of the song, we have to refer to Isaiah's earlier career, while he was still unknown as a prophet. The response is that the strategy of the *example* is not foreign to Isaiah and the audience should not be surprised by the prophet's use of figures and tropes of speech, especially vineyard (compare also 1:8).

Concerning the place of social criticism, the objective of the song in Isaiah's prophecy, we should realize that the complexity of the argument and its literary development correspond with the place and function of the song and its surrounding context. The clue for grasping the argument's point of departure, the rhetorical situation, is the first speech, 1:2–20. There the emphasis is on moral-ethical behavior that dominates even cultic devotion (vv. 10–15). The moral-ethical misbehavior is the cause of the painful war (vv. 4–9). We should realize that an argument that dismisses the significance of a cult in such a society is extremely unpopular. Hence, Isaiah devotes a series of speeches, chapters 1–5, to the importance and the political consequences of moral-ethical misbehavior. Disregarding the popular crucial function of cult and stressing instead the moral-ethical issue as the predominant criterion for God's punishment or reward (see mainly 1:18–20) is the substance of Isaiah's political and domestic message. This difficult rhetorical task explains the need for repeated speeches concerning the issue of behavior and justice. It also clarifies Isaiah's employment of a specific strategy of stories, metaphors, and examples. We notice that the examples mirror nature: domestic animals, vineyard, and so forth. The comparisons to natural phenomena are effective since those examples signify order. There is no disorder in nature. The motif of ingratitude negates nature, and the analogy to human behavior is, therefore, forceful; nature always responds properly.

So Isaiah tells a story, reciting first a concrete episode that correlates with daily experience. However, he opens the song uncharacteristically, placing himself in the first person: "Let me sing for my beloved." Isaiah repeats this personal autobiographical style in chapter 6, and in his song about the farmer in 28:23ff.

Thus Isaiah, both in the farmer's example and the song of the vineyard, does not start in his customary manner, by quoting or referring to God. On the contrary, he speaks about his experience. The point that the speaker does not talk theoretically is self-evident. We may assume, therefore, that with the application of the story to a specific biographical situation, realizing that the poet is, in fact, the prophet, a fundamental change takes place in it, for in this way it is not merely a song, an entertainment; it now acquires allegorical features and each element challenges the listener to provide an appropriate interpretation.

I have already called attention to the symbolic use of vineyard in 1:8, and one may add 27:1ff. as further symbolic reference. The point is, therefore, that even if the original song is a love song (see the relationship between the vineyard and the lover in the Song of Songs 1:6, 2:15, 8:1,2, 8:11) about a disappointed lover, its setting in this context as a personal experience of Isaiah, determines the allegorical features of the song and accordingly the audience's reaction. In short, methodologically it is a mistake to isolate a specific discourse, to ignore its context, and then to draw conclusions on the basis of certain formal features or semantics about the meaning. The question of meaning is disconnected from the literary context.

Now let me refer to the difficult combination: "a song of a lover for his vineyard." "Lover," *dôd*, may be read either as an uncle, patron, or a lover with sexual connotation (compare the Song of Songs 1:2). Scholars who compare our song with Nathan's parable, suggest reading the song as the same literary type at least until the turning point in verse 3, "judge," in which the text functions as a prophetic judgment speech, "juridical parable." The comparison is, however, not too helpful. There is a major difference that is reflected in the opening line of the song, which has a certain sexual allusion. Recited, however, by the prophet it produces an ambiguity, an awareness for a dual meaning, and an allegorical feature.

Isaiah starts by introducing his intention: "Let me sing." The form differs from his other citations of songs or parables. In 26:1 he recites the verb "sing" in passive: "This song shall be sung." The use of the *cohortative* in 5:1, is effective; it lays stress on the determination underlying the action and the personal interest in it. Furthermore, Ehrlich's remark that the song is simple, prosaic, is partially correct. We shall discover that the attempt to reach the audience is not limited to form; there is a clear effort to attract the listener's attention through specific stylistic devices as well.

Let us look first at the structure of the song, which is short but enriched with details. Verse 2, for instance, outlines three sorts of agricultural works together with the building of a tower and a wine-cellar. The description of the destruction at verse 5 suggests further work such as a fence. The emphasis on details intends to establish not only an authentic climate but also a feeling of ingratitude and anger. A number of scholars call attention to the lack of harmony between the construction and the destruction; however, a close reading reveals a symmetry. The song outlines twelve kinds of agricultural works in two parallels, or more precisely, two sets of five actions plus a consequence: (1) He broke the ground, (2) cleared it of stones, (3) planted it with choice vines, (4) built a watchtower, (5) hewed a vine press in it, but: it yielded wild grapes [v. 2]. On the other hand: (1) removes its hedge, (2) it may be ravaged, (3) break down its wall, (4) it may be trampled [v. 5], (5) it shall not be pruned or hoed, hence: "it shall be overgrown with briers and thistles" [v. 6].

The internal structure of the song is curious. We have noticed the simple uncomplicated description of events as well as the almost harmonic structure; the language, however, is quite unusual. The verb '*zq* (v. 2) is *hapaxlegomenon*; the Hebrew of the combination "on a fruitful hill" (v. 1) is unique. The Hebrew for "wild grapes" (vv. 2,4) used as a noun in such a context is irregular, *bth* is also *hapaxlegomenon*, and there are other unusual combinations, which I shall refer to below. Such crowded irregular usage suggests an aim. The intention is rhetorical: there is a danger that a familiar song may sound cliché. Thus any shift or tendency for variety is affective. It directs the audience to concentrate on each word or combination of the song. The question is, what is an affective style?

> "A good style is first of all clear," writes Aristotle, Variations from ordinary usage make the style more impressive. . . . It is well to give the ordinary idiom an air of remoteness; the hearers are struck by what is out of the way, and like what strikes them. In verse there are many things to produce this effect, and to verse they are fitting; — for there the subject-matter — both things and persons is more remote from daily life.
>
> (Aristotle, *Rhetoric*)

Another significant rhetorical device employed in our song is sound-effect. *Yedîdî* (my friend) and *dôdî* (my beloved, lover) are related as a pun (The Septuagint read: "I shall sing to my beloved a song of my beloved.") The chain of verbs: *vy'zqehû, vysqlehû, vyt'hû* (v. 2) is a series of *assonances* and *alliterations*,which provides an aesthetic musical sound. Again, when a poet recites a common motif, the strategy, in order to avoid the routine, is to provide an aesthetic effect.

Hitherto, I have discussed the form and the stylistic principles of drawing the audience's attention. The following will be a closer look at the content furnished with further comments on the structure of the song. The series of verbs in verse 2 provides a feeling of continuity and urgency. The first agricultural work, expressed by the unique *vy'zqebû*, which has to be understood as deep digging, hoeing, preceded by *vysqlebû* (cf. Isa. 62:10) indicates the unusually hard work required before the planting itself. The point is obvious — to stress the amount of hard labor preparation requires, and consequently, the deep disappointment, the feeling of unfaithfulness. Furthermore, the building of a tower inside the vineyard is impressive. First, in comparison with 1:8: "like a booth in a vineyard/like a lodge in a cucumber field," we are struck by the sharp contrast between booth or lodge, which connotes temporarily even weakness, and a tower, which connotes power. Second, tower, which indicates a permanent building, correlates with the owner's hope: "he hoped it would yield grapes" (v. 2). The course of nature invites a permanent building, hence the vineyard betrayed is absurd. Moreover, the pair *yqb* ("vineyard") and *mgdl* ("tower") is unusual (v. 2). The conventional biblical combination is "city"/ "tower" (2 Kings 17:9, 18:8, Gen. 11:4) or "wall"/"tower" (Ezek. 26:4, for instance). Concerning the vineyard, the formula is "vineyard"/"barn" (2 Kings 6:27, Hos. 9:2, Deut. 15:14) or "winepress"/"vineyard" (Joel 4:13). Thus the pair "vineyard"/"tower" is a further example of the intention to break the routine, and to create the unexpected. The verb "hewed" functions in this context to demonstrate the owner's assurance and self-confidence. The entire structure of verse 2 leads to the feeling of total frustration. It is a structure of three lines, not the regular two, which means that the third line lacks the expected parallel. Hence, the verse ends suddenly. It provides, therefore, a feeling of unfulfillment; a structure that fits with the owner's mood of discontinuity.

"And now" (v. 3), which indicates the turning point, the call for judgment, connoting the argument between the lovers, conveys as well a characteristic prophetic judgment (compare "now, therefore, hear the word of the Lord," Amos 7:16).

The transfer to the first person: "Judge, I pray you" (v. 3) switches the focus on the speaker himself. I do not suggest that the transfer from the third to the first person is merely poetic style, but rather, that it is an intentional rhetorical device (*Aversio = Apostrophe*), that is, the turning of the speech to a new person, thus giving life to the new character. Such a device allows the prophet to confront his audience gradually: to hide himself behind his beloved one, and then, at the right moment, to appear on the stage as the opponent. Earlier, the audience, knowing the nature of Isaiah's prophecy, may dismiss him, but by focusing the audience's attention on a third person, Isaiah gradually paves the way for his direct involvement. Now the audience confronts the prophet himself.

The series of actions taken against the vineyard is delivered forcefully. The verbs of verse 5 are in the infinitive absolute, a useful device for emphasis.

The result, "it shall be overgrown with briers and thistles" (v. 6), is expressed in characteristic Isaiahic language (compare 7:25).

Mention should be made to the remarkable *assonance šāmîr/šayît* ("briers"/ "thistles"), which intends to increase the effect at the end of the song: *mišpāt/ mispāh* ("justice"/"injustice"), *ṣdāqāh/ṣeʿāqāh* ("equity"/"iniquity"), a series of *puns*. The play on sound contrasts the terms, stressing the different ideas that sharpen the definition of the proper concept.

To conclude, there is a sharp contrast between the ethical demands and the people's practice, which explains Isaiah's concentration on the motif of injustice in the context of chapters 1–5. (compare 1:16–17, 2:21–28, 3:13–15). We have realized the prophet's difficulties concerning the reception of his criticism. His sensitivity to communication is reflected in his rhetoric. Isaiah employs a specific literary strategy in order to affect his audience. I have mentioned the genre of the lament (1:21ff.) as a vehicle for drawing the listener's attention, and we have discussed another literary form, the *māšāl*, whose function is to evoke the listener's own experience of awareness. It is important to remember, what many seem to ignore, that metaphor, parable, allegory, fable and so on, may be included within the *māšāl* form.

The conclusion is that the song of the vineyard should be studied in a context, which means the song is a product of what has preceded as well as the continuing social criticism (5:8ff.). The form, the song, is a rhetorical strategy, commonly employed by Isaiah, in order to influence his listeners.

GEOFFREY HARTMAN

The Poetics of Prophecy: Jeremiah

In our honorific or sophomoric moods, we like to think that poets are prophets. At least that certain great poets have something of the audacity and intensity — the strong speech — of Old Testament prophets who claimed that the word of God came to them. "The words of Jeremiah, the son of Hilkiah . . . To whom the word of the Lord came in the days of Josiah . . . " It is hard to understand even this introductory passage, for the word for "words," *divre* in Hebrew, indicates something closer to "acts" or "word events," while what the King James version translates as "to whom the word of the Lord came," which hypostatizes the Word, as if it had a being of its own, or were consubstantial with what we know of God, is in the original simply *hajah devar-adonai elav*, "the God-word was to him." We don't know, in short, what is going on; yet through a long tradition of translation and interpretation we feel we know. Similarly, when Wordsworth tells us that around his twenty-third year he "received" certain "convictions," which included the thought that despite his humbler subject matter he could stand beside the "men of old," we seek gropingly to make sense of that conviction. "Poets, even as Prophets," Wordsworth writes,

> each with each
> Connected in a mighty scheme of truth,
> Have each his own peculiar faculty,
> Heaven's gift, a sense that fits him to perceive
> Objects unseen before . . .
> An insight that in some sort he possesses,
> A privilege whereby a work of his,
> Proceeding from a source of untaught things

From *High Romantic Argument: Essays for M. H. Abrams.* © 1981 by Cornell University Press.

Creative and enduring, may become
A power like one of Nature's.
[1850 *Prelude* 13.301–12]

In the earlier (1805) version of *The Prelude* "insight" is "influx," which relates more closely to a belief in inspiration, or a flow (of words) the poet participates in yet does not control: "An influx, that in some sort I possess'd."

I will somewhat neglect in what follows one difference, rather obvious, between poet and prophet. A prophet is to us, and perhaps to himself, mainly a *voice*—as God himself seems to him primarily a voice. Even when he does God in many voices, they are not felt to stand in an equivocal relation to each other: each voice is absolute, and vacillation produces vibrancy rather than ambiguity. In this sense there is no "poetics of prophecy"; there is simply a voice breaking forth, a quasivolcanic eruption, and sometimes its opposite, the "still, small voice" heard after the thunder of Sinai. I will try to come to grips with that difference between poet and prophet later on; here I should only note that, being of the era of Wordsworth rather than of Jeremiah, I must look back from the poet's rather than from the prophet's perspective, while acknowledging that the very concept of poetry may be used by Wordsworth to reflect on—and often to defer—the claim that he has a prophetic gift.

There is another passage in *The Prelude* that explores the relation between poet and prophet. Wordsworth had been to France during the Revolution, had followed that cataclysmic movement in hope, had seen it degenerate into internecine politics and aggressive war. Yet despite the discrediting of revolutionary ideals, something of his faith survived, and not only faith but, as he strangely put it, "daring sympathies with power." In brief, he saw those terrible events in France as necessary and even divinely sanctioned. To explain his mood Wordsworth writes a confessional passage that also gives his most exact understanding of prophecy:

> But as the ancient Prophets, borne aloft
> In vision, yet constrained by natural laws
> With them to take a troubled human heart,
> Wanted not consolations, nor a creed
> Of reconcilement, then when they denounced,
> On towns and cities, wallowing in the abyss
> Of their offences, punishment to come;
> Or saw, like other men, with bodily eyes,
> Before them, in some desolated place,
> The wrath consummate and the threat fulfilled;
> So, with devout humility be it said,

So, did a portion of that spirit fall
On me uplifted from the vantage-ground
Of pity and sorrow to a state of being
That through the time's exceeding fierceness saw
Glimpses of retribution, terrible,
And in the order of sublime behests:
But, even if that were not, amid the awe
Of unintelligible chastisement,
Not only acquiescences of faith
Survived, but daring sympathies with power,
Motions not treacherous or profane, else why
Within the folds of no ungentle breast
Their dread vibration to this hour prolonged?
Wild blasts of music thus could find their way
Into the midst of turbulent events;
So that worst tempests might be listened to.
                [1850 *Prelude* 10.437–63]

This eloquent statement has many complexities; but it is clear that though
Wordsworth felt himself "uplifted from the vantage-ground/Of pity and sorrow," he did not leave them behind in this moment of sublime vision and terrible purification. It is certainly a remarkable feature of a prophet like Jeremiah
that "borne aloft/In vision" he yet takes with him "a troubled human heart."
Like Jonah, he tries to evade the commission, though not, like Jonah, by running
away but rather by claiming he is not of age when it comes to speech ("Then
said I, Ah, Lord GOD! behold, I cannot speak: for I am a child"). Jeremiah
even accuses God, in bitterness of heart, of the very thing of which God accused
Israel: of seducing the prophet, or of being unfaithful (Jer. 20:7ff.).

Wordsworth expresses most strongly a further, related aspect of prophetical
psychology: the ambivalent sympathy shown by the prophet for the powerful
and terrible thing he envisions. This sympathy operates even when he tries
to avert what must be, or to find a "creed of reconcilement." The poet's problem
vis-à-vis the Revolution was not, principally, that he had to come to terms
with crimes committed in the name of the Revolution or of liberty. For at
the end of the passage from which I have quoted he indicates that there had
been a rebound of faith, a persuasion that grew in him that the Revolution
itself was not to blame, but rather "a terrific reservoir of guilt/And ignorance
filled up from age to age" had "burst and spread in deluge through the land."
The real problem was his entanglement in a certain order of sensations which
endured to the very time of writing: he owns to "daring sympathies with power,"
"motions," whose "dread vibration" is "to this hour prolonged," and whose

harmonizing effect in the midst of the turbulence he characterized by the oxymoron "Wild blasts of music."

We understand perfectly well that what is involved in Wordsworth's sympathy with power is not, or not simply, a sublime kind of *Schadenfreude*. And that no amount of talk about the pleasure given by tragedy, through "cathartic" identification, would do more than uncover the same problem in a related area. The seduction power exerts, when seen as an act of God or Nature, lies within common experience. It does not of itself distinguish poets or prophets. What is out of the ordinary here is the "dread vibration": a term close to music, as well as one that conveys the lasting resonance of earlier feelings. How did Wordsworth's experience of sympathy with power accrue a metaphor made overt in "wild blasts of music"?

The tradition that depicts inspired poetry as a wild sort of natural music ("Homer the great Thunderer, [and] the voice that roars along the bed of Jewish Song") circumscribes rather than explains these metaphors. When we take them to be more than commonplaces of high poetry we notice that they sometimes evoke the force of wind and water as blended sound (cf. "The stationary blasts of waterfalls," 1850 *Prelude* 6.626), a sound with power to draw the psyche in, as if the psyche also were an instrument or element, and had to mingle responsively with some overwhelming, massive unity. Despite the poet's imagery of violence, the ideal of harmony, at least on the level of sound, is not given up. The soul as a gigantic if reluctant aeolian harp is implicitly evoked.

How strangely this impulse to harmony is linked with violent feelings can be shown by one of Wordsworth's similes. Similes are, of course, a formal way of bringing together, or harmonizing, different areas of experience. From Coleridge to the New Critics the discussion of formal poetics has often focused on the valorized distinction between fancy and imagination, or on the way difference is reconciled. Shortly before his reflection on the ancient prophets, and when he is still describing the indiscriminate carnage unleashed by Robespierre, Wordsworth has recourse to a strange pseudo-Homeric simile comparing the tempo of killings to a child activating a toy windmill:

> though the air
> Do of itself blow fresh, and make the vanes
> Spin in his eyesight, *that* contents him not,
> But, with the plaything at arm's length, he sets
> His front against the blast, and runs amain,
> That it may whirl the faster.
> [1850 *Prelude* 10.369–74]

An aeolian toy is used, explicitly now, to image a sublime and terrible order of events. The instrument is given to the wind, so that it may go faster;

yet this childish sport is set in an ominous context. The innocent wish to have something go fast reflects on the child whose mimicry (as in the Intimations Ode) suggests his haste to enter the very world where that haste has just shown itself in heinous form. Though there is something incongruous in the simile, there is also something fitting: or at least a drive toward fitting together incongruous passions of childhood and adulthood; and may this drive not express the dark "workmanship that reconciles/Discordant elements" by a mysterious, quasi-musical "harmony" (1850 *Prelude* 1.340ff.)? Here the reconciling music, by which the mind is built up, is already something of a "wild blast"; and when we think of the passage on prophecy to follow, on Wordsworth's "daring sympathies with power," we realize that what is involved in these various instances—lust for carnage, vertigo-sport, the child's impatience to grow up, the poet's fit of words, and the prophet's sympathy with the foreseen event, however terrible—is an anticipatory relation to time, a hastening of futurity.

The music metaphor, associated with wind and water sound, occurs in yet another context close to apocalyptic feelings. (By "apocalyptic" I always mean quite specifically an anticipatory, proleptic relation to time, intensified to the point where there is at once desire for and dread of the end being hastened. There is a potential inner turning against time, and against nature insofar as it participates in the temporal order.) Wordsworth's dream in *Prelude* V of the Arab saving stone and shell from the encroaching flood, also identified as the two principal branches of humane learning, mathematics and literature, is given an explicitly apocalyptic frame. The poet is meditating on books "that aspire to an unconquerable life," human creations that must perish nevertheless. Quoting from a Shakespeare sonnet on the theme of time, he reflects that we "weep to have" what we may lose: the weeping represents both the vain effort and the proleptic regret, so that the very joy of possessing lies close to tears, or thoughts deeper than tears. Only one detail of the ensuing dream need concern us. It comes when the Arab asks the dreamer to hold the shell (poetry) to his ear. "I did so," says the dreamer,

> And heard that instant in an unknown tongue,
> Which yet I understood, articulate sounds,
> A loud prophetic blast of harmony;
> An Ode, in passion uttered, which foretold
> Destruction to the children of the earth
> By deluge, now at hand.
> [1850 *Prelude* 5.93–98]

A "blast of harmony" is not only a more paradoxical, more acute version of the metaphor in "blast of music," but we recognize it as an appropriate figure for the shouting poetry also called prophecy. In the lines that follow,

Wordsworth stresses the dual function of such poetry: it has power to exhilarate and to soothe the human heart. But this is a gloss that conventionalizes the paradox in "blast of harmony" and does not touch the reality of the figure.

Our task is to understand the reality of figures, or more precisely, the reality of "blast of harmony," when applied to prophecy, or prophetic poetry. I will suggest, on the basis of this figure, that there is a poetics of prophecy; and I will study it by reading closely two episodes in *The Prelude* entirely within the secular sphere: the "spot of time" alluding to the death of the poet's father, and the ascent of Snowdon. After that a transition to the prophetic books, and to Jeremiah in particular, may lie open.

II

The death of Wordsworth's father is not attended by unusual circumstances. As Claudius says in a play we shall refer to again: a "common theme/Is death of fathers." Yet it is precisely the commonplace that releases in this case the "dread vibration." The thirteen-year-old schoolboy is impatient to return home for the Christmas holidays, and climbs a crag overlooking two highways to see whether he can spot the horses that should be coming. From that bare, wind-blown crag he watches intensely, and shortly after he returns home his father dies. That is all: a moment of intense, impatient watching, and then, ten days later, the death. Two things without connection except contiguity in time come together in the boy, who feels an emotion that perpetuates "down to this very time" the sights and sounds he experienced waiting for the horses. Here is Wordsworth's account in full:

> There rose a crag,
> That, from the meeting-point of two highways
> Ascending, overlooked them both, far stretched;
> Thither, uncertain on which road to fix
> My expectation, thither I repaired,
> Scout-like, and gained the summit; 'twas a day
> Tempestuous, dark, and wild, and on the grass
> I sate half-sheltered by a naked wall;
> Upon my right hand couched a single sheep,
> Upon my left a blasted hawthorn stood;
> With those companions at my side, I watched,
> Straining my eyes intensely, as the mist
> Gave intermitting prospect of the copse
> And plain beneath. Ere we to school returned,—
> That dreary time,—ere we had been ten days

Sojourners in my father's house, he died,
And I and my three brothers, orphans then,
Followed his body to the grave. The event,
With all the sorrow that it brought, appeared
A chastisement; and when I called to mind
That day so lately past, when from the crag
I looked in such anxiety of hope;
With trite reflections of morality,
Yet in the deepest passion, I bowed low
To God, Who thus corrected my desires;
And, afterwards, the wind and sleety rain,
And all the business of the elements,
The single sheep, and the one blasted tree,
And the bleak music from that old stone wall,
The noise of wood and water, and the mist
That on the line of each of those two roads
Advanced in such indisputable shapes;
All these were kindred spectacles and sounds
To which I oft repaired, and thence would drink,
As at a fountain; and on winter nights,
Down to this very time, when storm and rain
Beat on my roof, or, haply, at noon-day,
While in a grove I walk, whose lofty trees,
Laden with summer's thickest foliage, rock
In a strong wind, some working of the spirit,
Some inward agitations thence are brought,
Whate'er their office.
                    [1850 *Prelude* 12.292–333]

The secular and naturalistic frame of what is recorded remains intact. Yet the experience is comparable in more than its aura to what motivates prophecy. Though there is no intervention of vision or voice, there is something like a special, burdened relation to time. Wordsworth called the episode a "spot of time," to indicate that it stood out, spotlike, in his consciousness of time, that it merged sensation of place and sensation of time (so that time was *placed*), even that it allowed him to physically perceive or "spot" time.

The boy on the summit, overlooking the meeting point of two highways, and stationed between something immobile on his right hand and his left, is, as it were, at the center of a stark clock. Yet the question, How long? if it rises within him, remains mute. It certainly does not surface with the ghostly, prophetic dimension that invests it later. At this point there is simply a boy's impatient hope, "anxiety of hope," as the poet calls it (1.313), a straining of eye and mind that corresponds to the "far-stretched" perspective of the roads. But the father's death, which supervenes as an "event" (1.309), converts that moment of hope into an ominous, even murderous anticipation.

In retrospect, then, a perfectly ordinary mood is seen to involve a sin against time. The boy's "anxiety of hope," his wish for time to pass (both the "dreary time" of school and now of watching and waiting) seems to find retributive fulfillment when the father's life is cut short ten days later. The aftermath points to something unconscious in the first instance but manifest and punishing now. The child feels that his "desires" have been "corrected" by God. What desires could they be except fits of extreme—apocalyptic—impatience, brought on by the very patience or dreary sufferance of nature, of sheep and blasted tree? That the boy bowed low to God, who corrected his desires, evokes a human and orthodox version of nature's own passion.

A similar correction may be the subject of "A slumber did my spirit seal," where a milder sin against time, the delusion that the loved one is a "thing" exempt from the touch of years, is revealed when she dies and becomes a "thing" in fact. The fulfillment of the hope corrects it, as in certain fairy tales. In Wordsworth, hope or delusion always involves the hypnotic elision of time by an imagination drawn toward the "bleak music" of nature—of a powerfully inarticulate nature.

Yet in both representations, that of the death of the father and that of the death of the beloved, there is no hint of anything that would compel the mind to link the two terms, hope against time and its peculiar fulfillment. The link remains inarticulate, like nature itself. A first memory is interpreted by a second: the "event" clarifies an ordinary emotion by suggesting its apocalyptic vigor. But the apocalyptic mode, as Martin Buber remarked, is not the prophetic. Wordsworth's spots of time are said to renew time rather than to hasten its end. A wish for the end to come, for time to pass absolutely, cannot explain what brought the two happenings together, causally, superstitiously, or by a *vaticinum ex eventu*.

Perhaps the apocalyptic wish so compressed the element of time that something like a "gravitation" effect was produced, whereby unrelated incidents fell toward each other. It is, in any case, this process of conjuncture or binding that is mysterious. Not only for the reader but for Wordsworth himself. A more explicit revelation of the binding power had occurred after the death of the poet's mother. Wordsworth's "For now a trouble came into my mind/From unknown causes" (1850 *Prelude* 2.276–77) refers to an expectation that when his mother died the world would collapse. Instead it remains intact and attractive.

> I was left alone
> Seeking the visible world, nor knowing why.
> The props of my affection were removed,
> And yet the building stood, as if sustained
> By its own spirit!
>
> [1850 *Prelude* 2.277–81]

What he had previously named, describing the relationship between mother and infant, "the gravitation and the filial bond," continues to operate without the mother. This event contrary to expectation is the "trouble"; and the "unknown causes" allude to the gravitation, or glue or binding, that mysteriously sustains nature, and draws the child to it in the mother's absence. Even loss binds; and a paradox emerges which focuses on the fixative rather than fixating power of catastrophe, on the nourishing and reparative quality of the "trouble." Wordsworth, too benevolent perhaps, suggests that time itself is being repaired: that the pressure of eternity on thought (the parent's death) creates an "eternity of thought" (1850 *Prelude* 1.402). The survivor knows that the burden of the mystery can be borne, that there is time for thought.

Whether or not, then, we understand Wordsworth's experience fully, the "spots of time" describe a trauma, a lesion in the fabric of time, or more precisely, the trouble this lesion produces and which shows itself as an extreme consciousness of time. Not only is there an untimely death in the case of the father, but it follows too fast on the boy's return home. As in *Hamlet*, "The time is out of joint. O cursed spite/That ever I was born to set it right!" The righting of the injury somehow falls to the poet. "Future restoration" (1850 *Prelude* 12.286), perhaps in the double sense of a restoration of the future as well as of a restoration still to come, is the task he sets himself.

Prophecy, then, would seem to be anti-apocalyptic in seeking a "future restoration," or time for thought. But time, in Wordsworth, is also language, or what the Intimations Ode calls "timely utterance." That phrase contains both threat and promise. It suggests the urgent pressure that gives rise to speech; it also suggests that an animate response, and a harmonious one, is possible, as in Milton's "answerable style," or the pastoral cliché of woods and waters mourning, rejoicing or echoing in timely fashion the poet's mode. Ruskin referred to it as the pathetic fallacy but Abraham Heschel will make pathos, in that large sense, the very characteristic of prophetic language.

More radically still "timely utterance" means an utterance, such as prophecy, or prophetic poetry, which founds or repairs time. The prophet utters time in its ambiguity: as the undesired mediation, which prevents fusion, but also destruction. It prevents fusion by intruding the voice of the poet, his troubled heart, his fear of or flight from "power"; it prevents destruction by delaying God's decree or personally mediating it. Wordsworth speaks scrupulous words despite his sympathy with power and his attraction to the muteness or closure foreseen. By intertextual bonding, by words within words or words against words, he reminds us one more time of time.

We cannot evade the fact that the anxious waiting and the father's death are joined by what can only be called a "blast of harmony." The two moments are harmonized, but the copula is poetic as well as prophetic. For the conjunction of these contiguous yet disparate happenings into a "kindred" form is due to a "working of the spirit" that must be equated with poetry itself. While in the boy of thirteen the process of joining may have been instinctual, the poet recollects the past event as still working itself out; the incident demonstrated so forceful a visiting of imaginative power that later thought is never free of it. What is remarkable in this type-incident—and so remarkable that it keeps "working" on the mind "to this very time"—is not only the "coadunation," as Coleridge would have said, or "In-Eins-Bildung" (his false etymology for the German *Einbildungskraft*, or imagination), but also that it is a "blast," that the workmanship reconciling the discordant elements anticipates a final, awesome unification. Hope is always "anxious" in that it foresees not just unity but also the power needed to achieve unity, to blast things into that state. The fear, then, that mingles with apocalyptic hope also stills it, or brings it close to "that peace/Which passeth understanding" (1850 *Prelude* 14.126–27), because of the uncertain, terrible nature of this final bonding, which evokes in the episode on the crag a bleak and bleating music and images of stunned, warped, blasted, inarticulate being.

III

I turn to the climatic episode of *The Prelude*, the ascent of Snowdon in book 14. Disregarding all but its barest structure, we see that it again presents a sequence of two moments curiously harmonized. The theme of time enters *as elided* when the moon breaks through the mist and into the absorbed mind of the climber. "Nor was time given to ask or learn the cause,/For instantly a light upon the turf/Fell like a flash . . . " (14.37–39). This moment of prevenient light is followed as suddenly by a wild blast of music: the roar of waters through a rift in the mist. The second act or "event" is here an actual sound, separated off from sight and almost hypostatized as a sound. It is quite literally a "blast of harmony": "The roar of waters . . . roaring with one voice."

The appearance of the moon out of the mist is not, however, as unmotivated as might appear. It realizes an unuttered wish, "Let there be light," as the poet climbs through the darkness to "see the sun rise." Spotting the moon fulfills his hope in an unexpected way, which also foreshortens time. The mind of the poet is disoriented; but then time is lengthened as the sight of the moonstruck scene takes over in a kind of silent harmonization. If my hypothesis is correct, there is something truly magical here. The effect ("And there was light") utters the cause—that is, utters the scriptural text ("Let there be light") lodging as desire in the poet. Silence emits a "sound of harmony" (14.98–99) analogous to the music of the spheres. Not the poet but heaven itself declares the glory, the "And there was light" as "night unto night showeth knowledge." Wordsworth seems to behold visibly the "timely utterance" with which Genesis begins—the very harmony between cause and effect, between fiat and actualizing response—and this spectacle seems to be so ghostly a projection of nature itself (rather than of his own excited mind) that he claims it was "given to spirits of the night" and only by chance to the three human spectators (14.63–65).

Yet if the first act of the vision proper proves deceptive, because its motivation, which is a scriptural text, or the authority of that text, or the poet's desire to recapture that fiat power, remains silent and inward, the second act, which is the rising of the voice of the waters, also provides deceptive, even as it falsifies the first. The sound of the waters (though apparently unheard) must have been there all along, so that what is shown up by the vision's second act is a premature harmonizing of the landscape by the majestic moon: by that time-subduing object all sublime. Time also becomes a function of the desire for harmony as imagination now foreshortens and now enthrones the passing moment, or, to quote one of many variants, "so moulds, exalts, indues, combines,/Impregnates, separates, adds, takes away/And makes one object sway another so . . . " In the poet's commentary there is a further attempt at harmonizing, when moon and roaring waters are typified as correlative acts, the possessions of a mind

> That feeds upon infinity, that broods
> Over the dark abyss, intent to hear
> Its voices issuing forth to silent light
> In one continuous stream
>
> [14.71–74]

An image of communion and continuity is projected which the syntax partially subverts, for "its" remains ambiguous, and we cannot say for sure whether the voices belong to the dark abyss or the heavenly mind. What remains of this rich confusion are partial and contradictory structures of unification, which meet us "at every turn" in the "narrow rent" of the text, and add up less to a "chorus of infinity" than again to a "blast of harmony."

IV

For prophet as for poet the ideal is "timely utterance," yet what we actually receive is a "blast of harmony." In Jeremiah a double pressure is exerted, of time on the prophet and of the prophet on time. The urgency of "timely utterance" cuts both ways. Moreover, while the prophet's words must harmonize with events, before or after the event, the word itself is viewed as an event that must harmonize with itself, or with its imputed source in God and the prophets. A passage such as Jer. 23:9–11 describes the impact of the God-word in terms that not only are conventionally ecstatic but also suggest the difficulty of reading the signs of authority properly, and distinguishing true from false prophet. "Adultery" seems to have moved into the word-event itself.

> Concerning the prophets:
> My heart is broken within me,
> all my bones shake;
> I am like a drunken man,
> like man overcome by wine,
> because of the LORD
> and because of his holy words.
> For the land is full of adulterers;
> because of the curse the land mourns.

The time frame becomes very complex, then. On an obvious level the God-word as threat or promise is interpreted and reinterpreted in the light of history, so that Jeremiah's pronouncements are immediately set in their time. "The words of Jeremiah, the son of Hilkiah . . . to whom the word of the Lord came in the days of Josiah . . . " The ending *jah*, meaning "God," reveals from within these destined names the pressure for riming events with God. Jeremiah's prophecies are political suasions having to do with Israel's precarious position between Babylon on one border and Egypt on the other in the years before the destruction of Jerusalem by Nebuchadnezzar. The very survival of Israel is in question; and the prophet is perforce a political analyst as well as a divine spokesman. He speaks at risk not only in the hearing of God but also in that of Pashur, who beat him and put him in the stocks (20:1–4), in that of so-called friends who whisper "Denounce him to Pashur," and in that of King Zedekiah, the son of Josiah, king of Judah, who sends Pashur (the same or another) to Jeremiah, saying, "Inquire of the Lord for us" about Nebuchadnezzar, king of Babylon (21:1–3).

On another level, however, since the book of Jeremiah knows that the outcome is "the captivity of Jerusalem" (1:3), a question arises as to the later force of such prophecy. Near the onset of Jeremiah's career a manuscript of what may have been a version of Deuteronomy was found, and a dedication ceremony took place which pledged Judah once more to the covenant. The issue of the covenant—whether it is broken, or can ever be broken—and the part played in this issue by the survival of a book such as Jeremiah's own is another aspect of the prophet's utterance. Can one praise God yet curse oneself as the bearer of his word (20:13–14)? Or can Judah follow God into the wilderness once more, showing the same devotion as when it was a bride (2:2)? "I utter what was only in view of what will be. . . . What is realized in my history is not the past definite of what was, since it is no more, or even the present perfect of what has been in what I am, but the future anterior of what I shall have been for what I am in the process of becoming." That is Jacques Lacan on the function of language.

Indeed, the contradictions that beset "timely utterance" are so great that a reversal occurs which discloses one of the founding metaphors of literature. When Jacques Lacan writes that "symbols . . . envelop the life of man in a network so total that they join together, before he comes into the world, those who are going to engender him 'by flesh and blood'; so total that they bring to his birth, along with the gifts of the stars, if not with the gifts of the fairies, the shape of his destiny; so total that they give the words that will make him faithful or renegade, the law of the acts that will follow him right to the very place where he *is* not yet and even beyond his death; and so total that through them his end finds its meaning in the last judgment, where the Word absolves his being or condemns it," he is still elaborating Jer. 1:4. "Now the word of the LORD came to me saying, 'Before I formed you in the womb I knew you, and before you were born I consecrated you; I appointed you a prophet to the nations.' " This predestination by the word and unto the word—the "imperative of the Word," as Lacan also calls it, in a shorthand that alludes to the later tradition of the Logos—is then reinforced by Jer. 1:11–12. "And the word of the LORD came to me saying, 'Jeremiah, what do you see?' And I said, 'I see a rod of almond.' Then the LORD said to me, 'You have seen well, for I am watching over my word to perform it.' "

Here the pun of "rod of almond" (*makel shaqued*) and "[I am] watching" (*shoqued*) is more, surely, than a mnemonic or overdetermined linguistic device: it is a rebus that suggests the actualizing or performative relationship between words and things implied by the admonition: "I am watching over my word to perform it." The admonition is addressed to the prophet, in whose care the word is, and through him to the nation; while the very image of the rod of almond projects not only a reconciliation of contraries, of punishment (rod) and pastoral peace (almond), but the entire problem of timely utterance, since the almond tree blossoms unseasonably early and is as exposed to blasting as is the prophet, who seeks to avoid premature speech: "Ah, Lord God! Behold, I do not know how to speak, for I am only a child."

The forcible harmonizing of *shaqued* and *shoqued*, the pressure of that pun, or the emblematic abuse of a pastoral image, alerts us to the difficult pathos of prophetic speech. What does "watching over the word" involve? The prophets are politically and psychically in such a pressure-cooker situation ("I see a boiling pot," Jer. 1:13) that a powerful contamination occurs. Their words cannot always be distinguished from those of God in terms of who is speaking. The prophet identifies now with God and now with his people; moreover, his only way of arguing with the Lord is through words and figures given by the latter. Lacan would say that there is an inevitable inmixing of the Discourse of the Other. Jeremiah argues with God in God's language; and such scripture formulas as "according to thy word" recall this confused and indeterminate situation.

When, in famous lyric verses, Jeremiah admits that he cannot speak without shouting, and what he shouts is "violence and destruction" (20:8), it is as if the God-word itself had suffered a crisis of reference. For this typical warning is now directed not against Israel but against God: it refers to the condition of the prophet who feels betrayed as well as endangered. Jeremiah's hymn begins: "O Lord, you seduced me, and I was seduced," where "seduce," *pittiytani*, can mean both sexual enticement and spiritual deception—as by false prophets. No wonder that at the end of this hymn, the most formal and personal in the entire book, there is a surprising and unmotivated turn from blessing ("Sing to the LORD; praise the LORD") to cursing ("Cursed be the day on which I was born!" 20:13–18). However conventional such a curse may be, and we find a famous instance in Job, it cannot but be read in conjunction with "Before I formed you in the womb I knew you." Jeremiah's "Cursed be the day" is a Caliban moment; God has taught the prophet to speak, and so to curse; or it is a Hamlet moment, the prophet being "cursed" by his election to set the time right. But more important, the curse is the word itself, the violence done by it to the prophet. He feels it in his heart and bones as a burning fire (20:9). The word that knew him before he was conceived has displaced father and mother as begetter: when he curses his birth his word really curses the word. Jeremiah is not given time to develop; he is hurled untimely into the word. The words of the prophet and the words of God can be one only through that "blast of harmony" of which Wordsworth's dream still gives an inkling.

V

When even an intelligent contemporary discussion of "The Prophets as Poets" talks of a "symphony of the effective word" and "the gradual union of person and word," and sees prophecy advancing historically from "word as pointer to word as the thing itself," it adopts metaphors as solutions. The animating fiat spoken by God in the book of Genesis, which founds the harmonious correspondence of creative principle (word) and created product (thing), is literalized by a leap of faith on the part of the intelligent contemporary reader.

Yet with some exceptions—Wolfgang Binder and Peter Szondi on the language of Hölderlin, Erich Auerbach on Dante and figural typology, Northrop Frye on Blake, M. H. Abrams and E. S. Shaffer on the Romantics, Stanley Cavell on Thoreau—it is not the literary critics but the biblical scholars who have raised the issue of secularization (or, what affinity is there between secular and sacred word?) to a level where it is more than a problem in commuting: how to get from there to here, or vice versa. Since Ambrose and Augustine, and again since the Romantic era, biblical criticism has developed together with literary criticism; and still we are only beginning to appreciate their mutual concerns.

It is no accident that the career of Northrop Frye has promised to culminate in an Anatomy of the Bible, or in a summa of structural principles that could harmonize the two bodies of the logos: scripture and literature. By labeling an essay "The Poetics of Prophecy," I may seem to be going in the same direction, and I certainly wish to; yet I think that the relationship between *poetics* and *prophetics* cannot be so easily accommodated. The work of detail, or close reading, ever remains, and quite possibly as a task without an ending. Even when we seek to climb to a prospect where secular and sacred hermeneutics meet on some windy crag, we continue to face a number of unresolved questions that at once plague and animate the thinking critic.

One question is the status of figures. They seem to persist in language as indefeasible sedimentations or as recurrent necessity, long after the megaphone of prophetic style. Moreover, because of the priority and survival of "primitive" or "oriental" figuration, such distinctions as Coleridge's between fancy and imagination tend to become the problem they were meant to resolve. Strong figurative expression does not reconcile particular and universal, or show the translucence of the universal in the concrete: there is such stress and strain that even when theorists value one mode of imaginative embodiment over another—as symbol over allegory or metaphysical wit—they admit the persistence and sometimes explosive concurrence of the archaic or depreciated form.

Another important question is the status of written texts in the life of society or the life of the mind. Almost every tradition influenced by Christianity has aspired to a spiritualization of the word, its transformation and even disappearance as it passes from "word as pointer to word as thing itself." A logocentric or incarnationist thesis of this kind haunts the fringes of most studies of literature, and explains the welcome accorded at present to semiotic counterperspectives. Textual reality, obviously, is more complex, undecidable, and lasting than any such dogma; and the dogma itself is merely inferred from historically ramified texts.

A last question concerns intertextuality. From the perspective of scripture intertextuality is related to canon formation, or the process of authority by which the bibles (*biblia*) we call the Bible were unified. The impact of scripture on literature includes the concept of (1) peremptory or preemptive texts and (2) interpreters who find the unifying principle that could join books into a canon of classics. From a secular perspective these books, whether classified as literature or as scripture, have force but no authority; and to bring them together into some sort of canon is the coup of the critic, who harmonizes them by the force of his own text. His work reveals not their canonicity but rather their intertextuality; and the most suggestive theory along these lines has been that of Harold Bloom.

The impact, according to him, of a preemptive poem on a later one is always "revisionary": the one lives the other's death, deviating its meaning, diverting its strength, creating an inescapable orbit. "Revisionary" suggests, therefore, a relationship of force: again, a blast of harmony rather than a natural or authoritative unification.

For a reason not entirely clear to me, Bloom wishes to establish English poetry after Milton as a Milton satellite. Milton becomes a scripture substitute with the impressive and oppressive influence of scripture itself. Later poets must harmonize with Milton, willingly or unwillingly: even their deviations are explained by attempts to escape the Milton orbit. Yet I have shown that Wordsworth may imitate a scripture text ("Let there be light") with a power of deviousness that is totally un-Miltonic. Milton and Nature, Wordsworth saw, were not the same. His return to scripture is not to its precise verbal content, though it is an implicit content (Genesis, light, voice) that infuses the texture of the vision on Snowdon. The form of the fiat, however, predominates over its content; and what we are given to see is not scripture reenacted or imaginatively revised—new testamented—but the unuttered fiat in its silent yet all-subduing aspect. What Wordsworth names and represents as Nature is the fiat power working tacitly and harmoniously, reconciling discordant elements, building up the mind and perhaps the cosmos itself.

Snowdon's Miltonic echoes, therefore, which recapitulate a portion of the story of creation as retold in the seventh book of *Paradise Lost*, are allusions whose status is as hard to gauge as those to *Hamlet* in the "spot of time" referring to the father's death. The converging highways, moreover, in that spot of time could lead the contemporary reader (perhaps via Freud) to Oedipus, so that a question arises on the relation of revisionary to hermeneutic perspectives, making the intertextual map more tricky still. Yet Wordsworth's vision, natural rather than textual in its apparent motivation, can still be called revisionary because a prior and seminal text may be hypothetically reconstituted.

The act of reconstitution, however, now includes the reader in a specific and definable way. The *poet* as reader is shown to have discovered from within himself, and so recreated, a scripture text. The *interpreter* as reader has shown the capacity of a "secular" text to yield a "sacred" intuition by a literary act of understanding that cannot be divided into those categories. On the level of interpretation, therefore, we move toward what Schleiermacher called *Verstehen*, on the basis of which a hermeneutic is projected that seeks to transcend the dichotomizing of religious and nonreligious modes of understanding and of earlier (prophetic) and later (poetic-visionary) texts.

VI

Returning a last time to Wordsworth: much remains to be said concerning the "gravitation and the filial bond" that links earlier visionary texts to his own. The reader, in any case, also moves in a certain gravitational field; and I have kept myself from being pulled toward a Freudian explanation of the nexus between the boy's "anxiety of hope" and the guilty, affective inscription on his mind of a natural scene. My only finding is that should a God-word precede in Wordsworth, it is rarely foregrounded, but tends to be part of the poem's ground as an inarticulate, homeless or ghostly, sound. It becomes, to use one of his own expressions, an "inland murmur."

In the second act of Snowdon this sound comes out of the deep and is suddenly the very subject, the "Imagination of the whole" (1805 *Prelude* 13.65). Though the text behind that sound cannot be specified, it is most probably the word within the word, the Word that was in the Beginning (John 1:1), and which uttered as from chaos, "Let there be light." In Milton the first words of the "Omnific Word" are "Silence, ye troubl'd Waves, and thou Deep, peace" (*Paradise Lost* 7.216), a proto-fiat Wordsworth may have absorbed into his vision of silence followed by his more radical vision of the power in sound.

When the poet writes, "The sounding cataract haunted me like a passion" ("Tintern Abbey"), there is again no sense of a proof text of any kind. We recognize a congruity of theme between this waterfall and the "roar of waters" heard on Snowdon, and perhaps associate both with Psalm 42: "Deep calls unto deep at the thunder of thy cataracts." Such allusions may exist, but they are "tidings" born on the wave of natural experience. Yet a prophetic text does enter once more in the way we have learned to understand. The word "passion," by being deprived òf specific reference, turns back on itself, as if it contained a muted or mutilated meaning. By a path more devious than I can trace, the reader recovers for "passion" its etymological sense of "passio"—and the word begins to embrace the pathos of prophetic speech, or a suffering idiom that is strongly inarticulate or musical, like the "earnest expectation of the creature . . . subjected . . . in hope" of which Paul writes in Romans (8:19–20), like sheep, blasted tree, and the boy who waits with them, and the barely speaking figures that inhabit the poet's imagination. The event, in Wordsworth, is the word of connection itself, a word event (the poem) that would repair the bond between human hopes and a mutely remonstrant nature, "subjected in hope."

"Do you know the language of the old belief?" asks Robert Duncan. "The wild boar too/turns a human face." Today the hope in such a turning includes the very possibility of using such language. A mighty scheme not of truth but of troth—of trusting the old language, its pathos, its animism, its fallacious figures—is what connects poet and prophet. When Wordsworth apostrophizes nature at the end of the Intimations Ode, he still writes in the old language, yet how precariously, as he turns toward what is turning away:

> And O, ye Fountains, Meadows, Hills and Groves,
> Forebode not any severing of our loves!

BIBLIOGRAPHICAL NOTE

The locus classicus of Coleridgean poetics is found in chapters 13 and 14 of the *Biographia Literaria* (1818), "On the Imagination, or Esemplastic Power," etc. *Aids to Reflection* (1824) and a mass of miscellaneous lectures and readings contain many subtle and varying attempts to distinguish between symbolical and allegorical, analogous and metaphorical language, and so forth. Coleridge's reflections on the subject of style and unity are much more intricate than my general comment suggests; see, for one example, "On Style," reprinted in *Coleridge's Miscellaneous Criticism*, ed. T. M. Raysor (Cambridge, Mass., 1936). Yet even there German-type speculation is mixed with practical and preacherly admonition. The major German influence in regard to art, revelation, and the question of unity (or "identity philosophy") was, of course, Schelling. Martin Buber's distinction between apocalyptic and prophetic is made in "Prophecy, Apocalyptic, and the Historical Hour," in *On the Bible* (New York, 1968). For Abraham Heschel on pathos, see *The Prophets* (New York, 1962). The intelligent contemporary discussion on prophets as poets is in David Robertson's chapter of that title in *The Old Testament and the*

Literary Critic (Philadelphia, 1977). Robertson acknowledges his debt to Gerhard von Rad's *Old Testament Theology*, volume 2. To the literary scholars mentioned in my essay, I should add Paul de Man's and Angus Fletcher's work on the theory of allegory; Walter Benjamin's seminal reconsideration of baroque allegory in *The Origin of German Tragic Drama* (originally published in 1928); and articles by Robert W. Funk on the parable in the New Testament and in Kafka. Frank Kermode is also working on the parable and has begun publishing on the idea of canon formation. Elinor Shaffer's *Kubla Khan and the Fall of Jerusalem* (Cambridge, England, 1976) links up more specifically than Basil Willey movements in Bible criticism and considerations of literary form. Her chapter entitled "The Visionary Character" is especially valuable in summarizing the movement of thought whereby poets, critics, and theologians came to consider Holy Writ as composed of different poetic and narrative genres, and faced the question of how to value nonapostolic (generally "apocalyptic" rather than "prophetic") visionariness. My quotations from Jacques Lacan can be found in *Ecrits: A Selection* (New York, 1977). The issue of secularization in literary history is central to M. H. Abrams's *Natural Supernaturalism* (1971) and has elicited, in the Anglo-American domain, many partial theories from Matthew Arnold to Daniel Bell. Stanley Cavell's *The Senses of Walden* (1971) reveals a Wordsworthian type of underwriting in Thoreau, and one so consistent in its allusions to earlier epics and scriptures that *Walden* begins to emerge as a sacred book.

LEO STRAUSS

On Socrates and the Prophets

Fifty years ago, in the middle of World War I, Herman Cohen, the greatest representative of German Jewry and spokesman for it, the most powerful figure among the German professors of philosophy of his time, stated his view on Jerusalem and Athens in a lecture entitled "The social ideal in Plato and the prophets" [*Hermann Cohens Jüdische Schriften* (Berlin, 1924)]. He repeated that lecture shortly before his death. We may then regard it as stating his final view on Jerusalem and Athens and therewith on *the* truth. For, as Cohen says right at the beginning, "Plato and the prophets are the two most important sources of modern culture." Being concerned with "the social ideal," he does not say a single word on Christianity in the whole lecture. Crudely but not misleadingly one may restate Cohen's view as follows. *The* truth is the synthesis of the teaching of Plato and that of the prophets. What we owe to Plato is the insight that the truth is in the first place the truth of science but that science must be supplemented, overarched by the idea of the good which to Cohen means, not God, but rational, scientific ethics. The ethical truth must not only be compatible with the scientific truth; the ethical truth even needs the scientific truth. The prophets are very much concerned with knowledge: with the knowledge of God, but this knowledge as the prophets understood it, has no connection whatever with scientific knowledge; it is knowledge only in a metaphorical sense. It is perhaps with a view to this fact that Cohen speaks once of the divine Plato but never of the divine prophets. Why then can he not leave matters at Platonic philosophy? What is the fundamental defect of Platonic philosophy that is remedied by the prophets and only by the prophets? According to Plato, the cessation of evils requires the rule of the philosophers,

---

From *Jerusalem and Athens: Some Preliminary Reflections* (The City College Papers, no. 6, 1967).
© 1967 by the City College of New York.

of the men who possess the highest kind of human knowledge, i.e., of science in the broadest sense of the term. But this kind of knowledge, as to some extent all scientific knowledge, is according to Plato the preserve of a small minority: of the men who possess certain gifts that most men lack—of the few men who possess a certain nature. Plato presupposes that there is an unchangeable human nature. As a consequence, he presupposes that there is such a fundamental structure of the good human society as is unchangeable. This leads him to assert or to assume that there will be wars as long as there will be human beings, that there ought to be a class of warriors and that that class ought to be higher in rank and honor than the class of producers and exchangers. These defects are remedied by the prophets precisely because they lack the idea of science and hence the idea of nature, and hence they can believe that men's conduct toward one another can undergo a change much more radical than any change ever dreamt of by Plato.

Cohen has brought out very well the antagonism between Plato and the prophets. Nevertheless we cannot leave matters at his view of that antagonism. Cohen's thought belongs to the world preceding World War I. Accordingly he had a greater faith in the power of modern Western culture to mold the fate of mankind than seems to be warranted now. The worst things that he experienced were the Dreyfus scandal and the pogroms instigated by Czarist Russia: he did not experience Communist Russia and Hitler Germany. More disillusioned regarding modern culture than Cohen was, we wonder whether the two ingredients of modern culture, of the modern synthesis, are not more solid than that synthesis. Catastrophes and horrors of a magnitude hitherto unknown, which we have seen and through which we have lived, were better provided for, or made intelligible, by both Plato and the prophets than by the modern belief in progress. Since we are less certain than Cohen was that the modern synthesis is superior to its pre-modern ingredients, and since the two ingredients are in fundamental opposition to each other, we are ultimately confronted by a problem rather than by a solution.

More particularly, Cohen understood Plato in the light of the opposition between Plato and Aristotle—an opposition that he understood in the light of the opposition between Kant and Hegel. We, however, are more impressed than Cohen was by the kinship between Plato and Aristotle on the one hand and the kinship between Kant and Hegel on the other. In other words, the quarrel between the ancients and the moderns seems to us to be more fundamental than either the quarrel between Plato and Aristotle or that between Kant and Hegel.

We prefer to speak of Socrates and the prophets rather than of Plato and the prophets, for the following reasons. We are no longer as sure as Cohen was that we can draw a clear line between Socrates and Plato. There is traditional support for drawing such a clear line, above all in Aristotle; but Aristotle's statements on this kind of subject no longer possess for us the authority that they formerly possessed, and this is due partly to Cohen himself. The clear distinction between Socrates and Plato is based, not only on tradition, but on the results of modern historical criticism; yet these results are in the decisive respect hypothetical. The decisive fact for us is that Plato as it were points away from himself to Socrates. If we wish to understand Plato, we must take him seriously; we must take seriously in particular his deference to Socrates. Plato points not only to Socrates' speeches but to his whole life, to his fate as well. Hence Plato's life and fate does not have the symbolic character of Socrates' life and fate. Socrates, as presented by Plato, had a mission; Plato did not claim to have a mission. It is in the first place this fact—the fact that Socrates had a mission—that induces us to consider, not Plato and the prophets, but Socrates and the prophets.

I cannot speak in my own words of the mission of the prophets. Surely here and now I cannot do more than remind you of three prophetic utterances of singular force and grandeur.

> In the year that King Uzziah died I saw also the Lord sitting upon a throne, high and lifted up, and his train filled the temple. Above it stood the seraphim: each one had six wings; with twain he covered his face, and with twain he covered his feet, and with twain he did fly. And one cried unto another, and said, Holy, holy, holy is the Lord of hosts: the whole world is full of his glory. And the posts of the door moved at the voice of him that cried, and the house was filled with smoke. Then I said, Woe is me! for I am undone; because I am a man of unclean lips, and I dwell in the midst of a people of unclean lips: for mine eyes have seen the King, the Lord of hosts. Then flew one of the seraphim unto me, having a live coal in his hand, which he had taken with the tongs from off the altar: And he laid it upon my mouth, and said, Lo, this hath touched thy lips; and thine iniquity is taken away, and thy sin purged. Also I heard the voice of the Lord, saying, Whom shall I send, and who will go for us? Then said I, Here am I; send me.
>   (Isa. 6)

Isaiah, it seems, volunteered for his mission. Could he not have remained silent? Could he refuse to volunteer? When the word of the Lord came unto Jonah, "Arise, go to Nineveh, that great city, and cry against it; for their wickedness is come up before me," "Jonah rose up to flee unto Tarshish from the presence of the Lord"; Jonah ran away from his mission; but God did not allow him to run away; He compelled him to fulfill it. Of this compulsion we hear in different ways from Amos and Jeremiah. Amos 3:7–8: "Surely the Lord God will do nothing but he revealeth his secret unto his servants the prophets. The lion hath roared, who will not fear? the Lord God hath spoken; who will not prophesy?" The prophets overpowered by the majesty of the Lord, by His wrath and His mercy, bring the message of His wrath and His mercy:

> Then the word of the Lord came unto me, saying, Before I formed thee in the belly I knew thee and before thou camest out of the womb I sanctified thee, and I ordained thee a prophet unto the nations. Then said I, Ah, Lord God! behold, I cannot speak; for I am a child. But the Lord said unto me, Say not, I am a child; for thou shalt go to all that I shall send thee, and whatsoever I command thee thou shalt speak. Be not afraid of their faces; for I am with thee to deliver thee, saith the Lord. Then the Lord put forth his hand, and touched my mouth. And the Lord said unto me, Behold, I have put my words in thy mouth. See, I have this day set thee over the nations and over the kingdoms, to root out, and to pull down, and to destroy, and to throw down, to build, and to plant.
>
> (Jer. 1:4–10)

The claim to have been sent by God was raised also by men who were not truly prophets but prophets of falsehood, false prophets. Many or most hearers were therefore uncertain as to which kinds of claimants to prophecy were to be trusted or believed. According to the Bible, the false prophets simply lied in saying that they were sent by God: "they speak a vision of their own heart, and not out of the mouth of the Lord. They say . . . the Lord hath said, Ye shall have peace" (Jer. 23:16–17). The false prophets tell the people what the people like to hear; hence they are much more popular than the true prophets. The false prophets are "prophets of the deceit of their own heart" (ibid. 26); they tell the people what they themselves imagined (consciously or unconsciously) because they wished it or their hearers wished it. But: "Is not my word like as a fire? saith the Lord, and like a hammer that breaketh the rock in pieces?" (ibid. 29). Or, as Jeremiah put it when opposing the false prophet Hananiah: "The prophets that have been before me and before thee of old prophesied both against many countries, and against great kingdoms, of war, and of evil, and of pestilence." (28:8) This does not mean that a prophet is true only if he is a prophet of doom; the true prophets are also prophets of ultimate salvation. We understand the difference between the true and the false prophets if we listen to and meditate on these words of Jeremiah: "Thus saith the Lord; Cursed is the man, that trusteth in man, and makes flesh his arm, and whose heart departeth from the Lord. . . . Blessed is the man that trusteth in the Lord, and whose hope the Lord is." The false prophets trust in flesh, even if that flesh is the temple in Jerusalem, the promised land, nay, the chosen people itself, nay, God's promise to the chosen people if that promise is taken to be an unconditional promise and not as a part of a Covenant. The true prophets, regardless of whether they predict doom or salvation, predict the unexpected, the humanly unforeseeable—what would not occur to men, left to themselves, to fear or to hope. The true prophets speak and act by the spirit and in the spirit of *Ehyeh-asher-ehyeh*. For the false prophets on the other hand there cannot be the wholly unexpected, whether bad or good.

Of Socrates' mission we know only through Plato's *Apology of Socrates*, which presents itself as the speech delivered by Socrates when he defended himself against the charge that he did not believe in the existence of the gods worshipped by the city of Athens and that he corrupted the young. In that speech he denies possessing any more than human wisdom. This denial was understood by Yehudah ha-levi among others as follows: "Socrates said to the people: 'I do not deny your divine wisdom, but I say that I do not understand it; I am wise only in human wisdom.' " While this interpretation points in the right direction, it goes somewhat too far. At least Socrates refers immediately after having denied possessing any more than human wisdom, to the speech that originated his mission, and of this speech he says that it is not his but he seems to ascribe to it divine origin. He does trace what he says to a speaker who is worthy of credence to the Athenians. But it is probable that he means by that speaker his companion Chairephon who is worthy of credence to the Athenians, more worthy of credence to the Athenians than Socrates, because he was attached to the democratic regime. This Chairephon, having once come to Delphi, asked Apollo's oracle whether there was anyone wiser than Socrates. The Pythia replied that no one was wiser. This reply originated Socrates' mission. We see at once that Socrates' mission originated in human initiative, in the initiative of one of Socrates' companions. Socrates takes it for granted that the reply given by the Pythia was given by the god Apollo himself. Yet this does not induce him to take it for granted that the god's reply is true. He does take it for granted that it is not meet for the god to lie. Yet this does not make the god's reply convincing to him. In fact he tries to refute that reply by discovering men who are wiser than he. Engaging in this quest he finds out that the god said the truth: Socrates is wiser than other men because he knows that he knows nothing, i.e., nothing about the most important things, whereas the others believe that they know the truth about the most important things. Thus his attempt to refute the oracle turns into a vindication of the oracle. Without intending it, he comes to the assistance of the god; he serves the god; he obeys the god's command. Although no god had ever spoken to him, he is satisfied that the god had commanded him to examine himself and the others, i.e., to philosophize, or to exort everyone he meets to the practice of virtue: he has been given by the god to the city of Athens as a gadfly.

While Socrates does not claim to have heard the speech of a god, he claims that a voice—something divine and demonic—occurs to him from time to time, his daimonion. This daimonion, however, has no connection with Socrates' mission, for it never urges him forward but only keeps him back. While the Delphic oracle urged him forward toward philosophizing, toward examining his fellow men, and thus made him generally hated and thus brought him into mortal danger, his daimonion kept him back from political activity and thus saved him from mortal danger.

The fact that both Socrates and the prophets have a divine mission means or at any rate implies that both Socrates and the prophets are concerned with justice or righteousness, with the perfectly just society which as such would be free from all evils. To this extent Socrates' figuring out of the best social order and the prophets' vision of the Messianic age are in agreement. Yet whereas the prophets predict the coming of the Messianic age, Socrates merely holds that the perfect society is possible: whether it will ever be actual, depends on an unlikely, although not impossible, coincidence, the coincidence of philosophy and political power. For, according to Socrates, the coming-into-being of the best political order is not due to divine intervention; human nature will remain as it always has been; the decisive difference between the best political order and all other societies is that in the former the philosophers will be kings or that the natural potentiality of the philosophers will reach its utmost perfection. In the most perfect social order as Socrates sees it, knowledge of the most important things will remain, as it always was, the preserve of the philosophers, i.e., of a very small part of the population. According to the prophets however, in the Messianic age "the earth shall be full of knowledge of the Lord, as the waters cover the earth" (Isa. 11:9), and this will be brought about by God Himself. As a consequence, the Messianic age will be the age of universal peace: all nations shall come to the mountain of the Lord, to the house of the God of Jacob, "and they shall beat their swords into plowshares, and their spears into pruning hooks: nation shall not lift up sword against nation, neither shall they learn war any more." (Isa. 2:2–4) The best regime, however, as Socrates envisages it, will animate a single city which as a matter of course will become embroiled in wars with other cities. The cessation of evils that

Socrates expects from the establishment of the best regime will not include the cessation of war.

The perfectly just man, the man who is as just as is humanly possible, is according to Socrates the philosopher and according to the prophets the faithful servant of the Lord. The philosopher is the man who dedicates his life to the quest for knowledge of the good, of the idea of the good; what we would call moral virtue is only the condition or by-product of that quest. According to the prophets, however, there is no need for the quest for knowledge of the good: God "hath shewed thee, o man, what is good; and what doth the Lord require of thee, but to do justly, and to love mercy, and to walk humbly with thy God." (Mic. 6:8) In accordance with this the prophets as a rule address the people and sometimes even all the peoples, whereas Socrates as a rule addresses only one man. In the language of Socrates the prophets are orators while Socrates engages in conversations with one man, which means he is addressing questions to him.

There is one striking example of a prophet talking in private to a single man, in a way addressing a question to him.

> And the Lord sent Nathan unto David. And he came unto him, and said unto him, There were two men in one city; the one rich, and the other poor. The rich man had exceeding many flocks and herds: But the poor man had nothing, save one little ewe lamb, which he had brought and nourished up: and it grew up together with him, and with his children; it did eat of his own meat, and drank of his own cup, and lay in his bosom, and was unto him as a daughter. And there came a traveller unto the rich man and he spared to take of his own flock and of his own herd, to dress for the wayfaring man that was come unto him; but took the poor man's lamb, and dressed it for the man that was come unto him. And David's anger was greatly kindled against the man; and he said to Nathan, As the Lord liveth, the man that hath done this thing shall surely die; And he shall restore the lamb fourfold, because he did this thing, and because he had no pity. And Nathan said to David, Thou art the man.
>
> (2 Sam. 12:1–7)

The nearest parallel to this event that occurs in the Socratic writings is Socrates' reproof of his former companion, the tyrant Critias. "When the thirty were putting to death many citizens and by no means the worst ones, and were encouraging many in crime, Socrates said *somewhere*, that it seemed strange that a herdsman who lets his cattle decrease and go to the bad should not admit that he is a poor cowherd; but stranger still that a statesman when he causes the citizens to decrease and go to the bad, should feel no shame nor think himself a poor statesman. This remark was *reported* to Critias." (Xenophon, *Memorabilia* I 2.32–33.)

DOUGLAS ROBINSON

Jonah and Moby-Dick

The Book of Jonah presents a striking alternative to the eschatological thrust of OT prophecy. In its historical context of emergent postexilic apocalypticism, of passionately ethnocentric messianic expectation, the Book of Jonah stands out as an exceptional call for cosmopolitan tolerance, a tolerance that would place personal spiritual growth ahead of racial discrimination, ethics ahead of apocalypse. Jonah is the perfect Jew of his time—his messianic expectation is strong, his ethnocentrism implacable—and so, in the world of this book, he becomes an apocalyptic prophet against his will, a rebel against God's holy command: not because he has any particular antipathy toward the doomsayer's role, but because he is afraid that his apocalyptic preaching might prevent apocalypse. He is an apocalyptic bigot, a Jew who resists preaching anything to the great Gentile city, Nineveh, lest it repent and be spared. In an OT context, of course, the Gentiles are of the company of the NT Antichrist, the forces of earthly evil whose destruction is eagerly awaited as the prerequisite of apocalyptic restoration. To encourage their repentance, therefore, was to postpone the messianic kingdom, the elevation of the Jewish nation out of bondage into paradise. And so, when the word comes down to Jonah, he flees it:

> Now the word of the LORD came to Jonah the son of Amittai, saying "Arise, go to Nineveh, that great city, and cry against it; for their wickedness has come up before me." But Jonah rose to flee to Tarshish from the presence of the LORD. He went down to Joppa and found a ship going to Tarshish; so he paid the fare,

From *American Apocalypses: The Image of the End of the World in American Literature.* © 1985 by The Johns Hopkins University Press.

and went on board, to go with them to Tarshish, away from the
presence of the LORD.

(Jon. 1:1–3)

Being a rather literal-minded chauvinist, Jonah believes that God *lives* in
Israel and can be escaped by geographical flight. As soon as the ship gets out
to sea, however, God raises a tempest that threatens to destroy it—an
"apocalypse" that can be averted only through Jonah's repentance, just as the
destruction of Nineveh can be averted by *their* repentance. Jonah does not
immediately come forward; only after lots have been cast and Jonah singled
out as the cause of the ship's distress does he reluctantly offer himself as
propitiatory sacrifice: "Take me up and throw me into the sea," he tells the
crew; "then the sea will quiet down for you" (Jon. 1:12). With anticipatory
irony, the sailors are portrayed as Gentiles (praying to their *gods*) who are yet
decent men, more selfless than Jonah. Whereas Jonah is willing to let the crew
die lest Nineveh be *spared*, they would rather risk death than cast out a stranger
who admits his own guilt. Jonah finally convinces them to heave him over-
board, however, and the first apocalyptic threat passes: the sea is calmed. As
a result, the sailors are awed by the power of Jonah's God, and offer sacrifices
not to their gods, but to Yahweh. God's purpose is not to destroy the Gentiles,
but to convert them.

Jonah is now swallowed by the whale, remaining in its belly for three
days and three nights, until finally he sends up a prayer of repentance and
is deposited on dry land, where God again instructs him to preach doom to
the Ninevites. He does, and as he feared, they do repent, and God does spare
them. This angers Jonah considerably; ostensibly repentant, he retains his
chauvinism, and so he removes himself outside the city to sulk—and, he hopes,
to watch the Gentile city's demise. There God comes to him in a final attempt
to teach him a larger perspective: raising a plant to shade Jonah from the sun,
God causes it to wither overnight as a kind of material allegory for Jonah's
edification:

But God said to Jonah, "Do you do well to be angry for the plant?"
And he said, "I do well to be angry, angry enough to die." And
the LORD said, "You pity the plant, for which you did not labor,
nor did you make it grow, which came into being in a night, and
perished in a night. And should I not pity Nineveh, that great city,
in which there are more than a hundred and twenty thousand
persons who do not know their right hand from their left, and also
much cattle?"

(Jon. 4:9–11)

One wonders just how intentional this concluding bathos is; to describe the Ninevites as not knowing their right hand from their left is to *reduce* them to the status of cattle, and to end the book on the bathetic note of "and also much cattle" reduces the enterprise it describes to absurdity. God is a Humane Society liberal who feels sorry for a bunch of dumb animals. By implication, however, the *opposite* to this animal state, represented by Israel through Jonah, is not much dearer to God; Jonah does know his right hand from his left, knows God from idols, Jews from Gentiles, but that knowledge generates only an apocalyptic selfishness . . . that hungers for the destruction of enemies. God's is a broader perspective that encompasses both the knowledge and the bitter ethnocentrism of the Jews, and both the ignorance and the humble repentance of the Ninevites, and that implicitly *equates* the two peoples in such a way as to hint at a human brotherhood. God threatens to destroy the Gentile city for their ignorant wickedness—but also threatens to destroy Jonah, the tale's figure for Israel, for his knowledgeable chauvinism, and finally *spares* and *teaches* both. Read in terms of image and theme, the Book of Jonah points clearly to an imagistic reversal of the apocalypse—an invocation of apocalyptic threats (structural collapse in ship and city) in order to replace the ideology of apocalypse with a "liberal," antiapocalyptic tolerance.

This reading, however, neglects the tale's most famous episode—Jonah's descent into the belly of the whale. Why must Jonah be swallowed up? How is his repentance tied to the mythic descent? A look at the tale's rhetoric clarifies much of its obscurity. As is twice emphasized in the opening paragraph of the book, Jonah flees "from the presence of the LORD," which is to say, in Hebrew terms, from God's face. He seeks a place where God cannot *see* him—where he can *absent* himself from God's command and thus also from God's wrath at his disobedience. This ironic inversion of the religious desire for presence into a desire for absence is symbolically a death wish; the only place of absence in the Hebrew cosmology is Sheol, the land of the dead. And when Jonah is swallowed up by the whale, he *figures* his absence in terms of Sheol:

> I called to the LORD, out of my distress,
>   and he answered me;
> out of the belly of Sheol I cried,
>   and thou didst hear my voice. . . .
> Then I said, "I am cast out
>   from thy presence;
> how shall I again look
>   upon thy holy temple?"
>
>   (Jon. 2:1, 4)

But with Jonah's death comes also conversion:

> When my soul fainted within me,
>   I remembered the LORD;
> and my prayer came to thee,
>   into thy holy temple. . . .
> Deliverance belongs to the LORD!
>   (Jon. 2:7, 9)

The absence of Sheol is thus converted here into presence in God's holy temple; cast out of God's presence into the land of the dead, Jonah *prays*, and the prayer (synecdoche of Jonah, whose name means "dove") flies from Sheol-absence to temple-presence, leading ultimately to deliverance. Tropologically speaking, the irony of Jonah's flight from presence into absence has been converted into the synecdoche of prayer, outward flight from God's face into inner mental speech, which flies back to God's presence. In the whale's belly, the absence Jonah seeks is revealed as *internality*, specifically the internality of a prison; to escape, Jonah must unlearn his simplistic notions of externality, and go *out* by first going *in*. That is, Jonah's path out of the whale's belly lies not through the whale's skin, an outward direction that a mythic hero (or an Ahab) would take, but through the inwardness of his own mind. When Jonah prays, he imagistically turns inside out, the outward predicament of being trapped in a whale's belly becoming itself the illusion that is replaced with an internal dialogue, an inward communion between Jonah-as-prayer and God-as-spirit. That this inwardness delivers Jonah back into the outside world suggests that activity in that world without the inward journey Jonah undergoes is doomed to insubstantiality; one goes out by first going in, and synecdochically inverting internality into externality.

When Jonah emerges from the whale's belly, however, his learning is far from complete. When God stops the apocalypse, Jonah's bigotry reemerges as an angry death wish—he again prefers to die rather than see a Gentile city spared. As Jonah sees it, God has cheated Israel and made a liar out of him: he had, after all, predicted no contingent destruction but a predetermined apocalypse: "Yet forty days, and Nineveh shall be overthrown" (Jon. 3:4). But another way of conceiving Nineveh's salvation is to imagine Jonah's prophecy not as a metaleptic projection, Jonah's bigotry *become* future [in] the form of destruction, but as metonymical reduction, in which Nineveh's wickedness is destroyed not by the apocalypse *imaged* by Jonah, but by the apocalyptic image itself—by signifier rather than by signified, in the structuralist idiom. In other words, frightened by the apocalyptic image, the Ninevites destroy their *own* wickedness metonymically in repentance; cataclysm, etymologically the "washing down" of the world in the Flood, becomes the "washing away" of the Ninevites' evil. And Jonah is taught, this time, by the same metonymical process: instead of having him swallowed up by another whale, God presents Jonah with a metonymic image of destruction, a plant that grows and dies *next to* the great city. And, one assumes (the book ends on the rhetorical question that presumably precedes Jonah's final insight), just as Jonah's image of the end of the world instructed Nineveh, so also will this image instruct Jonah.

Rhetorically, then, the Book of Jonah records a three-phase movement from ignorance to wisdom. In the first, or ironic, phase, Jonah flees a presence that is at once a *fullness* and a *limitation* (a limitation of perspective to the ethnocentrism sanctified by Jewish tradition) into a deathly absence, a psychological isolation from both God and his Holy Nation, that is revealed as *inward*. The constrictions of this inwardness, however, impinge on Jonah's mind in the image of prison, motivating the second, or synecdochic, phase. Here Jonah escapes mental imprisonment by inverting inside and outside, going out by going in, thus learning to operate in the outside world with a broader perspective gained through his inward journey. But in order to carry "insight," inward vision, into the outside world, he must understand the nature of *signs*. This is the lesson learned in the third, or metonymical, phase. Responsible activity in the world requires neither a solipsistic withdrawal into an inward fantasy world nor a projective drive to transform the world into an image of one's inwardness, but a metonymical compromise between image and reality. One offers an image of the end of the world not in the belief that (through the supernatural intervention of a sympathetic God) reality will conform to it, but in the hope that the image might encourage others to undergo one's own transitional experience. Like Augustine's allegorical displacement of the Book of Revelation, the Book of Jonah traces the internalization of apocalyptic threats into a learning process in which the learner progresses by discovering first the inward path to expanded perspectives and then the necessity of *compromising* with inward vision in confrontation with the world. . . .

Melville's first extended interpretation of the Book of Jonah in *Moby-Dick* is, interestingly enough, an ironic misinterpretation of the book, in the form of Father Mapple's Puritan sermon on that text. By making Father Mapple get it all wrong, Melville at once distances the unbendingly dualistic Puritan interpretation and moves hermeneutically back closer to the spirit of the original text. Father Mapple's reading of the book, in fact, most nearly approximates the eschatological mind-set of the intractable Jonah, for he presents as the message of the book precisely the religious bigotry that the writer seeks to demolish. Jonah's task, according to Father Mapple, is "to preach the Truth to the face of Falsehood!" Truth and falsehood: Israel and Nineveh, that is, Jews and

Gentiles, Christians and heathens, Puritans and papists—which is all to say, *my side* and *the other side*. Significantly, however, truth is precisely what Jonah does *not* preach to the Ninevites. When his prediction of doom does not bring on doom, he is proved a liar, at least within the terms of his naive dualism. It is this naive dualism that Father Mapple presents as the vision of Jonah's God:

> This, shipmates, this is that other lesson; and woe to that pilot of the living God who slights it. Woe to him whom this world charms from Gospel duty! Woe to him who seeks to pour oil upon the waters when God has brewed them into a gale! Woe to him who seeks to please rather than to appal! Woe to him whose good name is more to him than goodness! Woe to him who would not be true, even though to be false were salvation! Yea, woe to him who, as the great Pilot Paul has it, while preaching to others is himself a castaway!

This may be good Puritanism, but it is not the Book of Jonah; Father Mapple is wrong on every point. He cries "Woe!"—but the God of the Book of Jonah called not for destruction but repentance; not for punishment and exclusion but forgiveness and integration; not for bigoted dualism but liberal tolerance. Jonah does pour oil on the waters when God has brewed them into a gale, by repenting—and so too do the Ninevites. Jonah refuses to preach apocalypse to Nineveh not because he is "appalled at the hostility he should raise"—what better hostility than the hostility of the Gentiles?—but because he *wants* to appal and is afraid his preaching will *please* his enemies the Ninevites by saving them. Truth and falsehood are a bit more complex in the Book of Jonah than they are for Father Mapple: for to be true to Jewish law, as Jonah is, is to be false to God, and to be false for Jonah is not salvation but imprisonment in the whale's belly. As Bainard Cowan points out, this alignment of Father Mapple with the apocalyptic bigot Jonah itself points forward to Ahab:

> Mapple's twisting of the message of Jonah to its opposite in an earnest conviction of personal rightness and an intolerance of opposition suggests in its largest lineaments the attitudes of Ahab. Mapple and Ahab share a hatred for profane darkness, a desire to "kill, burn, and destroy all sin," and an assumption that one can infallibly discern the ultimate import of things. Allegorical in the crude sense of substituting a value-term for a reality, theirs is ultimately a profoundly anti-allegorical attitude in rejecting the activity of interpretation as the condition whereby man lives in the world. It is a position that finally rejects mediation—truth is not to be gained from the created world, or from the words of others, nor,

finally, as with Jonah's intransigence, even from the interposing word of God.

We will return to the significant problem of mediation later; for now, let me emphasize the uncompromising dualism of Ahab, Father Mapple, and Jonah alike, their apocalyptic fanaticism that tends toward the splitting off and destruction of all that opposes their will.

Ishmael, clearly, presents a highly desirable imaginative alternative to this fanaticism. Ishmael, one might even say, stands for something like the easy tolerance God would teach Jonah. Certainly Ishmael's theological sophistry in the very next chapter, by which he persuades himself to join Queequeg in idolatry, is meant to conceal (playfully, and very thinly) a total disregard for moral and cosmic dualisms:

> I was a good Christian; born and bred in the bosom of the infallible Presbyterian Church. How then could I unite with this wild idolator in worshipping his piece of wood? But what is worship? Do you suppose, now, Ishmael, that the magnanimous God of heaven and earth—pagans and all included—can possibly be jealous of an insignificant bit of black wood? Impossible! But what is worship?— to do the will of God—*that* is worship. And what is the will of God?—to do to my fellow men what I would have my fellow man do to me—*that* is the will of God. Now, Queequeg is my fellow man. And what do I wish that this Queequeg would do to me? Why, unite with me in my particular Presbyterian form of worship. Consequently, I must then unite with him in his; ergo, I must turn idolator.

The "magnanimous God of heaven and earth" that Ishmael invokes, of course, is a far cry from the jealous Puritan God, as he is also from the God of most OT prophets; but he *is* the God of the Book of Jonah, and it is significant that Ishmael should tacitly reject Father Mapple's reading of Jonah here only a few pages later. Ishmael's sophistry is a mask for *flexibility*, the spirit of compromise—and flexibility is motivated by friendship, human ties ousting a priori principle as the ground for action.

It would not be unreasonable to assert, therefore, that in bifurcating his voyager into a narrator who survives and an actor who does not, as Grace Farrell Lee puts it, Melville was specifically bifurcating a Jonah figure into a compromiser capable of tolerance and a fanatic who is not; a representative of excluded middles and a representative of extremes; a prophet of something like "love," or human contiguity, and a prophet of apocalypse, of destructive discontinuity. This interpretation, of course, simplifies Ishmael and Ahab considerably—and I want to try to maintain a light touch here, not insisting too strongly on my character typology. The reason I find it useful to think of Ahab and Ishmael as two faces of a composite Jonah figure, however, is that it then becomes possible to place each at a crucial *transition point* in the Jonah motif, the progress of the Book of Jonah. Ahab, as we shall see, stands somewhere at the juncture between the ironic and the synecdochic phases, Ishmael at the juncture between the synecdochic and the metonymical phases.

Why is this useful? In his discussion of *Moby-Dick*, Daniel Hoffman provides a truncated account of the Book of Jonah, ending—like most accounts of the book, in fact—with Jonah's deliverance from the whale's belly. The result is, tellingly, an incisive reading of Ahab that fails to do justice to Ishmael. "Where Narcissus proves a solipsist," Hoffman writes, "the rebel Jonah at last acknowledges the God beyond himself. In consequence Jonah is not, like Narcissus, a suicide, but is reborn, literally resurrected from his death inside the whale. These experiences of Jonah's prove to be prototypes of several adventures suffered not only by Ishmael and Ahab but also by the harpooners Tashtego and Queequeg and by the demented cabin-boy Pip." Ishmael does move past the suicidal tendencies of Narcissus, as we saw earlier; but it is crucial to see how he also moves past the repentance of Jonah in the whale's belly, past the inside-outside inversion that Ahab never achieves, to a metonymical compromise with visionary insight. Ishmael survives the destruction of the *Pequod*, but it is doubtful whether he is "reborn, literally resurrected from his death inside the whale"—and in the context of the complete tale of Jonah it is equally doubtful whether Jonah's deliverance from the whale's belly is a literal rebirth either. Like Jonah, Ishmael emerges from the belly of the whale with one problem—Ahab's—solved, but with the greatest problem of all yet unsolved: how to live in the world with the complex knowledge his confrontations with Ahab and the whale have afforded him.

Hoffman notes, quite rightly, that "Melville consistently presents Ahab, his Antichrist, in the guise of an unrepentant Jonah," even of an "Anti-Jonah." As Ahab presents himself, certainly, he is anything but the rather odious little vermin portrayed in Jonah: "Now, then, be the prophet and the fulfiller one," he cries. "That's more than ye, ye great gods, ever were. I laugh and hoot at ye, ye cricket-players, ye pugilists, ye deaf Burkes and Bendigoes!" Here is no man who turns tail and runs; here is no shirking prophet, afraid to prophesy lest his threats not be fulfilled: Ahab hyperbolizes himself into a Romantic world-recreating hero and, swallowing his crew as the whale swallowed Jonah, sails straight into calamity.

But Ahab is a Jonah, finally, his own hyperbolic self-presentations to the contrary. He is less powerful, less in control of his own fate, less a match for the gods than he thought. His defeat by the white whale exposes his quest as finally little more than Jonah's ironic flight. He is not fleeing, as Jonah is, from God's face; he is rather fleeing from the recognition that God's face is not his own: that he *is* only mortal. But it is still flight. And if the final destruction marks his swallowing by the whale, his imprisonment in the dark interiority of death, he himself recognizes at isolated moments that he is always already imprisoned by the whale: "How can the prisoner reach outside," he says, "except by thrusting through the wall?"

Ahab's problem, of course, is that the wall behind which he is imprisoned, the whale in which he is trapped, is material existence, nature or *phusis*, the physical reality of the whale, the ship, and his own body, which conspire, he thinks, to thwart his inner vision. "And as when Spring and Summer had departed," Ishmael remarks at the end of "The Cabin-Table," "that wild Logan of the woods, burying himself in the hollow of a tree, lived out the winter there, sucking his own paws; so, in this inclement, howling old age, Ahab's soul, shut up in the caved trunk of his body, there fed upon the sullen paws of its gloom!" As Ahab finds himself trapped in the prison of his vengeance, in the interiority of the pasteboard mask taken as an enclosure to be smashed, so also does he find his frail old body imprisoning a soul that would be divine. This Platonic and Christian anger at the soul's bodily incarceration leads in Ahab both to a self-destructive anger at the body, a desire to discipline and finally to demolish the body that the soul might be freed—even if only into nonexistence—and toward a Romantic desire to expand the body to match the soul's self-conception:

> Hold; while Prometheus is about it, I'll order a complete man after a desirable pattern. Imprimis, fifty feet high in his socks; then, chest modelled after the Thames Tunnel; then, legs with roots to 'em, to stay in one place; then, arms three feet through the wrist; no heart at all, brass forehead, and about a quarter of an acre of fine brains; and let me see—shall I order eyes to see outwards? No, but put a sky-light on top of his head to illumine inwards. There, take the order, and away.

Here is Emerson's visionary giant reduced to a mechanical contrivance—a Frankenstein, a Talus, a gigantic cyborg made to order—whose magnitude will sustain the soul's strivings toward divinity and whose eyes are programmed to see only what the soul introjects: not life, but divine *desire*. Even this, however, constitutes a radical destruction of the body; where Emerson saw his giant body in the magic glass of nature, Ahab would scrap his old frail one in order to replace it with a heartless monster. Trapped in a carnal prison that constrains his fulfillment of desire, Ahab's divine-willing soul would thrust through the wall—and in so doing, of course, self-destruct. The whale as the mask that hides the "unknown but still reasoning thing," the body as the prison that restrains Ahab's self-engendered purpose—both must be destroyed that spirit might be conjoined with spirit, the NOT ME with the ME, God with man in a transformative apocalypse whose issue is the deification of the hero. Like Jonah, Ahab flees toward freedom, toward a self-contained freedom where God's absence will empower Ahab's divinity—but with every step he takes the walls close in on him. Locked into a vision of the world in which heroic action— violent reprisal as the "living act," the glorious transformative deed—is the only conceivable response to reality's encroachments on the human condition, Ahab strikes out at the walls that enclose him, and is buried under their rubble. Close as he occasionally comes to Jonah's synecdochic inversion of outside and inside— with Starbuck in "The Symphony," for example—Ahab never quite allows himself that "easy" way out. He is symbolically trapped in the whale's belly throughout the novel, trapped in the world, trapped in life itself—so that his incarceration becomes finally a living death, a death in life itself. His death and final descent into the watery depths, lashed to his enemy's side, only seals his failure to learn.

Indeed the infrequent moments when Ahab is seriously tempted by visions of compromise seem almost the influence of his narrator, Ishmael; for it is precisely that path from inside to outside, from synecdoche to metonymy, that Ishmael finds and Ahab does not. One might almost say that Ishmael finds the American escape from the endless hostility of Harold Bloom's family romance of influence, and nearly teaches it to Ahab, paradoxically, in the narration of Ahab's story. Ahab's soliloquy at the end of "The Deck," for example, is obviously a thrust in the direction finally taken by Ishmael:

> Oh! how immaterial are all materials! What things real are there, but imponderable thought? Here now's the very dreaded symbol of grim death, by a mere hap, made the expressive sign of the help and hope of most endangered life. A life-buoy of a coffin! Does it go further? Can it be that in some spiritual sense a coffin is, after all, but an immortality-preserver? I'll think of that. But no. So far gone am I in the dark side of death, that its other side, the theoretic bright side, seems but uncertain twilight to me.

FRANK KERMODE

The Boy in the Shirt

Let us now [consider] the Boy in the Shirt (*sindōn*, a garment made of fine linen; not precisely a shirt, rather something you might put on for a summer evening, or wrap a dead body in, if you were rich enough). The Boy (actually a young man, *neaniskos*) is found only in Mark (14:51–52). At the moment of Jesus' arrest, says Mark—and Matthew agrees—all the disciples forsook him and fled. And both agree further that his captors then led him to the high priest. But between these two events Mark alone inserts another: "And a young man followed him, with nothing but a linen cloth about his body; and they seized him, but he left the linen cloth and ran away naked." And that is all Mark has to say about this young man.

The difficulty is to explain where the deuce he popped up from. One way of solving it is to eliminate him, to argue that he has no business in the text at all. Perhaps Mark was blindly following some source that gave an inconsistent account of these events, simply copying it without thought. Perhaps somebody, for reasons irrecoverably lost, and quite extraneous to the original account, inserted the young man later. Perhaps Matthew and Luke omitted him (if they had him in their copies of Mark) because the incident followed so awkwardly upon the statement that *all* had fled. (It is also conjectured that the Greek verb translated as "followed," *sunēkolouthei*, might have the force of "continued to follow," though all the rest had fled.) Anyway, why is the youth naked? Some ancient texts omit the phrase *epi gumnou*, which is not the usual way of saying "about his body" and is sometimes called a scribal corruption; but that he ran away naked (*gumnos*) when his cloak was removed is not in doubt. So we have to deal with a young man who was out on a

From *The Genesis of Secrecy: On the Interpretation of Narrative.* © 1979 by Frank Kermode. Harvard University Press, 1979.

chilly spring night (fires were lit in the high priest's courtyard) wearing nothing but an expensive, though not a warm, shirt. "Why," asks one commentator, "should Mark insert such a trivial detail in so solemn a narrative?" [Cranfield, *St. Mark*]. And, if the episode of the youth had some significance, why did Matthew and Luke omit it? We can without difficulty find meanings for other episodes in the tale (for instance, the kiss of Judas, or the forbidding of violent resistance, which makes the point that Jesus was not a militant revolutionist) but there is nothing clearly indicated by this one.

If the episode is not rejected altogether, it is usually explained in one of three ways. First, it refers to Mark's own presence at the arrest he is describing. Thus it is a sort of reticent signature, like Alfred Hitchcock's appearances in his own films, or Joyce's as MacIntosh [in *Ulysses*]. This is not widely believed, nor is it really credible. Secondly, it is meant to lend the whole story verisimilitude, an odd incident that looks as if it belongs to history-like fortuity rather than to a story coherently invented—the sort of confirmatory detail that only an eyewitness could have provided—a contribution to what is now sometimes called *l'effet du réel*. We may note in passing that such registrations of reality are a commonplace of *fiction*; in their most highly developed forms we call them realism. Thirdly, it is a piece of narrative developed (in a manner not unusual, of which I shall have something to say later) from Old Testament texts, notably Gen. 39:12 and Amos 2:16. Taylor, with Cranfield concurring, calls this proposition "desperate in the extreme." I suppose one should add a fourth option, which is, as with MacIntosh, to give up the whole thing as a pseudoproblem, or anyway insoluble; but although commentators sometimes mention this as a way out they are usually prevented by self-respect and professional commitment from taking it.

Now we have already noticed that Mark, for all the boldness of its opening proclamation ("The beginning of the good news of Jesus Christ") is, to say the least, a reticent text, whether its reserve is genuinely enigmatic or merely the consequence of muddle. Moreover, . . . where enigmas are credibly thought to exist in a text, it is virtually impossible to maintain that some parts of it are certainly not enigmatic. This is a principle important to the history of interpretation, and it was by carefully violating it with his fractured-surface theory [that a work of art may incorporate incoherencies on purpose, so to speak] that Robert Adams upset people. Let us then look at two attempts that have been made to treat the boy in the shirt as enigmatic and functional.

The first of these very well illustrates one alarming aspect of the business of interpretation, which is that by introducing new senses into a part of the text you affect the interpretation of the whole. And this "whole" may be not simply Mark, but the history of early Christianity. It has lately been shown

that there was more than one version of Mark. Morton Smith found, in a
Judean monastery, an eighteenth-century Greek manuscript in which was copied
a letter written by Clement of Alexandria at the end of the second century.
After demonstrating that this letter was indeed written by Clement, Smith
studies a passage in it that purports to be a quotation from Mark, though it
is nowhere to be found in the gospel as we have it. The context is as follows:
Clement is commending his correspondent Theodore for taking a firm line
with the Carpocratian Gnostics, a contemporary libertine sect which believed
it right to sin that grace might abound; indeed they were "unafraid to stray
into . . . actions whose very names are unmentionable," as Irenaeus, speaking
of Carpocratians and Cainites alike, reports. Now Clement wishes to distinguish
his authentic secret Mark from the inauthentic and conceivably licentious secret
Mark of the Carpocratians. He explains that Mark first wrote his gospel in
Rome, drawing on the reminiscences of Peter (we know from other evidence
that Clement, like most other people, accepted this account of the origin of
the gospel). But on that occasion Mark left out certain secrets. After Peter's
martyrdom, says Clement, Mark went to Alexandria, where he "composed
a more spiritual gospel" for the exclusive use of those who were "being initiated
into the great mysteries." Carpocrates had presumably taken over this secret
gospel and adulterated it with his own interpretations. In the circumstances,
says Clement, it will be best for the faithful to deny the very existence of a
secret version.

He then quotes a passage from the authentic Alexandrian version. It must
have come somewhere in the present tenth chapter of the gospel, and it tells
of a visit to Bethany. In response to the plea of a woman, Jesus rolled back
the door of a tomb and raised a rich young man from the dead. The young
man, looking upon him, loved him, and begged to be with him. After six days
he was commanded to go to Jesus at night. This he did, wearing a linen garment
(*sindōn*) over his naked body (*epi gumnou*). During the night Jesus instructed
the young man in "the mystery of the kingdom of God." Then the text continues
at 10:35 as we now have it.

Clement goes out of his way to deny that the true, as distinct from the
spurious, secret text contains the words *gumnos gumnou*, which might suggest
that the master as well as the catechumen was naked. Whether this suggestion
bore on baptismal practice, or had other magical and sexual import, is a matter
for conjecture in the light of what is known of Carpocratian habits; for of
course if Clement is telling the truth the words have no place in his genuine
text, only in the spurious version of Carpocrates.

In Morton Smith's opinion the initiation in question was baptism. The
story of the young man raised from the dead is obviously related to that of

Lazarus, which occurs only in John, and Smith believes they have a common original older than the Mark we now have. He also thinks that our young man in the linen shirt is this same young man in Clement's gospel who had looked and loved and worn a *sindōn* over his naked body. In the extant gospels Jesus never baptizes, but in Clement's version of Mark baptism must have been a central rite; and Clement would want to preserve this initiation ceremony from contamination by the libertine Gnostics. Anyway, the young man in Mark's account of the arrest is on his way to be baptized; that is why he is naked under his *sindōn*, a garment appropriate to symbolic as well as to real burial, and appropriate also to symbolic resurrection, both to be enacted in the ceremony. His baptism would take place in a lonely garden, under cover of night. We know that Jesus set guards (on this theory, to prevent interruption) and we know that the guards fell asleep. He was then surprised with the naked youth.

Thus the entire narrative is altered to make sense of a part of it. But the account I have so far given is a very inadequate account of Smith's hypothesis. He also proposes the view that the secretiveness of Mark's Jesus almost throughout the gospel is related to this use of baptism as initiation into the mysteries of the kingdom. Jesus is here regarded as a magician or shaman, the Transfiguration is explained as a shamanistic ascent. Now the Gnostic libertine interpretation of the secret gospel can be seen as an attempt to preserve or recover an original mystery concealed by the expurgated "Roman" version of Mark in general circulation. Like Clement, only more so, the Gnostics could think of the popular text as corrupt and imperfect in consequence of its attempt to keep the secrets. And whatever may be said about the provenance of these Alexandrian secret texts, they do provide a reason why the text as we have it appears both to reveal and proclaim, and at the same time to obscure and conceal.

We see, then, that an interpretation of our two Marcan verses along the lines proposed by Morton Smith entails a drastic revision of the received idea of a much larger text. We might want to ask some low-level questions about plausibility: for example, why did the hand that so expertly curtailed the tenth chapter fail to deal with the anomalous verses about the young man in the shirt? And perhaps there could be other explanations for the repetition of *epi gumnou*. This, as I said, has been thought unacceptable; it is absent from some good manuscripts at 14:51, and Taylor drops it from his text; but its recurrence in Clement's letter must mean either that it was right, and that Mark used it twice, or that whoever wrote the secret version of chapter 10 did so with the story of the young man in mind. At any rate it seems not unlikely that in the two verses we have been considering the secret gospel is showing through, a radiance of some kind, merely glimpsed by the outsider. And we should not be unduly surprised that the gospel, like its own parables, both reveals and conceals.

It is obvious by now that the story of the young man in the shirt cannot be *simply* interpreted; and complex interpretations, whether or not they have the seismic historical effects of Morton Smith's, will always have consequences that go far beyond the local problem. The most elegant interpretation known to me is that of Austin Farrer [Austin Farrer, *A Study in St. Mark* (London, 1951); *St. Matthew and St. Mark* (London, 1954)]. It uses as evidence Mark's linguistic habits, but it also finds in the gospel an occult plot, this time typological in style. Farrer was writing before the discovery of Clement's letter. It would probably have changed his argument in some ways, though he would doubtless have found useful to his purposes the occurrence, in the secret Mark, of the words *neaniskos* (not the most usual word for a young man) and *sindōn*. Mark uses *neaniskos*, in the public gospel, only for the young man who fled, and for the one who, at the end of the gospel, greets the women at Jesus' empty tomb.

Behind Farrer's interpretation is the knowledge that many of the crucial events in the gospel, especially in the Passion narrative, are closely related to Old Testament texts. They fulfill these texts, and the narrative as we have it records, and is in a considerable measure founded upon, such fulfillments. . . . An event in the gospel stories may originate, and derive some of its value from, a relationship with an event in an earlier narrative. The force of the connection may be evident only if we are aware of the conditions governing such relationships, for example that the relation of Jesus to the Law, and of Christian to Jewish history, is always controlled by the myth of fulfillment in the time of the end, which is the time of the gospel narratives. If this is granted, there is always a possibility that the sort of relationship Taylor called "desperate in the extreme"—between the story of the young man and the texts in Genesis and Amos—exists. Moreover, if the gospel contains allusions so delicate and recondite to earlier and uncited texts, why should there not be internal allusions and dependencies of equal subtlety? By seeking out such occult structural organizations one might confer upon Mark, after centuries of complaint at his disorderly construction, the kind of depth and closure one would hope to find in what has come to be accepted as the earliest and, in many ways, the most authoritative of the gospels.

Farrer's theories about Mark—numerological, typological, theological—are far too complicated to describe here, though to a secular critic they are exceptionally interesting. He himself altered them and then more or less gave them up, partly persuaded, no doubt, by criticisms of them as farfetched, partly disturbed by the imputation that a narrative of the kind he professed to be discussing would be more a work of fiction than an account of a crucial historical event. Neither of these judgments seems to me well founded. But let me say briefly what he made of the young man in the cloak. He sets him in a literary pattern of events preceding and following the Passion: for example, the unknown woman anoints Jesus at Bethany, and he says this anointing is an early anointing for burial; afterwards the women make a futile attempt to anoint his corpse. The youth who flees in his *sindōn* forms a parallel with the youth (also *neaniskos*) the women find in the tomb. The first youth deserted Jesus; the second has evidently been with him since he rose. Furthermore, the linen in which Joseph of Arimathea wraps the body is called a *sindōn*, so there seems to be an intricate relationship between the *neaniskos* in his *sindōn* and the body in the tomb, now risen. As I say, the relation might have been made still more elaborate had Farrer known of the passage in Clement, which also involves a *neaniskos* in a tomb. He tells us that the punishment of a temple watcher who fell asleep on duty was to be beaten and stripped of his linen garment; which may have a bearing on the boy's losing his. He also accepts the affiliation which Taylor rejected, believing that the young man is related to (he does not say "invented to accord with") two Old Testament types, one in Amos (2:16)—"on that day the bravest of warriors shall be stripped of his arms and run away"—and the other in Genesis (39:12), where Joseph escapes from the seduction attempt of Potiphar's wife by running away and leaving his cloak in her hands.

In such patterns as these, Farrer detected delicate senses, many of them ironical. And since he was not an adherent of the latest school of hermeneutics, he believed that Mark must have intended these senses, and that he must have had an audience capable of perceiving them. So far from being a bungler, awkwardly cobbling together the material of the tradition, Mark developed these occult schemes "to supplement logical connection," by which I take it Farrer meant something like "narrative coherence." He let his imagination play over the apparently flawed surface of Mark's narrative until what Adams calls fractures of the surface became parts of an elaborate design.

I do not doubt that Farrer's juggling with numbers gets out of hand. But even that has a basis in fact. He was confronting a problem that earlier exegetes had experienced. Since there is certainly a measure of arithmological and typological writing in the New Testament (twelve apostles and twelve tribes, Old Testament types sometimes openly cited, sometimes not) is there not reason to think that intensive application may disclose more of it than immediately meets the eye? Yet the more complex the purely literary structure is shown to be, the harder it is for most people to accept the narratives as naively transparent upon historical reality.

At one point Farrer even suggests that the young man deserting is a figure representing the falling off of all the others. This seems to me a fine interpretation. We have, at this moment in the narrative, three principal themes: Betrayal, Flight, and Denial. Judas is the agent of the first and Peter of the third. . . . Peter, halfway through the gospel, was the first to acknowledge the Messiah, though the acknowledgment was at once followed by a gesture of dismissal by Jesus: "Get behind me, Satan—you care not for the things of God but the things of man." Now he apostasizes and perhaps even curses Jesus, exactly at the moment when his master is for the first time asserting his true identity and purpose before the Sanhedrin. The implication, first made at the moment of recognition, and followed by the first prophecy of the Passion, is that the chief apostle will, when the Passion begins, deny the master. On both occasions he stands for the wholesale denial of Jesus, almost for Denial in the abstract. So too this young man, who is Desertion. The secret passage enhances this reading; the typical deserter is one who by baptism or some other rite of initiation has been reborn and received into the Kingdom. Nevertheless he flees. Thus we may find in this sequence of betrayal, desertion, and denial, a literary construction of considerable sophistication, one that has benefited from the grace that often attends the work of narration—a grace not always taken into account by scholars who seek to dissolve the text into its elements rather than to observe the fertility of their interrelations. It must, however, be said again that these narrative graces entail some disadvantages if one is looking more for an historical record than for a narrative of such elaborateness that it is hard not to think of it as fiction.

How do the interpretations of Smith and Farrer differ? The first assumes that Mark built up an esoteric plot, using material that was somehow also available to John, who developed it differently in the story of Lazarus and his sisters. The second argues that Mark worked an existing Passion narrative, presumably quite simple, into a complex narrative structure so recherché that between the first privileged audience and the modern interpreter himself no one ever understood it in its fullness. The frame of reference of the first is provided by the techniques of historiography, that of the second by literary criticism. Each is in its own way imaginative, though the quality of imagination differs greatly from one to the other. A Schweitzer might place Smith's work in the tradition of lives of Jesus, beginning two centuries ago with Bahrdt and Venturini, which assumed that what made sense of the gospel narratives was something none of them ever mentioned: for example, that Jesus was the instrument of some secret society. As to Farrer, his work was rejected by the establishment, and eventually by himself, largely because it was so literary. The institution knew intuitively that such literary elaboration, such emphasis on elements that must be called fictive, was unacceptable because damaging to what remained of the idea that the gospel narratives were still, in some measure, transparent upon history.

The constructions of Smith are historical; those of Farrer are literary. But they both assume that there is an enigmatic narrative concealed in the manifest one. Each suggests that an apparent lack of connection, the existence of narrative elements that cannot readily be seen to form part of a larger organization, must be explained in terms of that hidden plot, and not regarded as evidence of a fractured surface, or mere fortuities indicating that reality may be fortuitous. Joyce once said of *Ulysses*: "I've put in so many enigmas and puzzles that it will keep the professors busy for centuries over what I meant, and that's the only way of ensuring one's immortality." This is a shrewd joke, but the suggestion that enigmas and puzzles have necessarily to be "put in" is false. Joyce was only imitating the action of time. It would be more accurate to say that whatever remains within the purview of interpretation—whether by the fiat of the professors or of some other institutional force—will have its share of enigmas and puzzles. Whatever is preserved grows enigmatic; time, and the pressures of interpretation, which are the agents of preservation, will see to that. Who was the man in the macintosh [in *Ulysses*]? Mr. Duffy, Stanislaus Joyce, Mr. Wetherup, Bloom's doppelganger, Theoclymenos, Hermes, Death, a mere series of surface fractures? Each guess requires the construction of an enigmatic plot, or, failing that, a declaration that the text is enigmatically fortuitous. Who was the boy in the linen shirt, and where did he pop out of? The answers are very similar: a candidate for baptism, an image of desertion, a fortuity that makes the surface of narrative more like the surface of life. . . .

Why do we labor to reduce fortuity first, before we decide that there is a way of looking which provides a place for it? I have still no satisfying answer; but it does appear that we are programmed to prefer fulfillment to disappointment, the closed to the open. It may be that this preference arises from our experience of language-learning; a language that lacked syntax and lacked redundancy would be practically unlearnable. We depend upon well-formedness—less so, it must be confessed, in oral than in written language: in the written story there is no visible gesture or immediate social context to help out the unarticulated sentence, the aposiopesis. There are modern critics who think our desire for the well formed—or our wish to induce well-formedness where it is not apparent—is in bad faith. They hold that it is more honest to experience deception, disappointment, in our encounters with narrative. They have not yet prevailed; we are in love with the idea of fulfillment, and our interpretations show it. In this we resemble the writers of the New Testament and their immediate successors, who were, though much more strenuously, more exaltedly, in love with fulfillment; the verb meaning to fulfill, and the noun *pleroma*, full measure, plenitude, fulfillment, are endlessly repeated, and their senses extend from the fulfillment of prophecy and type to the complete attainment of faith.

Such expectations of fullness survive, though in attenuated form, in our habitual attitudes to endings. That we should have certain expectations of endings, just as we have certain expectations of the remainder of a sentence we have begun to read, has seemed so natural, so much a part of things as they are in language and literature, that (to the best of my knowledge) the modern study of them begins only fifty years ago, with the Russian Formalist Viktor Shklovsky. It was he who showed that we can derive the sense of fulfilled expectation, of satisfactory closure, from texts that actually do not provide what we ask, but give us instead something that, out of pure desire for completion, we are prepared to regard as a metaphor or a synecdoche for the ending that is not there: a description of the weather or the scenery, he says, will do, say the rain at the end of Hemingway's *Farewell to Arms*, or the river at the end of Matthew Arnold's *Sohrab and Rustum*. These are matters that still require investigation; the fact that they do so testifies to the truth of the statement that we find it hardest to think about what we have most completely taken for granted.

Now it happens that Mark is never more enigmatic, or never more clumsy, than at the end of his gospel; and I can best bring together the arguments of this [essay] by briefly considering that ending. Too briefly, no doubt; for whole books have been written about it, and it has been called "the greatest of all literary mysteries" [D. E. Nineham, *Saint Mark* (Harmondsworth, 1963)]. It is worth saying, to begin with, that nobody thought to call it that until after Mark had come to be accepted as the earliest gospel and Matthew's primary source; we do not recognize even the greatest literary mysteries until the text has gained full institutional approval. When Mark was thought to derive from Matthew it was easy to call his gospel a rather inept digest, as Augustine did; and then the abruptness of the ending was merely an effect of insensitive abridgment, and not a problem at all, much less a great mystery. Even now there are many who are impatient of mystery, and wish to dispose of it by asserting that the text did not originally end, or was not originally intended to end, at 16:8. But very few scholars dare to claim that the last twelve verses, 9–20, as we still have them in our Bibles, are authentic, for there is powerful and ancient testimony that they are not.

The gospel we are talking about ends at 16:8. In the previous verse the young man in the tomb gives the women a message for Peter and the disciples concerning their meeting with the risen Jesus. But they flee the tomb in terror and say nothing to anybody. This ending must soon have come to seem strange, which is why somebody added the extra twelve verses. We are not entitled to do anything of that kind; we can argue that the gospel was, for some reason, left unfinished; or we can interpret the ending as it stands.

The last words of the gospel are: "for they were afraid," *ephobounto gar*. It used to be believed that you could not end even a sentence with such a construction; and to this day, when it is accepted that you could do so in popular Greek, nobody has been able to find an instance, apart from Mark, of its occurrence at the end of a whole book. It is an abnormality more striking even than ending an English book with the word "Yes," as Joyce did. Joyce's explanations of why he did so are interestingly contradictory. *Ulysses*, he told his French translator, "must end with the most positive word in the human language." Years later he told Louis Gillet something different: "In *Ulysses*," he said, "to represent the babbling of a woman as she falls asleep, I tried to end with the least forceful word I could possibly find. I found the word *yes*, which is barely pronounced, which signifies acquiescence, self-abandonment, total relaxation, the end of all resistance." Here again Joyce gives the professors a license to interpret which they would have had to take anyway. The only positive inference to be made from these two remarks is that Joyce knew, as Shklovsky did, that we all want to make a large interpretative investment in the end, and are inclined to think the last word may have a quite disproportionate influence over the entire text. Later he ended *Finnegans Wake* with the word *the*; in one sense it is as weak as Mark's enclitic *gar*, though in another it is definite though barely pronounced, and deriving strength from the great *ricorso*, which makes it the first word in the book as well as the last. These ambiguities are not unlike those of Mark's problematical ending.

Let us pass by the theories which say the book was never finished, that Mark died suddenly after writing 16:8, or that the last page of his manuscript fell off, or that there is only one missing verse which ties everything up (such a verse in fact survives, but it is not authentic and will probably not be in your Bible), or that Mark had intended to write a sequel, as Luke did, but was prevented. Let us also skirt round the more congenial theory of Jeremias, that Mark went no further because he thought that what happened next should be kept from pagan readers [J. Jeremias, *The Eucharistic Words of Jesus* (London, 1966)]. We can't deny that this fits in with a pattern of revelation and deception observable elsewhere in Mark; nor that there is evidence of secrets reserved to the initiate, or expressed very cryptically, as in Revelation. Still, it's hard to see why the gospel, which is a proclamation of the good news, should stop before it had fairly reached the part that seemed most important to Paul; by Mark's time it had been preached for an entire generation.

So let us assume that the text really does end, "they were scared, you see," and with *gar* as the last word, "the least forceful word" Mark "could possibly find." The scandal is, of course, much more than merely philological. Omitting any post-Easter appearance of Jesus, Mark has only this empty tomb and the terrified women. The final mention of Peter (omitted by Matthew) can only remind us that our last view of him was not as a champion of the faith but as the image of denial. Mark's book began with a trumpet call: "This is the beginning of the gospel of Jesus Christ, the son of God." It ends with this faint whisper of timid women. There are, as I say, ways of ending narratives that are not manifest and simple devices of closure, not the distribution of rewards, punishments, hands in marriage, or whatever satisfies our simpler intuitions of completeness. But this one seems at first sight wholly counter-intuitive, as it must have done to the man who added the twelve verses we now have at the end.

A main obstacle to our accepting "for they were scared" as the true ending, and going about our business of finding internal validation for it, is simply that Mark is, or was, not supposed to be capable of the kinds of refinement we should have to postulate. The conclusion is either intolerably clumsy; or it is incredibly subtle. One distinguished scholar, dismissing this latter option, says it presupposes "a degree of originality which would invalidate the whole method of form-criticism" [W. L. Knox, quoted in Taylor, *St. Mark*]. This is an interesting objection. Form-criticism takes as little stock as possible in the notion of the evangelists as authors; they are held to be compiling, according to their lights, a compact written version of what has come to them in oral units. The idea that they shaped the material with some freedom and exercised on the tradition strong individual talents was therefore foreign to the mode of criticism which dominated the institution throughout the first half of the present century. And that alone is sufficient to dispose of the idea as false. Now all interpretation proceeds from prejudice, and without prejudice there can be no interpretation; but this is to use an institutional prejudice in order to disarm exegesis founded on more interesting personal prejudices. If it comes to a choice between saying Mark is original and upholding "the whole method of form-criticism" the judgment is unhesitating: Mark is not original. To be original at all he would have had to be original to a wholly incredible extent, doing things we know he had not the means to do, organizing, alluding, suggesting like a sort of ancient Henry James, rather than making a rather clumsy compilation in very undistinguished Greek.

Yet if we look back once more to the beginning of Mark, we might well have the impression that this brief text, so much shorter than any of the other gospels, at once gave promise of both economy and power. First, an exultant announcement of the subject, then the splendidly wrought narrative of John the Baptist, which, though heavy with typology, has memorable brevity and force. It is a world away from the overtures of other gospels. Matthew and

Luke were not content with it, perhaps it did not seem a true beginning, this irruption of a hero full grown and ready for action; so they prefixed their birth stories and genealogies. We are so used to mixing the gospels up in our memory into a smooth narrative paste that laymen rarely consider the differences between them, or reflect that if we had only Mark's account there would be no Christmas, no loving virgin mother, no preaching in the temple — nothing but a clamorous prologue, the Baptist crying in the wilderness, with his camel-skin coat and his wild honey. Matthew and Luke started earlier, with Jesus' ancestry, conception, and birth; John exceeded them both, and went back to the ultimate possible beginning, when, in the pre-existence of Jesus, only the Word was.

Mark, it appears, could not maintain this decisiveness, this directness. He grows awkward and reticent. There are some matters, it seems, that are not to be so unambiguously proclaimed. The story moves erratically, and not always forward; one thing follows another for no very evident reason. And a good deal of the story seems concerned with failure to understand the story. Then, after the relative sharpness and lucidity of the Passion narrative, the whole thing ends with what might be thought the greatest awkwardness of all, or the greatest instance of reticence: the empty tomb and the terrified women going away. The climactic miracle is greeted not with rejoicing, but with a silence unlike the silence enjoined, for the most part vainly, on the beneficiaries of earlier miracles — a stupid silence. The women have come to anoint a body already anointed and two days dead. Why are they so astonished? Jesus has three times predicted his resurrection. Perhaps they have not been told? Perhaps their being dismayed and silent is no stranger than that Peter should have been so disconcerted by the arrest and trial? He knew about *that* in advance. And we might go on in this way, without really touching the question.

Farrer, extending the argument I've already mentioned, finds the answer in the double pattern of events before and after the Crucifixion. Before it, Jesus said he would go to Galilee; spoke of the anointing; gave to the disciples at the Last Supper a sacramental body which should have made it clear to them that the walling up of a physical body was unimportant. The disciples fled before the Crucifixion, the women after it. And all in all, says Farrer, the last six verses of the gospel (3–8) form "a strong complex refrain, answering to all the ends of previous sections in the Gospel to which we might expect it to answer." So for him the ending, like everything else in this strange tacit text, is part of an articulate and suggestive system of senses which lies latent under the seemingly disjointed chronicle, the brusquely described sequence of journeyings and miracles. Farrer may persuade us that even if he is wrong in detail there is an ending here at the empty tomb, and it is for us to make sense of it.

[Earlier], I used the term "fore-understanding." It is a translation of the German word *Vorverständnis*, and its value in hermeneutics is obvious. Even at the level of the sentence we have some ability to understand a statement before we have heard it all, or at any rate to follow it with a decent provisional sense of its outcome; and we can do this only because we bring to our interpretation of the sentence a pre-understanding of its totality. We may be wrong on detail, but not, as a rule, wholly wrong; there may be some unforeseen peripeteia or irony, but the effect even of that would depend upon our having had this prior provisional understanding. We must sense the genre of the utterance.

Fore-understanding is made possible by a measure of redundancy in the message which restricts, in whatever degree, the possible range of its sense. Some theorists, mostly French, hold that a fictive mark or reference inevitably pre-exists the determination of a structure; this idea is not so remote from *Vorverständnis* as it may sound, but it is so stated as to entitle the theorist to complain that such a center must inevitably have an ideological bearing. "Closure . . . testifies to the presence of an ideology" [Jonathan Culler, *Structuralist Poetics* (London, 1975)]. To restrict or halt the free movement of senses within a text is therefore thought to be a kind of wickedness. It may be so; but it is our only means of reading until revolutionary new concepts of writing prevail; and meanwhile, remaining as aware as we can be of ideological and institutional constraints, we go about our business of freezing those senses into different patterns. Of course the inevitability of such constraints, which increase with every increase of ideological or institutional security, is a reason why outsiders may produce the most radiant interpretations.

The conviction that Mark *cannot* have meant this or that is a conviction of a kind likely to have been formed by an institution, and useful in normal research; the judgments of institutional competence remove the necessity of considering everything with the same degree of minute attention, though at some risk that a potential revolution may be mistaken for a mere freak of scholarly behavior. But there are occasions when rigor turns to violence. The French scholar Etienne Trocmé, steeped in Marcan scholarship and the methods of modern biblical criticism, can argue that an understanding of the structure of Mark depends upon our seeing that in its original form it ended, not at 16:20, and not at 16:8 either, but at the end of the thirteenth chapter, which forms the so-called Marcan apocalypse, and immediately precedes the Passion narrative. Given the religious and political situation at the moment of writing, this is where the gospel ought to end, with an allusion to the genre of apocalypse current at that time, and a solemn injunction to watch, which refers to a particular first-century community of Christians and not to the historical narrative as such. If one accepts this position it becomes possible to show that the preceding part of the text is consonant with this ending; and what is not consonant can be explained as the work of the editor who later revised the gospel and added the Passion narrative for a "second edition, revised and supplemented by a long appendix" [Etienne Trocmé, *The Formation of the Gospel According to Mark* (London, 1975)]. By such means one may, without violating the institutional consensus, prepare a text that conforms with one's own rigid fore-understanding of its sense. On the other hand, Farrer's reading is condemned as it were by institutional intuition; we may therefore call it an outsider's interpretation. I find it preferable to interpretations that arise from the borrowed authority of the institutionalized corrector, and presuppose that the prime source of our knowledge of the founder of Christianity will necessarily be compliant with whatever, for the moment, are the institution's ideas of order.

Farrer's notions of order were literary, and although his tone is always reverent, and occasionally even pious, he makes bold to write about Mark as another man might write about Spenser, except that he has some difficulty with the problem of historicity, for he could certainly not accept Kant's word for it that the historical veracity of these accounts was a matter of complete indifference. Of course his motive for desiring fulfillment was related to his faith and his vocation. But his satisfaction of that desire was to be achieved by means familiar to all interpreters, and like the rest he sensed that despite, or even because of, the puzzles, the discontinuities, the amazements of Mark (and the gospel is full of verbs meaning "astonish," "terrify," "amaze," and the like), his text can be read as somehow hanging together.

If there is one belief (however the facts resist it) that unites us all, from the evangelists to those who argue away inconvenient portions of their texts, and those who spin large plots to accommodate the discrepancies and dissonances into some larger scheme, it is this conviction that somehow, in some occult fashion, if we could only detect it, everything will be found to hang together. When Robert Adams challenged this conviction he was thought bold. The French utopians challenge it in a different way, condemning the desire for order, for closure, a relic of bourgeois bad faith. But this is an announcement of revolutionary aims: they intend to change what is the case. Perhaps the case needs changing; but it is the case. We are all fulfillment men, *pleromatists*; we all seek the center that will allow the senses to rest, at any rate for one interpreter, at any rate for one moment. If the text has a great many details that puzzle us, we ask where they popped up from. Our answers will be very diverse: . . . a candidate for baptism; a lover; a mimesis of actuality; a signature. We halt the movement of the senses, or try to. Sometimes the effort is great.

NORTHROP FRYE

Phases of Revelation

The Biblical religions are strongly moral and voluntaristic, and throw their main emphasis on salvation, whether individual or social. The two forms are interconnected, of course, and social organization and individual duty keep alternating with each other. They also preserve the tension of creature and creator to the limits of their revelation, and they are theistic, in that they deny that any category of being higher than the personality of God can exist. To many people today, some of these characteristics seem rather primitive in contrast to what is provided by certain forms of Hindu and Buddhist belief. Here we are expected to pass beyond the external and objective barrier of the divine personal creator, who is usually thought of in these Oriental religions as largely a projection of the ego, and seek instead what is generally called enlightenment. This enlightenment is attained by destroying the notion of the individual subject, for whom all the rest of the world is objective, a mirror that reflects back to the subject all its desires and aggressions. If attained, enlightenment brings about the same kind of obedience to the moral code (*dharma*) that "salvation" does in the West, but without the legalism that Christianity is regarded as having abolished only in theory. In the Western world, it is urged, such a conception as salvation by the will implies at once a prolonged argument over whether it is man's will or God's will or some proportion of both that gets involved in the saving: in the Eastern quest for enlightenment all such either-or questions are simply left behind.

Such Oriental perspectives have made a good deal of headway in the West, where they are removed from their own social context. In that context how-ever, we noted, Marxism, which we have characterized as a Western gospel

From *The Great Code: The Bible and Literature.* © 1981, 1982 by Northrop Frye. Harcourt Brace Jovanovich and Routledge & Kegan Paul, 1982.

descended from the social aspect of the Biblical religions, has been a major influence. Still, it would perhaps be profitable to inquire what elements in the Biblical tradition correspond to the more metaphorical and less conceptual appeal of the Oriental conception of enlightenment. This is part of our central question, What in the Bible particularly attracts poets and other creative artists of the Western world? If this interest on my part is kept in view, some of the emphases in what follows may be easier to understand.

The content of the Bible is traditionally described as "revelation," and there seems to be a sequence or dialectical progression in this revelation, as the Christian Bible proceeds from the beginning to the end of its story. I see a sequence of seven main phases: creation, revolution or exodus (Israel in Egypt), law, wisdom, prophecy, gospel, and apocalypse. Five of these phases have their center of gravity in the Old Testament and two in the New. Each phase is not an improvement on its predecessor but a wider perspective on it. That is, this sequence of phases is another aspect of Biblical typology, each phase being a type of the one following it and an antitype of the one preceding it.

FIRST PHASE: CREATION

We have noted [previously] the main characteristics of the creation myth in the Bible: it is an artificial creation myth in which the world was originally made by a sky-father, in contrast to sexual creation myths in which it is brought into being by (frequently) an earth-mother. In Genesis, however, the forms of life are *spoken* into existence, so that while they are made or created, they are not made out of something else. Christian doctrine speaks of a creation *ex nihilo*, and denies that the waste and empty chaos we meet at the beginning could have been coeternal with God. So we should not oversimplify the antithesis between making and bringing to birth. Another antithesis is more important. Sexual creation myths tend to become cyclical, because the conception of birth leads us only to an earlier birth in the past and a renewal of birth in the future. The Genesis myth starts with what Artistotle would call the *telos*, the developed form toward which all living things grow, and the cycle of birth and death follows after.

Three questions arise in studying the creation myth in the Bible. First, why is the deity to whom exclusive devotion is to be paid so intolerably patriarchal? We know only of a world in which every human and animal form is born from a female body; but the Bible insists, not only on the association of God with the male sex, but that at the beginning the roles of male and female were reversed in human life, the first woman having been made out of the body of the first man. Second, why is creation contained within the image of the week, and alleged to have occupied six days? Third, what is meant by saying that death came into the world with the fall of man? All these questions have immediate answers. God is male because that rationalizes the ethos of a patriarchal male-dominated society; creation took six days because that rationalizes the law of the sabbath; death came with the fall because that rationalizes the very primitive feeling that death, the most natural and inevitable of all events, is still somehow unnatural, and that if we die someone or something else must be responsible. All these answers are true as far as they go, so we shall ignore their truth in order to try to get a little farther.

In the older, or Jahwist, account of the Creation, which begins in Gen. 2:4, not all the imagery of sexual creation is eliminated. That account begins with the watering of a garden, and Adam emerges from the dust of the ground, the *adamah* or mother earth. The association between gardens and female bodies runs all through literature, and is found elsewhere in the Bible, notably in the Song of Songs. If we look at the imagery of *Paradise Lost*, we can see how subtly and delicately Milton has associated the body of the garden of Eden with the body of Eve; Adam is associated rather with the lower sky. The maleness of God seems to be connected with the Bible's resistance to the notion of a containing cycle of fate or inevitability as the highest category that our minds can conceive. All such cycles are suggested by nature, and are contained within nature—which is why it is so easy to think of nature as Mother Nature. But as long as we remain within her cycle we are unborn embryos.

The chief point made about the creation of Eve is that henceforth man is to leave his parents and become united with his wife (2:24). The parent is the primary image of the extension of what we are beyond ourselves in time, but that image has to give way to the image of the sexual union of bridegroom and bride. This is a modulation of a principle to be dealt with farther on, that the anxiety of continuity in time has to be superseded sooner or later by a break with it. Of the two parents, the mother is the one we have to break from in order to get born at all. The embryonic life in Mother Nature, enclosed in the mechanical cycle of repetition, is also mechanical, with no freedom to escape. The embryo is mentioned in Psalm 139:16, where the Hebrew word is *golem*, and in later Jewish legend the *golem* became, very appropriately, a mechanical monster like the one in Mary Shelley's *Frankenstein*.

From this point of view we can see how important it is that the first word of the Bible is "beginning." Nature itself suggests no beginning: it exists in an indefinite dimension of time and space. Human life is a continuum that we join at birth and drop off at death. But, because *we* begin and end, we insist that beginnings and endings must be much more deeply built into the reality of things than the universe around us suggests, and we shape our myths accordingly. We have [previously] noted how tenaciously Christianity clung to the notion of a finite beginning and end in time and space, as part of the emphasis it gave to the eternal and infinite beyond it. It gained little by that emphasis, we saw, because, at least in the general social imagination, the usual views of the eternal and infinite did not get beyond the perspective of endless time and space.

We get a little closer to this question when we realize that the central metaphor underlying "beginning" is not really birth at all. It is rather the moment of waking from sleep, when one world disappears and another comes into being. This is still contained within a cycle: we know that at the end of the day we shall return to the world of sleep, but in the meantime there is a sense of self-transcendence, of a consciousness getting "up" from an unreal into a real, or at least more real, world. This sense of awakening into a greater degree of reality is expressed by Heraclitus, in an aphorism referred to earlier, as a passing from a world where everyone has his own "logos" into a world where there is a common "logos." Genesis presents the Creation as a sudden coming into being of a world through articulate speech (another aspect of logos), conscious perception, light and stability. Something like this metaphor of awakening may be the real reason for the emphasis on "days," and such recurring phrases as "And the evening and the morning were the first day," even before the day as we know it was established with the creating of the sun. The fact that this phrase starts with the evening, too, follows the rhythm of awakening.

In the earth-mother, or sexual, type of creation myth, death is not a problem. Death is built into a myth that concerns only living things, all of which die; and in fact death is the only element that makes either the process itself or the myth about it intelligible. But an intelligent God, it is felt, can have made only a model world, a world he could see to be "good" (1:10, etc.), and consequently it could not have had any death or sin or misery originally in it. Such a myth therefore must have an alienation myth of a "fall" to account for the contrast between the perfect world God must have made with the world we live in now.

The story of the fall of man in Genesis seems originally to have been one of the sardonic folktales of the Near East that explain how man once had immortality nearly within his grasp, but was cheated out of it by frightened or malicious deities. We have earlier versions from Sumerian times on that are less rationalized than the one in Genesis. But the Genesis account, in its turn, has very little of the desperate anxiety to prove that the Fall was all man's fault and not the least little bit God's fault that we find, for example, in *Paradise Lost*. The Genesis account permits itself a verse (3:22) in which God seems to be telling other gods that man is now "one of us," in a position to threaten their power unless they do something about it at once, with a break in the syntax that suggests genuine terror. On the other hand, it is not easy to hear either in the Genesis story what Paul and the author of II Esdras heard in it, the terrible clang of an iron gate shut forever on human hopes. To make the "fall" story an intelligible account of man's present alienation from nature, a very complex fall within nature itself has to be postulated. Milton devotes the tenth book of *Paradise Lost* to showing how every inconvenience man suffers in nature, from frostbite to thorns on the rose bushes, resulted from a fall of nature that completed the human fall. But this is pure reconstruction: there is not a word about any such fall in Genesis, the cursing of the ground in 3:17 being removed in 8:21.

What man acquires in the Fall is evidently sexual experience as we know it, and something called the knowledge of good and evil, obviously connected with sex but not otherwise explained. Man becomes ashamed of his body and performs his sexual acts in secret: certain features of that body, such as the fact that in most climates he needs clothing and consequently is the world's only naked animal, indicate a uniquely alienated relation to his environment. The reason for the creation of woman, we are told (2:24), is that in the sexual relation man should be not alone and yet "one flesh" with his wife. In sex as we know it there is no complete union of bodies, and therefore sex, even with synchronized orgasms, has a residual frustration built into it. The knowledge that accompanied the discovery of sex in its present form seems to have been a genuine wisdom that put man, at least potentially, on the level of the true gods or angels (see 2 Sam. 14:17). But it was clearly a knowledge founded on self-consciousness, as is sexual knowledge itself, in which man becomes a subject confronting an objective environment. Consciousness of this sort, the philosophers tell us, is founded on a consciousness of death, so that mortality is a part of it. The "subtle" serpent, with its ability to renew its vitality by shedding its skin, is the symbol of the cyclical world of objective nature that man entered with his "fall." In the Genesis account the world of the Fall is symbolized only by the serpent: the assumption that the serpent was a disguise for Satan comes much later. Man's chief and most distinctive assets are his sense of sex as an imaginative experience and his consciousness: these two are closely connected, but have a common and fatal flaw.

It is with the "fall" that the legal metaphor begins that persists all through the Bible, of human life as subject to a trial and judgment, with prosecutors and defenders. In this metaphor Jesus is the counsel for the defense, and the primary accuser is Satan the *diabolos*, a word from which our word devil comes, and which originally included a sense of the person opposed to one in a lawsuit.

In the emotional response to Christianity at any rate, the role of God as Father, however defined in dogma, keeps shifting from the benevolent to the diabolical, from a being genuinely concerned for man to an essentially malicious being compounded of wrath and condemnation. One consequence of having a creation myth, with a fall myth inseparable from it, has been the sense of being objective to God, or, more specifically, of being constantly watched and observed, by an all-seeing eye that is always potentially hostile.

Such emotional uncertainty, it could be said, is the result of a fallen state in which there are radical limitations to our vision. But when we move back from the story of the Fall to the Priestly account of creation in the first chapter, we meet some puzzling features there too. The world God made was so "good" that he spent his seventh day contemplating it—which means that his Creation, including man, was already objective to God, even if we assume that man acquired with his fall a new and more intense feeling of the "otherness" of both God and nature. The Creation, we are told, imposed light and order on a chaotic darkness, a deep symbolized by the sea of death. Yet the acts of creation include the separating of land from sea and the alternating of light and darkness with the creation of the sun and moon. So chaos and darkness can be thought of in two ways. They may be thought of as enemies of God outside his creation; but they are dialectically incorporated into creation, and are creatures of God as well. The second is the view taken in the Book of Job; the first is the more usual view of the prophets. But the prophets also suggest that God is above such distinctions as those that the knowledge of good and evil provides:

> I form the light, and create darkness; I make peace, and create evil:
> I the Lord do all these things.
>
> (Isa. 45:7)

Perhaps, then, the sense of alienation traditionally attached to the fall may be latent in the original creation too, with its recurrent darkness and its stability menaced by the sea and other images of chaos (see Job 38:11). Furthermore, it is not said that man was immortal before his fall, only that there is danger of his becoming so after it. . . . The traditional Christian view of the verse "And God said, Let there be light, and there was light" is that it is the Word of God that creates, and that therefore Christ, identified with the Word of God in John and elsewhere, was the original creator. But to speak is to enter the conventions of language, which are a part of human death-consciousness; so if we push the image far enough, we come to the possibility that as soon as God speaks, and transforms himself into a Word of God, he has already condemned himself to death.

The fact that modern English has preserved the two words "sunlight" and "daylight" may suggest that at one time daylight was not causally associated with the sun at all. Similarly, the primordial light of Gen. 1:3 is not the light of the sun or moon. The emphasis on the sacredness of the week, the period of the lunar phase, is one of several indications of an original lunar cult among the Hebrews, as would be natural for desert dwellers for whom the sun is a killer and the moon a friendly guide in darkness. Jesus is described as a light shining in darkness (John 1:5), which suggests the moon or a bright star like the one heralding his birth. And yet the "Day of the Lord" imagery often recurs to a catastrophe in which "the sun shall be turned into darkness, and the moon into blood" (Joel 2:31, quoted in Acts 2:20). After that, the new light that would enlighten the redeemed survivors would have to come from the fire of life which was neither sun nor moon but rather the original light of creation. In Psalm 72:7 it is said in the ["Authorized Version" of 1611, source of all quotations here except where it is wrong or inadequate, abbreviated as AV] that God's people will have peace "as long as the moon endureth," but the sense of the original is closer to "until the moon is destroyed." It seems almost as though in the last phase of revelation the first phase, the artificial creation, will become a gigantic illusion to be swept away.

The Creation, in short, seems to belong to the complex we have associated [elsewhere] with the metaphor of integration. To create is to create a designed unity, with the craftsman's care in which every detail acquires a function, a distinctive relationship to a whole. Critics from Elizabethan times at least have noted the analogy between God as Creator and the poet, whose name means "maker." We should be more inclined now to reverse the analogy, and say that the conception of God as Creator is a projection from the fact that man makes things. The analogy was originally intended to confer dignity on the poet, but it ends by cutting God down to a bargain-basement demiurge. As Wallace Stevens says, one confides in what has no concealed creator: the sense of the beauty and majesty and splendor of nature is in the long run cheapened by what used to be called the argument from design. The argument from design did not survive the evolutionary structures of thought in the nineteenth century, but the assumption that the only alternative vision to a designing deity is something mindless and random seems also a trifle glib. Clearly there is something essential about the place of creation in the total Biblical vision, but our ways of comprehending it seem to be grossly inadequate. When we turn to human creative power, we see that there is a quality in it better called re-creation, a transforming of the chaos within our ordinary experience of nature.

The ambiguity in the Biblical conception of creation is a very deep-seated one, and in the New Testament period those who pressed the issue hardest

were the Gnostics. They maintained that the created order was essentially alien
to man and could therefore never have been produced by a God who had
any interest in man's redemption or emancipation. There were pagan and Jewish
Gnostics as well as Christian ones, and it was not their Christian opponents
but Plotinus who attacked them most sharply on this point. Plotinus reproaches
them for adopting what seems to us an utterly obvious principle: that all men
are brothers, "including the base," as he says, but that men are not brothers
to the stars. The beauty and perfection of the established order of nature was
a central element of faith to him, however that order may be obscured by
human ignorance.

Christianity clearly had to steer some sort of middle course between the
Gnostic contempt for nature and the pagan adoration of it. Paul speaks of
Jesus' teaching as a new creation, one that puts the old creation in the position
of a mother in childbirth (Rom. 8:20–22), although the latter is still a manifestation, or secondary Word of God (Rom. 1:20). Down to the eighteenth
century, Christianity worked out this position on the basis of a conception
of two levels of nature. The upper level was the "good" divine creation of
Genesis; the lower level was the "fallen" order that Adam entered after his
sin. Man is born now on the lower level, and his essential duty in life is to
try to raise himself to the higher one. Morality, law, virtue, the sacraments
of the Church, all help to raise him, as does everything genuinely educational.
Whether the arts are genuinely educational in this sense was disputed, but
the general principle remained: Milton, for example, defines education as the
attempt to repair the fall of Adam by regaining the true knowledge of God.

The "good" creation, in this view, was the world man was intended to
live in, and is therefore the order specifically of human nature. The world of
animals and plants we now inhabit is a physical nature that human nature is
in but not of: man is confronted with a moral dialectic at birth and must either
rise above physical nature or sink below it into sin. The nature around us is
permeated by death and corruption, but we can discern within it the original
"good" creation. The symbol of this original nature, and all that is now really
left of it, is the sky. The stars give out, according to legend, a music or harmony
that expresses the sense of perfected structure. The two levels of nature thus
make up for man a purgatorial order, a means whereby he attains his own
"true nature."

This symbolic structure wore out in the eighteenth century for two main
reasons. First, the images of the sky's perfection disappeared: the stars were
not made out of immortal quintessence, and the planets did not revolve around
the earth in perfect circles. The sky joined the rest of nature as an image of
alienation, often in fact as the most extreme form of it. Second, there was

no real evidence that the "natural" on the upper human level really was natural to man except the assertions of custom and established authority. The Lady in Milton's *Comus* regards her chastity as natural on her level of nature, but arguments used are circular: she wishes to remain chaste, and that is that. For us, human creativity is still thought of as purgatorial, as a way of raising the level of human nature. But that it imitates or restores an original divine creation of nature is not a principle now defended with much confidence. The essential meaning of the creation story, for us, seems to be as a type of which the antitype is the new heaven and earth promised in Rev. 21:1.

SECOND PHASE: REVOLUTION

In the Book of Genesis God makes a series of contracts or testaments with Adam, with Noah, with Abraham, with Isaac (Gen. 26:3), and with Jacob (Gen. 35:11). The sixth, with Moses, begins the Book of Exodus and the real story of Israel, and the seventh comes with the law itself, delivered in the wilderness after the Exodus. In many respects it would have been much simpler if the Biblical story had begun with the colloquy with Moses from the burning bush. Such a beginning would have wiped out at once the dreary chess problem of "theodicy," of how to derive a bad world from a good God without making God responsible in any way for its badness, that we have just been stumbling over. In the burning-bush story a situation of exploitation and injustice is already in existence, and God tells Moses that he is about to give himself a name and enter history in a highly partisan role, taking sides with the oppressed Hebrews against the Egyptian establishment.

The burning-bush contract introduces a revolutionary quality into the Biblical tradition, and its characteristics persist through Christianity, through Islam, and survive with little essential change in Marxism. Of these characteristics, the most important are, first, a belief in a specific historical revelation as a starting point. Israel's story begins here and in this way; Christianity begins with Christ and not, say, with the Essenes; Islam begins with the Hegira of Mohammed, Communism with Marx and not, say, with Owen or Fourier. Second is the adoption of a specific canon of texts, clearly marked off from apocryphal or peripheral ones, along with a tendency to regard the heretic who differs on minor points of doctrine as a more dangerous enemy than the person who repudiates the whole position. Third is the dialectical habit of mind that divides the world into those with us and those against us.

The Israelites made their great contribution to history, as is the wont of human nature, through their least amiable characteristic. It was not their belief that their God was the true God but their belief that all other gods were false that proved decisive. I spoke [earlier] of the contrast between the revolutionary monotheism of the Bible and the imperial monotheisms in Egypt, Persia, Rome, and elsewhere. For an educated and tolerant monotheist of the latter type, the conception "false god" would be almost unintelligible, certainly in bad taste. In Japan, when Buddhism was introduced, there was a good deal of tension with the indigenous Shinto religion, until a Buddhist theologian proposed that the *kami*, the miscellany of gods, nature spirits, and ancestral spirits in Shinto, could all be regarded as emanations of the Buddha, after which the two religions coexisted. No such compromise was ever possible for Judaism, Christianity, Islam, or (*mutatis mutandis*) Marxism.

Israel's Syrian neighbors, like most ancient peoples, assumed that when they went to war with Israel they would be fighting Israel's gods as well, whose existence and reality they did not question, and that they should, for example, try to get the Israelites into flat country because the gods of a hilly country would be expert hill-fighters (1 Kings 20:23). The assumption proved disastrous for them because Jehovah took offense at the suggestion that he was not equally good in valleys. The great story of the contest of Elijah and the priests of Baal on Mount Carmel, on the other hand, is designed to show that Baal does not exist at all, not that Jehovah is the stronger god. True, an earlier story about a contest between Jehovah and the Philistine god Dagon (1 Sam. 5) does not appear to deny the reality of Dagon. There is a good deal of flexibility in such matters, because logically the reality of a "false god" would have to be a devil, and elaborate demonologies belong to a later period.

The main historical preoccupation of both Judaism and Christianity was not with demonology but with the expectation of a *culbute générale* in the future, a kind of recognition scene when those with the right beliefs or attitudes would emerge on top with their now powerful enemies rendered impotent. The simplest version of this *culbute* is the one given in the Book of Esther, when a proposed anti-Jewish pogrom with Haman for its leader and Mordecai for its chief victim is reversed by a stratagem. Haman is hanged on the gallows he built for Mordecai, and the resulting massacre is of his party. But even this intransigent book reflects the general tendency of Judaism to come to terms with the secular power rather than colliding with it. The king of Persia is left in possession of his kingdom, as are Nebuchadnezzar and Darius in Daniel. Paul, we saw, also urged compliance with secular power. But the general feeling persists, in Christianity, in Islam, and now in Marxism, that nothing will ever go right until the entire world is united in the right beliefs.

There is one obvious feature of the Bible that is of great importance in considering its revolutionary aspect: its strong emphasis on metaphors of the ear as compared with those of the eye. Much is said about the word of God, and there is never any difficulty about God's speaking. But any suggestion that God has been seen is hedged about with expurgation and other forms of editorial anxiety: the explanation is generally that it was only an angel of God that was seen. The miraculously burning bush, as a visible object, is there only to catch Moses' attention: it is what is said from within it that is important. Similarly, Hagar's confused question in Gen. 16:13, rendered by the AV as "Have I also here looked after him that seeth me?" probably means "Have I really seen God and lived?" Similarly, Gideon and the parents of Samson assume that seeing the face of God means death (Judg. 6:23 and 13:22). In Exod. 33:20ff., God, aware of a similar danger to Moses, considerately turns around and presents the prophet with his "back parts," carefully explained in later exegesis as the symbol of the material world. The importance of the invisibility of God's presence in the Holy of Holies has already been noted.

We come a little closer to an actual vision of God in the two great epiphanies of Isaiah 6 and Ezekiel 1. The AV ascribes to Isaiah the statement "I saw also the Lord sitting upon a throne, high and lifted up." There is an ancient legend, which could conceivably be more than a legend, that Isaiah was martyred by King Manasseh on the charge of having claimed to have had a direct vision of God. Ezekiel's vision of God's chariot, however, is diverted to the "wheels within wheels" (giving rise to a later tradition of a separate class of angels called "wheels") and to the four "living creatures" drawing it, identified as a man, a bull, a lion, and an eagle. In Christianity there would be less difficulty about such a vision, because what was seen would be the Son or Word of God, and it would be typologically easy for Christians to identify the four living creatures of Ezekiel (which reappear in Rev. 4:6ff.) with the writers of the four Gospels, that is, the carriers of the divine Word.

But even Christianity had its difficulties, as we see in the curious wording of John 1:18: "No man hath seen God at any time; the only begotten Son . . . hath declared him." The spoken words of Christ are recorded with great care, but his physical appearance, the fact that he was bound to resemble some people more closely than others, could never have been anything but an embarrassment. It is different with his second and final coming, when "every eye shall see him" (Rev. 1:7). The eye was satisfied before the beginning of history, in Eden where God made every tree "that is pleasant to the sight" (Gen. 2:9), and the eye will be satisfied again in the last day, when all mysteries are revealed. But history itself is a period of listening in the dark for guidance through the ear.

The revolutionary context of this is clear enough. The word listened to and acted upon is the starting point of a course of action: the visible object brings one to a respectful halt in front of it. We have noted the persistent association of the world ruler with the sun, the starting point of the visible world; and the salute is said to have developed out of the ritual shading of one's eyes before the glory of a superior countenance. The metaphors "capital city" and "head of state" indicate how our social life is bound up with seeing heads, or more precisely faces. Greek culture focused on two powerful visual stimuli: the nude in sculpture, and the drama in literature. However important what is heard in a theater may be, the theater itself is primarily a visual experience as the origin of the word "theater" (*theasthai*, to see) indicates. A polytheistic religion, again, must have statues or pictures to distinguish one god from another. The revolutionary tradition in Judaism, Christianity, and Islam has tended to a good deal of prudery about the naked body, to iconoclasm, and to a rejection of spectacular art, especially when representational.

The second commandment prohibits the making of "graven images" to represent either the true or any false god, and in Judaic and Islamic traditions particularly this has restricted, even eliminated, many aspects of representational art. In Christianity the intensifying of the original revolutionary impulse, such as we have in left-wing ("Puritan") Protestant movements, is regularly associated with iconoclasm. The use of icons in Christian churches was, of course, carefully protected by dogma against any confusion with idolatry, but that, also of course, did not prevent left-wing reformers from calling it idolatry, and going on periodic rampages of smashing stained glass and burning religious pictures. There were also some ferocious outbreaks of iconoclasm in Eastern Churches. Again, the Christian campaign against gladiatorial shows was prompted less by humanitarian motives than by a prejudice against spectacles. Tertullian, for example, urges the faithful to stay away from such spectacles and wait for the real spectacle, the sight of their enemies writhing in the torments of hell. The Puritan and Jansenist prejudice against "stage shows" is familiar, and needs only an allusion. The influence of the Greek tradition, or some aspects of it, has been of immense value to the Western world in counteracting the neuroses of its revolutionary religious tradition.

In all this it is easy to lose sight of the genuine feeling that underlies the hatred of idolatry. We have tried to show that the root of this hatred is a revolutionary impatience with a passive attitude toward nature and the gods assumed to be dominating it. This attitude of acceptance of external power, it is felt, assumes it to be far stronger than it is. Paul speaks (Gal. 4:9) of "the weak and beggarly elements, whereunto ye desire again to be in bondage." There is a great deal of visual imagery in the Bible, but that imagery has to be internalized, made the imaginative model of a transformed world. Of course the energy thereby withdrawn from nature is projected on God, but the attitude toward God is not intended to be passive. In the Old Testament God is naturally assumed to be capable of doing what Israel cannot do for itself, but his willingness to do it depends on their obedience to his law, and that is a strenuous and full-time activity. In the New Testament the activity described as faith is similarly assumed to be capable of generating miraculous results. Both are or include protests against any lotus-eating surrender to fate and the cycles of nature.

THIRD PHASE: LAW

Whatever the historical facts may have been, the Old Testament's narrative sequence, in which the giving of the law comes so soon after the Exodus, is logically and psychologically the right one. Mount Sinai follows the spoiling of the Egyptians as the night the day. A shared crisis gives a community a sense of involvement with its own laws, customs, and institutions, a sense of being a people set apart. Tocqueville noted, and Dickens in *Martin Chuzzlewit* satirized, this element in American life after the Revolution. The Revolution itself built a good deal on the New England Puritan feeling that their colony was an attempt to construct a new society in spite of the devil, so to speak, and was consequently exposed to his greater malice. A country founded on a revolution acquires a deductive way of thinking which is often encoded in constitutional law, and the American reverence for its Constitution, an inspired document to be amended and reinterpreted but never discarded, affords something of a parallel to the Old Testament sense of Israel as a people created by its law.

More extreme, more primitive, and to most of us far less desirable, is the sense of purity in a people linked together by common acts and beliefs. The conception of purity sets up an uncompromising superego model for human actions, which means that no society can live in a state of purity of any kind for very long. Hence the sense of purity soon modulates to the sense of a need for purging. The passages in Ezra and Nehemiah about Jews who are compelled to put away their foreign wives read very unpleasantly in this century of racism; yet the parallel with racism is not quite relevant. Any revolutionary society may have purges that are not necessarily on a racial basis. Closely associated with the purge is the idea of the saving remnant, a curiously pervasive theme in the Bible from the story of Gideon's army in Judges 7 to the exhortations to the seven churches of Asia Minor in Revelation. The feeling that a pure or homogeneous group, no matter how small, is the only socially effective one, and in times of crisis is the one to be kept for seed, so to speak, until a new age dawns, is an integral part of the revolutionary consciousness.

A society with a human hierarchy may be full of, or even founded on, injustice and exploitation. But the corruption that is bound to grow up in such a society at least affords loopholes that the wily, the indolent, and occasionally the genuinely honest, can take advantage of. The primitive Israelite society under Moses and Joshua is presented as living in the full glare of a theocratic dictatorship, where every rebellion is known to God and instantly annihilated. In the story of Achan in Joshua 7 we see how the acquisitiveness of one man, in keeping back for himself what is to be devoted to God, brought disaster to all Israel, and had to be atoned for by the destruction of Achan's entire family. The terrorism of an incorruptible society revived in the first generation of Christianity, and the corresponding story in the New Testament is that of Ananias and Sapphira in Acts 5.

The conception of law in the Bible is immensely complex, and we are concerned with it only as the third in our sequence of phases. We distinguish between two aspects of law: our obligations to society and the human observation of the repeating processes in nature. These two areas have little in common, and the grotesque pun on the word "law" which has connected or identified them entered our cultural heritage as the result of a conspiracy, so to speak, of Classical and Biblical tendencies. The conception of "natural law" was developed to establish a link between human law and the so-called laws of nature, but that belongs to the history of Western thought rather than to the study of the Bible. We have suggested [previously] that such a conception assumes two levels of nature, one intended by God for humanity alone, and the other the "fallen" or alienated nature that we see around us. Hence what is "natural" to man is not natural in the context of the world of animals and plants and stones, but includes the elements of culture and civilization. But as these are interpreted by the voice of established authority in human society, all arguments about what is really natural to man on the higher level are completely circular.

We spoke [previously] of the Greek sense of social contract, most obviously present at the end of the *Oresteia*, in which the gods, or at least the goddess of wisdom, are shown as endorsing a justice that extends over both moral and natural orders. At the heart of this justice is the sense of *nemesis*, the tendency in nature to recover its balance after an act of human aggression. This recovery of balance makes a tragic action in Greek drama not only morally but almost physically intelligible. Such *nemesis* may operate on the mechanical or *lex talionis* principle, as with the Furies, or in accordance with a higher form of equity; but in either case it demonstrates the return to balance that makes the scales the central emblem of justice. Such balance is very deeply rooted in nature: the Ionian philosopher Anaximander suggests that birth itself is a disturbance of balance, and that death is its inevitable *nemesis*.

The Bible has a very different view of nature, but it regards moral and natural orders as controlled by the same divine will, and hence it also identifies moral and natural law, in its own fashion. In a polytheistic religion there can be a clash of divine interests and wills, as there is a clash between Aphrodite and Artemis in *Hippolytus*, or a near-clash between Apollo and Athene in the *Oresteia* — to say nothing of the divine civil war provoked by the golden apple of the goddess Discord. Such clashes open the way to the conception of a fate overruling a variety of divine wills, and fate is really a metaphor for natural "law." Hence science develops more readily out of a polytheistic religion. In Homer there are sometimes suggestions that fate and the will of Zeus are the same thing, but there are other suggestions that the two are really different, and that fate is the stronger.

With an omnipotent personal God, however, we cannot really distinguish a miracle from a natural event, except by its rarity. Even after the rise of science, we suggested [earlier], there is a persisting residual notion that in "natural law" too there is commanding and obedience, although it is clear that laws of nature are not "broken." If they appear to be, it is because there are other "laws" operating that we have not yet identified. Natural law in particular is traditionally regarded as the continuing of the divine creation in time, a view quite consistent with thinking of nature as having its own legal code which it automatically obeys. Hence in certain types of religious mind the right of God to suspend the "laws of nature" is vigorously defended, because law implies constraint and necessity, and overruling it affords a glimpse of a higher "providential" order manifesting the state before the fall, especially if the overruling is made in our favor. Natural law, however, like the divine creation of which it is an extension, is a conception we no longer know very clearly how to deal with, except to point out the difficulties of the metaphor involved and to say, with Sartre, that the problem of human freedom cannot be worked out wholly within the categories of man as we know him and nature as we see it.

FOURTH PHASE: WISDOM

The conception of wisdom in the Bible, as we see most clearly in some of the psalms, starts with the individualizing of law, with allowing the law, in its human and moral aspect, to permeate and inform all one's personal life. Law is general: wisdom begins in interpreting and commenting on law, and applying it to specific and variable situations. There are two wider principles in such wisdom. In the first place, the wise man is the one who follows in the accepted way, in what experience and tradition have shown to be the right way. The fool is the man with the new idea that always turns out to be an old fallacy. Such wisdom is dominated throughout by what may be called the anxiety of continuity. It goes with the authority of seniors, whose longer experience in the tried and tested modes of action makes them wiser than the young. The Book of Proverbs, traditionally assigned to Solomon, recommends the corporal punishment of one's sons, in a verse (19:18) that has probably been responsible for more physical pain than any other sentence ever written. In Ben Sirach's Ecclesiasticus, in the Apocrypha, this principle is expanded into a general enthusiasm for beating anyone within reach, including daughters and servants. What is behind this is not sadism but the attitude that has given so curiously penal a quality to the education of the young down to our own century. Education is the attaining of the right forms of behavior and the persistence in them, hence, like a horse, one has to be broken into them.

The second element in wisdom is inseparable from the first. The sense of continuity, or persistence in the right ways, relates primarily to the past: wisdom facing the future is prudence (Prov. 8:12), a pragmatic following of the courses that maintain one's stability and balance from one day to the next. Perhaps the serpent is a symbol of wisdom because there is a good deal of wriggling and insinuating about choosing the wisest course of action. Prudent advice is communicated by the proverb, which is normally addressed to those without supreme advantages of birth or wealth, and provides advice on how to meet the various crises of social life. It is closely related to the fable, one of the few literary genres that are popular in the sense of possessing a genuine affinity with the lower ranks of society. The best-known purveyors of fables, Aesop and Phaedrus, were both slaves. The fable is not very prominent in the Old Testament, except that the Book of Job is an enormous expansion of one, but it comes into its own, as a vehicle of instruction, in the parables of Jesus. The proverb, on the other hand, is the kernel of wisdom literature, which consists largely of collections of proverbs. There seems to be something about the proverb that stirs the collector's instinct—which is natural if one accepts its usefulness as a key to success in life. Wisdom, as noted, is not knowledge: knowledge is of the particular and actual, and wisdom is rather a sense of the potential, of the way to deal with the kind of thing that may happen. It is this sense of the potential that the proverb is specifically designed to assist.

All the Near Eastern civilizations seem to have cultivated the proverb a good deal: the Egyptians, with their rigidly stratified society, were especially fond of it. Some ancient Egyptian proverbial material reappears in the Book of Proverbs, where it is already centuries old. Often the containing form is that of a father giving advice to his son, transmitting the ancestral and traditional wisdom of the culture in the manner of Polonius instructing Laertes in *Hamlet*, or, still later, Lord Chesterfield trying, in a series of letters, to make another

Lord Chesterfield out of his lumpish offspring. Elsewhere it is a teacher instructing a pupil.

One typical piece of wisdom literature is the story of Ahikar, the sage and of course elderly counselor of the king of Nineveh (Assyria). Having no son, he adopts a nephew who turns out to be a scoundrel, plots against him, and manages to get him condemned to death. Ahikar escapes, through the usual romance formula in which a hired assassin develops a conscience, and goes to Egypt, where he also becomes a counselor. The king of Nineveh soon finds himself in difficulties, wishes audibly he had his adviser back, is told that Ahikar is still alive, sends for him and restores him to favor. Ahikar then takes a terrible revenge on his nephew by placidly reciting one proverb after another to him, an appreciable number of them concerned with the sin of ingratitude, until, the text demurely informs us, the nephew blows up and bursts. For a popular tale one can hardly miss with these ingredients: it has the superior wisdom and virtue of seniors, the dangers of trusting anyone under thirty, and any number of proverbs thrown in to improve the reader's mind. Ahikar has left his mark on at least the Apocrypha (Tobit is said to be Ahikar's uncle); on Greek literature, where he is identified with Aesop; and on the Koran (Sura 10), which as a rule has even less interest in secular literature than other sacred books.

The center of the conception of wisdom in the Bible is the Book of Ecclesiastes, whose author, or rather chief editor, is sometimes called Koheleth, the teacher or preacher. Koheleth transforms the conservatism of popular wisdom into a program of continuous mental energy. Those who have unconsciously identified a religious attitude either with illusion or with mental indolence are not safe guides to this book, although their tradition is a long one. Some editor with a "you'd better watch out" attitude seems to have tacked a few verses on to the end suggesting that God trusts only the anti-intellectual, but the main author's courage and honesty are not to be defused in this way. He is "disillusioned" only in the sense that he has realized that an illusion is a self-constructed prison. He is not a weary pessimist tired of life: he is a vigorous realist determined to smash his way through every locked door of repression in his mind. Being tired of life is in fact the only mental handicap for which he has no remedy to suggest. Like other wise men, he is a collector of proverbs, but he applies to all of them his touchstone and key word, translated in the AV as "vanity." This word (hebel) has a metaphorical kernel of fog, mist, or vapor, a metaphor that recurs in the New Testament (James 4:14). It thus acquires a derived sense of "emptiness," the root meaning of the Vulgate's vanitas. To put Koheleth's central intuition into the form of its essential paradox: all things are full of emptiness.

We should not apply a ready-made disapproving moral ambience to this word "vanity," much less associate it with conceit. It is a conception more like the *shunyata* or "void" of Buddhist thought: the world as everything within nothingness. As nothing is certain or permanent in the world, nothing either real or unreal, the secret of wisdom is detachment without withdrawal. All goals and aims may cheat us, but if we run away from them we shall find ourselves bumping into them. We may feel that a saint is a "better" man than a sinner, and that all our religious and moral standards would crumble into dust if we did not think so; but the saint himself is most unlikely to take such a view. Similarly, Koheleth went through a stage in which he saw that wisdom was "better" than folly, then a stage in which he saw that there was really no difference between them, as death lies in wait for both, and finally realized that both views were equally "vanity." As soon as we renounce the expectation of reward, in however refined a guise, for virtue or wisdom, we relax and our real energies begin to flow into the soul. Even the great elegy at the end over the failing bodily powers of old age ceases to become "pessimistic" when we see it as part of the detachment with which the wise man sees his life in the context of vanity.

We take what comes: there is no choice in the matter, hence no point in saying "we should take what comes." We soon realize by doing so that there is a cyclical rhythm in nature. But, like other wheels, this is a machine to be understood and used by man. If it is true that the sun, the seasons, the waters, and human life itself go in cycles, the inference is that "there is a time for all things," something different to be done at each stage of the cycle. The statement "There is nothing new under the sun" applies to wisdom but not to experience, to theory but not to practice. Only when we realize that nothing is new can we live with an intensity in which everything becomes new.

The creation began with air and light, the two symbols of "spirit." Air is the first thing we think of when we think of things that we can't see but know to exist, and in a sense we do not see light either: what we see is metaphorically fire, a source or reflection of light. We see by means of light and air: if we could see air we could see nothing else, and would be living in the dense fog that is one of the roots of the word "vanity." In the Bible the invisible world is not usually thought of as a separate and higher order of reality: it is thought of rather as the medium by which the world becomes visible (see Rom. 1:20 and Heb. 11:2). The invisible world, like the cyclical machinery of nature, is an opportunity for human energy, not a stifling darkness or a concealed revelation.

In Koheleth's inexhaustible treasury of common sense one of the shrewdest comments is that God has put *'olam* into man's mind (3:11). This word usually means something like "eternity," but in this context has rather the sense of mystery or obscurity. Eternity is a mental category that, in Keats's phrase, teases us out of thought: we do not know what it means, but as long as it is there we can never be satisfied with simplistic solutions. We are all born lost in a forest: if we assume either that the forest is there or that it is not there, we shall follow the rhythm of nature and walk endlessly in circles. The metaphor of fog or mist present in "vanity" suggests that life is something to find a way through, and that the way of wisdom is the way out.

The teaching of this book comes to a focus on a "work ethic" of "whatsoever thy hand findeth to do, do it with thy might" (9:10). The Preacher is not recommending activity for its own sake, but pointing to the release of energy that follows the giving up of our various excuses for losing our way in the fog: "Better is the sight of the eyes than the wandering of the desire" (6:9), as he says. But the phrase "work ethic" suggests the question of what is not work, and our normal habits of language tell us that one opposite of work, at least, is play. Work, as we usually think of it, is energy expended for a further end in view; play is energy expended for its own sake, as with children's play, or as a manifestation of the end or goal of work, as in "playing" chess or the piano. Play in this sense, then, is the fulfillment of work, the exhibition of what the work has been done for.

The Preacher is well aware of this connection, and emphasizes that we should "live joyfully" (9:9). But the point is even clearer in the Book of Proverbs, where Wisdom is personified as an attribute of God from the time of creation, expressing in particular the exuberance of creation, the spilling over of life and energy in nature that so deeply impresses the prophets and poets of the Bible. The AV speaks of this wisdom as "rejoicing in the habitable part of his earth" (8:31), but this is feeble compared to the tremendous Vulgate phrase *ludens in orbe terrarum, playing* over all the earth. Here we finally see the real form of wisdom in human life as the *philosophia* or *love* of wisdom that is creative and not simply erudite. We see too how the primitive form of wisdom, using past experience as a balancing pole for walking the tightrope of life, finally grows, through incessant discipline and practice, into the final freedom of movement where, in Yeats's phrase, we can no longer tell the dancer from the dance.

FIFTH PHASE: PROPHECY

Wisdom, with its sense of continuity, repetition, precedent, and prudence, is the highest form of the ordinary functioning level of society. The revolution is far in the past; it is a part of tradition now, and without the fifth stage of prophecy the culture reflected in the Old Testament would have nothing unique about it. For prophecy is the individualizing of the revolutionary impulse, as wisdom is the individualizing of the law, and is geared to the future as wisdom is to the past.

Our earliest historical glimpse of the prophets of Western Asia is in the autobiographical account of the Egyptian envoy Wen-Amon, who encountered one at the court of Sidon in Phoenicia. They first appear in the Old Testament in ecstatic groups, working themselves into trance-like states with the aid of music, and then speaking with a different voice, no doubt assumed originally to have been the voice of the local god. Samuel says to Saul:

> Thou shalt meet a company of prophets coming down from the high place with a psaltery, and a tabret, and a pipe, and a harp, before them; and they shall prophesy:
> And the Spirit of the Lord will come upon thee, and thou shalt prophesy with them, and shall be turned into another man.
>
> (1 Sam. 10:5-6)

The prophets, then, like the oracle priestesses in Greece, arose out of a primitive reverence for people with ecstatic powers. Not unnaturally there were those who discovered that there was a comfortable living to be made by the not very difficult effort of developing these powers, as long as one did not go far enough under to forget what the king wanted to hear. The great majority of prophets, the Old Testament itself makes clear, were well-broken-in functionaries either of the court or of the temple. So it is all the more interesting that the Old Testament should highlight so strongly a number of prophets who spoke out against royal policies and exposed themselves to persecution as a result. In the superbly told story of Micaiah (1 Kings 22), in the dialogues with King Ahaz in the early part of Isaiah, in the account of Jeremiah's collisions with the last kings of Judah, the same point in constantly made: the prophet with the authentic message is the man with the unpopular message.

Many prophets, "cultic prophets" as they are called by scholars, were attached to the temple and spoke from within the orbit of priestly authority. But the distinction between prophetic and priestly authority is already established in the Pentateuch, where Moses is described as the greatest of Hebrew prophets (Deut. 34:10), the priestly functions assigned to Aaron being quite separate. It is also Moses who wishes that all the Lord's people would become prophets (Num. 11:29). Left to himself, Aaron goes wrong and makes an idolatrous golden calf; but though Moses makes human mistakes, the voice of prophecy in itself is conventionally regarded as infallible. Jesus, again, thinks of the prophetic tradition as one of martyrs to the testimony of God (Matt. 5:12), and clearly regards it as superior in authority to that of the "chief priests and the scribes."

Such prophets, though "called" by God and invariably claiming to speak with the voice or authority of God, are no longer simply ecstatics. They are advisers to princes even when their advice is furiously rejected, and they are rather people with what seems to be an open channel of communication between the conscious and the unconscious, if this way of putting it is not too anachronistic. As such, they represent an authority in society that most societies find the greatest difficulty in absorbing. The story of Cassandra is an example from a non-Biblical culture. Most prophets have to be accredited by either secular or spiritual authority as already established, because by what other criteria can a society distinguish a superior authority from an inferior one? Any self-deluded crank can call himself a prophet, and even the psychotics who assert that God has told them to murder somebody may appear sane enough at other times.

Both testaments reflect this difficulty: even in Saul's time there is a sharp distinction between the accredited prophets, whom Saul himself joined briefly, and such ecstatics as the Witch of Endor, who communicated with the spirits of the dead, conventionally assumed to have knowledge of the future. This contrast recurs also in Greek culture in a different form. There are gods above who appear in the *Iliad* and elsewhere in the disguise of a familiar person, in broad daylight, and giving advice on an immediate and specific situation. There are also sinister gods below who live with the spirits of the dead, and have to be invoked by midnight sacrifices of black animals and the like: these can reveal a more distant future, as when Odysseus consults the shade of Tiresias for information about his own death. The popular notion of a prophet is that of a man who can foretell the future, but the Biblical prophets as a rule take fairly short views, except when prophesying the future restoration of Israel.

The New Testament, like the Old, warns frequently against false prophets, but its criteria for distinguishing the genuine ones are not very precise. Paul, dealing with the ecstatic manifestations in the church of Corinth, says that "the spirits of the prophets are subject to the prophets" (1 Cor. 14:32), which apparently means that authentic prophets can control their ecstatic powers and are not taken over by them. The contrast between those inspired by the Holy Spirit and those who are possessed by devils recurs in 1 John 4, where it is proposed that spirits unwilling to testify to the Christian faith are to be known as evil, it being assumed that there are subjects on which even a lying spirit is afraid to lie. An uneasy transition is marked here between the early Christian detaching of prophetic authority from Jewish priestly authority and its later absorption into Christian priestly authority.

In the post-Biblical period both Christianity and Rabbinical Judaism seem to have accepted the principle that the age of prophecy had ceased, and to have accepted it with a good deal of relief. Medieval Europe had a High King

and a High Priest, an Emperor and a Pope, but the distinctively prophetic
third force was not recognized. The exceptions prove the rule. The career of
Savonarola is again one of martyrdom, and the same is true of Joan of Arc,
who illustrates the inability of a hierarchical society to distinguish a Deborah
from a Witch of Endor. The liberty of prophesying was supposed to be one
of the issues of the Reformation, but it can hardly be said that Protestantism
succeeded in developing a prophetic authority distinct from a priestly one: its
prophets never strayed very far from pulpits. It is Milton in the *Areopagitica*
who, perhaps without fully realizing it, gives us a clue to some of the sources
of the prophetic element in modern society. They may come through the
printing press, more particularly from writers who arouse social resentment
and resistance because they speak with an authority that society is reluctant
to recognize. Such authority, in this context, is certainly not infallible, but
it may be genuine insight nonetheless. Tolerance for creative minds as potentially
prophetic, even without ready-made standards and certainly without any belief
in their infallibility, seems to be a mark of the most mature societies. In the
modern world, therefore, what corresponds to prophetic authority is the growth
of what we called [earlier] a cultural pluralism, where, for example, a scientist
or historian or artist may find that his subject has its own inner authority,
that he makes discoveries within it that may conflict with social concern, and
that he owes a loyalty to that authority even in the face of social opposition.

Prophecy in the Bible is a comprehensive view of the human situation,
surveying it from creation to final deliverance, and it is a view which marks
the extent of what in other contexts we could call the creative imagination.
It incorporates the perspective of wisdom but enlarges it. The wise man thinks
of the human situation as a kind of horizontal line, formed by precedent and
tradition and extended by prudence: the prophet sees man in a state of alienation
caused by his own distractions, at the bottom of a U-shaped curve. We shall
come to this U-shaped curve [elsewhere] as the unit of narrative in the Bible.
It postulates an original state of relative happiness, and looks forward to an
eventual restoration of this state, to, at least, a "saving remnant." The wise
man's present moment is the moment in which past and future are balanced,
the uncertainties of the future being minimized by the observance of the law
that comes down from the past. The prophet's present moment is an alienated
prodigal son, a moment that has broken away from its own identity in the
past but may return to that identity in the future. We can see from this that
the Book of Job, though it is classed with wisdom literature and includes a
eulogy of wisdom, cannot be understood by the canons of wisdom alone, but
needs the help of the prophetic perspective.

SIXTH PHASE: GOSPEL

The gospel (restricting our comment on it to the perspective of this [essay])
is a further intensifying of the prophetic vision. That vision, we suggested,
had two levels: the level of the present moment and a level above it. The latter
is both that of the original identity symbolized by the garden of Eden (along
with . . . the Promised Land and the Temple), and the ultimate identity
symbolized by the return to these things after the "Day of the Lord" and the
restoring of Israel. Jesus' teaching centers on the conception of a present spiritual
kingdom that includes all these upper-level images, and on earth he is thought
of as living simultaneously in it and among us.

To express this there have to be secondary metaphors of "descending" from
the higher level, or "heaven," and of "ascending" back into it again. Prophecies
of the restoration of Israel such as Isaiah's prophecy of Emmanuel in Isaiah
7, and Ezekiel's vision of the valley of dry bones in Ezekiel 37, were interpreted
by Christians as types of the Incarnation or the Resurrection. Paul's brilliant
phrase for the Incarnation is "He emptied himself" (Phil. 2:7; the AV's rendering
is not a translation but an inept gloss). That is, he "descended" or was born
into the world of vanity or total emptiness. The return to the spiritual world
is "resurrection," a conception which, though it is a return from death, can
hardly be confined to the revival of a dead body in a tomb. Jesus sometimes
speaks of his central doctrine of a spiritual kingdom as a mystery, a secret
imparted to his disciples (though they often got it wrong too), with those outside
the initiated group being put off with parables (Mark 4:11). It seems clear,
however, that the real distinction between initiated and uninitiated is between
those who think of achieving the spiritual kingdom as a way of life and those
who understand it merely as a doctrine.

The way of life is described as beginning in *metanoia*, a word translated
"repentance" by the AV, which suggests a moralized inhibition of the "stop
doing everything you want to do" variety. What the word primarily means,
however, is change of outlook or spiritual metamorphosis, an enlarged vision
of the dimensions of human life. Such a vision, among other things, detaches
one from one's primary community and attaches him to another. When John
the Baptist says "Bring forth fruits worthy of *metanoia*" (Matt. 3:8), he is
addressing Jews, and goes on to say that their primary social identity (descent
from Abraham) is of no spiritual importance. What one repents of is sin, a
word that means nothing outside a religious and individualized context. That
is, sin is not illegal or antisocial behavior. The "deadly" or mortal sins that
destroy the soul were classified in the Middle Ages as pride, wrath, sloth, envy,

avarice, gluttony, and lechery; and of these, heavily moralized as they are, not one necessarily results in criminal or antisocial acts. Sin is rather a matter of trying to block the activity of God, and it always results in some curtailing of human freedom, whether of oneself or of one's neighbor.

The dialectic of *metanoia* and sin splits the world into the kingdom of genuine identity, presented as Jesus' "home," and a hell, a conception found in the Old Testament only in the form of death or the grave. Hell is that, but it is also the world of anguish and torment that man goes on making for himself all through history. Jesus describes it in imagery of an undying worm and an unquenched fire, taken from the last verse of Isaiah, which speaks of the dead bodies of those overthrown in the final *culbute*. As a form of vision, *metanoia*s reverses our usual conceptions of time and space. The central points of time and space are now and here, neither of which exists in ordinary experience. In ordinary experience "now" continually vanishes between the no longer and the not yet; we may think of "here" as a hazy mental circumference around ourselves, but whatever we locate in ordinary space, inside it or outside it, is "there" in a separated alien world. In the "kingdom" the eternal and infinite are not time and space made endless (they *are* endless already) but are the now and the here made real, an actual present and an actual presence. Time vanishes in Jesus' "Before Abraham was, I am" (John 8:58); space vanishes when we are told, in an aphorism previously referred to, that the kingdom is *entos hymon* (Luke 17:21), which may mean among you or in you, but in either case means here, not there.

In its relation to the previous phrases, the gospel of *metanoia* makes man a "new creature" (2 Cor. 5:17), in which the original and now fallen order of nature becomes a mother bringing to birth a re-creation made through a union of God and man (Rom. 8:21). It is the reappearance in human life of the higher or transfigured nature, the innocent world before the fall. The revolutionary thrust of the Exodus is also preserved, and Jesus often speaks of "faith" as though it gave the individual as much effective power as the Exodus gave the whole society of Israel. Such faith clearly includes a power of action informed by a vision transcending time and space. In the Old Testament law and wisdom follow the deliverance from Egypt. The totalitarian conception of law, in which the breaker of an obligation to God is to be wiped out with his family (Josh. 7:24), had already given way to the principle that the individual alone was responsible for what he did (Ezek. 18:20). One of the pseudepigrapha, 2 Baruch, speaks of the law among us and the wisdom within us (48:24). But the gospel is a different kind of individualizing of the law, founded on the category of prophecy. We remarked earlier that Christianity thinks of the Old Testament as primarily a book of prophecy rather than of law; and the principle involved here needs careful stating.

We spoke [earlier] of the latent terrorism in the rule of law, which has been seen many times in history since the Old Testament, and is often a post-revolutionary feeling. A great experience has been shared: the society feels drawn together into a single body, and social and individual standards become, for a necessarily brief period, assimilated. Plato's *Republic* outlines an ideal society on the analogy of the wise man's mind, where the reason is a dictatorial philosopher-king, the will a ruthless thought-police hunting down every subversive impulse, and the natural impulses of appetite, though allowed to function, are rigidly controlled. At the end of the ninth book Socrates suggests that such a society could perhaps never exist, but that wise men may and do exist, and the wise man would live by the laws of such a republic, whatever his actual social context. As an allegory of the wise man's mind, the *Republic* is a powerful vision; as an ideal social order, it would be a fantastic tyranny.

Similarly, the Sermon on the Mount is in part a commentary on the Ten Commandments in which the negative commands not to kill or commit adultery or steal are positively stated as an enthusiasm for human life, a habitual respect for the dignity of a woman, a delight in sharing goods with those who need them. Such a gospel, Paul says, sets one free of the law—and of course we do not get free of the law by breaking the law, only more fouled up with it than ever. But the standards of the highly integrated individual are far more rigorous than those that apply to society in general, hence the gospel made into a new social law would again be the most frightful tyranny. Thus, according to Milton, Jesus condemns divorce because "marriage" for him means spiritual marriage, the model of which is Adam and Eve in Eden, for each of whom there was, very exactly, no one else. Such a marriage would not be "consummated," which means finished, at the first sexual union, but only by the death of one of the partners. But to assume that every sexual liaison or marriage contract in ordinary society is a spiritual marriage of this type would pervert the gospel into a new law.

Whether Milton is right or wrong, he is assuming a prophetic rather than a legal basis for the gospel. Let us go back to Plato for another illustration. The one thing which has caught everyone's imagination in Plato is the figure of Socrates, the archetypal teacher and prophet, "corrupting" the youth of Athens by showing them that when they express social stereotypes about love or courage or justice or pleasure they have not the faintest idea what they are talking about. We see this Socrates, in the *Apology* and the *Phaedo*, facing martyrdom without making any concession to the ignorance and stupidity of his accusers. But Plato himself was a revolutionary thinker, and in the *Laws* he draws up a blueprint for his own post-revolutionary society. In that society all teachers are to be most strictly supervised and instructed what to teach: everything depends on their complete subservience to the overall social vision. Socrates does not appear in the *Laws*, and no such person as Socrates could exist in such a society. We should be careful to understand what Plato is doing here. He is really assuming that those who condemned Socrates were right in principle, and wrong only—if wrong at all by that time—in their application of it.

Similarly, Christianity is founded on a prophet who was put to death as a blasphemer and a social menace, hence any persecuting Christian is assuming that Pilate and Caiaphas were right in principle, and should merely have selected a different victim. The significance of the life of Jesus is often thought of as a legal significance, consisting in a life of perfect morality, or total conformity to a code of right action. But if we think of his significance as prophetic rather than legal, his real significance is that of being the one figure in history whom no organized human society could possibly put up with. The society that rejected him represented all societies: those responsible for his death were not the Romans or the Jews or whoever happened to be around at the time, but the whole of mankind down to ourselves and doubtless far beyond. "It is expedient that one man die for the people," said Caiaphas (John 18:14), and there has never been a human society that has not agreed with him.

What primarily distinguishes Christianity (and Judaism) from most Oriental religions, it seems to me, is this revolutionary and prophetic element of confrontation with society. This element gives meaning and shape to history by presenting it with a dialectical challenge. From this point of view, the root of evil in human life cannot be adequately described as ignorance, or the cure for it correctly described as enlightenment. The record of human cruelty and folly is too hideous for anything but the sense of a corrupted will to come near to a diagnosis. Hence Jesus was not simply the compassionate Jesus as Buddha was the compassionate Buddha. His work, though it includes the teaching of ways of enlightenment, does not stop there, but goes through a martyrdom and a descent into death. Two implications here are of especial importance for our present purpose. One, a specifically historical situation is latent in any "enlightenment": man has to fight his way out of history and not simply awaken from it. Two, the ability to absorb a complete individual is, so far, beyond the capacity of any society, including those that call themselves Christian.

Anti-Semitism is a long-standing corruption of Christianity, and one of the more rationalized pretexts for it is the notion that the legalism condemned in the New Testament is to be identified with Judaism. But this is a very dubious interpretation of even the most polemical parts of the New Testament, and is not found at all in the teaching of Jesus. Jesus always attacks a quite specific elite or pseudo-elite of chief priests, scribes, lawyers, Pharisees, Sadducees, and other "blind guides" (Matt. 23:24), but not the precepts of the religion he was brought up in himself. What Jesus condemned in Pharisaism is as common in Christianity as in any other religion. The attack on legalism is in a quite different context: it means accepting the standards of society, and society will always sooner or later line up with Pilate against the prophet.

In the Book of Leviticus the ritual for the Day of Atonement . . . consisted in separating a symbolic figure of a goat ("scapegoat," as the AV calls it), which represented their accumulated sin, from the community of Israel. The antitype of this, in the Christian view, is the separation of Christ from the human community, an atonement that reunites God with man. It was unfortunate for the English language that the originally comic pronunciation of "one" as "wun" should have caught on, as it obscures the connection of "one" with other words derived from it, such as "alone" and "only." More relevant for us at the moment is its obscuring of the fact that the radical meaning of "atonement" is "unifying." The AV speaks of atonement mainly in the sense of making reparation for sin, and in an Old Testament context. The "unifying" implications of atonement take us much further than this. They suggest that a channel of communication between the divine and the human is now open, and hence the whole metaphorical picture of the relation of man and God has to be reversed. Man does not stand in front of an invisible but objective power making conciliatory gestures of ritual and moral obligation to him: such gestures express nothing except his own helplessness.

Let us take an example from outside the Biblical area. The Roman Saturnalia festival, in which masters waited on their slaves in memory of the golden age of Saturn, was a dumb, helpless gesture which said symbolically that the slave structure of Roman society was all wrong, but that nothing could or would be done about it. For Paul and the author of Hebrews the old sacrificial rituals, like the Saturnalia, were "vanity": empty actions in an empty world, even though the good will they expressed had a symbolic or typical value. In the changed metaphor man has an infinite energy behind him that is now available to him: a God who is invisible because he does the seeing. The metaphor of a God behind, a power that can do anything through man, seems implicit in Jesus' strong emphasis on God as a "Father," the hidden source of his own energy. Once again, changes in metaphor are fundamental changes, and here we may glimpse the possibility of getting past the pseudo-issues growing out of the metaphor of a divine presence in front of us, who may be believed or disbelieved "in" because he may or may not be "there." Theist and atheist are at one in regarding personality as the highest category known to experience. Whether it is possible for human personality to be connected with and open to a divine one that is its own infinite extension may still be a question, but the more solid the metaphorical basis for either side, the more possibility there is of mutual understanding.

So far we have spoken in individual terms, but the gospel also brings in a new conception of "Israel" as the citizens of the kingdom of God. The notion that any group of such citizens, such as women or slaves, is inherently second-class is nonsense (Gal. 3:28). Such a society is not the ordinary society out of which we grow from birth, but a re-created society growing out of an individual. Its type is the society descended from an eponymous ancestor, as the society of Israel grew out of the body of Jacob. The conception of a possible social resurrection, a transformation that will split the world of history into a spiritual kingdom and a hell, is a part of the gospel teaching itself, though an easy part to misunderstand. I think we do misunderstand it if we assume that everyone in the New Testament period thought that the world was coming to an end at once, and that consequently Jesus himself must have been equally confused about the matter. No doubt there were many for whom the "end of the world" was a simply future event, but we have suggested that a rather subtler notion of time than that seems to be involved in Jesus' teachings.

SEVENTH PHASE: APOCALYPSE

The Greek word for revelation, *apocalypsis*, has the metaphorical sense of uncovering or taking a lid off, and similarly the word for truth, *aletheia*, begins with a negative particle which suggests that truth was originally thought of as also a kind of unveiling, a removal of the curtains of forgetfulness in the mind. In more modern terms, perhaps what blocks truth and the emerging of revelation is not forgetting but repression. We have noted that the last book in the Bible, the one explicitly called Revelation or Apocalypse, is a mosaic of allusions to the Old Testament: that is, it is a progression of antitypes. The author speaks of setting down what he has seen in a vision, but the Book of Revelation is not a visualized book in the ordinary sense of the word, as any illustrator who has struggled with its seven-headed and ten-horned monsters will testify. What the seer in Patmos had a vision of was primarily, as he conceived it, the true meaning of the Scriptures, and his dragons and horsemen and dissolving cosmos were what he saw in Ezekiel and Zechariah, whatever or however he saw on Patmos.

The general material of the vision is the familiar material of prophecy: there is again a *culbute générale* in which the people of God are raised into recognition and the heathen kingdoms are cast into darkness. There are portentous events in both social and natural orders: plagues, wars, famines, great stars falling from heaven, and an eventual transformation, for those who persist in the faith, of the world into a new heaven and earth. We are greatly oversimplifying the vision, however, if we think of it simply as what the author thought was soon going to happen, as a firework show that would be put on for the benefit of the faithful, starting perhaps next Tuesday. For him all these incredible wonders are the inner meaning or, more accurately, the inner form of everything that is happening now. Man creates what he calls history as a screen to conceal the workings of the apocalypse from himself.

St. John the Divine sees all this "in the spirit" (1:10), with his spiritual body, and the spiritual body is the most deeply repressed element of experience. The *culbute* he describes is political in only one of its aspects. The chief enemy, symbolized as a "Great Whore," is "spiritually" called Babylon, but she is also called "Mystery" (17:5). The word "mystery" is extensively used in the New Testament in both a good and a bad sense: there is a mystery of the kingdom (Matt. 13:11 and elsewhere) and a mystery of iniquity (2 Thess. 2:7). Nothing is more mysterious to the world than the half-esoteric beliefs of the primitive Christians, and nothing more obvious and apparent than, say, the power of the Emperor Nero. But the mystery turns into a revelation of how things really are, and the obvious power of Nero rolls into the darkness of the mystery of the corrupted human will from whence it emerged. The vision of the apocalypse is the vision of the total meaning of the Scriptures, and may break on anyone at any time. It comes like a thief in the night (Rev. 16:15, cf. 1 Thess. 5:2: this phrase is one of the few links between Revelation and the rest of the New Testament). What is symbolized as the destruction of the order of nature is the destruction of the way of seeing that order that keeps man confined to the world of time and history as we know them. This destruction is what the Scripture is intended to achieve.

There are, then, two aspects of the apocalyptic vision. One is what we may call the panoramic apocalypse, the vision of staggering marvels placed in a near future and just before the end of time. As a panorama, we look at it passively, which means that it is objective to us. This in turn means that it is essentially a projection of the subjective "knowledge of good and evil" acquired at the fall. That knowledge, we now see, was wholly within the framework of law: it is contained by a final "judgment," where the world disappears into its two unending constituents, a heaven and a hell, into one of which man automatically goes, depending on the relative strength of the cases of the prosecution and the defense. Even in heaven, the legal vision tells us, he remains eternally a creature, praising his Creator unendingly.

Anyone coming "cold" to the Book of Revelation, without context of any kind, would probably regard it as simply an insane rhapsody. It has been described as a book that either finds a man mad or else leaves him so. And yet, if we were to explore below the repressions in our own minds that keep us "normal," we might find very similar nightmares of anxiety and triumph. As a parallel example, we may cite the so-called Tibetan Book of the Dead, where the soul is assumed immediately after death to be going through a series of visions, first of peaceful and then of wrathful deities. A priest reads the book into the ear of the corpse, who is also assumed to hear the reader's voice telling him that all these visions are simply his own repressed mental forms now released by death and coming to the surface. If he could realize that, he would immediately be delivered from their power, because it is his own power.

If we take a similar approach to the Book of Revelation, we find, I think, that there is a second or participating apocalypse following the panoramic one. The panoramic apocalypse ends with the restoration of the tree and water of life, the two elements of the original creation. But perhaps, like other restorations, this one is a type of something else, a resurrection or upward metamorphosis to a new beginning that is now present. We notice that while the Book of Revelation seems to be emphatically the end of the Bible, it is a remarkably open end. It contains such statements as "Behold, I make all things new" (21:5); it describes God as the Alpha and Omega, the beginning and end of all possibilities of verbal expression; it follows the vision of the restoring of the water of life with an earnest invitation to drink of it. The panoramic apocalypse gives way, at the end, to a second apocalypse that, ideally, begins in the reader's mind as soon as he has finished reading, a vision that passes through the legalized vision of ordeals and trials and judgments and comes out into a second life. In this second life the creator-creature, divine-human antithetical tension has ceased to exist, and the sense of the transcendent person and the split of subject and object no longer limit our vision. After the "last judgment," the law loses its last hold on us, which is the hold of the legal vision that ends there.

We suggested [earlier] that the Bible deliberately blocks off the sense of the referential from itself: it is not a book pointing to a historical presence outside it, but a book that identifies itself with that presence. At the end the reader, also, is invited to identify himself with the book. Milton suggests that the ultimate authority in the Christian religion is what he calls the Word of God in the heart, which is superior even to the Bible itself, because for Milton this "heart" belongs not to the subjective reader but to the Holy Spirit. That is, the reader completes the visionary operation of the Bible by throwing out the subjective fallacy along with the objective one. The apocalypse is the way the world looks after the ego has disappeared.

In our discussion of creation we were puzzled by the paradox in the word when applied to human activity. God, we are told, made a "good" world; man fell into a bad world and the good one vanished; consequently *human* creativity has in it the quality of *re*-creation, of salvaging something with a human meaning out of the alienation of nature. At the end of the Book of Revelation, with such phrases as "I make all things new" (21:5) and the promise of a new heaven and earth, we reach the antitype of all antitypes, the real beginning of light and sound of which the first word of the Bible is the type.

HAROLD BLOOM

"Before Moses Was, I Am":
The Original and the Belated Testaments

Your father Abraham rejoiced that he was to see my day; he saw
it and was glad." The Jews then said to him, "You are not yet fifty
years old, and have you seen Abraham?" Jesus said to them, "Truly,
truly, I say to you, before Abraham was, I am."

(John 8:56–58)

This exchange from The Gospel According to St. John will be my text. In
the Christian triumph over the Hebrew Bible, a triumph which produced that
captive work, the Old Testament, there is no more heroic stroke than the
transumptive trope of John's Jesus: "Before Abraham was, I am." Too much
is carried by that figuration for any range of readings to convey, but one reading
I shall give is the implied substitution: "Before Moses was, I am." To my reading,
the author of the Gospel of John was and is a more dangerous enemy of the
Hebrew Bible than even Paul, his nearest rival. But I can hardly go on until
I explain what I intend to mean by "an enemy of the Hebrew Bible."

It is now altogether too late in Western history for pious or humane self-
deceptions on the matter of the Christian appropriation of the Hebrew Bible.
It is certainly much too late in Jewish history to be other than totally clear
about the nature and effect of that Christian act of total usurpation. The best
preliminary description I have found is by Jaroslav Pelikan:

What the Christian tradition had done was to take over the Jewish
Scriptures as its own, so that Justin could say to Trypho that the
passages about Christ "are contained in your Scriptures, or rather
not yours, but ours." As a matter of fact, some of the passages were

From *Notebooks in Cultural Analysis: An Annual Review.* © 1984 by Duke University Press.

contained only in "ours," that is, in the Christian Old Testament.
So assured were Christian theologians in their possession of the
Scriptures that they could accuse the Jews not merely of misunderstanding and misinterpreting them, but even of falsifying scriptural
texts. When they were aware of differences between the Hebrew
text of the Old Testament and the Septuagint, they capitalized on
these to prove their accusation. . . . The growing ease with which
appropriations and accusations alike could be made was in proportion to the completeness of the Christian victory over Jewish
thought.

　Yet that victory was achieved largely by default. Not the superior
force of Christian exegesis or learning or logic but the movement
of Jewish history seems to have been largely responsible for it.

Pelikan's dispassionate judgment on this matter is beyond disputation.
Though the Christians were to "save" the Old Testament from those like
Marcion who would cast it out completely, that is precisely what they saved—
their Old Testament. The New Testament is to a considerable extent a reading of that Old Testament, and I would judge it a very mixed reading indeed.
Some of it is a strong misreading, and much of it is a weak misreading, but
I will concern myself here entirely with strong misreadings, because only strong
misreadings work so as to establish lasting enmities between texts. The author
of the Gospel of John is an even stronger misreader than St. Paul, and I want
to compare John's and Paul's strengths of what I call poetic misprision before
I center upon John. But before commencing, I had better declare my own stance.

　"Who is the interpreter, and what power does he seek to gain over the
text?" That Nietzschean question haunts me always. I am an enemy of the
New Testament. My enmity is lifelong, and intensifies as I study its text more
closely. But I have no right to assert that my own enmity carries the force
of the normative Jewish tradition, because I am not a representative of that
tradition. From a normative Jewish perspective, let us say from the stance of
the great Akiba, I am one of the *minim*, the Jewish Gnostic heretics. My own
reading of the Hebrew Bible, even if I develop it into a strong misreading,
is as unacceptable in its way to the normative tradition as all Christian readings necessarily are. I state this not to posture, but to make clear that I do
not pretend to the authority of the normative tradition. In my view, the
Judaism that moves in a continuous line from the Academy of Ezra through
the Pharisees and on to the religion of my own parents is itself a very powerful misreading of the Hebrew Bible and so of the religion of the Yahwist,
whatever we might take that religion to have been. But my subject here is
not the text of the Yahwist.

What kind of authority can a literary critic, whose subject is the secular literature of the English language, bring to a reading of the New Testament, particularly to a reading that sees the New Testament as a text in conflict and confrontation with the Hebrew Bible? I cannot speak for other literary critics, as here too I am a sect or party of one, and have no authority other than whatever my ideas and my writings can assert for me. But the central concern of my own literary theory and praxis, for some fifteen years now, has been the crisis of confrontation and conflict between what I have called strong poems, or strong texts. I cannot say that my formulations in this area have met with a very amiable reception, even in the most secular of contexts, and so I do not expect an amiable response as I cross the line into the conflict of scriptures. Still, I have learned a great deal from the response to my work, a response that necessarily has become part of my subject. One lesson has been that there are no purely secular texts, because canonization of poems by the secular academies is not merely a displaced version of Jewish or Christian or Moslem canonization. It is precisely the thing itself, the investment of a text with unity, presence, form, and meaning, followed by the insistence that the canonized text possesses these attributes immutably, quite apart from the interpretive activities of the academies.

If so many partisans of Wordsworth or Whitman or Stevens find the offense of my work unbearable, then clearly I must expect a yet more pained response from the various custodians of the Hebrew Bible or the New Testament. I won't take more space here for unhappy anticipation or personal defense, yet I do want to make the modest observation that several years spent intensely in reading as widely as I can in Biblical scholarship have not left me with the impression that much authentic *literary* criticism of Biblical texts has been written. To make a clean sweep of it, little seems to me to have been added by recent overt intercessions by literary critics, culminating in Northrop Frye's *The Great Code*, a work in which the triumph of the New Testament over the Hebrew Bible is quite flatly complete. Frye's code, like Erich Auerbach's *figura*, which I have attacked elsewhere, is only another belated repetition of the Christian appropriation and usurpation of the Hebrew Bible.

But these matters I will argue elsewhere. I come back again to the grand proclamation of John's Jesus: "Before Abraham was, I am." What can an antithetical literary criticism (as I call my work) do with the sublime force of that assertion? Or how should that force be described? It is not the New Testament's antithetical reply to the Yahwist's most sublime moment, when Moses agonizingly stammers: "If I come to the people of Israel and say to them, 'The God of your fathers has sent me to you,' and they ask me, 'What is his name?' what shall I say to them?" God said to Moses, "I AM WHO I AM." This is the Revised Standard Version, and like every other version, it cannot handle Yahweh's awesome, untranslatable play upon his own name: *ehyeh asher ehyeh*. I expand upon a suggestion of Martin Buber's when I render this as "I will be present wherever and whenever I will be present." For that is the Yahwist's vision of *olam* as "a time without boundaries," and of the relation of Yahweh to a dynamics of time that transcends spatial limitations.

The Yahwist's vision of his God certainly would seem to center with a peculiar intensity upon the text of Exodus 3:13–14. But the entire history of ancient Jewish exegesis hardly would lead anyone to believe that this crucial passage was of the slightest interest or importance to any of the great rabbinical commentators. The *Exodus Rabbah* offers mostly midrashim connecting the name of God to his potencies which would deliver Israel from Egypt. But *ehyeh asher ehyeh* as a phrase evidently did not have peculiar force for the great Pharisees. Indeed, Jewish tradition does very little with the majestic proclamation until Maimonides gets to work upon it in *The Guide for the Perplexed*. One of my favorite books, Marmorstein's fascinating *The Old Rabbinic Doctrine of God*, has absolutely not a single reference to Exodus 3 in its exhaustive one-hundred-fifty-page section on "The Names of God." Either we must conclude that *ehyeh asher ehyeh* has very little significance for Akiba and his colleagues, which I think probably was the case, or we must resort to dubious theories of taboo, which have little to do with the strength of Akiba.

This puzzle becomes greater when the early rabbinical indifference to the striking *ehyeh asher ehyeh* text is contrasted to the Christian obsession with Exodus 3, which begins in the New Testament and becomes overwhelming in the Church Fathers, culminating in Augustine's endless preoccupation with that passage, since for Augustine it was the deepest clue to the metaphysical essence of God. Brevard Childs, in his commentary on Exodus, has outlined the history of this long episode in Christian exegesis. Respectfully, I dissent from his judgment that the ontological aspects of Christian interpretation here really do have any continuity whatsoever either with the biblical text or with rabbinical traditions. These "ontological overtones," as Childs himself has to note, stem rather from the Septuagint's rendering of *ehyeh asher ehyeh* as the very different ἐγώ εἰμι 'ὁ ὤν and from Philo's very Platonized paraphrase in his *Life of Moses*: "Tell them that I am He Who is, that they may learn the difference between what is and what is not." Though Childs insists that this cannot be dismissed as Greek thinking, it is nothing but that, and explains again why Philo was so crucial for Christian theology and so totally irrelevant to the continuity of normative Judaism.

The continued puzzle, then, is the total lack of early rabbinical interest in the *ehyeh asher ehyeh* text. I labor this point because I read John's greatest subversion of the Hebrew Bible as what I call this transumption of Yahweh's words to Moses in the extraordinary outburst of John's Jesus, "Before Abraham was, I am," which most deeply proclaims: "Before Moses was, I am." To me, this is the acutest manifestation of John's palpable ambivalence toward Moses, an ambivalence whose most perceptive student has been Wayne Meeks. John plays on and against the Yahwist's grand word-play on Yahweh and *ehyeh*. However, when I assert even that, I go against the authority of the leading current scholarly commentary upon the Fourth Gospel, and so I must deal with this difficulty before I return to the Johannic ambivalence toward the Moses traditions. And only after examining John's agon with Moses will I feel free to speculate upon the early rabbinic indifference to God's substitution of *ehyeh asher ehyeh* for his proper name.

Both B. Lindars and C. K. Barrett in their standard commentaries on John insist that "Before Abraham was, I am" makes no allusion whatsoever to "I am that I am." A literary critic must begin by observing that New Testament scholarship manifests a very impoverished notion as to just what literary allu- ion is or can be. But then here is Barrett's flat reading of this assertion of Jesus: "The meaning here is: Before Abraham came into being, I eternally was, as now I am, and ever continue to be." Perhaps I should not chide devoted scholars like Lindars and Barrett for being inadequate interpreters of so extraordinary a trope, because the master modern interpreter of John, Rudolf Bultmann, seems to me even less capable of handling trope. Here is his reading of John 8:57–58:

> The Jews remain caught in the trammels of their own thought. How can Jesus, who is not yet 50 years old, have seen Abraham! Yet the world's conception of time and age is worthless, when it has to deal with God's revelation, as is its conception of life and death. "Before Abraham was, I am." The Revealer, unlike Abraham, does not belong to the ranks of historical personages. The ἐγώ which Jesus speaks as the Revealer is the "I" of the eternal Logos, which was in the beginning, the "I" of the eternal God himself. Yet the Jews cannot comprehend that the ἐγώ of eternity is to be heard in an historical person, who is not yet 50 years old, who as a man is one of their equals, whose mother and father they knew. They cannot understand, because the notion of the Revealer's "pre- existence" can only be understood in faith.

In a note, Bultmann too denies any allusion to the "I am that I am" declaration of Yahweh. I find it ironical, nearly two thousand years after St. Paul accused the Jews of being literalizers, that the leading scholars of Christian- ity are hopeless literalizers, which of course the great rabbis never were. I cannot conceive of a weaker misreading of "Before Abraham was, I am" than Bultmann's sneering retreat into "faith," a "faith" in the "pre-existence" of Jesus. If that is all John meant, then John was a weak poet indeed. But John is at his best here, and at his best he is a strong misreader and thus a strong writer. As for Bultmann's polemical point, I am content to repeat a few amiable remarks made by Rabbi David Kimhi almost eight hundred years ago:

> Tell them that there can be no father and son in the Divinity, for the Divinity is indivisible and is one in every aspect of unity unlike matter which is divisible.
>
> Tell them further that a father precedes a son in time and a son is born through the agency of a father. Now even though each of the terms "father" and "son" implies the other . . . he who is called the father must undoubtedly be prior in time. Therefore, with reference to this God whom you call Father, Son, and Holy Spirit, that part which you call Father must be prior to that which you call Son, for if they were always coexistent, they would have to be called twin brothers.

I have cited this partly because I enjoy it so much, but also because it raises the true issue between Moses and John, between Abraham and Jesus, which is the agonistic triple issue of priority, authority, and originality. As I read John's trope, it asserts not only the priority of Jesus over Abraham (and so necessarily over Moses), but also the priority, authority, and originality of John over Moses, or as we would say, of John as writer over the Yahwist as writer. That is where I am heading this account of the agon between the Yahwist and John, and so I turn now to some general observations upon the Fourth Gospel—observations by a literary critic, of course, and not by a qualified New Testament believer and/or scholar.

John does seem to me the most anxious in tone of all the gospels, and its anxiety is as much what I would call a literary anxiety as an existential or spiritual one. One sign of this anxiety is the palpable difference between the attitude of Jesus toward himself in the Fourth Gospel as compared to the other three. Scholarly consensus holds that John was written at the close of the first century, and so after the Synoptic Gospels. A century is certainly enough time for apocalyptic hope to have ebbed away, and for an acute sense of belatedness to have developed in its place. John's Jesus has a certain obsession with his own glory, and particularly with what that glory ought to be in a Jewish context. Rather like the Jesus of Gnosticism, John's Jesus is much given to saying "I am," and there are Gnostic touches throughout John, though their extent is disputable. Perhaps, as some scholars have surmised, there is an earlier, more

Gnostic gospel buried in the Gospel of John. An interesting article by John Meagher of Toronto, back in 1969, even suggested that the original reading of John 1:14 was "And the Word became *pneuma* and dwelt among us," which is a Gnostic formulation, yet curiously more in the spirit and tone of much of the Fourth Gospel than is "And the Word became flesh."

The plain nastiness of the Gospel of John toward the Pharisees is in the end an anxiety as to the spiritual authority of the Pharisees, and it may be augmented by John's Gnostic overtones. A Jewish reader with even the slightest sense of Jewish history, feels threatened when reading John 18:28–19:16. I do not think that this feeling has anything to do with the supposed pathos or problematic literary power of the text. There is a peculiar wrongness about John's Jesus saying, "If my kingship were of this world, my servants would fight, that I might not be handed over to the Jews" (18:36); it implies that Jesus is no longer a Jew, but something else. This unhappy touch is another sign of the pervasive rhetoric of anxiety in the Fourth Gospel. John's vision seems to be of a small group—his own, presumably—which finds its analogue and asserted origin in the group around Jesus two generations before. In the general judgment of scholars, the original conclusion of the gospel was the parable of doubting Thomas, a manifest trope for a sect or coven undergoing a crisis of faith.

It is within that anxiety of frustrate expectations, perhaps even of recent expulsion from the Jewish world, that John's agon with Moses finds its context. Wayne Meeks has written very sensitively of the Fourth Gospel's ambivalence toward the Moses traditions, particularly those centered upon the image of Moses as prophet–king, a unique amalgam of the two roles that John seeks to extend and surpass in Jesus. My interest in John's handling of Moses is necessarily different in emphasis, for I am going to read a number of John's namings of Moses as being tropes more for the text than for the supposed substance of what the New Testament (following the Septuagint) insists upon calling the Law. I myself will call it not Torah but J or the Yahwist, because that is where I locate the agon. Not theology, not faith, not truth is the issue, but literary power, the scandalous power of J's text, which by synecdoche stands for the Hebrew Bible as the strongest poem that I have ever read in any language I am able to read. John, and Paul before him, took on an impossible precursor and rival, and their apparent victory is merely an illusion. The aesthetic dignity of the Hebrew Bible, and of the Yahwist in particular as its uncanny original, is simply beyond the competitive range of the New Testament as a literary achievement, as it is beyond the range of the only surviving Gnostic texts that have any aesthetic value—a few fragments of Valentinus and the Gospel of Truth that Valentinus may have written. But I will return to the end of this discourse to the issue of rival aesthetic achievements. John's struggle with Moses is at last my direct concern.

There are so many contests with Moses throughout the New Testament that I cannot contrast John in this regard to all of the other texts, but I do want to compare him briefly with Paul, if only because I intend later to consider some aspects of Paul's own struggle with the Hebrew Bible. I think there is still nothing so pungent in all commentary upon Paul as the remarks made by Nietzsche in 1888, in *The Antichrist*:

> Paul is the incarnation of a type which is the reverse of that of
> the Savior; he is the genius in hatred, in the standpoint of hatred,
> and in the relentless logic of hatred. . . . What he wanted was power;
> with St. Paul the priest again aspired to power, – he could make
> use only of concepts, doctrines, symbols with which masses may
> be tyrannised over, and with which herds are formed.

Of course Nietzsche is extreme, but can he be refuted? Paul is so careless, hasty, and inattentive a reader of the Hebrew Bible that he very rarely gets any text right; and in so gifted a person this kind of weak misunderstanding can come only from the dialectics of the power drive, of the will to power over a text, even when the text is as formidable as Torah. There is little agonistic cunning in Paul's misreadings of Torah; many indeed are plain howlers. The most celebrated is his weird exegesis of Exod. 34:29–35, where the text has Moses descending from Sinai, tablets in hand, his face shining with God's glory – a glory so great that Moses must veil his countenance after speaking to the people, and then unveil only when he returns to speak to God. Normative Jewish interpretation, surely known to Paul, was that the shining was the Torah restoration of the *zelem*, the true image of God that Adam had lost, and that the shining prevailed until the death of Moses. But here is 2 Cor. 3:12–13:

> Since we have such a hope, we are very bold, not like Moses, who
> put a veil over his face so that the Israelites might not see the end
> of the fading splendor.

There isn't any way to save this, even by gently calling it a "parody" of the Hebrew text, as Wayne Meeks does. It isn't a transumption or lie against time, which is the Johannine mode; it is just a plain lie against the text. Nor is it uncharacteristic of Paul. Meeks very movingly calls Paul "the Christian Proteus," and Paul is certainly beyond my understanding. Proteus is an apt model for many other roles, but perhaps not for an interpreter of Mosaic text. Paul's reading of what he thought was the Law increasingly seems to me oddly Freudian, in that Paul identifies the Law with the human drive that Freud wanted to call Thanatos. Paul's peculiar confounding of the Law and death presumably keeps him from seeing Jesus as a transcending fulfillment of Moses. Instead, Paul contrasts himself to Moses, hardly to his own disadvantage. Thus, Rom. 9:3:

> For I could wish that I myself were accused and cut off from Christ
> for the sake of my brethren, my kinsmen by race.

It may seem at first an outburst of Jewish pride, of which I would grant the Protean Paul an authentic share, but the Mosaic allusion changes its nature. All exegetes point to Exod. 32:32 as the precursor text. Moses offers himself to Yahweh as atonement for the people after the orgy of the golden calf: "But now, if thou wilt forgive their sin—and if not, blot me, I pray thee, out of thy book which thou hast written." How do the two offers of intercession compare? After all, the people *have* sinned, and Moses would choose oblivion to save them from the consequences of their disloyalty. The allusive force of Paul's offer is turned against both his own Jewish contemporaries and even against Moses himself. Even the Pharisees (for whom Paul, unlike John, has a lingering regard) are worshippers of the golden calf of death, since the Law *is* death. And all Moses supposedly offered was the loss of his own prophetic greatness, his place in the salvation history. But Paul, out of supposed love for his fellow-Jews, offers to lose more than Moses did, because he insists he has more to lose. To be cut off from Christ is to die eternally, a greater sacrifice than the Mosaic offer to be as one who had never lived. This is what I would call the daemonic counter-Sublime of hyperbole, and its repressive force is enormous and very revelatory.

But I return again to John, whose revisionary warfare against Moses is subtler. Meeks has traced the general pattern, and so I follow him here, though of course he would dissent from the interpretation I am going to offer of this pattern of allusion. The allusions begin with John the Baptist chanting a typical Johannine metalepsis, in which the latecomer truly has priority ("John bore witness to him, and cried, 'This was he of whom I said: He who comes after me ranks before me, for he was before me' "), to which the author of the Fourth Gospel adds: "For the law was given through Moses; grace and truth came through Jesus Christ" (John 1:15, 17). Later, the first chapter proclaims: "We have found him of whom Moses in the law and also the prophets wrote, Jesus of Nazareth" (1:45). The third chapter daringly inverts a great Mosaic trope in a way still unnerving for any Jewish reader: "No one has ascended into heaven but he who descended from heaven, the Son of man. And as Moses lifted up the serpent in the wilderness, so must the Son of man be lifted up" (3:13–14). John's undoubted revisionary genius is very impressive here merely from a

technical or rhetorical point of view. No heavenly revelations ever were made
to Moses, whose function is reduced to a synecdoche, and indeed to its lesser
half. To use one of my revisionary ratios, Jesus on the cross will be the *tessera*
or antithetical completion of the Mosaic raising of the brazen serpent in
the wilderness. Moses was only a part, but Jesus is the fulfilling whole. My
avoidance of the language of typology, here and elsewhere, is quite deliberate,
and will be defended in my conclusion, where I will say a few unkind words
about the Christian and now Auerbachian trope of *figura*.

The same ratio of antithetical completion is invoked when Jesus announces
himself as the fulfiller of the sign of manna, as would be expected of the Messiah.
But here the gratuitous ambivalence toward Moses is sharper: "Truly, truly,
I say to you, it was not Moses who gave you the bread from heaven; my
Father gives you the true bread from heaven. For the bread of God is that
which comes down from heaven, and gives life to the world" (6:32–33). As
the trope is developed, it becomes deliberately so shocking in a Jewish context
that even the disciples are shocked; but I would point to one moment in the
development as marking John's increasing violence against Moses and all the
Jews: "Your fathers ate the manna in the wilderness, and they died. . . . I am
the living bread . . . if any one eats of this bread, he will live for ever; and
the bread which I shall give for the life of the world is my flesh" (6:49, 51).
It is, after all, gratuitous to say that our fathers ate the manna and died; it
is even misleading, since had they not eaten the manna, they would not have
lived as long as they did. But John has modulated to a daemonic counter-
Sublime, and his hyperbole helps to establish a new, Christian sublimity, in
which Jews die and Christians live eternally.

Rather than multiply instances of John's revisionism, I want to conclude
my specific remarks on the Fourth Gospel by examining in its full context
the passage with which I began: "Before Abraham was, I am." I am more than
a little unhappy with the sequence I will expound, because I find in it John
at nearly his most unpleasant and indeed anti-Jewish, but the remarkable
rhetorical strength of "Before Abraham was, I am" largely depends upon its
contextualization, as John undoes the Jewish pride in being descended from
Abraham. The sequence, extending through most of the eighth chapter, begins
with Jesus sitting in the temple, surrounded both by Pharisees and by Jews
who are in the process of becoming his believers. To those he has begun to
persuade, Jesus now says what is certain to turn them away:

> "If you continue in my word, you are truly my disciples, and
> you will know the truth, and the truth will make you free." They
> answered him, "We are descendants of Abraham, and have never

been in bondage to any one. How is it that you say, 'You will
be made free'?"

(8:31–32)

It seems rather rhetorically weak that Jesus should then become aggressive,
with a leap into murderous insinuations:

"I know that you are descendants of Abraham; yet you seek
to kill me, because my word finds no place in you. I speak of what
I have seen with my Father, and you do what you have heard from
your father."

(8:37–38)

As John's Jesus graciously is about to tell them, the Jews' father is the devil.
They scarcely can be blamed for answering, "Abraham is our father," or for
assuming that their accuser has a demon. I look at the foot of the page of
the text I am using, *The New Oxford Annotated Bible, Revised Standard Version*
(1977), and next to verse 48, on having a demon, the editors helpfully tell
me, "*The Jews* turn to insult and calumny." I reflect upon how wonderful a
discipline such scholarship is, and I mildly rejoin that by any dispassionate
reading John's Jesus has made the initial "turn to insult and calumny." What
matter, since the Jews are falling neatly into John's rhetorical trap? Jesus has
promised that his believers "will never see death" and the astonished children
of Abraham (or is it children of the devil?) protest:

"Abraham died, as did the prophets; and you say, 'If any one
keeps my word, he will never taste death.' Are you greater than
our father Abraham, who died?"

(8:52–53)

Jesus responds by calling them liars, again surely rather gratuitously, and then
by ensnaring them in John's subtlest tropological entrapment, which will bring
me full circle to where I began:

"Your father Abraham rejoiced that he was to see my day; he
saw it and was glad." The Jews then said to him, "You are not yet
fifty years old, and have you seen Abraham?" Jesus said to them,
"Truly, truly, I say to you, before Abraham was, I am."

(8:57–58)

It is certainly the most remarkable transumption in the New Testament,
though I had better explain what I mean by transumption, which is a little
exhausting for me, since I have been explaining the term endlessly in eight

books published over the last nine years. Very briefly, transumption or metalepsis is the traditional term in rhetoric for the trope that works to make the late seem early, and the early seem late. It lies against time, so as to accomplish what Nietzsche called the will's revenge against time, and against time's assertion, "It was." Uniquely among figures of speech, transumption works to undo or reverse anterior tropes. It is therefore the particular figure that governs what we might call "interpretive allusion." Ultimately, it seeks to end-stop allusiveness by presenting its own formulation as the last word, which insists upon an ellipsis rather than a proliferation of further allusion.

When John's Jesus says, "Before Abraham was, I am," the ultimate allusion is not to Abraham but to Moses, and to Yahweh's declaration made to Moses, "I am that I am." The transumption leaps over Abraham by saying also, "Before Moses was, I am," and by hinting ultimately: "I am that I am"—because I am one with my father Yahweh. The ambivalence and agonistic intensity of the Fourth Gospel achieves an apotheosis with this sublime introjection of Yahweh, which simultaneously also is a projection or repudiation of Abraham and Moses. I am aware that I seem to be making John into a Gnostic Christian, but that is the transumptive force of his rhetoric, as opposed perhaps to his more overt dialectic. His Gospel, as it develops, does seem to me to become as Gnostic as it is Christian, and this is the kind of Gnosticism that indeed was a kind of intellectual or spiritual anti-Semitism. Obviously, I believe that there are Gnosticisms and Gnosticisms, and some I find considerably more attractive than others. Just as obviously, the Gnostic elements in John, and even in St. Paul, seem to me very shadowed indeed.

Earlier in this discourse, I confessed my surprise at the normative rabbinical indifference, in ancient days, to Yahweh's sublime declaration, *ehyeh asher ehyeh*. If the great Rabbi Akiba ever speculated about that enigmatic phrase, he kept it to himself. I doubt that he made any such speculations, because I do not think that fearless sage was in the habit of hoarding them, and I am not enough of a Kabbalist to think that Akiba harbored forbidden or esoteric knowledge. To the normative mind of the Judaism roughly contemporary with Jesus, there was evidently nothing remarkable in Yahweh's declining to give his name, and instead almost playfully asserting: "Tell them that I who will be when and where I will be am the one who has sent you." That is how Yahweh talked, and how he was. But to the belated author of the Fourth Gospel, as to all our belated selves, "I am that I am" was and is a kind of *mysterium tremendum*, to use Rudolf Otto's language. That mystery John sought to transcend and transume with the formulation, "Before Abraham was, I am." Prior to the text of Exodus was the text that John was writing, in which the Jews were to be swept away into the universe of death, while Jesus led John on to the universe of life.

This transformation is an instance of just how the New Testament reduced the Hebrew Bible to that captive work, the Old Testament. Though the reduction is necessarily of great theological influence, it of course does not touch the Hebrew Bible. I have read the Hebrew Bible since I was a child, and the New Testament since I first took a course in New Testament Greek as an undergraduate. Clearly, I am not a dispassionate reader of the New Testament, though I do not read the Hebrew Bible as the normative Jewish tradition had read it, either. I come back to the issue of the interpreter's authority. When I read, I read as a literary critic, but my concerns have little in common with those of any other contemporary critic. Idealizations of any text, however canonical, or of the reading process itself are not much to my taste. Emerson said he read for the lustres. I follow him, but I emphasize even more that the lustres arise out of strife, competition, defense, anxiety, and the author's constant need for survival *as an author*. I don't see how any authentic literary critic could judge John as anything better than a very flawed revisionist of the Yahwist, and Paul as something less than that, despite the peculiar pathos of his protean personality. In the aesthetic warfare between the Hebrew Bible and the New Testament, there is just no contest, and if you think otherwise, then bless you.

But surely the issue is not aesthetic, I will be reminded. Well, we are all trapped in history, and the historical triumph of Christianity is brute fact. I am not moved to say anything about it. But I am moved to reject the idealized modes of interpretation it has stimulated, from early typology on to the revival of *figura* by Erich Auerbach and the Blakean Great Code of Northrop Frye. No text, secular or religious, fulfills another text, and all who insist otherwise merely homogenize literature. As for the relevance of the aesthetic to the issue of the conflict between sacred texts, I doubt finally that much else is relevant to a strong reader who is not dominated by extraliterary persuasions or convictions. Reading *The Book of Mormon*, for instance, is a difficult aesthetic experience, and I would grant that not much in the New Testament subjects me to rigors of quite that range. But then John and Paul do not ask to be read against *The Book of Mormon*.

Can the New Testament be read as less polemically and destructively revisionary of the Hebrew Bible than it actually is? Not by me, anyway. But don't be too quick to shrug off a reading informed by an awareness of the ways of the antithetical, of the revisionary strategies devised by those latecomers who seek strength, and who will sacrifice truth to get strength even as they proclaim the incarnation of the truth beyond death. Nietzsche is hardly the favorite sage of contemporary New Testament scholars, but perhaps he still has something vital to teach them.

What do Jews and Christians gain by refusing to see that the revisionary desperation of the New Testament has made it permanently impossible to identify the Hebrew Bible with the Christian Old Testament? Doubtless there are social and political benefits in idealizations of "dialogue," but there is nothing more. It is not a contribution to the life of the spirit or the intellect to tell lies to one another or to oneself in order to bring about more affection or cooperation between Christians and Jews. Paul is hopelessly equivocal on nearly every subject, but to my reading he is clearly not a Jewish anti-Semite; yet his misrepresentation of Torah was absolute. John is evidently a Jewish anti-Semite, and the Fourth Gospel is pragmatically murderous as an anti-Jewish text. Yet it is theologically and emotionally central to Christianity. I give the last word to the sage called Radak in Jewish tradition, that David Kimhi whom I cited earlier. He quotes as proof-text Ezek. 16:53: "I will turn their captivity, the captivity of Sodom and her daughters." And then Radak comments, rightly dismissing from his perspective all Christians as mere heretics from Judaism: "This verse is a reply to the Christian heretics who say that the future consolations have already been fulfilled. *Sodom is still overturned as it was and is still unsettled.*"

HERBERT MARKS

Pauline Typology
and Revisionary Criticism

Concern over the problem of intertestamental continuity goes back to the paradoxical attitude of the earliest Christian writers, who in the New Testament presented their teachings on the one hand as a confirmation of the scriptural word, on the other as a decisively new revelation. Unlike the more overtly theological paradoxes professed in the creeds, this literary paradox, for which the term "typology" may serve as a convenient flag, has never been dogmatically defined. The most influential proposals from the second century on share a common dependence on Paul's letter-spirit antithesis; yet differing theological presuppositions have led, in circular fashion, to quite different theories of interpretation. Unfortunately, the rich legacy of hermeneutic debate tends to color our reading of Paul himself, whose letters contain examples of and directives for a way of reading scripture (and by extension other literature) that cannot be comfortably reconciled with any normative mode of interpretation.

To argue a contrast between Paul and the Church is itself a venerable tradition, and Harnack's remark that the history of dogma is "a history of Pauline reactions in the Church" is justly celebrated. However, the opposition I have in mind is not offered as a critique of a theological institution, but rather as a demonstration of the motives governing a kind of creative interpretation whose source is the impulse toward imaginative autonomy, or, to use the language of the New Testament, toward *exousia* (power or freedom). Such an impulse produces a deep though often disguised ambivalence toward the primary text; for it is only at the text's prior instigation and within its matrix of given forms

From *Journal of the American Academy of Religion* 52, no. 1 (March 1984). © 1984 by *The American Academy of Religion*.

that the interpreter, whether poet or theologian, can conceive his own vision. In his studies of modern poetry, Harold Bloom has described such ambivalence as an "anxiety of influence," relating it to the generic principle, first formulated by Vico, that priority in the natural order is equivalent to authority in the spiritual order. While interpreters unaffected by it tend to promote "the idealizing process that is canonization," the "strong" or creative reader, by willfully distorting the antecedent text succeeds in arrogating to himself some measure of its authority. It will be my contention here that Paul's subordination of the Jewish scriptures to their "spiritual" understanding is a paradigmatic instance of revisionary power realized in the process of overcoming a tyranny of predecession.

In historical terms, this approach leads to conclusions that might be characterized vaguely as Marcionite. More precisely, it would salvage a central insight from the position of Marcion's foremost expositor, Adolf von Harnack, who (with the exception of Nietzsche) was the modern writer most sensitive to the antithetical aspect of the Pauline writings. In Harnack's view, Paul never intended the Hebrew Bible to become the *Erbauungsbuch* of Christianity; the faith he envisioned would have been entirely "spiritual" and not a book-religion at all, although his actual use of scripture, particularly his typological exegesis, contributed to the opposite effect. Admittedly, the reasoning on which this conclusion is based is often dubious (the significance of the scarcity of Old Testament quotations in the shorter letters is debatable as is the uncritical identification of "letter" with scripture), but the estimation of Paul's fundamentally agnostic stance toward scriptural tradition seems to me accurate. I would suggest however, in disagreement with Harnack, that it is precisely in his typological exegesis that Paul's stance is most apparent. Literal and spiritual represent opposing terms, but the literary is one of the realms in which both may be defined. Indeed, "in the Judaeo-Christian development," as James Barr has written, the very "possibility of being radical or revolutionary is connected with being a book religion."

THE CANONICAL PERSPECTIVE

For the most part, modern students of Paul have neglected this idea—a neglect I would like to examine briefly, as it will help to bring out the deeper tendency of Paul's own thinking. One may begin by distinguishing three types of interpretation. A reading that is not revisionary, in the sense defined above, is apt to be either expository or apologetic. Since modern New Testament scholarship, for all its avowed objectivity, has allowed these latter to intermingle, it is hardly surprising that the distinctively antithetical character of Paul's hermeneutics has not been properly appreciated.

Precritical discussion of the relationship between the two testaments was by derivation an apologetic enterprise. It began as a response to Jewish critics, on the one hand, and to those radicals, on the other, whose aggressive emphasis on discontinuity was perceived to be a corollary of gnostic dualism. With the rise of historical criticism and the attendant redefinition of the *sensus litteralis*, Old and New ceased to be a prominent focus of attention. Questions of signification gave way to questions of verification, and the drive to uncover the historical facts (*wie es eigentlich gewesen*) fostered scholarly indifference to textual correspondences. At the same time, the emergence of Old Testament and New Testament criticism as separate academic disciplines created a special obstacle to intertestamental study.

Modern efforts to bridge this gap are based on the essentially empirical premise that scriptural exegesis played an important part in the life of the early Christian communities. It is generally assumed that members of the incipient churches were searching the scriptures, first, for ways to interpret events in the life of Jesus which impressed them as extraordinary, and, second, for ways to make the proclamation of their interpretation acceptable to their con-temporaries. C. H. Dodd, whose book *According to the Scriptures* has been the starting point for a succession of impressive studies on the historical use of the Old Testament in the New, announces this hypothesis in his opening chapter. In Dodd's words, "the Church was committed, by the very terms of its *kerygma*, to a formidable task of biblical research, primarily for the purpose of clarifying its own understanding of the momentous events out of which it had emerged, and also for the purpose of making its Gospel intelligible to the outside public." In short, the Church's primary interpretive task is assumed to have been one of assimilation, of harmonizing its primitive *kerygma* with the existing body of Jewish tradition, and such familiar New Testament features as introductory formulae, typological correspondences, and prophecy fulfillments are credibly explained as responses to this descriptive or apologetic challenge.

It should be noted, however, that this critical approach, which leads natu-rally to an emphasis on continuities between Old and New, is not without apologetic overtones of its own. Most obvious is the explicit bias toward what C. F. D. Moule calls "the pressure of events": "The Christians thus found themselves pushed by the pressure of events into a new way of selecting, re-lating, grouping, and interpreting what we call 'Old Testament' passages; and while the scriptures of the Jews undoubtedly exercised a great influence upon the form in which they presented their material, and ultimately upon the very writing and collecting of the Christian scriptures, this influence was evidently subordinate both to the influence of the apostolic witness to Jesus and to the living inspiration of the Christian prophets in the Church." Here, the insistence on the priority of the Church's witness, the sharp distinction between form and content, and the reluctance to allow that scriptural interpretation might have played an initiatory or constitutive rather than a merely expository role in the New Testament's evolution all testify to the desire of historical criticism to save the phenomena at any cost. Although, as Hans Frei has demonstrated, this interest may be traced to the failure of post Enlightenment Protestant theology to differentiate history-likeness from history, or meaning from historical truth, the hypothesis advanced has more in common with precritical efforts to define the relationship between the two testaments than is commonly supposed. For orthodox Christian commentators, Old and New Testament, whatever their relative merits, were the two parts of a determined canon whose unique authority, aside from Eastern debates over the Apocrypha, was virtually established from the time of Irenaeus. Canonicity was the starting point of biblical hermeneutics. The task of the theologian was to link the two parts of the canon together in a static bond, and to this end correspondences were observed or invented. Modern scholars construct a parallel to this situation when, from the flexible body of oral traditions, liturgical practices, and social alliances embedded in the New Testament, they hypostasize an original "kerygma," which functions hermeneutically much like a canonical text. In this way, the predicament of the New Testament authors comes to resemble the more familiar predicament of the established Church. Viewed through the correspondent lenses of the canonical spectacles, the earliest Christian exegetes seem also to be engaged in a labor of assimilation, selecting and interpreting likely Old Testament texts in accordance with an external principle.

This bias has been most evident in studies of the synoptic gospels. But it has colored the discussion of Paul's hermeneutics as well, where it has had the acknowledged effect of assimilating Pauline exegesis to early Christian (and Qumran) exegesis as a whole. Thus, D. Moody Smith, reviewing recent research on the use of the Old Testament in the New, can write of Paul's "conviction that the Old Testament finds its fulfillment in a new event or series of events which have occurred or are about to occur," and, further, that of the several heads under which Paul's relation to the Old Testament may be summarized the "first, and most important . . . is his general prophetic and kerygmatic understanding of the Old Testament as the precursor, prefiguration, and promise of the Gospel." Such a summary is only justified on the premise that in Paul the messianic proof-texts characteristic of the gospels are, as E. E. Ellis says, "presupposed," thus freeing the apostle to focus his attention on "the next step— the significance of the Scriptures for the Messianic Age and Messianic Community." In this way, the difference between Paul and the synoptic tradition is limited to a difference in topical emphasis, while the basic presupposition of Dodd, that the significance of the Jewish scriptures for Christianity was primarily descriptive or apologetic, remains intact. One recognizes its influence in the pragmatic views of Paul's hermeneutics set forth by critics as different as Willi Marxsen, who stresses that Paul never starts out from a scriptural text but rather uses scriptural references to clarify particular Christian messages—a method he characterizes as "implicitly apologetic"—and Barnabas Lindars, who goes so far as to assert that "the curse of the Law was an aspect of the Passion apologetic."

In sum, the majority of modern scholars have taken a nicely domesticated view of Paul's position. One might call this the Lukan view; for in the Book of Acts Paul too appears to resort to the allegedly fundamental practice of using biblical prophecy to explain the identity and significance of Jesus. We see him preaching the gospel according to scripture to the Jewish congregations in Antioch (13:16–41), Thessalonica (17:2f.), and Rome (28:23), as well as in his self-defense before Agrippa (26:22f.), developing correspondences between the messianic prophecies and the life of Jesus. However, appeals to scripture markedly similar in form are also ascribed to Peter (2:22–36), to Philip (8:30–35), and to the risen Christ (Luke 24:27, 44–47), suggesting that such testimonies are part of a literary pattern rather than a record of actual words or styles. (The fact that all the passages, except for Peter's, call special attention to the exegetical process itself may indicate that Luke was anxious to endow that method of reading on which his own gospel tradition depended with a legitimizing pedigree.) Moreover, when one examines Paul's own letters, one finds that despite the density of scriptural quotations—approximately one third of the New Testament total, mostly concentrated in the four *Hauptbriefe*—not one is ever used as testimony to establish the identity of Jesus. This holds even if one includes, in addition to overt citations, general allusions to Old Testament episodes or themes and the many formulaic appeals to scriptural authority. The two apparent exceptions, 1 Cor. 15:3–5 and Rom. 1:3f., both occur in the context of creedal summaries adopted from common liturgical tradition. The use of fulfillment words, such as the verb *pleroun* so prevalent in Acts and elsewhere, to connect biblical prophecy with a more recent event is likewise uncharacteristic.

The fact is, Paul's writing gives little indication that he concerned himself at all with the events of Jesus' life. What we today might call the question of facticity had for him a subtler consequence, hinted, for example, in Gal. 2:19f., where the conviction that Jesus was actually crucified according to the law is the implicit premise behind the claim that his own death to the law is a revitalization. For Paul, the given belief in a crucified messiah was the *punctum stans* from which to project that otherwise groundless series of dia-lectical revisions (power in weakness, wisdom in folly, life in death, fulfillment in abrogation) of which his hermeneutics are an integral part. One thus searches in vain through the extant letters for a literal or historical apologetics. It is from his soteriology that his Christology has largely to be inferred, and evidence for the specific influence of biblical prophecy is purely conjectural.

THE AUTHORITY OF SCRIPTURE

Paul most often appeals to the authority of scripture to reinforce ethical precepts or to adjudicate specific questions of personal conduct and church policy (Rom. 13:9f., 14:11; 1 Cor. 5:13, 9:9; 2 Cor. 8:15, 9:9; and elsewhere). Such parenetic uses, while suggesting that Paul continued to recognize the law's directive or regulatory function, have a limited bearing on the question of the deeper relationship between the two testaments. However, a few of them demonstrate a peculiar reversal, by which the text, though cited as authoritative, seems to owe its significance not to its own intrinsic merit but to something in the situation of the interpreter. These passages, though not unprecedented in first-century Jewish exegesis, reveal features of the more original orientation that governs Paul's attitude toward scripture as a whole. The best example is Paul's parenetic use of aspects of the exodus tradition in 1 Cor. 10:1–11 to admonish his readers against backsliding and moral laxity: "I want you to know, brethren, that our fathers were all under the cloud, and all passed through the sea, and all were baptized into Moses in the cloud and the sea, and all ate the same supernatural food and all drank the same supernatural drink. For they drank from the supernatural Rock which followed them, and the Rock was Christ. Nevertheless with most of them God was not pleased; for they were overthrown in the wilderness." Paul's identification of the rock with Christ subordinates the scriptural text to a group of midrashic traditions, including perhaps the "rejected stone" tradition of the early Church. More centrally, the Israelites, "baptized into Moses" but still liable to destruction, are important only insofar as readers of scripture are capable of seeing in their predicament a prefiguration of their own situation: "Now these things are warnings to us, not to desire evil as they did. Do not be idolaters as some of them were; as it is written, 'The people sat down to eat and drink and rose up to dance.' We must not indulge in immorality as some of them did, and twenty-three thousand fell in a single day. We must not put the Lord to the test, as some of them did and were destroyed by serpents; nor grumble, as some of them did and were destroyed by the Destroyer. Now these things happened to them as a warning, but they were written down for our instruction, upon whom the end of the ages has come."

Here then it is the special understanding of the interpreter that determines the significance of the text, which only assumes its exemplary or prescriptive role by virtue of that understanding (cf. Rom. 15:4; 4:23f.). As with the Qumran sectarians, the eschatology highlighted in the final phrase emphasizes the communal or ecclesiastical dimension in opposition to the realized eschatology of the "spirituals." But it is hard to see how such reasoned convictions affect the interpretive act itself. Paul does not simply interpret the exodus events as instructive examples to Christians. He suggests, more boldly than the *pesharim* or their New Testament counterparts, that the biblical events were recorded in written form for the specific purpose of eliciting the interpretation he gives them: that insofar as they are scripture, they originated "as a warning," the principal meaning and interest of which lay in its anticipatory quality.

The word translated "warning" in the [Revised Standard Version] is *tupos* in Greek, and it is this passage together with Rom. 5:14 that has given Paul his reputation as the originator of typological interpretation. (The same word, which derives ultimately from the verb *tuptein* meaning "to strike," also occurs with its ordinary meaning of "example" or "standard" elsewhere in the letters.) In the classic definition of Erich Auerbach, a typological or figural interpretation "establishes a connection between two events or persons, the first of which signifies not only itself but also the second, while the second encompasses or fulfills the first." This connection is a dialectical one, involving a strong negative contrast between type and antitype, which Gerhard von Rad has aptly designated the "element of supersession" (cf. Eichrodt in Westermann). Since the precursor is asserted to be less substantial than the successor, the "fulfillment" of the Old Testament text may be said to entail its simultaneous annulment. Auerbach exaggerates the case when he writes that Paul's use of typology "intended to strip the Old Testament of its normative character and show that it is merely a shadow of things to come." The rebuke to the "spirituals" in 1 Cor. 4:6 (*mē huper ha gegraptai*), for example, preserves the premise of scriptural authority without which vital response would have slipped into solipsism. But the patent effect of the antitype was to narrow the social and spiritual order within which the normative character of scripture continued to obtain.

It is common to present Pauline typology in contrast with its Philonic counterpart. When Justin Martyr writes that the brazen serpent raised on a pole (Num. 21:9) is a type of Christ, for example, he is held to be interpreting in the Pauline or Palestinian tradition (*Trypho* 112). When his contemporary Theophilus of Antioch writes that the three days of creation preceding the appearance of the sun and stars are "types of the trinity, god, his word, and his wisdom," he is said to be using a Philonic or Alexandrian kind of typology, otherwise known as allegory (*Autol.* 2.15). Definitions of the two are legion. To continue with Auerbach: "The two poles of the figure are separate in time, but both, being real events or figures are within time, within the stream of historical life. . . . Since one thing represents and signifies the other [typological] interpretation is 'allegorical' in the widest sense. But it differs from most of the allegorical forms known to us by the historicity both of the sign and what it signifies." One may appreciate this difference by comparing Paul's identification of the rock of Massah with Christ, and Philo's interpretation of the rock as a symbol of divine wisdom (*Leg. alleg.* 2.86; cf. Wis. 11.4). In Paul's reading, there is a radical actualization, a drastic evacuation of the past into the present, which "strikes" indirectly at the priority, and hence the authority, of the scriptural text. In Philo, on the other hand, the temporal dimension is irrelevant, and, as a result, the antithetical impulse is of a less aggressive order. Whereas the Platonic dialectic which lies behind allegorical reading is cognitive (to use the vocabulary of William Hamilton), the Pauline dialectic is conative. Thus, for Philo, the discovery of the hidden meaning of the rock is an end in itself, while Paul, having appropriated the scriptural figure, incorporates it as part of a dramatic sequence in which he and his contemporaries are the ultimate term.

Revisionary correspondences of this order do not originate with the New Testament. Repeated breaks characterize the whole history of Yahwism, and one can trace the revolution of patterns and motifs that recapitulate earlier traditions without dissolving their historical status at almost every stage in the development of the biblical text. This is especially true of the prophets, who were consciously looking for a new David, a new exodus, a new covenant, and a new city of God. To Hosea, for example, the intimacy of the early wilderness period foreshadowed Israel's final union with Yahweh (2:14–23), while to Second Isaiah, the exodus from Egypt, the covenant with Noah, and the foundation of Zion all appeared as types of Israel's ultimate redemption. For the Hebrew writers, no less than for Paul, the second term of these analogies was meant to supersede the first. A prophecy of the new exodus in Second Isaiah provides the most dramatic illustration, with its injunction to "remember not the former things nor consider the things of old" directly preceding its announcement of the "new thing" (43:18f. – a passage that in its entirety may have inspired the Pauline doctrine of a "new creation" [2 Cor. 5:17; Gal. 6:15]).

Even here, however, one must recognize that the prophetic oracle refers to a *future* act of Yahweh, a work he is on the point of inaugurating, rather than to an actual consummation. This future orientation is generally characteristic of the Hebrew Bible, where fulfillments are constantly being postponed or sublated into ever more figurative promises. Accordingly, a contrast may be drawn between Old Testament typology, which continues to direct the reader's expectations toward a continually receding future—"into the void" as Karl Barth has put it—and Christian typology, in which the act of fulfillment will already have been accomplished.

From one point of view, such "actualized" typology is more ambiguous than its Old Testament prototype; for while its antithetical potential remains appreciable, it may also serve (in fact, most often serves) to establish continuities, as in the apologetic writings of the church fathers. The New Testament writers themselves all maintain the tension between these two possibilities (continuity and discontinuity). But just as Matthew, embellishing his picture of Jesus as a second Moses, leans to one side of the balance, so Paul, with his concern for the situation of the interpreter, leans sharply to the other. Since both make use of temporally grounded correspondences, the difference is less a matter of practice than of intention. Matthew's principal concern is the identity of Jesus; hence, he remains attached to the content of scripture. In Paul's letters on the other hand, not the kerygma but the interpreter is the primary focus, and the attitude toward scripture is therefore more aggressive.

Otherwise stated, for Paul interpretation is first and foremost an occasion for the exercise of "Christian freedom" or *exousia*—that ambiguous catchword whose root means "being" and whose English equivalents include "license" and "autonomy" as well as "authority" and "power." Paul's concern with autonomy operates at various levels. It shows itself most obviously in his polemical and ecclesiastical activity, leading him to disclaim emphatically any connection with the hierarchy of the Jerusalem church, and perhaps determining his denial in Gal. 1:22 that he was known by sight to the churches of Judaea. At a more personal level, it stimulated his impatience with the attitude, if not the practices, of contemporary Jewish exegesis, which had made the cessation of direct revelation the implicit foundation for its "hedge about the torah" (Aboth 1.1). In contrast to the rabbis, Paul saw himself as carrying on the prophetic line, proclaiming to a generation engrossed in religious conventions and intimidated by its own past that divine intervention was a current reality. Accordingly, he speaks of being "set apart" before birth (Gal. 1:15; cf. Isa. 49:1; Jer. 1:5), and compares himself to Moses, the archetypal prophet (2 Cor. 3:7ff.; Rom. 9:3, 10:1), and to David, the author of the Psalms (2 Cor. 4:13). But at the level that concerns us here, Paul's impulse toward spiritual autonomy prompted a deep ambivalence toward the Bible itself, making him not an apologist— dependent on scripture for legitimating testimony—but a dogmatist—affirming the priority of his own conceptions by imposing them on the earlier tradition. Like Jesus, according to the testimony of Mark, he wished to teach *hōs exousian echōn*, "as one who had authority, and not as the scribes" (1:22).

EXOUSIA AND INTERPRETATION

Paul employs the word *exousia* repeatedly in elaborating his theory of Christian conduct, and, though he never uses it in a hermeneutic context, his most explicit discussion of scriptural interpretation insists on the importance of freedom (*eleutheria*) as a concomitant of spiritual understanding (2 Cor. 3:17). Significantly, this discussion begins with Paul's attempt to authenticate his own authority: "For we are not, like so many, peddlers of God's word; but as men of sincerity, as commissioned by God, in the sight of God we speak in Christ. . . . Not that we are competent of ourselves to claim anything as coming from us; our competence is from God, who has made us competent to be ministers of a new covenant, not in a written code but in the Spirit; for the written code kills, but the Spirit gives life" (2 Cor. 2:17; 3:5f.). Despite the subtle disclaimer in 3:5a (cf. Phil. 3:9), this position is tantamount to a proclamation of autonomy; for the direct commission from God frees the apostle from acknowledging any lesser power, including, as it turns out, the power of sacred scripture (cf. Gal. 1:11f.). This becomes clearer in the sequel, where the declaration of competence provides the ground for Paul's elaboration of a distinctive theory of interpretation, geared to the recipients of the "new covenant."

The idea of a new covenant is a prominent motif in the Hebrew Bible itself. It appears most notably in Jeremiah, where its antithetical implications are already developed: "Behold, the days are coming, says the Lord, when I will make a new covenant with the house of Israel and the house of Judah, not like the covenant which I made with their fathers when I took them by the hand to bring them out of the land of Egypt, my covenant which they broke, though I was their husband, says the Lord. But this is the covenant which I will make with the house of Israel after those days, says the Lord: I will put my law within them, and I will write it upon their hearts; and I will be their God, and they shall be my people" (31:31–33). The point here is not that the content of the Sinai covenant is to be nullified, but rather that the manner in which it is apprehended is to change (cf. 24:7; 32:39f.). The same position is taken by Ezekiel when he opposes the "heart of flesh" to the "heart of stone" and makes inspired understanding the sign of divine acceptance (36:26f.; cf. 11;19f.). Thus, in the major prophets, the dynamics of supersession are already asserted within a hermeneutic context.

Paul puts this tradition to an extremely personal (and, it may seem, whimsical or reductive) use when he writes to the Corinthians that, although he has presented no apostolic credentials, they themselves are his "letter of recommendation" (perhaps because Paul has converted them to Christianity, perhaps because he has continued to care for them affectionately), "written not with ink but with the Spirit of the living God, not on tablets of stone but on tablets of human hearts" (3:3). In introducing the scriptural allusion, Paul writes, as a rhetorician might, to embellish his claim of competence. But the prophetic text, once invoked, continues to haunt him, and within three lines he returns to confront it via the "new covenant" of which he has been qualified by God to be a minister. "Not in the written code but in the spirit," he adds, rounding out the "letter of recommendation" figure; for authenticity can never be bound to a determined tenor. On the contrary, it is a self-accrediting power that only subsists by constant revision, and its manifestations are ever evolving "from one degree of glory to another" (3:18).

The Hebrew Bible contains a variety of covenant traditions, but theologically they can be divided into two principal types. On the one hand, there is the Davidic–Abrahamic tradition, in which Yahweh promises to bless his people but no reciprocal obligation is imposed. On the other hand, there are the covenants at Sinai and Shechem, in which Israel commits itself to adhere strictly to the conditions set forth by Yahweh. George E. Mendenhall has spoken of the new covenant in Jeremiah, with its emphasis on divine forgiveness, as a product of the amalgamation of these two traditions. Israel had broken its covenant obligations according to the Mosaic tradition, and so forfeited its right to protection; according to the Abrahamic tradition, however, Yahweh's protection was inalienable. The renewal of the covenant in such a manner was to eliminate the danger of disobedience satisfied both allegations. Where Jeremiah harmonizes the two traditions, Paul's procedure, however, is to set them at odds. One observes this most readily in Galatians 3 and 4, where the more remote covenant of grace—likened to Sarah, bearing children for freedom—is adduced in subversion of the more immediate Mosaic law—likened to Hagar, "bearing children for slavery." In 2 Corinthians, the same subversive procedure is working, but here no positive model from scripture is proposed. Rather, the "emphasis upon direct responsibility to God, upon freedom and self-determination," which Mendenhall finds characteristic of the Abrahamic covenant tradition, is appropriated to a new "dispensation of righteousness" which prevails in despite of all written authority. Paul's revisionary strategy is thus twofold: he factors the scriptural tradition and uses one part of it to discredit the other; and he presents the remaining benefits as exclusive prerogatives of his new life in Christ. In addition, of course, he revises the covenant's temporal status: what was prophecy in Jeremiah is actuality in Paul.

The fact that in the Galatians passage Paul's concern is clearly with the law as commandment or demand, and that the authority of scripture as such is hardly questioned, raises the possibility that his polemic against the "written code" in 2 Corinthians is of more limited application than I have been arguing. A correlation between *gramma* and a more strictly theological sense of *nomos* appears for example in Rom. 7:6: "But now we are discharged from the law, dead to that which held us captive, so that we serve not under the old written code but in the new life of the Spirit." The meanings of "the law" in Paul's writings is too large a question to treat adequately here. As the Greek translation of *torah*, however, *nomos* was at least potentially synonymous with the Bible as a whole, and this is obviously the sense it is intended to have in Rom. 3:19, where the passages from the prophets and psalms quoted in the preceding verses are regarded jointly as *nomos*. Presumably the "old covenant" of which Paul speaks in 2 Cor. 3:14 also has this meaning (cf. Mekilta Pisha 5, "By covenant is meant nothing else but the Torah"). Moreover, just as Paul implicitly acknowledges the authority of scripture in passages where the motivation of the interpreter is not in question, so he can refer to the law as "holy" and "spiritual" (Rom. 7:12, 14) apart from its oppressive effect on those who serve it. As E. E. Ellis writes, "*Graphē* and *nomos* both signify for Paul the revealed will of God. But the law understood as a legal system apart from Christ could only bring death; so also the whole Old Testament understood and applied without the illumination of the *pneuma* often resulted not in *graphē* but only in *gramma*. . . . The issue of the Law versus Christ here passed into Paul's understanding of the nature of Scripture itself." Freedom from the law as command and freedom from the law as text are finally interchangeable for Paul, because both are metonymic on a kind of freedom that has no identifiable locus in rational or sensual experience. Its locus is the gospel—something unknown and inconceivable—whose content is either the dramatic paradox of the messiah crucified or the subtler enigma of its own proclamation. Whether the negative term in Paul's antitheses appears to have a legal or a hermeneutic referent is thus a matter of relative indifference. An emphasis on the law as command would, Paul felt, inevitably be accompanied by a transformation of writings (*graphē*) into a written code (*gramma*)—i.e., into a canonized, and therefore "petrified," order of compulsion. In this connection, Paul's attitude might be compared to that of Moses in the imaginative view of some early writers when, observing the idolatry of the Israelites, and recognizing that it would extend to the torah as well, he chose to shatter the tablets, thus initiating the process that culminated in the "tablets of the heart."

Paul's own "shattering," however, as appears from his elaboration of the letter-spirit antithesis in the chapter we have been discussing, involves an active depreciation of Moses foreign to the apologetic reading of his successors: "Now if the dispensation of death, carved in letters on stone, came with such splendor that the Israelites could not look at Moses' face because of its brightness, fading as this was, will not the dispensation of the Spirit be attended with greater splendor?" (2 Cor. 3:7f.). At first appearance, this is a fairly straightforward contrast between the Mosaic law and the new covenant. "Carved in letters on stone" emphasizes the written, formulaic quality of the former and helps explain why it is a "dispensation of death" in opposition to the dynamic "dispensation of the Spirit." But the idea that the light shining in Moses' face, that is, the power and glory of the Mosaic writings, was a *fading* splendor is not found in the passage from Exodus to which Paul alludes (34:29–35). In fact, the prevailing Jewish interpretation insisted that Moses' face shone undiminished until his death.

Here then is an example of the kind of exegetical freedom Paul advocates; for his "competence" has allowed him willfully to revise the scriptural text, conforming it to his own antithetical purposes. This revision becomes the very core of Paul's argument in the following lines. It is, he admits, his own "hope" of a splendor that will outshine Moses' that makes him "very bold": "not like Moses, who put a veil over his face so that the Israelites might not see the end of the fading splendor. But their minds were hardened; for to this day, when they read the old covenant, that same veil remains unlifted, because only through Christ is it taken away" (3:13f.). In the Priestly account of the descent from Sinai which underlies this passage, Moses assumes the veil not because his glory is fading but because it is too awesome for the Israelites to face. The veil is analogous in this respect to the veil set up in the tabernacle, as in Solomon's temple, to screen off the holy of holies (Exod. 26:31–33; 40:21), or the wings of the guardian cherubim which overshadow the mercy seat on top of the ark itself (25:18–22). It is the condition of Yahweh's self-revelation to an impure or stiff-necked people, too mistrustful to embrace its covenanted role or realize the full meaning of its liberation. By its agency, the divine glory, of which Moses' glory is a reflection, is at the same time objectively present yet imperfectly accessible to generations that must still endure a wilderness wandering and, with one exception (Joshua; the high priest), perish in exile.

Paul allows a part of this idea to come through when he asserts a connection between the veil and the hardness of the Israelites. But the full meaning only resurfaces at the beginning of the next chapter, when it is no longer a question of the Mosaic code but of Paul's own gospel! These lines ostensibly mark the resumption of his self-defense against the rival apostles; but beneath this topical struggle for recognition, the engagement with Moses reaches its crisis: "Therefore, having this ministry by the mercy of God, we do not lose heart. We have renounced disgraceful, underhanded ways; we refuse to practice cunning or to tamper with God's word, but by the open statement of the truth we would commend ourselves to every man's conscience in the sight of God. And even if our gospel is veiled, it is veiled only to those who are perishing" (4:1-3). Again, the disclaimer is a warning; for what Paul has done is underhanded indeed. By claiming for his own gospel an attribute of the Mosaic code, he has appropriated to himself the glory of the scriptural tradition. He began, as we have seen, by introducing a distorted reading of that tradition so as to discredit Moses, but he concludes here by assuming its legitimate meaning, thus displacing the veiled splendor of the old covenant with the veiled "light of the gospel of the glory of Christ" (4:4).

Paul effects a similar reversal in Rom. 10:5ff., when he interprets the words of Moses' farewell address, "It is not in heaven. . . . But the word is very near you; it is in your mouth and in your heart" (Deut. 30:12-14), as a reference to Christ, "the word of faith which we preach." It is easy to confuse Paul's meaning here with the common early Christian view that Jesus was himself the "new torah" personified. But Paul knows Christ less conventionally, as an operant virtue rather than a hypostasized essence: as an imperative to actualizing exegesis ("Christ the evolver" in Coleridge's phrase) who also integrates the ego-centric into the representative "I"—the I "in Christ." As a result, the antitype of the old covenant for Paul is always the gospel, and the antitype of Moses, Paul himself.

When Christ appears as an antitype, it is in conjunction with Adam, "who was a type of the one who was to come" (Rom. 5:14). Though the typological relation remains temporal, the context here is more properly mythical than historical (cf. 1 Cor. 15:22, 45ff.). Paul's purpose is to convince us that grace will prevail over sin. "As [Adam's] trespass led to condemnation for all men, so [Christ's] act of righteousness leads to acquittal and life for all men" (Rom. 5:18). The supersessive element is made explicit in the three verses contrasting the free gift of righteousness with the "original" gratuitous trespass. Since it must overcome a resistance, the counteraction or revision is the stronger act (*pollō mallon*). Resistance, in this case, may be identified with the law, which functions as an agent of repression. Like the interpreter's text, law provides for the dialectical antithesis, without which supersession would be mere repetition. Its power is potentially stifling, but since Christ, as the antitype, is "prior" to Adam, its final effect is an intensification: "Law came in, to increase the trespass; but where sin increased, grace abounded all the more" (5:20).

THE PROSPECTIVE STANCE

Typology, as Harold Bloom has recognized in *Poetry and Repression*, is a revisionary mode, which works by making the later perpetually earlier than its predecessors. (One might say that in typology the later text becomes the cause [*aitia*] of the earlier text's subsistence.) If one is willing to use the terminology adapted after Quintilian, it can be defined more narrowly as a form of transumption or *metalepsis*, from the "trope-reversing trope," in which "a word is substituted metonymically for a word in a previous trope. . . . Metalepsis leaps over the heads of other tropes and becomes a representation set against time, sacrificing the present to an idealized past or hoped-for-future." "Properly accomplished, this stance figuratively produces the illusion of having fathered one's own fathers, which is the greatest illusion, the one that Vico called 'divination,' or that we could call poetic immortality." Bloom goes on to insist that the New Testament lacks such a stance in regard to the Old. But as our whole discussion has suggested, the contrary is patently the case, at least so far as Paul is concerned. According to Bloom's own definition in the same essay, "the scheme of transumption . . . demands a juxtaposition of three times; a true one that was and will be . . . ; a less true one that never was . . . ; and the present moment, which is emptied out of everything but the experiential darkness against which the poet-prophet struggles." In Milton's description of the Chariot of Paternal Deitie in book 6 of *Paradise Lost*, which Bloom cites as an example, these times are respectively occupied (1) by the ultimately primary texts in Ezekiel and Revelation, which *Paradise Lost* contrives to rival as a result of the transumption; (2) by the antecedent texts of Virgil, Dante, and Petrarch, which Milton overleaps; and (3) by the allusion to Milton's own self-portrait as "the invincible warriour Zeale" riding "over the heads of Scarlet Prelats" in his *An Apology Against a Pamphlet*. Since Paul is a theoretician rather than a poet, the correlative instances from his writings are overt rather than allusive. In the case of the Romans passage just discussed, they could be enumerated as follows: (1) Adam unfallen, which is the moment of creation with which fallen mankind is reconciled as a result of the transumptive stance (the "true" time "that was and will be"); (2) Adam fallen, or the Old Testament history, ending in Christ crucified (the "less true one that never was"); and (3) the "all men" represented by Paul himself as he is "buried" and "crucified" with Christ (Rom. 6:4, 6) (the "present moment" of strife and "experiential darkness"). To reiterate, Paul is not concerned here with who Christ is, but with what Christ does. He is "the one who was to come," and what he does (overleaping his own death) makes what he is a continual possibility.

It is an axiom of revisionary criticism that "a creative interpretation is . . . necessarily a misinterpretation." Such deliberate misreadings arise, according to Bloom, "out of the illusion of freedom, out of a sense of priority being possible." The torah, as the dominant literary influence on Paul's thinking, had to be challenged if Paul was to realize the autonomy he desired; for it was at least partly the experience of its mediating power that had awakened his own yearning for an unmediated covenant. Of course, such a situation was finally an impossible one, as Paul well understood. No matter how boldly he proclaimed his "new creation," its presence had always to remain a lie since it could never relieve him from the burden of indebtedness to its own scriptural sources. Yet in contempt of all logic, Paul continued to brave the verdict of reprobation, announcing his ministry to be greater than that of his precursors, as if the spiritual freedom of which he boasted could be gained by sheer strength of desire. It was a defiant and precarious stance, whether one calls it hermeneutic heroism, or more poetically holy folly.

Paul never ceases to revere the Jewish scriptures, but he maintains that to read them in a vitalizing rather than a stupefying fashion one has need of a special dispensation. This dispensation is inseparable from the prospective stance toward revelation which Paul affirms in his letter to the Philippians, "forgetting what lies behind and straining forward to what lies ahead" (3:13). His subordination of scripture to its "spiritual" understanding thus implies a profound conviction that what matters most is not the conclusion or content of the interpretation, but the occurrence of the interpretive act itself. "Although the history of the nation and the world has lost interest for Paul," writes Bultmann, "he brings to light another phenomenon, the historicity of man." "Historicity" here carries the existential conviction that man creates his own essence through his personal acts — acts which are necessarily incursions against his own past. The act of interpretation does not exhaust or define this self-creation, but it epitomizes it more perspicuously than most kinds of activity; since in interpretation the "past" takes the form of a recognizable text and need not be retrieved from a chaos of unannealed events and impressions.

Before this monumental past, those who would study interpretation with Paul are faced with two options: they can apprehend and vindicate his readings, or they can emulate his method. Most common expositors take the former path. They accept Christ, the *content* of Paul's revision, as a given and follow his directive to read the Old Testament by the light of the New. There are some, however, who would prefer to take Paul's *act* or attitude as authoritative. They would know the "dispensation of the spirit" as a straining toward freedom, knowing that this always involves a struggle against one's own patrimony in the deepest sense — "the inevitable struggle," to use Barth's words, "of revelation against the religion of revelation." Within the temporal framework that the Bible insists on, they would recognize that the content of the gospel is never fixed. Something like this stance has been implicit in the biblical interpretation of such sects as the Montanists and the Spiritual Franciscans, but for the most part their insights have been intermixed with a tendency toward historical literalism. For the true disciples of Paul on this second path, one should rather turn to the poets, in whose hands an interpretation, as one poet reminds us, is always "a horde of destructions."

D. H. LAWRENCE

Apocalypse

W hen you start to teach individual self-realisation to the great masses of people, who when all is said and done are only *fragmentary* beings, *incapable* of whole individuality, you end by making them all envious, grudging, spiteful creatures. Anyone who is kind to man knows the fragmentariness of most men, and wants to arrange a society of power in which men fall naturally into a collective wholeness, since they *cannot* have an individual wholeness. In this collective wholeness they will be fulfilled. But if they make efforts at individual fulfilment, they *must fail* for they are by nature fragmentary. Then, failures, having no wholeness anywhere, they fall into envy and spite. Jesus knew all about it when he said: To them that have shall be given, etc. But he had forgotten to reckon with the mass of the mediocre, whose motto is: We have nothing and therefore nobody shall have anything.

But Jesus gave the ideal for the Christian individual, and deliberately avoided giving an ideal for the State or the nation. When he said, "Render unto Caesar that which is Caesar's," he left to Caesar the rule of men's bodies, willy-nilly: and this threatened terrible danger to a man's mind and soul. Already by the year 60 A.D. the Christians were an accursed sect; and they were compelled, like all men, to sacrifice, that is to give worship to the living Caesar. In giving Caesar the power over men's bodies, Jesus gave him the power to compel men to make the act of worship to Caesar. Now I doubt if Jesus himself could have performed this act of worship, to a Nero or a Domitian. No doubt he would have preferred death. As did so many early Christian martyrs. So there, at the very beginning was a monstrous dilemma. To be a Christian meant death at the hands of the Roman State; for refusal to submit to the cult of

From *Apocalypse.* © 1931 by the Estate of David Herbert Lawrence, renewed 1960, 1966 by Viking Press, Inc. Viking Press, 1966.

the Emperor and worship the divine man, Caesar, was impossible to a Christian. No wonder, then, that John of Patmos saw the day not far off when *every* Christian would be martyred. The day would have come, if the imperial cult had been absolutely enforced on the people. And then when *every* Christian was martyred, what could a Christian expect but a Second Advent, resurrection, and an absolute revenge! There was a condition for the Christian community to be in, sixty years after the death of the Saviour.

Jesus made it inevitable, when he said that the money belonged to Caesar. It was a mistake. Money means bread, and the bread of men belongs to no men. Money means also power, and it is monstrous to give power to the virtual enemy. Caesar was *bound*, sooner or later, to violate the soul of the Christians. But Jesus saw the individual only, and considered only the individual. He left it to John of Patmos, who was up against the Roman State, to formulate the Christian vision of the Christian State. John did it in the Apocalypse. It entails the destruction of the whole world, and the reign of saints in ultimate bodiless glory. Or it entails the destruction of all earthly power, and the rule of an oligarchy of martyrs (the Millennium).

This destruction of all earthly power we are now moving towards. The oligarchy of martyrs began with Lenin, and apparently others also are martyrs. Strange, strange people they are, the martyrs, with weird, cold morality. When every country has its martyr-ruler, either like Lenin or like those, what a strange, unthinkable world it will be! But it is coming: the Apocalypse is still a book to conjure with.

A few vastly important points have been missed by Christian doctrine and Christian thought. Christian fantasy alone has grasped them.

1. No man is or can be a pure individual. The mass of men have only the tiniest touch of individuality: if any. The mass of men live and move, think and feel collectively, and have practically no individual emotions, feelings or thoughts at all. They are fragments of the collective or social consciousness. It has always been so. And will always be so.

2. The State, or what we call Society as a collective whole *cannot* have the psychology of an individual. Also it is a mistake to say that the State is made up of individuals. It is not. It is made up of a collection of fragmentary beings. And *no* collective act, even so private an act as voting, is made from the individual self. It is made from the collective self, and has another psychological background, non-individual.

3. The State *cannot* be Christian. Every State is a Power. It cannot be otherwise. Every State must guard its own boundaries and guard its own prosperity. If it fails to do so, it betrays all its individual citizens.

4. Every *citizen* is a unit of worldly power. A *man* may wish to be a pure Christian and a pure individual. But since he *must* be a member of some political

State, or nation, he is forced to be a unit of worldly power.

5. As a citizen, as a collective being, man has his fulfilment in the gratification of his powersense. If he belongs to one of the so-called "ruling nations," his soul is fulfilled in the sense of his country's power or strength. If his country mounts up aristocratically to a zenith of splendour and power, in a hierarchy, he will be all the more fulfilled, having his place in the hierarchy. But if his country is powerful and democratic, then he will be obsessed with a perpetual will to assert his power in interfering and *preventing* other people from doing as they wish, since no man must do more than another man. This is the condition of modern democracies, a condition of perpetual bullying.

In democracy, bullying inevitably takes the place of power. Bullying is the negative form of power. The modern Christian State is a soul-destroying force, for it is made up of fragments which have no organic whole, only a collective whole. In a hierarchy each part is organic and vital, as my finger is an organic and vital part of me. But a democracy is bound in the end to be obscene, for it is composed of myriad disunited fragments, each fragment assuming to itself a false wholeness, a false individuality. Modern democracy is made up of millions of frictional parts all asserting their own wholeness.

6. To have an ideal for the individual which regards only his individual self and ignores his collective self is in the long run fatal. To have a creed of individuality which denies the reality of the hierarchy makes at last for more anarchy. Democratic man lives by cohesion and resistance, the cohesive force of "love" and the resistant force of the individual "freedom." To yield entirely to love would be to be absorbed, which is the death of the individual: for the individual must hold his own, or he ceases to be "free" and individual. So that we see, what our age has proved to its astonishment and dismay, that the individual *cannot* love. The individual cannot love: let that be an axiom. And the modern man or woman *cannot* conceive of himself, herself, save as an individual. And the individual in man or woman is *bound* to kill, at last, the lover in himself or herself. It is not that each man kills the thing he loves, but that each man, by insisting on his own individuality, kills the lover in himself, as the woman kills the lover in herself. The Christian *dare not love*: for love kills that which is Christian, democratic, and modern, the individual. The individual *cannot* love. When the individual loves, he ceases to be purely individual. And so he *must* recover himself, and cease to love. It is one of the most amazing lessons of our day: that the individual, the Christian, the democrat *cannot love*. Or, when he loves, when she loves, he *must* take it back, she *must* take it back.

So much for private or personal love. Then what about that other love, "caritas," loving your neighbour as yourself?

It works out the same. You love your neighbour. Immediately you run the risk of being absorbed by him: you must draw back, you must hold your own. The love becomes resistance. In the end, it is all resistance and no love: which is the history of democracy.

If you are taking the path of individual self-realisation, you had better, like Buddha, go off and be by yourself, and give a thought to nobody. Then you may achieve your Nirvana. Christ's way of loving your neighbour leads to the hideous anomaly of having to live by sheer resistance to your neighbour, in the end.

The Apocalypse, strange book, makes this clear. It shows us the Christian in his relation to the State; which the gospels and epistles avoid doing. It shows us the Christian in relation to the State, to the world, and to the cosmos. It shows him in mad hostility to all of them, having, in the end, to will the destruction of them all.

It is the dark side of Christianity, of individualism, and of democracy, the side the world at large now shows us. And it is, simply, suicide. Suicide individual and *en masse*. If man could will it, it would be cosmic suicide. But the cosmos is not at man's mercy, and the sun will not perish to please us.

We do not want to perish, either. We have to give up a false position. Let us give up our false position as Christians, as individuals, as democrats. Let us find some conception of ourselves that will allow us to be peaceful and happy, instead of tormented and unhappy.

The Apocalypse shows us what we are resisting, unnaturally. We are unnaturally resisting our connection with the cosmos, with the world, with mankind, with the nation, with the family. All these connections are, in the Apocalypse, anathema, and they are anathema to us. We *cannot bear connection*. That is our malady. We *must* break away, and be isolate. We call that being free, being individual. Beyond a certain point, which we have reached, it is suicide. Perhaps we have chosen suicide. Well and good. The Apocalypse too chose suicide, with subsequent self-glorification.

But the Apocalypse shows, by its very resistance, the things that the human heart secretly yearns after. By the very frenzy with which the Apocalypse destroys the sun and the stars, the world, and all kings and all rulers, all scarlet and purple and cinnamon, all harlots, finally all men altogether who are not "sealed," we can see how deeply the apocalyptists are yearning for the sun and the stars and the earth and the waters of the earth, for nobility and lordship and might, and scarlet and gold splendour, for passionate love, and a proper unison with men, apart from this sealing business. What man most passionately wants is his living wholeness and his living unison, not his own isolate salvation of his "soul." Man wants his physical fulfilment first and foremost, since now, once and once only, he is in the flesh and potent. For man, the vast marvel is to be alive. For man, as for flower and beast and bird, the supreme triumph is to be most vividly, most perfectly alive. Whatever the unborn and the dead may know, they cannot know the beauty, the marvel of being alive in the flesh. The dead may look after the afterwards. But the magnificent here and now of life in the flesh is ours, and ours alone, and ours only for a time. We ought to dance with rapture that we should be alive and in the flesh, and part of the living, incarnate cosmos. I am part of the sun as my eye is part of me. That I am part of the earth my feet know perfectly, and my blood is part of the sea. My soul knows that I am part of the human race, my soul is an organic part of the great human soul, as my spirit is part of my nation. In my own very self, I am part of my family. There is nothing of me that is alone and absolute except my mind, and we shall find that the mind has no existence by itself, it is only the glitter of the sun on the surface of the waters.

So that my individualism is really an illusion. I am a part of the great whole, and I can never escape. But I *can* deny my connections, break them, and become a fragment. Then I am wretched.

What we want is to destroy our false, inorganic connections, especially those related to money, and re-establish the living organic connections, with the cosmos, the sun and earth, with mankind and nation and family. Start with the sun, and the rest will slowly, slowly happen.

Chronology

TEXTUAL

HISTORICAL

?   The Creation and the Flood

1800 B.C.   The Patriarchs and the Sojourn in Egypt (c. 1800–1250)

1700 B.C.

1600 B.C.

1500 B.C.

1400 B.C.

1300 B.C.

1200 B.C.   The Exodus and the Conquest (c. 1250–1200)

Joshua (c. 1200–1150)

The Judges (c. 1150–1025)

1100 B.C.

1000 B.C.   The Monarchy (c. 1025–930)

The Two Kingdoms (c. 930–590)

The J Source (c. 950–900)

TEXTUAL		HISTORICAL
The E Source (c. 850–800)	900 B.C.	
	800 B.C.	
Amos, Proverbs 10–22:16 (c. 750)		The Fall of Samaria (c. 720)
Hosea (c. 725)		The Reformation of Josiah (c. 700–600)
Micah, Proverbs 25–29, Isaiah 1–31, JE redaction (c. 700)	700 B.C.	
Deuteronomy, Zephaniah (c. 650)		
Nahum, Proverbs 22:17–24 (c. 625)		
Deuteronomy-Kings (c. 600–500), Jeremiah, Habakkuk (c. 600)	600 B.C.	The Fall of Jerusalem and the Exile to Babylonia (c. 587–538)
Job 3–31, 38–42:6 (c. 575)		
Isaiah 40–55, Job 32–37 (c. 550)		
Isaiah 56–66, Jeremiah 46–52, Ezekiel 1–37, 40–48, Lamentations (c. 525)	500 B.C.	The Return (c. 538)
Job redaction, the P Source, Haggai, Zechariah 1–8, Jeremiah 30–31 (c. 500)		
Additions to Ezekiel 1–37, 40–48 (c. 475–400)		Nehemiah and Ezra (c. 475–350)
Joel, Malachi, Proverbs 30–31, Lists (c. 450)		
JEP redaction [Genesis–Numbers], Isaiah 32–35, Proverbs 1–9, Ruth, Obad (c. 425)		
JEPD redaction, Jonah, Psalms, Proverbs redaction Song of Songs, Chronicles, Ezra, Nehemiah (c. 400) Ecclesiastes (c. 350)	400 B.C.	
Zechariah 9–14 (c. 325)		The Hellenistic Period (c. 330–63)

TEXTUAL		HISTORICAL
Isaiah 24–27, Ezekiel 38–39 (c. 300) The Septuagint, a translation of the Hebrew Bible into Greek (c. 250–100)	300 B.C.	
	200 B.C.	
Daniel (c. 175)		The Maccabean Revolt (c. 165)
Esther (c. 100)	100 B.C.	Pompey takes Jerusalem (c. 63)
	10 B.C.	Birth of Christ (c. 6)
	B.C. ——— A.D.	
	A.D. 10	
	A.D. 20	Baptism of Christ and the beginning of John's Ministry (c. 26)
	A.D. 30	Crucifixion and resurrection of Christ and Pentecost (c. 30) Conversion of Paul (c. 32)
	A.D. 40	Martyrdom of James (c. 44) Paul and Barnabas visit Jerusalem during famine (c. 46)
Galatians (c. 49) Thessalonian Letters (c. 50)	A.D. 50	Paul's First Missionary Journey (c. 47–48) Paul's Second Missionary Journey (c. 49–52)

TEXTUAL		HISTORICAL
		Paul's Third Missionary Journey (c. 52–56)
Corinthian Letters (c. 53–55)		Paul is arrested in Jerusalem and is imprisoned
Romans (c. 56)		by Caesar (c. 56–58)
		Paul's voyage to Rome and shipwreck (c. 58)
		First Roman imprisonment of Paul (c. 59–60)
Philippians (c. 60)	A.D. 60	Paul's release and last travels (c. 61–63)
Colossians, Philemon (c. 61–62)		Paul's second Roman imprisonment,
		martyrdom, and death; death of Peter
		(c. 64–65)
Mark (65–67)		
	A.D. 70	Fall of Jerusalem (c. 70)
Matthew (75–80)	A.D. 80	
Canonization of the Hebrew Bible at Synod of Jamnia (c. 90)	A.D. 90	Persecutions under Emperor Domitian discussed
		in Revelation (c. 93–96)
Ephesians, Hebrews, Revelation, Luke, Acts (c. 95); 1 Peter	A.D. 100	
(c. 95–100), Fourth Gospel (c. 95–115)		
Johannine Epistles (c. 110–115)	A.D. 125	
James, Jude (c. 125–150)	A.D. 150	
2 Peter (c. 150)		
Timothy, Titus (c. 160–175)	A.D. 175	

TEXTUAL

Stabilization of the New Testament canon of twenty-seven books (c. 350–400)

Jerome completes the Latin Vulgate, a translation of the Bible based on the Septuagint and translated from the Hebrew (c. 400)

A.D. 200
A.D. 300

A.D. 400

A.D. 500
A.D. 600
A.D. 700
A.D. 800
A.D. 900
A.D. 1000
A.D. 1100
A.D. 1200
A.D. 1300

The first translation of the Bible into English, by John Wycliffe (c. 1382)

A.D. 1400

The Gutenberg Bible is printed from movable type, ushering in the new era of printing (1456)

A.D. 1500

Erasmus finishes a translation of the Bible into Greek (1516)
Martin Luther translates the Bible into German (1522)
William Tyndale and Miles Coverdale's English translations of the Bible (1535)

333

TEXTUAL

Matthew's Bible is produced, based on the Tyndale and
    Coverdale versions (1537)
The Great Bible is produced by Coverdale (1539)
The Geneva Bible, the first to separate chapters into verses (1560)
The Douay–Rheims Bible, a Catholic translation from Latin
    into English (1582–1610)
The King James Version is completed (1611)

A.D. 1600

A.D. 1700
A.D. 1800

The English Revised Version is coissued by English and
    American scholars (1885)

A.D. 1900

The American Standard Version (1901)
The Moffatt Bible (1924)
The Smith–Goodspeed Bible (1931)
The Confraternity Version, an Episcopal revision of the
    Douay–Rheims Bible (1941)
Knox's Version, based on the Latin Vulgate and authorized
    by the Catholic Church (1945–49)
The Revised Standard Version (1952)
The New English Bible, Protestant (1961)
The Jerusalem Bible, Catholic (1966)
The Modern Language Bible (1969)
The New American Bible, Catholic (1970)
Today's English Version (1976)
The New International Version (1978)
The New Jewish Version (1982)

Contributors

HAROLD BLOOM, Sterling Professor of the Humanities at Yale University, is the author of *The Anxiety of Influence, Poetry and Repression*, and many other volumes of literary criticism. His forthcoming study, *Freud: Transference and Authority*, attempts a full-scale reading of all of Freud's major writings. A MacArthur Prize Fellow, he is general editor of five series of literary criticism published by Chelsea House.

KENNETH BURKE is the author of such crucial works of theoretical and practical criticism as *Permanence and Change, Philosophy of Literary Form: Studies in Symbolic Action*, and *A Grammar of Motives*. He has taught at many American universities including Harvard, Princeton, and the University of Chicago.

ROBERT ALTER is Professor of Hebrew and Comparative Literature at the University of California, Berkeley. His books include *Defenses of the Imagination* and *Partial Magic: The Novel as a Self-Conscious Genre*.

ERICH AUERBACH was Sterling Professor of Romance Languages at Yale University. His highly acclaimed works of literary criticism include *Mimesis* and *Scenes from the Drama of European Literature*.

MEIR STERNBERG is Professor of Comparative Literature at Tel-Aviv University. He is the author of *Expositional Modes and Temporal Ordering in Fiction* and many studies in the Bible and literary theory.

ROLAND BARTHES was one of the most provocative French structuralists and a founder of the field of semiotics. Among his important critical studies are *Mythologies, S/Z*, and *The Pleasure of the Text*.

ROBERT POLZIN is Associate Professor of Religion at Carleton University in Ottawa, Canada. He is the author of *Biblical Structuralism, The Biblical Mosaic: Changing Perspectives*, and *The Late Biblical Hebrew*.

MARTIN BUBER is one of the most influential and prolific modern scholars of Judaism and the Hebrew Bible. His best known books include *Moses, Israel and Palestine,* and *The Prophetic Faith.*

ROBERT GORDIS, Seminary Professor of Bible at The Jewish Theological Seminary of America, is the author of *The Jew Faces a New World, Conservative Judaism, Judaism for the Modern Age,* and *The Root and the Branch.*

YEHOSHUA GITAY is Professor of Hebrew and of Bible Studies at Wesleyan University and the author of *Prophecy and Persuasion: A Study of Isaiah 40–48.*

GEOFFREY HARTMAN is Karl Young Professor of English and Comparative Literature at Yale University. His highly acclaimed critical works include *Saving the Text, Criticism in the Wilderness,* and *The Role of Reading.*

LEO STRAUSS was Robert Maynard Hutchins Distinguished Service Professor of Political Science at the University of Chicago. He is the author of *Persecution and the Art of Writing, What Is Political Philosophy?* and *The City and Man.*

DOUGLAS ROBINSON, Associate Professor of English Philology at the University of Tampere in Finland, is the author of *John Barth's Giles Goat-Boy: A Study.*

FRANK KERMODE was King Edward VII Professor of English Literature at Cambridge University, and is now Professor of English at Columbia University. His books include *The Classic, The Sense of an Ending,* and *The Genesis of Secrecy.*

NORTHROP FRYE is University Professor of English at the University of Toronto. His epochal books include *Fearful Symmetry: A Study of William Blake* and *Anatomy of Criticism.*

HERBERT MARKS teaches in the Comparative Literature Department at the University of Indiana, Bloomington. He is the author of an essay on Robert Frost in the Chelsea House *Modern Critical Views* series and is completing a book on representation in the Bible, Dante, and modern poetry.

D. H. LAWRENCE, the British writer best known for controversial novels like *The Rainbow* and *Women in Love,* was also a prolific poet, playwright, and essayist.

Bibliography

Alonzo Schokel, Luis. *The Inspired Word: Scripture and the Light of Language and Literature*. New York: Herder & Herder, 1965.

Alter, Robert. *The Art of Biblical Narrative*. New York: Basic Books, 1981.

———. *The Art of Biblical Poetry*. New York: Basic Books, 1985.

Arnold, Matthew. *God and the Bible: A Review of Objections to Literature and Dogma*. Repr. of 1875 ed. New York: AMS Press, 1975.

———. *Literature and Dogma: An Essay towards a Better Apprehension of the Bible*. Repr. of 1883 ed. New York: AMS Press, 1970.

Barr, J. *The Semantics of Biblical Language*. Oxford: Oxford University Press, 1961.

Barton, John. *Reading the Old Testament*. Philadelphia: Westminster Press, 1984.

Beardslee, William A. *Literary Criticism of the New Testament*. Philadelphia: Fortress Press, 1970.

Blenkinsopp, J. "Structure and Style in Judges 13–16." *Journal of Biblical Literature* 82 (1963): 72–73.

Brams, Steven J. *Biblical Games*. Cambridge: M.I.T. Press, 1980.

Brown, Norman O. *Love's Body*. New York: Vintage Press, 1968.

Burke, Kenneth. *The Rhetoric of Religion: Studies in Logology*. Berkeley: University of California Press, 1970.

Caird, G. B. *The Language and Imagery of the Bible*. Philadelphia: Westminster Press, 1980.

Campbell, Edward F., Jr. "The Hebrew Short Story: A Study of Ruth." In *"A Light unto My Path": Old Testament Studies in Honor of Jacob M. Myer*, edited by Howard N. Bream, et al. Philadelphia: Temple University Press, 1974.

Carmichael, Calum M. "A Ceremonial Crux: Removing a Man's Sandal as a Female Gesture of Contempt." *Journal of Biblical Literature* 96 (1977): 321–36.

Carmichael, Joel. *The Death of Jesus*. New York: The Macmillan Company, 1962.

Cassuto, Umberto. *A Commentary on the Book of Genesis*. Jerusalem: Magness Press, 1961.

Charity, A. C. *Events and Their Afterlife*. Cambridge: Cambridge University Press, 1966.

Chase, Mary Ellen. *Life and Language in the Old Testament*. New York: W. W. Norton & Company, 1955.

Culley, Robert. *Studies in the Structure of Hebrew Narrative*. Missoula, Mont.: Scholars Press, 1976.

Doty, William. "Linguistics and Biblical Criticism." *Journal of the American Academy of Religion* 41 (1973): 114–21.

Eissfeldt, Otto. *The Old Testament: An Introduction*. New York: Harper & Row, 1972.

Falk, Marcia. *Love Lyrics from the Bible: A Translation and Literary Study of the Song of Songs.* Sheffield, England: Almond Press, 1982.

Farrer, Austin. *A Rebirth of Images: The Making of St. John's Apocalypse.* Boston: Beacon Press, 1949.

Fox, Evereth. *In the Beginning.* New York: Schocken Books, 1983.

Frei, Hans W. *The Eclipse of Biblical Narrative.* New Haven: Yale University Press, 1974.

Frye, Northrop. *The Great Code: The Bible and Literature.* New York: Harcourt Brace Jovanovich, 1982.

Gardner, Helen. *Religion and Literature.* London: Faber & Faber, 1971.

Gitay, Yehoshua. *Prophecy and Persuasion.* Bonn: Linguistica Biblica, 1981.

Good, E. M. *Irony in the Old Testament.* Philadelphia: Westminster Press, 1965.

Gordis, Robert. *The Book of God and Man: A Study of Job.* Chicago: The University of Chicago Press, 1965.

——. *The Song of Songs and Lamentations: A Study, Modern Translation and Commentary.* New York: Ktav Publishing House, 1974.

Gottwald, Norman K. *The Hebrew Bible: A Socio-Literary Introduction.* Philadelphia: Fortress Press, 1985.

Gros-Louis, Kenneth R. R., ed. *Literary Interpretation of Biblical Narratives.* Nashville: Abingdon, 1982.

——. *Text and Texture: Close Readings of Selected Biblical Texts.* New York: Schocken Books, 1979.

Gunkel, Hermann. *The Legends of Genesis.* New York: Schocken Books, 1964.

Habel, Norman. *Literary Criticism of the Old Testament.* Philadelphia: Fortress Press, 1971.

Heidel, Alexander. *The Gilgamesh Epic and Old Testament Parallels.* Chicago: The University of Chicago Press, 1963.

Heiman, J., and S. Werses, eds. "Studies in Hebrew Narrative Art." *Scripta Heirosolymitana* 27 (1978): 9-26.

Henn, T. R. *The Bible as Literature.* New York: Oxford University Press, 1970.

Holbrook, Clyde A. *The Iconoclastic Deity.* London: Associated University Presses, 1984.

Kugel, James L. *The Idea of Biblical Poetry.* New Haven: Yale University Press, 1981.

——. "On the Bible as Literary Criticism." *Prooftexts* 1 (1981): 217-36.

Landy, Francis. *Paradoxes of Paradise: Identity and Difference in the Song of Songs.* Sheffield, England: Almond Press, 1983.

——. "The Song of Songs and the Garden of Eden." *Journal of Biblical Literature* 98 (1979): 513-28.

Leach, Edmund. "The Legitimacy of Solomon: Some Structural Aspects of Old Testament History." In *Introduction to Structuralism,* edited by Michael Lane. New York: Basic Books, 1970.

Licht, Jacob. *Storytelling in the Bible.* Jerusalem: Magness Press, 1978.

Long, Burke O. "Recent Field Studies in Oral Literature and Their Bearing on the Old Testament." *Vetus Testamentum* 26 (1976): 187-98.

McDonald, D. B. *The Hebrew Literary Genius.* Princeton: Princeton University Press, 1933.

McEvenue, Sean E. *The Narrative Style of the Priestly Writer.* Rome: Biblical Institute Press, 1971.

Miles, John. "Gagging on Job." *Semeia* 7 (1977): 71-126.

Moulton, R. G. *The Literary Study of the Bible.* Boston: D. C. Heath, 1895.

Muilenburg, James. "A Study in Hebrew Rhetoric: Repetition and Style." *Vetus Testamentum Supplement* 1 (1953): 97-111.

Nissim, Haviva. "On Analyzing the Biblical Story." *Hasifrut* 24 (1977): 136–43.

Patrides, C. A. *The Grand Design of God: The Literary Form of the Christian View of History.* London: Routledge, 1972.

Pfeiffer, Robert H. *Introduction to the Old Testament.* New York: Harper & Row, 1948.

Polzin, Robert M. *Biblical Structuralism.* Missoula, Mont.: Scholars Press, 1977.

———. *Moses and the Deuteronomist.* New York: Seabury, 1980.

Pope, Marvin H. *Song of Songs.* Garden City, N.Y.: Doubleday, 1977.

Price, Reynolds. *A Palpable God.* New York: Atheneum, 1978.

Radday, Yehuda T. "Chiasm in Joshua, Judges and Others." *Linguistica Biblica* 3 (1973): 7–9.

Rauber, D. F. "Literary Values in the Bible." *Journal of Biblical Literature* 89 (1970): 27–37.

Ricoeur, Paul. *Essays on Biblical Interpretation.* Philadelphia: Fortress Press, 1980.

Robertson, David. *The Old Testament and the Literary Critic.* Philadelphia: Fortress Press, 1977.

Rosenburg, Joel. "Meanings, Morals and Mysteries: Literary Approaches to Torah." *Response* 9 (1975): 81–94.

Sanders, Paul S., ed. *Twentieth Century Interpretations of the Book of Job.* Englewood Cliffs, N.J.: Prentice Hall, 1968.

Schneidau, Herbert N. *Sacred Discontent: The Bible and the Western Tradition.* Berkeley: University of California Press, 1976.

Simon, Uriel. "An Ironic Approach to a Biblical Story." *Hasifrut* 2 (1970): 598–607.

Sternberg, Meir. "Between the Truth and the Whole Truth in Biblical Narrative: The Rendering of Inner Life by Telescoped Inside View and Interior Monologue." *Hasifrut* 29 (1979): 110–46.

———. "Caution: A Literary Text! Problems in the Poetics and Interpretation of Biblical Narrative." *Hasifrut* 2 (1970): 608–63.

———. "Delicate Balance in the Rape of Dinah: Biblical Narrative and the Rhetoric of the Narrative Text." *Hasifrut* 4 (1973): 193–231.

———. "The King through Ironic Eyes: The Narrator's Devices in the Story of David and Bathsheba, and Two Excurses on the Theory of the Narrative Text." *Hasifrut* 1 (1968): 262–91.

———. "Language, World and Perspective in Biblical Art." *Hasifrut* 32 (1983): 88–131.

———. *The Poetics of Biblical Narrative.* Bloomington: Indiana University Press, 1985.

———. "The Structure of Repetition in Biblical Narrative: Strategies of Informational Redundancy." *Hasifrut* 25 (1977): 124–37.

Tribble, Phyllis, ed. "The Effects of Women's Studies on Biblical Scholarship." *Journal for the Study of the Old Testament* 22 (1982): 3–72.

———. *God and the Rhetoric of Sexuality.* Philadelphia: Fortress Press, 1978.

———. "The Radical Faith of Ruth." In *To Be a Person of Integrity*, edited by James Ogden. Valley Forge: Judson Press, 1975.

———. *Texts of Terror: Literary-Feminist Readings of Biblical Narratives.* Philadelphia: Fortress Press, 1984.

Via, Dan O., Jr. *The Parables: Their Literary and Existential Dimension.* Philadelphia: Fortress Press, 1967.

Walzer, Michael. *Exodus and Revolution.* New York: Basic Books, 1985.

Wilder, Amos N. *Early Christian Rhetoric: The Language of the Gospel.* Cambridge: Harvard University Press, 1971.

Wimsatt, W. K., and Monroe C. Beardsley. "The Intentional Fallacy." In *The Verbal Icon.* New York: Noonday, 1958.

Acknowledgments

"The First Three Chapters of Genesis: Principles of Governance Stated Narratively" by Kenneth Burke from *The Rhetoric of Religion: Studies in Logology* by Kenneth Burke, © 1961 by Kenneth Burke. © 1970 by the Regents of the University of California. Reprinted by permission of the University of California Press.

"Sacred History and the Beginnings of Prose Fiction" by Robert Alter from *The Art of Biblical Narrative* by Robert Alter, © 1981 by Robert Alter. Reprinted by permission of Basic Books, Inc., Publishers.

"Representations of Reality in Homer and the Old Testament" (originally entitled "Odysseus' Scar") by Erich Auerbach from *Mimesis: The Representation of Reality in Western Literature* by Erich Auerbach, and translated by Willard R. Trask. © 1953, © 1981 renewed by Princeton University Press. Reprinted by permission of Princeton University Press. This essay originally appeared in the *Partisan Review*.

"The Wooing of Rebekah" (originally entitled "View Points and Interpretations") by Meir Sternberg from *The Poetics of Biblical Narrative* by Meir Sternberg, © 1985 by Meir Sternberg. Reprinted by permission of Indiana University Press.

"The Struggle with the Angel: Textual Analysis of Genesis 32:22–32" by Roland Barthes from *Image, Music, Text* by Roland Barthes, © 1977 by Roland Barthes. Reprinted by permission of Hill & Wang.

"Wrestling Sigmund: Three Paradigms for Poetic Originality" by Harold Bloom from *The Breaking of the Vessels* by Harold Bloom, © 1982 by The University of Chicago. Reprinted by permission of The University of Chicago Press.

"The Second Address of Moses: Deuteronomy 5:1b–28:68" (originally entitled "The Book of Deuteronomy") by Robert Polzin from *Moses and the Deuteronomist: A Literary Study of the Deuteronomic History* (Part One) by Robert Polzin, © 1980 by Robert Polzin. Reprinted by permission of the author, Harper & Row Publishers, and The Seabury Press.

"Job" by Martin Buber from *On the Bible: Eighteen Studies* by Martin Buber, and edited by Nahom M. Glatzer, © 1968 by Schocken Books, Inc. Reprinted by permission. This essay orginally appeared in *The Prophetic Faith* by Martin Buber, translated by Carlyle Witton-Davies, © 1949 by The Macmillan Co.

"The Heart Determines: Psalm 73" by Martin Buber from *On the Bible: Eighteen Studies* by Martin Buber, and edited by Nahom M. Glatzer, © 1968 by Schocken Books, Inc. Reprinted by permission. This essay originally appeared in *Right and Wrong: An Interpretation of Some Psalms* and *Good and Evil* by Martin Buber, translated by Ronald Gregory Smith, © 1952, 1953 by Martin Buber. Reprinted by permission of SCM, Ltd. and Charles Scribner's Sons 1952.

"The Style of Koheleth" (originally entitled "The Style–His Religious Vocabulary" and "The Style–His Use of Quotations") by Robert Gordis from *Koheleth–The Man and His World* by Robert Gordis, © 1951 by Robert Gordis. Reprinted by permission of the author and Bloch Publishing Co.

"The Garden of Metaphor: The Song of Songs" (originally entitled "The Garden of Metaphor") by Robert Alter from *The Art of Biblical Poetry* by Robert Alter, © 1985 by Robert Alter. Reprinted by permission of Basic Books, Inc., Publishers.

"The Place and Function of the Song of the Vineyard in Isaiah's Prophecy" by Yehoshua Gitay, from *Isaiah and His Audience: The Structure and Meaning of Isaiah 1–12* by Yehoshua Gitay to be published by Indiana University Press. © 1986 by Yehoshua Gitay. Reprinted by permission of the author.

"The Poetics of Prophecy: Jeremiah" (originally entitled "Poetics of Prophecy") by Geoffrey Hartman from *High Romantic Argument: Essays for M. H. Abrams*, edited by Lawrence Lipking, © 1981 by Cornell University Press. Reprinted by permission of Cornell University Press.

"On Socrates and the Prophets" by Leo Strauss from *Jerusalem and Athens: Some Preliminary Reflections* (The City College Papers, no. 6, 1967), © 1967 by the City College of New York. Reprinted by permission.

"Jonah and *Moby-Dick*" (originally entitled "Call Me Jonah") by Douglas Robinson from *American Apocalypses: The Image of the End of the World in American Literature* by Douglas Robinson, © 1985 by The Johns Hopkins University Press, Baltimore/London. Reprinted by permission.

"The Boy in the Shirt" (originally entitled "The Man in the Macintosh, The Boy in the Shirt") by Frank Kermode from *The Genesis of Secrecy: On the Interpretation of Narrative* by Frank Kermode, © 1979 by Frank Kermode. Reprinted by permission of the author and Harvard University Press.

"Phases of Revelation" (originally entitled "Typology II: Phases of Revelation") by Northrop Frye from *The Great Code: The Bible and Literature* by Northrop Frye, © 1981, 1982 by Northrop Frye. Reprinted by permission of Harcourt Brace Jovanovich and Routledge and Kegan Paul Ltd.

" 'Before Moses Was, I Am': The Original and the Belated Testaments" by Harold Bloom from *Notebooks in Cultural Analysis: An Annual Review*, edited by Norman F. Cantor, © 1984 by Duke University Press. Reprinted by permission.

"Pauline Typology and Revisionary Criticism" by Herbert Marks from *Journal of the American Academy of Religion* 52, no. 1 (March 1984), © 1984 by *The American Academy of Religion*. Reprinted by permission.

"Apocalypse" (originally an untitled chapter) by D. H. Lawrence from *Apocalypse* by D. H. Lawrence, © 1931 by the Estate of David Herbert Lawrence, © renewed 1960, 1966 by Viking Press, Inc. Reprinted by permission of Viking Penguin, Inc.

Index